THE GREAT
ABOLITIONIST

THE GREAT
ABOLITIONIST

CHARLES SUMNER
AND THE FIGHT FOR
A MORE PERFECT UNION

STEPHEN PULEO

ST. MARTIN'S PRESS
NEW YORK

First published in the United States by St. Martin's Press, an imprint of St. Martin's Publishing Group

www.stmartins.com

Design by Meryl Sussman Levavi

Library of Congress Cataloging-in-Publication Data

Names: Puleo, Stephen, author.
Title: The great abolitionist : Charles Sumner and the fight for a more perfect union / Stephen Puleo.
Other titles: Charles Sumner and the fight for a more perfect union
Description: First edition. | New York : St. Martin's Press, 2024. Includes bibliographical references and index.
Identifiers: LCCN 2023056198 | ISBN 9781250276278 (hardcover) | ISBN 9781250276285 (ebook)
Subjects: LCSH: Sumner, Charles, 1811–1874. | Abolitionists—United States—Biography. | Legislators—United States—Biography. | United States. Congress. Senate—Biography. | Antislavery movements—United States—History—19th century. | United States—Politics and government—1845–1861.
Classification: LCC E415.9.S9 P95 2024 | DDC 326/.8092 [B]—dc23/eng/20231214
LC record available at https://lccn.loc.gov/2023056198

Our books may be purchased in bulk for promotional, educational, or business use. Please contact your local bookseller or the Macmillan Corporate and Premium Sales Department at 1-800-221-7945, extension 5442, or by email at MacmillanSpecialMarkets@macmillan.com.

First Edition: 2024

1 3 5 7 9 10 8 6 4 2

To Kate

Always have, always will, always us

CONTENTS

Author's Note on Usage   ix

Prologue   1

Part One: "Equality Before the Law"

Chapter 1. "We Are Becoming Abolitionists . . . Fast"   11

Chapter 2. "It Touched Me to the Soul"   21

Chapter 3. Texas Thunder   32

Chapter 4. A Daring Escape Attempt   43

Chapter 5. A New Doctrine Is Born   52

Chapter 6. Separate Is Inherently Unequal   61

Chapter 7. "Truth in the End Must Prevail"   71

Part Two: Unstoppable Peril

Chapter 8. Preserve the Union at Any Cost?   81

Chapter 9. "You Have Whipped Webster!"   90

Chapter 10. A Fugitive Slave Returned, a New Senator Elected   98

Chapter 11. "Slavery Is the Source of All Meanness Here"   109

Chapter 12. The Fugitive Slave Law Assailed   115

Chapter 13. Kansas and Nebraska—"At the Very Grave of Freedom"   126

Chapter 14. Bleeding Kansas   138

Chapter 15. The Crime Against Kansas   145

Chapter 16. Bleeding Sumner   153

Part Three: A Nation Split Asunder

Chapter 17. The Vacant Chair   163

Chapter 18. A Reelection and a Shocking Death   178

Chapter 19. The *Dred Scott* Decision and Trial by Fire   188

Chapter 20. Return from Exile   199

Chapter 21. "The Barbarism of Slavery"   205

Chapter 22. Lincoln's Election and Southern Secession   213

Chapter 23. "At Last the War Has Come"   221

Chapter 24. "Elevate the Condition of Men"   231

Chapter 25. "The Rebellion Is Slavery Itself!"   241

Chapter 26. British Treachery   246

Part Four:
Death of Slavery, Death of a Rebellion, Death of a President

Chapter 27. Emancipation in the Nation's Capital   261

Chapter 28. "At Last, the Proclamation Has Come"   271

Chapter 29. "The Result Is Certain—Sooner or Later"   283

Chapter 30. The Thirteenth Amendment and the End of the Fugitive
    Slave Law   289

Chapter 31. "Are You for Your Country, or Are You for
    the Rebellion?"   298

Chapter 32. With Malice Toward None?   307

Chapter 33. Richmond Has Fallen   319

Chapter 34. "We Are Near the End at Last"   324

Part Five:
"For All Everywhere Who Suffer from Tyranny and Wrong"

Chapter 35. Andrew Johnson's Betrayal   335

Chapter 36. The Fourteenth Amendment: "Freedom Without Suffrage
    Is Still Slavery"   345

Chapter 37. "I Begin to Live!"   351

Chapter 38. "My Home Was Hell . . ."   359

Chapter 39. "Guilty of All and Infinitely More!"   367

Chapter 40. "There Can Be No Backward Step"   376

Chapter 41. "Good-Bye and God Bless You!"   386

Epilogue: "Great Champion of Liberty"   392

Acknowledgments   405

Bibliographic Essay   409

Index   435

AUTHOR'S NOTE ON USAGE

My most important goal when writing about the past is to be sure my readers can place and "feel" themselves in the time period. Often, language usage plays a major role in achieving that goal. For that reason, you will note that I have chosen not to capitalize the word "black" when used in a racial context, though such usage is often embedded in books and articles about current events. However, this was not the case in Charles Sumner's world—far from it, in fact—and I believe such usage would produce a discordant note for readers. For example, capitalizing "black" in the same paragraph that references a "colored regiment" fighting for the Union Army is contradictory and immediately takes the reader out of the historical time period and into the present day. A similar strangeness would occur if a contemporaneous quote containing the lower-case "black"—from Sumner, for example—appeared close to a capitalized version in the author's voice. Readers with questions should feel free to reach out to me at spuleo@aol.com.

THE GREAT
ABOLITIONIST

PROLOGUE

Charles Sumner looked down upon Abraham Lincoln. The President, too tall for the bed, lay diagonally across the thin mattress, head lolling to one side, eyes half open, blood flowing freely from his wound, matting Lincoln's thick hair and staining the pillow. Sumner sat at the head of the bed, grasped the President's right hand in his own, bent closer to Lincoln, and spoke to him.

"It's no use, Mr. Sumner," said one of Lincoln's doctors. "He can't hear you."

"No," Sumner insisted, "he isn't dead. Look at his face; he is breathing." The physician replied softly: "It will never be anything more than this."

Sumner "sobbed like a woman" and bowed his own head until it nearly touched Lincoln's pillow. Though the unconscious President was covered with a heavy army blanket, his hand was already growing colder. Sumner listened to Lincoln's raspy breathing and would say later that it sounded almost like a melody. More than a dozen people filled the cramped bedroom, but—since Lincoln's wife, Mary Todd, had been removed earlier, her unnerving screams echoing long after she was escorted out—the night silence was punctuated only by an occasional cough or muffled cry.

Sumner remained at Lincoln's bedside all night, from 10:45 P.M. until after seven o'clock the following morning. The eerie quiet continued even as dawn broke. Just before Lincoln died, Mary Todd, now subdued in her shock, paid her last visit. At the moment of the President's death—7:22 A.M. on April 15—Lincoln's son, Robert, weeping uncontrollably, rested his head on Sumner's shoulder.

"He is gone; he is dead," one of the doctors said.

To the Reverend Dr. Phineas D. Gurley, the Lincoln family's minister, it seemed that four or five more minutes passed without "the slightest noise or movement" by anyone in the room. "We all stood transfixed in our positions, speechless, around the dead body of that great and good man."

✳ ✳ ✳

Secretary of War Edwin M. Stanton, standing at the foot of Lincoln's bed, spoke first and asked Dr. Gurley to offer a prayer. When he finished, everyone murmured "Amen," and again, no one dared speak. After a few moments, Stanton broke the silence: "Now he belongs to the angels." One by one, those who were with Lincoln at the end, Senator Charles Sumner included, filed out of the room, all but Stanton, who, while alone with the dead President, cut a lock of his hair and sealed it in a plain white envelope for posterity.

As shaken as Senator Charles Sumner was by Lincoln's assassination— what he would describe as a "transcendent event"—he found that the long overnight vigil helped cushion his initial shock at hearing the news. "The President was absolutely unconscious from the moment the ball entered his head till his heart ceased to beat," Sumner recalled later. "His death was, therefore, sudden, but not unprepared for."

During his time at Lincoln's bedside, Sumner contemplated the circumstances that led to the attack on the sixteenth President at nearby Ford's Theatre. His mind was not on the "humble criminal," John Wilkes Booth, who had fired the deadly shot before jumping to the stage and fleeing, but on the "agencies that directed the fatal bullet," the Confederate states and "belligerent slavery."

Both, Sumner noted, had been "defeated in battle" and thus had resorted to the most dishonorable, degrading, and cowardly act—assassination.

✳ ✳ ✳

The rebellion was over, the war nearly so after Robert E. Lee's surrender to Ulysses S. Grant at Appomattox Court House just days earlier, and now the rebels had murdered President Lincoln. For Sumner, the U.S. senator from Massachusetts and abolitionism's greatest proponent, the pain and irony were overpowering. He had dined recently with Lincoln and several cabinet members and noted that "down to the last, he had been gentle and forgiving" toward Confederate leaders. "He said nothing harsh even of [Confederate President] Jefferson Davis," despite protestations from some of his trusted advisors. Even when one cabinet member insisted that Davis "must not be spared" from the hangman's noose for his treasonous actions, Lincoln repeated words from his second inaugural address a month earlier:

"Judge not that ye be not judged."

Sumner, too, favored harsh retribution against the South, and while he truly mourned Lincoln's death, he also acknowledged that Lincoln's demise "will strengthen those who wish strong measures." As painful as the assassination was to the country in the moment, it could serve as a providential event to eradicate slavery forever and propel the drive for equal rights under the law, dual principles Sumner had championed virtually his entire public life.

Lincoln's death "will do more for the cause than any human life," he wrote, "for it will fix the sentiment of the country—perhaps of mankind."

In that sense, Sumner offered, macabre as it may sound, "few [deaths] have been happier."

✳ ✳ ✳

Charles Sumner and Abraham Lincoln had much in common, including their height; both men stood nearly six feet, four inches tall and often towered above others with whom they came in contact.

Beyond their physical similarities, the two men shared deep philosophical underpinnings. Both loved the Union and sought its preservation. Both cherished the Founding Fathers and the ideas promulgated in the Declaration of Independence and the Constitution. Both detested slavery, though it took Sumner's influence upon Lincoln to convince the President to publicly favor its outright abolition. Both employed words and ideas as their most powerful tools as they sought the elusive goal of equal rights for all. Both were leaders in the founding and shaping of the Republican Party into an antislavery political force. In the aftermath of the Civil War and Lincoln's death, Sumner carried on the party's mission through Reconstruction, a crusade he described as "the regeneration of the nation according to the promises of the Declaration."

And both paid a terrible price for their beliefs: Sumner was beaten within an inch of his life on the Senate floor in 1856 by a proslavery congressman wielding a cane; Lincoln made the ultimate sacrifice for vanquishing a rebellion whose foremost goal was the perpetuation of the South's "peculiar institution" of human bondage.

While President Lincoln has been, justifiably, the subject of countless biographies, thousands of essays, and lavish praise about his wisdom and leadership from scholars and schoolchildren alike, Charles Sumner's life and accomplishments have faded, an unfortunate historical occurrence—this is the first full biography of Sumner in more than a half century. This slight becomes more perplexing when Sumner's enormous contributions and his overall body of work during America's most dramatic and volatile era are taken into account.

His unrelenting efforts to abolish slavery and fulfill the nation's promise of civil, political, and racial equality; his expertise in foreign affairs that helped the United States avoid a potentially devastating war with England even as the country battled the Confederacy; his influence in virtually every major debate and issue that the country tackled in the decade prior to the Civil War, the war itself, and during Reconstruction— all of these place Charles Sumner among a handful of the most influential non-Presidents in American history, alongside Benjamin Franklin, Alexander Hamilton, Martin Luther King, Jr., and Susan B. Anthony.

✳ ✳ ✳

For a quarter of a century, including twenty-three consecutive years in the Senate from 1851 until his death (which encompassed a three-year absence as he recovered from his caning injuries), it was Charles Sumner— not Lincoln, William Lloyd Garrison, Frederick Douglass, Lydia Maria Child, or anyone else—who was the nation's most passionate and inexhaustible antislavery and equal rights champion.

Before and during the Civil War, at great personal sacrifice, he was the conscience of the North and the strongest and most influential voice in favor of abolition. Throughout Reconstruction, no one championed the rights of the emancipated freedmen more than Charles Sumner. Through the force of his words and his will, he moved first his state, and then the nation, toward the twin goals of abolitionism—which he achieved in his lifetime—and equal rights, which eluded him and the country, but for which he fought literally until the day he died.

In so doing, he laid the cornerstone arguments that civil rights advocates would build upon over the next century as the country strove to achieve equality among the races.

To Sumner, the two concepts of abolitionism and equal rights were inseparable and could not be untethered. Freedom and equality embodied the founding principles of the United States as stated in the Declaration of Independence and in the Constitution's guarantee of a republican form of government; only by enshrining these rights forever could the United States survive. This view was first considered radical and unworkable, dismissed as the ranting of rabble-rousers on the fringe—as a position held not even by Lincoln and other antislavery Republicans.

But Sumner's influence gradually took hold, permeated the party's dogma, and finally became the prevalent and official view of Lincoln and the nation.

✳ ✳ ✳

Charles Sumner stood tall and ramrod straight at the center of events that millions of Americans would learn about and study for the next century and a half: the Fugitive Slave Law; the Kansas-Nebraska Act; the battle for the soul of Kansas that became a symbol of abolitionist and proslavery tensions; the founding of the Republican Party; Lincoln's election in 1860; the secession of Southern states; the *Trent* Affair, in which he was the primary force in averting war with England; the Emancipation Proclamation, which he repeatedly beseeched Lincoln to issue and whose language he helped shape; Lincoln's remarkable and unexpected reelection in 1864; the President's assassination; the crafting of Reconstruction policy; the impeachment of President Andrew Johnson; and the Reconstruction amendments. He also served as head of the Radical Republicans throughout the war, as chairman of the Senate Foreign Relations Committee, and as the architect of a proposed sweeping civil rights bill that called for an end to all government and private sector discrimination.

As the nation literally fought for its life, Charles Sumner influenced, altered, and often defined America's course—in the moment and for the future. This biography (better described as a "biographical history"), rather than focusing on Sumner's every movement and utterance between childhood and death, traces the arc of his antislavery and equal rights leadership as he stood at the center of the storm that swept across the nation during the 1850s and 1860s.

From the moment he stepped onto the public stage, he made his fight America's fight.

Where others preached compromise and moderation, he never wavered in denouncing slavery's evils to all who would listen and demanding that it be wiped out of existence. Where others muttered cautious, even insipid, platitudes, his voice was clear and strong. Where others wilted under the onslaught of political attack, he stood fearless, a bulwark against the slings and piercing arrows of those who targeted him—Southern slaveholders, as well as many Northerners who placed economic interests ahead of their moral outrage.

He was beholden to no one, sought no ill-gotten gains, was unbribable and unbuyable, and had little interest in currying favor even to advance his own political fortunes.

His was a career, a life, supported by the twin pillars of courage and authenticity.

✳ ✳ ✳

Charles Sumner was the boldest, most controversial, and most influential voice of America's most turbulent two decades: the 1850s and 1860s. No one else came close.

As great events played out across the land during this period, Sumner seized the national narrative, refused to let go, and repeatedly held a mirror up to the country's aspirations and ideals. He inspired those who agreed with him, swayed fence-sitters, and eventually converted millions of naysayers. He had a particular understanding of the power of words and big themes to move people, to challenge their ways of doing things.

It was Charles Sumner who first used the phrase "equality before the law" in the United States, who first argued that "separate but equal" violated the precepts of the Declaration of Independence, and who infused the concept of "equal protection" for all into the language of the Fourteenth Amendment.

His oratory was his gift, if occasionally his undoing. He never backed down, never tempered his remarks, never prevaricated. Throughout his career, he was responsible for passing almost no significant legislation (though *as* a legislator, he is often underrated), and yet for two decades, in an era when senators often wielded more power than presidents, he was the most powerful man in the U.S. Senate.

Sumner understood politics, but he had little patience for the political *process* or in nourishing personal relationships that made the process run smoothly. Yet, merely uttering the words "U.S. Senator Charles Sumner of Massachusetts" was enough to stop both his allies and his enemies in their tracks. Supporters trumpeted his courage, his resilience, and his moral certitude. Detractors detested his arrogance, his seeming lack of empathy, and his utter contempt for those who disagreed with him.

But without question, when Charles Sumner spoke, everyone listened.

* * *

Like Winston Churchill during World War II and Martin Luther King, Jr., during the civil rights era, Charles Sumner, throughout the 1850s and 1860s, relied most heavily on the uncompromising clarity of his ideas, his relentless honesty, and his steadfastness as his most effective attributes as he sought to move the heart and mind of a country embroiled in crisis. Like Churchill and King, too, he employed rhetoric befitting big moments, and like both twentieth-century leaders, he shaped—and was shaped by—grand causes and occurrences.

He knew instinctively what was at stake and how to convey it. "The great hours of history seem to be tolling now," he wrote to his dear friend Henry Wadsworth Longfellow in 1859, understanding fully and capturing the gravity of deteriorating relations between North and South. After Lincoln's election in 1860, when it was clear that Southern states would secede and the union would break apart, Sumner recognized the momentousness of the occasion and reminded Longfellow that, even in the midst of such dire crisis, faintheartedness was not an option.

"There must be no yielding on our part," he said. "We are on the eve of great events."

* * *

Throughout his lifetime, in countless compelling moments, Charles Sumner's eloquence and inexhaustible zeal would shape the debate and ignite the passions of a nation.

No single individual did more to influence the antislavery movement on a national scale. No single person was more responsible for founding and fueling the growth of the antislavery Republican Party. No single lawmaker advocated for such broad and sweeping equal rights for African Americans or fought to make the discussion of such rights a reasonable and respectable option for their congressional colleagues.

His positions cost him dearly. Southerners despised him, sometimes feared him, and celebrated gleefully when Sumner was beaten unconscious in the Senate chamber. Northerners initially blanched at his abolitionism, later resisted his demands for equal rights as detrimental to the nation's attempts to heal, and often found his chafing personality off-putting. But most came to respect him and his positions, and near the end of his life, they elevated Sumner to revered elder-statesman status. His political courage and moral clarity established him as the national conscience on the issues of slavery and equal rights.

More than any other person of his era, perhaps of *any* era, Charles Sumner blazed the trail on the country's long, uneven, and ongoing journey toward realizing its full promise, its ever-striving quest to become a more perfect union.

PART ONE

"EQUALITY BEFORE THE LAW"

✳ CHAPTER 1 ✳

"WE ARE BECOMING ABOLITIONISTS . . . FAST"

Charles Sumner was saddened, though not overly sympathetic, when he saw his first slaves in 1834 at the age of twenty-three.

Fresh out of Harvard Law School, Sumner left Boston by stagecoach at 3:30 A.M. on February 17 for his first trip to Washington, D.C. His mentors, Harvard dean and associate Supreme Court justice Joseph Story and Professor Simon Greenleaf, had suggested the trip to the nation's capital, believing that for Sumner to excel at the law, he had to understand the way the country's politics worked and gain a broad acquaintance with judges and government leaders. Sumner also welcomed the trip as an opportunity to spread his wings after years of painstaking classroom study and cloying and overbearing supervision from his demanding father.

The long journey, portions of which were made by steamboat and railway (Sumner's first train ride), was tiring but exhilarating.

Departure night was so dark that Sumner, riding up front with the driver while eleven other passengers sat in the coach, did not realize until the break of dawn, ten miles from the city, that the wagon was pulled by six sturdy horses, a number Sumner marveled at in a letter to his family. Later, Sumner was the sole passenger on a "gig"—a small carriage pulled by a single horse—again riding alongside the driver "over roads nearly impassable to the best animals," while enduring "benumbing" cold. As the driver wrestled to keep the carriage on course, Sumner—at the driver's request—rained blows from his whip upon the horse to move the reluctant animal along, "literally *working* my passage . . . my shoulder was lame for its excessive exercise in whipping the poor brute." Changing horses every sixteen miles, the gig arrived in Hartford near 2:00 A.M. the next day, twenty-three hours after Sumner left Boston. Another stagecoach brought Sumner to New Haven, from which he boarded a steamer to New York City.

New York's "perpetual whirl and bustle" thrilled him. "I am now in the great Babel," he wrote to his parents, a young man on his own in the big city. "The streets flow with throngs, as thick and pressing as those of Boston on a gala day. Carriages of all sorts are hurrying by . . . omnibuses and Broadway coaches . . . are perpetually in sight. . . . One must be wide awake, or be run over by some of the crowd." Sumner then traveled by boat to Amboy, New Jersey, where he took his first train ride for nearly forty miles, "part of the way going at the rate of more than twenty miles an hour!" From there, he was on to Philadelphia and Baltimore by a combination of stage, railroad, and steamboat.

By the final leg of his exhausting six-day journey south, on a stagecoach ride from Baltimore to Washington—a stretch of only thirty-eight miles through "barren and cheerless country" that took all day over the "worst roads" Sumner had ridden upon—Sumner spotted a group of slaves toiling in a field. He appeared to view them with a combination of contempt and curiosity.

"My worst preconception of their appearance and ignorance did not fall as low as their actual stupidity," he wrote to his parents. "They appear to be nothing more than moving masses of flesh, unendowed with any thing of intelligence above the brutes." He concluded his reference with an ambiguous aside that may have been an indictment upon the South itself, the slave system, or the jarring sight of seeing enslaved people: "I have now an idea of the blight upon that part of the country in which they live."

He made no other direct reference to slavery, either in that letter or any others he wrote from Washington, D.C., in 1834.

＊ ＊ ＊

Upon reaching Washington, Sumner immersed himself in the city's political scene.

He settled into a routine wherein he rose at seven o'clock each morning, and after breakfast, visited a congressman or two. By late morning, he was in the Capitol building—a structure "that would look proud amidst any European palaces"—where he attended congressional debates or sat in on sessions of the Supreme Court, which met in a dark room on the lower floor, until late in the afternoon. In the evening, he often spent time with Justice Story and his legal associates and friends, dining at "well-furnished tables of the richest hotels," excited that at these lively and invigorating sessions "no conversation is forbidden . . . the world and all its things are talked of."

Sumner received a hands-on education about the legislative process and speechmaking. He sat rapt as Senator Henry Clay delivered a "splendid and thrilling" oration criticizing President Andrew Jackson, "without notes or papers of any kind . . . he showed *feeling*, to which, of course, his audience responded." South Carolina's John C. Calhoun employed his trademark "rugged language" to make an impression on his audience. Massachusetts senator Daniel Webster introduced Sumner to other senators and presented Sumner with his card, "which gives me access at all times to the floor." He watched attorney Francis Scott Key, author of "The Star-Spangled Banner," argue a case before the Supreme Court. He saw the original Declaration of Independence, which hung in the Patent Office, and "paid a pilgrimage to Mount Vernon on horseback."

Sumner described Washington as a "city of magnificent distances," and he walked for miles to take it all in, along the National Mall, up and down bustling and dust-choked Pennsylvania Avenue and the city's other main thoroughfares—and amid the numerous slave pens and auction sites that dotted the heart of the nation's capital.

✳ ✳ ✳

In fact, Washington at the time of Sumner's first visit was the nexus for a great slave migration—a slave "trail of tears," as it were—in which hundreds of thousands, perhaps up to one million, "Upper South" slaves, who worked in tobacco fields and as household servants in Virginia, Maryland, Delaware, and Kentucky, were sold to labor-hungry plantation owners in the rapidly growing Deep South cotton and sugarcane states of Alabama, Mississippi, Georgia, and Louisiana.

Between 1833 and 1836 alone, more than 150,000 Upper South slaves either walked overland for hundreds of miles—usually chained together—to Lower South owners or were transported by ship down the Eastern Seaboard, around Florida, and into the gulf ports of Mobile, Alabama, or New Orleans, where they awaited purchase and another trek to expanding plantations and farms across the Deep South. In Washington, D.C., slave pens were conspicuous in the heart of the city. Large D.C. slave brokers even purchased their own ships to support the coastal slave trade. "The District of Columbia is the great mart for the sale of men," said one antislavery activist in 1834, home to a "vast and diabolical slave trade."

For slave owners, Washington, D.C., was the perfect location through which to transport slaves to the Deep South. Its proximity to the slave states of Virginia and Maryland gave the city ready access to thousands of slaves—and free blacks who were often illegally rounded up and sold into slavery—as well as to the Potomac River and the Atlantic coast. Moreover, slavery proponents knew that if they kept the institution of slavery visible in the nation's capital, it would serve as a vivid symbol of their hold on the nation and the national government.

For antislavery advocates, abolitionists, and foreign guests, the city's slave auctions and pens had the opposite effect. Most expressed disgust at the site of chained slaves trudging past the White House and Capitol. Most turned away with shame as slaves awaited sale and relocation in crowded pens near and on the National Mall, as children were torn from their parents and families were broken apart.

All of the trading activity in Washington, D.C.—chained slaves forced under guard to pens near the National Mall; auctioneers offering men and women for sale as crowd members shouted their bids; newspaper advertisements that connected buyers and sellers of slaves—would have been impossible for Charles Sumner to miss.

Yet, strangely enough, Sumner—a prolific and descriptive writer who penned numerous letters home about virtually every aspect of his Washington trip—never explicitly articulated his feelings about the presence of such slave activity in the nation's capital.

✳ ✳ ✳

But he *alluded* to the issue, especially later in his trip.

"Signs of the deep distress of the country are received every day and proclaimed in both Houses," he wrote to his friend Professor Greenleaf on March 3. And again to Greenleaf on March 18: "The country is in a sad condition, without a discernible sign of relief. I cannot but have a sense or feeling that things cannot continue in this pass . . . the *very extremity of our distress shows the day of redemption to be near.*" A few days later,

Sumner confided to his father that, while one part of him felt "a little melancholy at leaving," he was ready to come home. "I feel in an unnatural state [in Washington]," he said.

Sumner attributed some of his sadness at the situation in D.C. to a growing dislike for politics as the days went along. His initial ebullience waned, and his letters became more cynical as he watched the political process at work, admitting to Greenleaf that he had felt "no envy" for the fame politicians acquired and "no disposition to enter into the unweeded garden in which they are laboring, even if its gates were wide open to me." To his father, Sumner acknowledged that the more he saw of Washington, the more he was convinced that "I shall probably never come here again. I have little desire ever to . . . in any capacity. Nothing I have seen of politics has made me look upon it with any feeling other than loathing."

It is hard to imagine that Charles Sumner's disgust for D.C. politics was separate from his feelings on slavery or the signs of slavery that surrounded him in the nation's capital, especially since, upon his return to Boston, the twenty-four-year-old Sumner began taking a deeper interest in the subject.

Sumner's father, Charles Pinckney Sumner, had strong antislavery sentiments, and though Charles and his father were not close, the elder Sumner's convictions carried great sway over his son's thinking. Young Charles denounced proslavery violence in the South, and he began reading William Lloyd Garrison's abolitionist newspaper, *The Liberator*. He also read abolitionist Lydia Maria Child's *An Appeal in Favor of That Class of Americans Called Africans*, first published in 1833, which further convinced him of the injustice of slavery and racial discrimination in the wake of his Washington trip.

Sumner was far from an antislavery champion in his mid-twenties, but there is little doubt that his first exposure to slavery stayed with him and had an important effect on his early thinking and throughout his life; his thoughts on the injustice of slavery pepper his early letters and other writings.

In January 1836, Sumner wrote a letter to his friend Dr. Francis Lieber, whom he met on his Washington trip and who was now a professor of political economy in South Carolina—in essence, an antislavery sympathizer in the heart of slave country. Lieber had as much influence over

Sumner's early thinking on slavery as anyone. Sumner shared his sentiments on the evils of slavery and also felt compelled to tell his friend:

"We are becoming abolitionists in the North fast."

✳ ✳ ✳

Not fast enough, apparently, for Europeans, who watched America's ongoing slavery debate with contempt.

And they let Charles Sumner know about it on his first trip to Europe in the late 1830s, a pilgrimage that accelerated his antislavery education and hardened his beliefs.

After his return from Washington, Sumner practiced law and taught at Harvard Law School, but he decided to interrupt both endeavors in 1837 to embark on a long European trip and "visit those scenes memorable in literature and history, and to see . . . the great men that are already on stage." The desire to cross the Atlantic had burned in Sumner "since the earlier days of memory"; such a trip would allow him to obtain knowledge of "languages . . . manners, customs, and institutions of other people than my own." Against the advice of his father, Justice Story, and other friends who believed Sumner would damage his career path by embarking on a whimsical journey, Sumner departed on December 8, 1837, aboard the *Albany*. "I tremble with hope, anticipation, and anxiety," he wrote as he was about to begin his European tour.

After overcoming seasickness that confined him to his cabin for a week on the early part of the voyage, Sumner recovered, relaxed, walked the decks, and engaged with other passengers. By the time the captain spied land on Christmas night, Sumner's spirits were high, and he could not wait to go ashore. "The life of life seems to have burst upon me," he wrote joyfully to a friend.

And indeed, Sumner did enjoy his visits to museums, palaces, libraries, drawing rooms, and cathedrals. But more memorable for him was that, for more than two years, from Paris to London to Rome to Munich to Vienna, Europeans told him repeatedly that American slavery was a disgrace unbefitting a civilized nation. People whom Sumner admired had strong abolitionist opinions and were not shy about expressing them. In London, the Duchess of Sutherland was unsurpassed among English nobility in using her position to argue against American slavery. And in Paris, Sumner met lecturer and author Jean Charles Léonard de

Sismondi, whom he described as a "thorough abolitionist" who was "astonished that our country will not take a lesson from the ample page of the past and eradicate slavery, as has been done in the civilized parts of Europe."

But what gave him pause—even more than the opinions of the political, social, and academic elites in his host countries—were the things Sumner saw with his own eyes.

On a freezing January day in Paris ("My hair is so cold that I hesitate to touch it with my hand," Sumner wrote), he attended a lecture at the Sorbonne and spotted "two or three blacks" in the audience. Sumner was surprised that they had the "easy, jaunty air of men of fashion, who were well received by their fellow students," and even more surprised that while they were standing amid their classmates, "their color seemed to be no objection" to the group. Sumner was "glad to see this" but acknowledged that such a scenario would be unlikely in America.

It was at that moment, in France in 1838 at the age of twenty-seven—reinforced by similar scenes in Italy—that Sumner recognized the full import of what he was witnessing and reached the conclusion that would anchor his antislavery and equal rights philosophy.

In his opinion, the camaraderie displayed between students of different races at the Sorbonne could only mean one thing—"that the distance between free blacks and whites among us is derived from education, and does not exist *in the nature of things.*"

For the remainder of his life, in personal letters and speeches and congressional debates, Sumner would reiterate, in some form, this profound observation and link it to his assertion that the promises of the Declaration of Independence and the Constitution applied to all people equally.

By the time he returned from Europe on Sunday, May 3, 1840, Charles Sumner was convinced that American society also would be far better if slavery were abolished.

✳ ✳ ✳

How to accomplish that was another matter.

Sumner sympathized with the moral purpose of abolitionists, and even initially gave merit to William Lloyd Garrison's calls to "dissolve the Union" if it could not abolish slavery. But as Sumner thought and read more about the issue, he found distasteful and counterproductive the position of Garrison and his acolytes that the Constitution was a pro-slavery instrument, "a covenant with death, and an agreement with Hell."

Sumner not only disagreed with Garrison's conclusions about the Constitution, but he also believed such language only served to array conservatives, moderates, and the country in general against the anti-slavery movement, even as these groups were all potential allies essential to its success. Sumner grew increasingly uncomfortable with the tone of the language used in the *Liberator*. "It has seemed to me often vindictive, bitter, and unchristian," he said. "I have been openly opposed to [its] doctrines on the Union and the Constitution."

To Sumner's way of thinking, the Constitution was a charter of human rights, a protector of freedom, the very guarantee of equality, for all races within the borders of the United States. It codified the linchpin "self-evident" and "all men are created equal" clauses in the Declaration of Independence. The Constitution's guarantee of a "republican form of government" applied to all men, black or white, and such a government could not exist if it embraced, or even tolerated, slavery.

In Sumner's view, the fact that the Constitution did not even contain the word "slavery" proved that the Founders refused to let it "pollute its text," sought to discredit the institution, and concurred with "prevailing opinion, which regarded Slavery as temporary, destined to pass away" of its own accord within a decade or two—unable to survive against the Constitution's guarantees of freedom; the fact that the Constitution included language that banned the slave trade as of 1808 was further evidence of this. Other elements of the Constitution that clearly contradicted the principles of equality—the Three-Fifths Compromise, the insertion of a fugitive slave law—were, in Sumner's view, essentially the same positions espoused by Madison and others—necessary compromises to placate Southern states and ensure the foundational document's passage in the first place.

This would be the essence of the argument Sumner would make throughout his life. Indeed, no other approach made sense to him, nor could any other argument serve as a catalyst for people from many different political persuasions to join, or at least support, the antislavery movement.

✳ ✳ ✳

In the early 1840s, Sumner began to more fully express his thoughts on the moral wrong of extending slavery beyond the current states that allowed and depended on the institution, and on refuting the notion that blacks were inherently inferior and thus could not become citizens. He had witnessed for himself in Europe that this belief, widely held both in the North and South, was an evil canard.

Sumner questioned how those who argued in favor of black inferiority reconciled their support for the U.S. Constitution. "If it be urged that the African cannot be a citizen of the U.S., it may be asked if the Constitution was intended to apply *only* to the Caucasian race," he concluded. If so, where did such limitations to one of America's founding documents end? "Is the Indian race also excluded?" Sumner asked. "Is the Mongolian excluded?"

Sumner's reasoning and the strength of his beliefs about the power within the Constitution to check—and perhaps end—slavery and ensure equal rights placed him in an odd position, sandwiched between conservatives and moderates, who were reluctant to tamper with the current uneasy alliance between North and South, and radicals like Garrison, who wanted to tear down the entire system and start over.

He was stung by criticism from both sides and often felt he was standing alone.

✳ ✳ ✳

After his eye-opening European trip, Sumner returned to Boston to practice law and quickly fell into a listlessness and ennui that worried his friends.

His heart wasn't in the law, and his clients and prospects noticed. His office became more of a social gathering spot than a focused place of business. Sumner often veered away from discussions of cases before him and launched into lengthy reminiscences of his European adventures. To a friend in Rome, he admitted his longing to again experience the "unspeakable charm of the place." Life was so much duller on Court Street, "with law books staring me in the face." He could not shake his lethargy or his doldrums, in or out of the office. Workdays were long, draining, and unfulfilling. "Though I earn my daily bread," he lamented to Lieber, "I lay up none of the bread of *life*."

Two years after returning from Europe, money became a problem.

His practice was so small that he accepted an appointment as a U.S. commissioner on bankruptcy proceedings, and he and his partner, George Hillard, made their "living on the blood and tears of those victims." His unhappiness at work spilled over to his social life, and his friends began avoiding him, or at least tiptoeing in his presence so as not to upset him further.

Soon Sumner began isolating himself from Boston society and even his closest friends, perceiving that people were talking behind his back and ridiculing him both for his antislavery positions and his lack of enthusiasm for his law practice. Only Henry Wadsworth Longfellow's company satisfied him, and when the poet sailed to Europe in 1842 to improve his health, Sumner was heartbroken. The euphoria of his own European trip long dissipated, Sumner was despondent, personally and professionally, lonely and discouraged, uncertain of his future, worried about criticism from allies and opponents alike. "I am more and more desolate and alone," he confided to Lieber. "I lead a joyless life, with very little sympathy."

Rapid mood swings, bouts of paranoia and depression, feelings of inferiority (even while professing his superiority), acerbic language, animus toward others, and a need to assume the martyr's mantle—these were all traits that shaped Charles Sumner's personality and influenced his actions.

As he emerged into public view in the 1840s and became a national force in the decades afterward, more and more people across America learned the full measure of Sumner's noble antislavery convictions, but many also saw a man whose personal struggles often derailed his brilliance.

Though Sumner's personality difficulties worsened in his late twenties, he had grappled with them for as long as he could remember.

✳ CHAPTER 2 ✳

"IT TOUCHED ME TO THE SOUL"

If psychoanalysis had been part of the American vocabulary in 1811, it would have been tempting to trace, almost literally to the day he was born, Charles Sumner's bouts of moodiness and depression and his difficulties empathizing with and relating to others.

On January 6 of that year, Charles and his twin sister, Matilda, entered the world prematurely, struggling to survive, each weighing barely three and a half pounds. They were the eldest of nine children who would eventually be born to Charles Pinckney Sumner and Relief Jacob Sumner of Boston. Charles was breastfed by his mother, but Matilda's care was turned over to a nurse.

Relief Sumner's decision to separate the children appeared to have long-standing consequences; Charles and Matilda were not close and never shared the deep and inexplicable bond that is often associated with twins. Sumner barely mentions Matilda in any of his writing, and when she died at age twenty-one from tuberculosis after a long illness, her twin brother, who wrote fiery letters expressing his outrage on many topics, reacted with cool detachment. "My grief, whatever it may be, has not the source that yours has," he wrote to a college chum who had expressed sympathy. "I have lost a sister; but I still have other sisters and brothers, entitled to my instruction and protection. I strive to forget my loss in an increased regard for the living."

Almost inconceivably, in the same letter in which he dismissed his friend's sympathy over Matilda's death, Sumner declared himself in excellent health.

"I was never better," he wrote.

✳ ✳ ✳

Sumner's coolness over the death of his twin sister was typical of his relationship with other members of his family.

His undemonstrative mother was never able to fully express her love for Charles (notwithstanding her preservation of a lock of his baby hair), and while the two maintained close ties to the end of her life, their relationship was stiff and formal. Most of his letters to her—only eighteen have been recovered—dealt with routine financial and household matters, and no letters have survived from Mrs. Sumner to Charles.

It is hard to believe she never wrote to her son. The remote possibility exists that all the letters from Sumner's mother were simply lost to history, but given the way he treated the correspondence of others, it is unlikely. Sumner meticulously preserved and organized virtually all of his correspondence; in many ways, his letters and speeches were his life. The simplest conclusions to draw are either that Sumner believed any letters from his mother were too mundane to include in his personal papers or that he wished to shield from future researchers the nature of their strained relationship. Some combination is likely.

As for his siblings, Sumner's relationships with virtually all of them were marked—or marred—by clumsiness and coldness. With the exception of his sister Mary, for whom Sumner developed a deep affection in 1844 when they both were being treated for serious illnesses, Sumner constantly lectured, admonished, tolerated, or outright ignored his siblings. Often, he reproached his brothers and sisters for what he perceived as their shortcomings or lack of discipline. He did not include them in important moments in his life—although as he grew older, his interactions increased with his brother George—made scant references to them in his autobiography, and penned letters to them that, while seemingly well-intentioned, were preachy and condescending.

For all but Mary, he had little to say when his siblings died (including two who perished in violent shipwrecks), and when he did mention them—as was the case when Matilda died—his words were most often either the impersonal musings of a philosopher or the arm's-length observations of a stranger. When his sister Jane died in 1837 at age seventeen from typhoid, Sumner was excitedly preparing for his trip to Europe and mentioned nothing about the loss.

In fact, Sumner rarely expressed love and tenderness to anyone. In this way, the eldest son mirrored his father, the person in the Sumner household who most affected Charles's personality as a young man, and whose outsized influence weighed on him for his entire life.

✳ ✳ ✳

"I have a son, named Charles Sumner, in his fifteenth year, and large of his age, but not of so firm and solid a constitution as I should wish him to have," wrote Charles Pinckney Sumner to Captain Alden Partridge, commander of the American Literary, Scientific, and Military Academy in Middletown, Connecticut. Although young Charles had good grades, at the time his father could not afford to send him to college, and in any case, he thought Partridge's academy might be a better fit for his son. "The life of a scholar would be too sedentary and inactive for him," Sumner's father said.

It was clear early that Charles Pinckney had questions about his son's ability to transition to manhood. Despite his strong academic performance at Boston Latin School, young Charles was uncoordinated and had no interest in sports or games. Boys nicknamed him "Gawky Sumner" and a friend later pointed out that he "never, so far as I know, fished or shot or rowed . . . in a word was without all those tastes which are almost universal with men of his age."

Maturity and accomplishment were paramount in Charles Pinckney's eyes. The Sumners could trace their Massachusetts lineage to the 1630s, and they took great pride in their deep roots and their contributions to the Commonwealth. Charles Pinckney did not demand so much of his other sons, but Charles, the eldest and bearing his father's name, carried a special burden to uphold the family's reputation.

"Charles," his father said, "upon your discretion and good deportment the happiness of *my* life will in no trifling measure depend."

Young Charles always resented his father for saddling him with this heavy and unfair burden.

✳ ✳ ✳

Charles Pinckney's fortunes improved when he became sheriff of Suffolk County, a position that paid more than $2,000 a year, and he was able to send young Charles to Harvard. Charles vacated his father's Beacon Hill home to study in Cambridge, but the elder Sumner did not let up on his son.

He required Sumner to report each week on what happened at school and kept meticulous account of his son's expenses. Anything less than perfection was unacceptable. Despite young Charles's absence for only three of 580 classes and chapel exercises during his first year of school—an enviable and remarkable attendance record—his father was far from impressed and chastised him for failing to devote his "*whole time* to the duties prescribed."

His father sought for Sumner an exalted and near unachievable well-roundedness. The elder Sumner loved the scholarly life, but as the son of a Revolutionary War hero himself, he wanted young Charles to excel physically and attain the proud bearing and strength of character that military training often produces. When Charles paid a visit to West Point during a Harvard recess, his father wrote a letter of introduction to the commander of the military academy in which he lamented that his son was "somewhat deficient in strength." No doubt looking to prove his father wrong about his physical prowess, in the summer before his final year as a Harvard undergraduate, Charles and four classmates hiked from Boston to Lake Champlain and then Albany, an exhilarating three-week journey during which he talked, sang, and laughed, free—for a short time at least—from Charles Pinckney's judgment and dominance.

But he was never free from the constant feeling that he would never be able to please his father.

After he graduated from Harvard at age nineteen and contemplated his future course in life, Charles complained to a friend that his father, who had spent years overseeing and attempting to manage the smallest details of his son's life, now offered "nought by way of encouragement."

Instead, he said, his father now seemed "determined to let me shape my own course, so that if I am wise, I shall be wise for myself; and if I am foolish, I alone shall bear it."

✳ ✳ ✳

To compensate for his inability to please his father, Sumner sought the company and mentoring of men who were his father's contemporaries—including Justice Joseph Story, whose influence and Harvard connections helped Sumner meet Unitarian reformer William Ellery Channing, and former President John Quincy Adams. It was under their tutelage that Sumner gained self-confidence, honed his ideas, and entered the world of Boston's elite.

Story, especially, was everything his father was not—warm, affectionate, complimentary. It is telling that Sumner, who does not mention his father in his autobiography, writes of Story: "Who could forget his bounding step, his contagious laugh, his exhilarating voice, his beaming smile, his countenance that shone like a benediction?" When Story died in September 1845, Sumner wrote that the loss created "a chasm which I shrink from contemplating."

Sumner's own father's death created no such chasm. Charles Pinckney raised a son who feared making mistakes, desperately needed the acceptance of others, and craved public attention and affirmation, all in response to a dreary upbringing and an iron rule at home. When Charles Pinckney died in April 1839 at the age of sixty-three, it was almost a relief to his eldest son.

Young Charles was traveling in Europe when he received word of his father's death and opted not to make the long trip home, "for I do not see any particular thing in which I could be useful." He admitted that the loss "has caused me many painful emotions—not the less painful because [it is] beyond the reach of ordinary sympathy." He simply was unable to feel the grief that other family members and friends had over the death of his father. Nonetheless, the memory of their relationship was a source of "unfeigned sorrow" to Sumner.

His friends tried to reassure him. "You were a good son," wrote Francis Lieber in his condolence letter. Another friend, who knew the circumstances of Sumner's difficult home life, wrote with brutal honesty what even Sumner may have been afraid to voice out loud, declaring that Sumner "was not as deeply afflicted by his [father's] death as you would have been if he had been *like a father* to you."

✳ ✳ ✳

Sumner's personal travails started with his family but did not end there. His friends—and he had many, especially in his Harvard days—were also familiar with his mood swings and his brooding, introverted, and often self-righteous manner. They enjoyed discussing politics and issues with him but worried about his inability or unwillingness to relax and engage in pleasant conversation or good-natured banter.*

Sumner's group of friends teased him about his lack of a sense of humor and his inability to enjoy or even recognize mirthfulness. Dr. Oliver Wendell Holmes joked that "if one told Charles Sumner that the moon was made of green cheese, he would controvert the alleged fact in all sincerity, and give good reasons why it could not be so." Holmes, who enjoyed Sumner's company and found him courteous and a good listener, like many others found it puzzling that "anything in nature of a jest came very hard to him. He would look bewildered and distressed with the pleasantry that set a company laughing."

Holmes astutely noted that Sumner was "less at ease with women" than with men. Painfully shy and fearful of rejection and humiliation, Sumner seemed unable to carry on even the most basic conversation with women he met in social situations. His intensity dampened light conversation in any setting, but his awkwardness became more pronounced when he was in the company of women. At one gathering, his friends noticed him talking uneasily to an attractive woman and wagered how long it would take for Sumner to turn away and revert to his more comfortable surroundings—conversing with men. They roared with laughter when it happened in a matter of minutes.

Though he was intimidated by strong women, Sumner was not hostile to them; he often admired them from afar. He held romantic notions about marriage and family and believed "that the only true love is love at first sight." But rather than seeking love, Sumner appeared terrified of female companionship and looked to avoid it.

It's also likely that women were less tolerant of Sumner's self-absorption than his male friends. In the matter of relationships, even when they did not involve him directly, Sumner made his own feelings paramount. When his friend Samuel Gridley Howe announced he would marry Julia Ward in 1843, Sumner's primary emotion was not happiness

---

* Any sort of historical medical diagnosis, especially nearly two hundred years after the fact, is fraught with peril. That said, Sumner displayed—and some historians have observed this—several symptoms of what today would be labeled as Asperger's syndrome, including awkwardness in social situations, difficulty expressing empathy, clumsiness, and the ability to hyperfocus on a specific topic.

for the couple but despair for himself. "My friends fall away from me," he wailed. "What will become of me?"

When Henry Wadsworth Longfellow announced his impending marriage to Fanny Appleton the same year, Sumner was distraught; the two men had shared long conversations and spent hours in each other's company. Sumner made no pretense of his unhappiness when Longfellow informed him of his engagement: "What shall I do these long summer evenings?" He hoped Longfellow would forgive his despair, but Sumner said, "Howe has gone . . . now you have gone, and nobody is left with whom I can have sweet sympathy."

Taking pity on Sumner, and with no intention of severing friendships now that they were married, the Longfellows—particularly Fanny, who enjoyed Sumner's company and recognized the importance of her husband's friend in his life—invited him to join them on their honeymoon to the Catskills. "We both earnestly hope you will be able, & willing to accompany us," Fanny wrote on the eve of their departure in the summer of 1843. "Henry promises to appear at the Office by 11 o'clock & hopes to find you with your trunk packed."

Sumner eagerly accepted, and on the train saw fit to read aloud to the newlyweds the funeral orations of French theologian Jacques-Bénigne Bossuet. If the Longfellows had any reaction to the train ride, or Sumner's selected subject matter, they kept it to themselves.

✳ ✳ ✳

For all his struggles with personal relationships, for all of his seeming incapability to assess the dynamics of a social situation—to "read the room" might be the appropriate modern expression—Charles Sumner demonstrated some moments of emotional support for friends and loved ones, offering them, in the words of his sister Julia, the "world of love and tenderness within him."

He enjoyed children and often entertained them and their parents with a lightness that rarely surfaced with adults. The Longfellow children loved spending time with him on his Sunday afternoon visits to Cambridge, especially laughing and playing games in the yard. Henry emphasized that the children always laughed in fun, never in malice, noting in his diary that his family was always "delighted to see him [Sumner] so often . . . the face of a friend—and such a friend!—is what one cannot see too much of; never too much." Years later, when Charley Longfellow was wounded fighting for the Union in the Civil War, Sumner made sure that he received the best care in the Washington, D.C., hospital to which he was confined.

At other times, Sumner sent autographs to young boys and girls who wrote to him, and he once stopped and autographed a sheet for a boy who approached him on the street. He also visited the homes of friends to celebrate, among other things, their children's birthdays and called on sick colleagues and friends; his letters are full of affectionate inquiries about and good wishes for his correspondents' families.

"I think very few people, unless they really knew him from first to last, understood his character," said one Boston woman who knew Sumner well. "His sweeter and gentler nature never had full development—but it was THERE, and those who loved him knew it."

✳ ✳ ✳

At no time was Sumner more expressive of his own emotions, and more affected by loss, than throughout the illness, decline, and death of his sister Mary, who, after a lengthy and painful ordeal, succumbed to tuberculosis. Sumner sat vigil, barely leaving his sister's bedside as she lingered on, often in considerable pain. On the night of October 10, 1844, Mary slept soundly, Sumner by her side, and when she awakened early on the morning of the eleventh, a Friday, Charles asked if she were in pain. "No," Mary replied, "angels are taking care of me."

Sumner grasped her hand and wept. At 9:00 A.M., without speaking again, his beloved Mary died.

His sister's death at age twenty-two devastated her thirty-three-year-old brother. "I had long expected this blow," he wrote, "but no preparation could render it other than bitter."

Sumner had a soft spot for Mary that he had for no one else. The two exchanged letters when Sumner visited Washington in 1834 (Mary was twelve), for which Sumner was grateful. Mary had been a girl when Sumner left for Europe in 1838, and she had grown into a beautiful, intelligent young woman by the time he returned two years later. Sumner enjoyed her conversation and her grace and was always proud to escort her to dinners, dances, and other society events in Boston.

Charles and Mary developed an even closer bond when Charles be-

came ill in the summer of 1844 and shared a room during his convalescence with his infirm and bedridden sister. For two months prior, Charles
had maintained a brutal pace on an editing and annotating project. He
labored day and night, withdrew from friends, developed headaches and
a cough, and ceased almost all exercise and recreation as he huddled in
his office and pored over his work. The physical strain, coupled with his
mental depression, was taking its toll—on one visit Longfellow found
him "in a desperate mood . . . wishing that some one would shoot [him]
through the heart."

By late June, Sumner's health began to break down, and he suffered a
"slow fever." He rallied by July 1 but returned to his backbreaking schedule
too soon, and, by mid-July, he fell seriously ill with fever and hallucina-
tions, "more so than ever before in my life." The family doctor immediately
diagnosed him with tuberculosis—the disease that was killing Mary—
although Sumner showed no apparent symptoms. The doctor also declared
Sumner's affliction hopeless and suggested death was only a matter of time.

Sumner thought otherwise, claiming physicians failed to "comprehend my case." When on July 31 he was finally able to dictate a letter
to Julia for their brother George ("I cannot yet hold a pen in my feverish fingers," he began), Sumner suggested that doctors were swayed by
Mary's illness when they mistakenly diagnosed him with tuberculosis.
Sumner offered his own opinion, which was likely closer to the truth: "I
consider my disease to have been a slow, nervous fever, brought on by
sitting and studying at my desk, till after the clock struck two at night."

Whatever the cause of Sumner's incapacitation—there is insufficient
evidence to offer a definitive diagnosis—for the last two weeks of July
1844, his family and his friends thought he was going to die.

"The doctors thought it was a case of galloping consumption," his sister
Julia recalled. Many friends called at his mother's house to pay their final
respects; others sent books, flowers, baskets of grapes, and letters of sympathy. One friend grieved when he entered Sumner's bedroom and saw Mary
sitting next to him. "It was an affecting sight to see brother and sister, thus
hand-in-hand, preparing to walk through the dark valley," he confided to
his diary. "I shall lose a good friend in Sumner." One of Longfellow's friends
wrote to the poet in late July: "I cannot believe God really means to deprive
humanity of so noble an example of all that is good and high-minded
and pure."

Longfellow's correspondent proved prescient—God was not yet ready for Charles Sumner. His recovery began in late July and continued rapidly for the next several weeks. By mid-August, though he continued to be plagued with night sweats and was still dictating letters to Julia, who also brought him meals and read to him, he was "slowly gaining in strength" and managing to take carriage rides up to ten miles to visit friends. In late August, despite Sumner feeling like "half a man . . . [with] the character of an invalid," and with his doctor's permission, he left Boston to recuperate at the home of his friend Nathan Appleton (Fanny Longfellow's father) in Pittsfield in western Massachusetts. There, he rode horses for hours through the hills of the Berkshires as a source of reinvigoration.

Even as his health improved, however, Sumner fretted about Mary. In early September, while still in Pittsfield, he received a letter from her informing Charles that she "had been obliged to part with her beautiful hair," a side effect from the scarring of bacterial tuberculosis.

"It touched me to the soul," Sumner said.

✳ ✳ ✳

In late September 1844, Sumner left the Berkshires and visited his brother Albert in Newport, Rhode Island, where he grew increasingly stronger. He slept long hours, read often, and rode horses on the beach, which exhilarated him.

He thought of Mary often. The notion of losing her seemed incomprehensible and inevitable at the same time. "I am sad at the thought of Mary, with a disease, like stern destiny, preying upon her," he acknowledged, "and yet, she has been spared longer than I had once ventured to hope." On September 30, he received a letter from Julia informing him that Mary had withdrawn to her bedchamber, "which she will never leave, except for Paradise." Sumner immediately returned to Boston, where he found Mary "weak, very weak—almost voiceless . . . the last sands of her most beautiful life were fast running out."

In his October 15 letter to his brother George, Sumner recapped Mary's final moments and her funeral two days after her death, and also tried to describe the impact of the loss on him and the family.

George had been away for so long that he did not "know the beauty and loveliness of the dear sister you have lost, for she was a child when you left home." Yes, Mary was a classical beauty; she possessed charm and grace, and, inarguably, her "bearing was a rare blending of dignity and modesty." But more important than all those traits, Sumner wrote to George, was Mary's strength of character, "which shone transparent" each day of her life, and the depth of her conscience, "which sat ruler of all [her] thoughts and acts."

Whether it was Mary's inherent gentleness, her long illness, or Charles's witnessing of her daily suffering even as he recovered from his own illness, she was the only member of the family with whom Charles developed a deep attachment.

Overwhelmed with grief for Mary, the normally self-centered Sumner conceded that he would have traded places with his sister. "I feel that it would have been far better had the health, which was unexpectedly renewed in my veins, been bestowed upon her in my stead," he wrote. It was the first time, and one of the only times, that Charles Sumner expressed unconditional love for a family member. No other death, before or after, affected Sumner so deeply, and thoughts of Mary stayed with him always.

Mary's death and his own recovery in 1844 deepened Charles Sumner's search for a meaningful pursuit beyond the law and changed his direction in life.

✳ CHAPTER 3 ✳

TEXAS THUNDER

His close brush with death, the painful loss of Mary, and a national crisis in 1845 combined to profoundly alter Charles Sumner's life and the course of the nation. Together, they served to transform his strong antislavery opinions into passionate political agitation on the issue, jar him from the complacency that had lingered since his return from Europe a few years earlier, and instill in the thirty-four-year-old a renewed sense of purpose that would propel him for nearly three decades.

During the early 1840s, Sumner dabbled in many issues, including progressive movements calling for reforms in prison, education, and mental health services. But by the latter half of 1845, no topic consumed his thoughts more than slavery and its attendant evils. He regarded slavery as a "sin, individual and national," and believed it was "the duty of each individual to cease committing it, and of course, of each State to do likewise."

Sumner argued privately to friends during this period that the best first step toward abolition was to "surround the South with a *moral* blockade," in which people of all walks of life—"the moralist, the statesman, the orator, and the poet"—expressed their public disapproval of slavery. Next, while he acknowledged that the national government could not constitutionally reach into a slave state to abolish the institution, it *could* establish antislavery laws within the District of Columbia, in territories, and as part of interstate commerce and coastal trade. And perhaps one day, Sumner argued, "the Constitution may be amended, so that it shall cease to render *any sanction* to slavery."

Still, prior to 1845, while the evolution of Sumner's beliefs was important in his own development as an antislavery voice, his views circulated only on the periphery of the national slavery debate. He put forth his opinions in letters to friends, associates, and, on occasion, local news-papers, but he remained on the sidelines of the political battle, mainly, he explained, because he disagreed with the scorched-earth approach of the Garrisonian radicals and, other than his membership in the Mas-sachusetts Whig Party, "had no relish for the strife of politics." He was hampered further when his debilitating illness hit in 1844.

But then came America's all-out effort to annex Texas from Mexico and admit it to the union as a slave state.

A fully recovered Charles Sumner could remain on the sidelines no longer.

✳ ✳ ✳

The United States had envisioned the annexation of Texas since the ad-ministration of Andrew Jackson in the 1830s; the effort sputtered under Martin Van Buren, then regained traction under President John Tyler, who convinced Congress to adopt a joint resolution to annex Texas days before President-elect James K. Polk was inaugurated.

While unrest among Texans was first fomented by genuine grievances against Mexico, an angry Sumner viewed the Texas plan as nothing more than a power grab by the proslavery Tyler to extend human bondage hundreds of miles west; many in Sumner's home state agreed. In fact, the movement to annex Texas stirred latent antislavery sentiment in New En-gland. In January 1845, the Massachusetts legislature approved a resolu-tion opposing the annexation and called for an anti-Texas convention at Faneuil Hall. Attendees of the Convention of the People of Massachusetts adopted an address, partially written by Senator Daniel Webster, declar-ing that the annexation was both proslavery and unconstitutional. In his own fiery speech, defiant abolitionist William Lloyd Garrison said that if Congress approved the plan, Massachusetts should consider the union dissolved and form a new government with other free states.

Public meetings and rallies against the admission of Texas as a slave state were held throughout the spring and summer across Massachusetts and other Northern states, and Sumner forwarded to Congress a peti-tion bearing the names of sixty thousand Massachusetts residents who opposed Texas's annexation and admission as a slave state.

Massachusetts was not uniformly against the annexation. Conserva-tive Massachusetts merchants were leery of overly strident anti-Texas annexation voices for fear of alienating Southern congressmen at precisely the time President Polk was proposing a reduction in trade tariffs that were hindering New England manufacturing. Sumner cared little for these arguments; for him, it was enough to believe that the annexation of Texas was wrong and immoral. As for many in the state's merchant class who supported the Texas annexation, including his brother George, Sumner accused them of considering only the "material interests" of the country.

The annexation of Texas would lead to war, Sumner argued—one immoral act would lead to another, surely, and underlying both of these was slavery, the greatest and most immoral evil of all.

✳ ✳ ✳

On a stormy November 1845 night at Boston's Faneuil Hall, before a huge crowd, Charles Sumner used the coming annexation of Texas to deliver his first public speech against the extension and perpetuation of slavery. Violent rain, roaring thunder, and crackling lightning were, in the words of one attendee, "emblematic of the present moral and political aspects of the country."

After commending the crowd for braving the inclement evening, Sumner wasted no time decrying the "scheme for the annexation of Texas" as one that began . . . in order to extend and strengthen slavery." All along, he argued, the move to annex Texas was an idea spawned, endorsed, and supported by Southern Democrats who were members or allies of the slaveocracy. Sumner's audience need look no further than the Texas constitution to see what Congress would de facto sanction with its admittance of Texas—the constitution not only supported slavery but also contained a clause prohibiting the state's legislature from abolishing the institution. "By welcoming Texas as a slave state we do make slavery *our own original sin*," he added. "Let us wash our hands of this great guilt."

Invoking patriotism, religion, and humanity, Sumner employed the rhetoric and passion that would become hallmarks of his career, language that would frighten his opponents and sometimes cause discomfort among his allies but left no ambiguity about where he stood.

He was likely recalling his early Washington, D.C., trip when he claimed that the annexation of Texas would "legalize a new slave-trade," in which "wretched coffles [would be] driven from the exhausted lands of the Northern slave states to the sugar plantations nearer the sun of the South." Sumner envisioned these slaves on their overland "fatal journey, chained in bands, and driven like cattle, leaving behind what has become to them a home and a country," exactly what had been happening as part of the Washington slave trade when Sumner visited in the mid-1830s.

Admitting Texas as a slave state would violate the promise of equal rights and the "brotherhood of all men" set forth in the Declaration of Independence, and as such Massachusetts must reject the notion.

Sumner thundered inside Faneuil Hall as the storm raged outside:

> If the slave-trade is to receive new adoption from our country, let us [in Massachusetts] have *no part or lot in it* . . . God forbid that the votes and voices of Northern freemen should help to bind anew the fetters of the slave! . . . God forbid that the lash of the slave-dealer should descend by any sanction from New England! . . . God forbid that the blood which spurts from the lacerated, quivering flesh of the slave should soil the hem of the white garments of Massachusetts!

Yes, it was late in the process—Texas admittance appeared to be a foregone conclusion—but Massachusetts must be "aroused," Sumner said. Neutrality was fine in ordinary politics, but on this topic, those who remained neutral were committing "treason to liberty, to humanity, and to the fundamental principles of free institutions." Massachusetts had always been a leader in the cause of freedom—it must not yield now.

The stirring rhetoric, along with the roaring storm, the wind rattling the windows of old Faneuil Hall, and the flashing lightning shooting streaks of fire across the black November sky—all of these made it easy for audience members to recall where they were when Charles Sumner became the newest and strongest antislavery voice in Massachusetts.

✳ ✳ ✳

Sumner's pleas were in vain.

On December 29, 1845, Congress, with little debate, admitted Texas to the union as a slaveholding state. In April 1846, General Zachary Taylor's men, provokingly marching through territory claimed by both the United States and Mexico, were fired upon—and President Polk announced that war with Mexico was underway. On May 13, a congressional declaration made it official, despite opposition from some Northern lawmakers.

That his country was fighting a war to essentially extend slavery left Sumner livid and unable to concentrate on much else. "In Sumner's alphabet just now there are only two words: Slavery and the Mexican War," wrote his friend, George Hillard. Sumner's law practice languished, and he increasingly lost interest in the law as a profession. Sumner advocated splitting the traditional Whig Party and became a leader of the so-called radical abolitionist "Conscience Whigs," who ridiculed and decried the old-guard "Cotton Whigs" as too moderate on slavery, even accusing the party's mercantile wing of desiring to preserve the institution. In Sumner's view, Whigs with textile interests—he called them the "lords of the loom"—were far too intertwined with the success of slave owners—the "lords of the lash"—because of Northern mill owners' need for cheap cotton.

Charles Sumner learned a great deal about himself from the Texas speech. For an intellectual who had previously expressed himself mainly through the written word, it taught him the full power of oratory and specifically the broad range of his own oratorical skills. For a rising talent whose name was known only to a few Boston political insiders, the Texas oration brought him national fame. For an attorney who had spent most of his early career huddled with dusty lawbooks, gloomy and unfulfilled professionally, the speech freed him from the constrictions of the legal profession, encouraged him to think about entering public life, and expanded his world in profound ways. The Texas speech demonstrated his towering intellect, his tenacity in argument, his capacity to deal with universal issues, and his moral courage.

The experience also taught him a valuable lesson: true leadership often requires expressing bold views and sentiments that engender discomfort. Throughout his career, rather than shrinking from controversy, Sumner would embrace it, grab it around the waist, and dance it across speaker platforms in Boston, New York, Washington, D.C., Europe, and elsewhere.

Emboldened by his Texas speech, Sumner in May 1846 ventured further into the political arena—as a harsh critic, not a candidate—and at the same time kicked a hornet's nest when he trained his sights and his scalding tongue on respected Boston congressman Robert C. Winthrop after the representative voted in favor of the Mexican War.

Sumner's actions, Winthrop's reaction, and the ensuing fallout make the incident the ideal microscope through which to view the competing facets of Charles Sumner's personality, characteristics he demonstrated to a wide audience in the latter half of the 1840s, traits he would carry with him for his entire life.

In this Sumner versus Sumner struggle, the unwavering antislavery crusader, the equal rights idealist, the visionary who foresaw a bright future few others thought possible, waged a constant internal battle against the sanctimonious egotist, the self-appointed martyr of righteousness, and the insecure, brooding, often lonely man who struggled mightily with personal relationships.

¥ ¥ ¥

As a lawmaker, Robert Winthrop, like the mercantile class who supported him, avoided controversy, confrontation, great moral questions, and, according to one contemporaneous writer, "any agitation which was likely to bring the masses to the front."

Like most traditional Boston Whigs, Winthrop held tepid antislavery positions, but also like many of his fellow party members, he viewed slavery as an unfortunate way of life that would eventually run its course rather than a monumental moral wrong that required immediate righting. He made this clear to abolitionists when he was first elected to Congress in 1839, informing them that he did not "regard it as any peculiar part of his duty to agitate the subject of slavery." Winthrop, whose bread was buttered by Boston's ruling class, was well aware that cheap Southern cotton, picked by slaves, oiled the wheels of his state's commerce both in Massachusetts textile factories and in the Boston financial houses whose capital was tied up in water turbines, woolen cards, power looms, and spinning jacks.

A loyal Cotton Whig, an ambitious lawmaker with aspirations for higher office who might someday need Southern support, Winthrop felt no need to alienate slave owners in any meaningful way. He was content to dip his toes along the water's edge of the slavery debate by politely opposing its extension, but he declined to venture into the deep, dark waters where dangerous abolitionists lurked.

But Winthrop found himself in a dilemma when it came time for a series of votes on the Mexican War. Wily Democrats, through parliamentary maneuvering, inserted a controversial preamble into a bill that provided $50,000 for supplies and 50,000 additional men for Zachary Taylor's army; and the bill's preamble declared that the war had been caused by Mexican aggression. As a Northern lawmaker who opposed slavery's extension, Winthrop opposed the preamble, but as a Whig politician who supported the military, he could hardly vote against supplies and reinforcements (never mind that Taylor neither requested nor needed either).

So, like most Whigs, Winthrop cast a "yes" vote. Winthrop insisted that he did so only after a pledge by President Polk that he was carrying on the war not for the purposes of aggression and conquest but only to achieve an honorable peace. But Winthrop's explanation rang hollow. Those who opposed his position believed that for partisan political purposes, for fear of being labeled by Democrats as unsupportive of the military in the 1848 presidential election, Winthrop and the other Whigs had demonstrated "weak submission in an hour which called for courage and faith."

In essence, even as he publicly denounced the U.S. invasion of Mexico, Winthrop's vote provided the means to carry it on.

Such craven hypocrisy Charles Sumner could not forgive.

✳ ✳ ✳

The battle was joined.

Writing under the pseudonym "Boston" on July 22, 1846, in the *Whig*, a party newspaper he and other Conscience Whigs had purchased to promote their aggressive antislavery views throughout Boston, Sumner first claimed he "cherished" Winthrop on a personal level, valued their cordial relationship, and never doubted the integrity of his character. However, by voting for the war bill, Winthrop had "told a lie" and committed "gross disloyalty to Truth and Freedom."

Sumner's rhetoric became more personal and animus-filled in a later article, in which he accused Winthrop of sanctioning "*unquestionably the most wicked act in our history.*"

Winthrop's vote was "wrong by the law of nations and by the higher law of God," Sumner declared. In language dripping with sanctimony,

Sumner compared Winthrop to a modern Pontius Pilate: "Blood! blood! is on the hands of the representative from Boston. Not all great Neptune's ocean can wash them clean." Nor did Sumner's verbal assault and personal attacks stop with newspaper articles. In a pointed letter to Nathan Appleton, an apoplectic Sumner described Winthrop as bereft of moral character and characterized the congressman's vote as *"the worst act that was ever done by a Boston representative."*

Appleton considered Sumner's assault to be "inconsistent with a proper Christian charity" and advised him to withdraw his charges against Winthrop. Sumner refused, claiming that Winthrop's vote led to an unjust war, "the greatest *crime* a nation can commit . . . I think it was the *imperative* of every Christian representative to oppose it, even if he stood *alone*."

Angry and hurt by the attacks, Winthrop responded with a letter that would terminate all communications with Sumner for the next sixteen years. He declared that Sumner's words were full of "the grossest perversions" because they attacked not just Winthrop's actions but also his integrity. He believed it inconceivable that a man who had professed to be his friend should "turn upon me with such ferocity."

✵ ✵ ✵

Winthrop was hardly alone in his anger toward Sumner. Members of Boston society, including influential political leaders, were shocked at Sumner's intemperate attitude and vituperative language against a sitting and respected congressman. Disagreement on issues was expected, but in the mid-nineteenth-century political arena, personal vitriol and character assassination were not.

Much of Boston society shunned Sumner after the Winthrop affair, and even close friends turned against him. The Winthrop controversy ended his regular and cordial visits to Appleton's house, and Boston educator and author George Ticknor never spoke to Sumner again. A Beacon Hill woman who had invited Sumner to a dinner party later received a withdrawal of an acceptance from a guest who'd learned that Sumner would be in attendance. Historian William Prescott still welcomed Sumner to his Beacon Street home but acknowledged that he selected his guests with care when Sumner was invited, "lest the feast should be marred by unseemly behavior on their part." The Longfellows, Henry and Fanny, remained devoted to Sumner and kept a room for his visits, but even they found it necessary to issue him a warning from Cambridge to stay away when Nathan Appleton visited his daughter and son-in-law.

Sumner was crushed both by the intensity of the reaction and the ostracism. A thirty-five-year-old bachelor with no family of his own and difficulties forming intimate friendships, he'd constructed his social life around conversations at men's clubs and dinner parties with Boston's intellectual and political elites. "There was a time when I was welcome at almost every house within two miles of us," he remarked to a friend while riding in a carriage down Beacon Street in Boston. "But now hardly any are open to me."

One of Boston's wealthiest and most venerable old-money party leaders who knew Sumner well said during this time: "His solitude is glacial. He has nothing but himself to think about."

Sumner acknowledged as much when he wrote on New Year's Eve 1846 to his brother George in Europe. Reinforcing his belief that the Mexican War was immoral, unconstitutional, and "wasteful of life and treasure," he remained puzzled that Winthrop and many Whigs placed politics ahead of party principles.

"The affairs of our country are now in a deplorable condition," he concluded to George.

✳ ✳ ✳

As isolated as he was after the Winthrop controversy, Sumner interpreted his condition as a type of social martyrdom, the price to pay for the sake of adhering to principle. He derived enormous satisfaction from "doing his duty."

He did not back off a single inch.

In Sumner's view, there was "no *real question now before the country*, except as to the Slave Power." He was frustrated at the lack of Whig action on the antislavery question. As his abolitionist views hardened, the Whigs seemed content to make speeches about issues that "fall below the occasion . . . they are superficial and do not really grasp the question."

At the Whig convention at Faneuil Hall in September 1846, young Conscience Whigs clambered for him to speak, and he did not disappoint, urging the party to cease its focus on mundane tariffs and other commercial interests and direct its full energies against the extension of slavery and, ultimately, to slavery's demise. Massachusetts Whigs must "not fear to stand alone" if need be. When Sumner finished, the estranged Appleton approached him as he left the podium and said, "Yours would have been a good speech in Virginia." Sumner replied that, sadly, "*we were* in Virginia, as to the [way Massachusetts interacted with the] Slave-Power."

Some Conscience Whigs had drafted Sumner as a congressional candidate in the 1846 election, but he declined on the grounds that such a political move would be seen as self-seeking and thus detract from the purity of his staunch antislavery message. He became despondent when Winthrop was reelected to Congress in a landslide, and he continued to alienate traditional Whigs when he accused them of being weak on the slavery issue and too loyal to traditional issues that the existential slavery debate had rendered all but meaningless. This elicited a fresh round of press attacks against Sumner—Cotton Whigs recognized him as the most dangerous leader of the radical antislavery wing of the party.

The split widened as the year went on.

✳ ✳ ✳

The rallying cry for Sumner and other Conscience Whigs throughout 1847 was the ongoing congressional debate over the Wilmot Proviso, the proposal to ban slavery in any territory acquired from Mexico. They made support of the proviso a minimum threshold for any future Whig candidate for president and threatened to break off and start their own party if Whigs failed to endorse it.

But at the Massachusetts Whig state convention in the fall, Sumner was disappointed when party loyalists applauded Daniel Webster's candidacy for the presidency in 1848, despite Webster's failure to endorse the Wilmot Proviso. Then, the final indignation: delegates rejected a Wilmot Proviso plank in the Whig party platform. Sumner expressed doubt that Conscience Whigs "would ever enter another convention of the [Massachusetts Whig] party."

Sumner was never more disheartened by the national Whigs' reluctance to tackle the slavery fight head-on than when the party nominated General Zachary Taylor for president in the spring of 1848—a man with, at best, ambiguous views on slavery whose main qualification was his performance in the Mexican War. "I will not vote for Taylor and I shall do all in my power to oppose his election," Sumner announced. He found the choice insulting and became more aggrieved when the Whigs nominated New York's Millard Fillmore, a moderate on the issue of slavery, as vice president.

He angered Cotton Whigs further when he accused Northern textile merchants and Southern slave owners of fashioning a secret conspiracy to ensure Taylor's election. An "unhallowed union" had formed, he insisted, "between the cotton planters and flesh-mongers in Louisiana and Mississippi and the cotton-spinners and traffickers of New England."

✳ ✳ ✳

Frustrated and thwarted by Cotton Whigs, Sumner and other Conscience Whigs realized, especially after Taylor's nomination, that their party would never embrace a forceful antislavery position. Timid lip service had preserved the old order, lined the pockets of Cotton Whigs, and maintained the delicate, though corrupt, balance between the Southern slave owners who sold cotton and the Northern merchants who purchased it. Merely relying on "hope" that such a partnership could be dissolved after Taylor's nomination was a fool's mission.

Events moved quickly in 1848. If Cotton Whigs and Conscience Whigs could not come together on the slavery issue, Charles Sumner believed it was time for the party to break apart. He finally left the Whigs altogether to become a leader of the fledgling Free Soil Party, whose ringing slogan, "Free Soil, Free Speech, Free Labor, and Free Men," Sumner believed—naively it turned out—would sweep the North with abolitionist fervor.

And if he needed more evidence of the rightness of his cause, a shocking episode that occurred in April, 450 miles southward in Washington, D.C., illustrated for him the inherent evil of slavery and reinforced his conviction that he held the moral high ground on the slavery debate.

He was not directly involved in the early stages of the notorious event, but he made his opinions known soon thereafter, and before long, Charles Sumner would be deeply mired in the aftermath of the largest attempted slave escape in American history.

✳ CHAPTER 4 ✳

A DARING ESCAPE ATTEMPT

APRIL 15, 1848, WASHINGTON, D.C., NIGHT

Light rain fell as dozens of slaves crept across the open fields and silently made their way through the dark and unpaved streets of the nation's capital. The group would grow to seventy-seven strong, from some forty households.

They had slipped undetected from their masters' homes in Washington City, Georgetown, and Alexandria and were hoping to reach the *Pearl*, a schooner moored at the Seventh Street Wharf on the Potomac River awaiting the arrival of its passengers.

By secret prearrangement, the runaways—old and young, parents with children, men and women who worked in homes, hotels, and boarding-houses—had been instructed to wait until dark to leave their quarters and, with as much stealth as possible, reach the *Pearl* no later than 11:00 P.M., when the 54-ton craft, now anchored at a remote dock about one mile from Pennsylvania Avenue, would shove off and carry them about 220 miles to Frenchtown, New Jersey, and freedom. To do so, the *Pearl* would have to travel undetected about 100 miles down the Potomac to Chesapeake Bay, then another 120 miles up the bay, across the Delaware Canal and along the Delaware River to the free state of New Jersey.

The *Pearl* had arrived two nights earlier, a Thursday, sailing up the Potomac to the Seventh Street wharf, carrying a load of wood, ostensibly for sale, to camouflage the real purpose of its mission. On board were three men: Captain Edward Sayres, owner of the *Pearl*; Daniel Drayton—sometimes called "captain"—a middle-aged veteran of the coastal trade with abolitionist sympathies, who had chartered the schooner for one hundred dollars; and Chester English, a young sailor and cook.

Sayres was responsible for the ship and in charge of English; Drayton was tasked with arranging for the safe passage of the runaway slaves—he was the lead architect of the most daring and audacious escape plan yet devised on the American continent.

✷ ✷ ✷

While Washington, D.C., was filled with slaveholders and slaveholding sympathizers, huge swaths of the District's population, as well as abolitionists across the country, were embarrassed not only that slavery was *allowed* in the nation's capital but also that human beings were bought and sold within sight of the Capitol Building—as Sumner had witnessed during his visit in 1834.

But because Washington was also surrounded by slaveholding states, most D.C. residents—like the national Cotton Whigs whom Charles Sumner vilified—accepted the existence of slavery as an essential element in maintaining sectional and regional peace and feared the shock to the system that the abolitionist philosophy could bring. Moreover, like Deep South slave owners, they also feared the notion of a servile black population rising up in rebellion.

It was ironic, then, that when the *Pearl* reached port, Washington was in the midst of a massive celebration to mark the recent overthrow of Louis Philippe's regime in France and the establishment of a free republic, raising the possibility of freedom spreading throughout other countries in Europe. America's capital could barely contain its jubilation. Bonfires blazed in public squares, a torchlight parade wound its way through Washington, and slaveholding U.S. congressmen missed the irony as they delivered speeches about a new dawn of freedom in Europe.

Drayton relied on newspaper accounts of the speeches because he did not hear them. "I came to Washington not to preach, nor to hear preached, emancipation, equality, and brotherhood, but to put them into practice," he wrote.

✷ ✷ ✷

The arrival of the *Pearl* in Washington was not a spontaneous act—it had actually been planned since February. Drayton repeatedly denied that the rescue plan was the work of any organized abolitionist plot, but that he had "been paid by others to take the slaves." He refused to say at first who these people were, only that he had received word from contacts in Philadelphia that a family in Washington was hoping to enlist his services. His reputation preceded him—Drayton had helped a woman and five children, all slaves, flee Washington the previous fall.

Later, Drayton confirmed that he had been approached by Daniel Bell, a free black resident of Washington, whose family, a wife and eight children, were in the midst of a legal battle to secure their freedom. The Bells had run out of money defending their status in court and faced the risk of being sold back into slavery. Daniel Bell convinced abolitionist William Chaplin to fund the effort to help his family flee Washington and reach freedom in the North. Through intermediaries, Bell reached Drayton.

When Drayton arrived in Washington, D.C, he met with Bell, who informed him that word had spread throughout the slave community of the *Pearl*'s mission and that "quite a number of others . . . wished to avail themselves of this opportunity of escaping." No one could say for sure just how many people wanted to flee, but thus far at least, the *Pearl*'s secret mission was known only to slaves; neither slave owners nor law enforcement officials were aware.

Undeterred at the potential increase in the number of passengers, Drayton reminded Bell of the need for a timely getaway. "All who [are] on board before eleven o'clock, I should take," he said. "The others would have to remain behind."

✴ ✴ ✴

Daniel Bell was just one person who organized the *Pearl*'s escape mission. Another was Samuel Edmonson, a "hired out" slave and one of fourteen children of Paul and Amelia Edmonson (Paul was a free black and Amelia was a slave, which under Maryland law made all fourteen children slaves). When they reached the appropriate age, their owner hired them out in Washington, D.C., as servants and laborers. Samuel and five of his siblings—including his sister Emily, who was hired out to a different family—planned to board the *Pearl*.

Samuel and Emily rendezvoused that night on a Washington street corner and arrived at the *Pearl* around the same time as a black carriage driver, Judson Diggs, who was carrying another runaway slave to the wharf. Much to Diggs's chagrin, two things occurred nearly simultaneously that left a bad taste in his mouth—and would have profound implications for the *Pearl* and its passengers. First, his penniless fare could not pay him and promised to send money later, which angered Diggs. Second, and more infuriating, Diggs spotted Emily Edmonson, to whom he had once proposed marriage; at the time, Emily could barely repress her laughter as she spurned his request.

Now, she was about to escape to freedom.

Diggs, a carriage driver who traded in both goods and information, would forget neither slight.

✳ ✳ ✳

Shortly after 10:00 P.M. on April 15, with the *Pearl*'s hold filled with seventy-seven runaway slaves, Drayton—convinced that the secrecy of his mission remained intact—ordered crew member English to cast off and make sail.

But a half mile upriver, the *Pearl* encountered both a strong tide and a dead calm, forcing it to lay up until daylight—a crucial delay. The wind picked up, and as the sun rose, the *Pearl* resumed sailing and passed by Alexandria. Feeling confident, Drayton went into the hold and distributed bread among his slave stowaways—"men and women in pretty equal proportions, with a number of boys and girls, and two small children."

Shortly after dinner, the *Pearl* encountered a steamer heading to Washington from Baltimore. As the schooner approached the mouth of the Potomac at Lookout Point, the wind roared to the north and, according to Drayton, "blew with such stiffness . . . it would make it impossible for us to go up the bay." He instead urged Sayres to go to sea, "with the intention of reaching the Delaware by the outside passage." Sayres refused, saying the vessel was not fit to venture into open ocean and that his contract called for the *Pearl* to sail along the prearranged route.

Drayton had no choice but to agree for the *Pearl* to drop anchor at 9:00 P.M. in Cornfield Harbor near Point Lookout, a common protected spot for craft to rest when encountering difficult winds in the area.

Exhausted after the tense escape and ensuing daylong voyage, Drayton, Sayres, English, and the *Pearl*'s runaway slaves fell fast asleep.

✳ ✳ ✳

Back in Washington at daybreak on Sunday the sixteenth, slave owners in the city and the surrounding towns woke to find "no breakfast was waiting for them" and worse, their slaves were missing, all "in one fell swoop," a district attorney would later say. The slave owners conferred and estimated that the value of the slaves lost, including many "prime hands," exceeded $100,000.

They organized a pursuing posse, which at first had no idea how or to where their slaves had escaped. Soon, though, the posse encountered Diggs, the carriage driver, still rankled about his passenger's lack of payment and thirsting for vengeance against Emily Edmondson. He wasted no time in pointing the posse toward the river. "It is very doubtful whether the pursuers would have got upon the right track had it not been for the treachery of [the] colored hackman," Drayton concluded later.

Constables and civilians alike, armed to the teeth with rifles, pistols, and bowie knives, jumped aboard the *Salem*, a steamboat operated by the prosperous Dodge family of Georgetown, who owned several runaway slaves aboard the *Pearl*. At noon on the sixteenth, the *Salem* steamed south with about thirty-five men aboard, where late in the day it encountered the ship from Baltimore, whose crew members revealed that they had crossed paths with the *Pearl*.

Still, when the *Salem* reached the mouth of the river it had not found the fleeing ship with the escaped slaves.

The slave owners, many of whom were drunk on brandy and other liquor, were about to abandon pursuit and turn back to Washington when someone had the idea to look in Cornfield Harbor.

✳ ✳ ✳

At 2:00 A.M. on Monday, April 17, 1848, Drayton was awakened suddenly by the sound of the *Salem* blowing off steam alongside the *Pearl*. "I knew at once that we were taken," he recalled.

Quickly, he heard loud shouts and the trampling of feet on deck as the posse boarded the *Pearl*. Several slaves hurried to Drayton's cabin and asked if they should fight, but he told them no; their pursuers would be armed, and Drayton feared a massacre if his passengers resisted. Suddenly the hatch opened and one of the men above yelled, "Niggers, by God!" to which his colleagues celebrated with resounding cheers and by banging their musket butts against the deck.

A group of men came to Drayton's berth, ordered him at gunpoint to get dressed, seized him and tied him up, along with Sayres and English, and took them prisoner aboard the *Salem*. The posse left the runaway slaves aboard the *Pearl,* to which the *Salem*'s crew attached a towline, and proceeded back up the river.

Throughout the return to Washington, Drayton and Sayres were harangued and threatened with lynching and daggers, while a frightened and overwhelmed English wept uncontrollably. Taking pity, Drayton explained to his captors that English had come to Washington "in perfect ignorance of the object of the expedition," whereupon they untied him.

The *Salem* arrived near Fort Washington at night and anchored until morning—the posse members preferring to make a triumphant entry into the nation's capital by daylight.

✳ ✳ ✳

As light dawned, Sayres and Drayton were tied together arm in arm, as were the slaves two by two, with their other arm bound behind their backs; as Drayton described them, thirty-eight men and boys, twenty-six women and girls, and thirteen small children. As the *Salem* passed Alexandria, the entire group was ordered on deck and exhibited to the hundreds of people who had gathered on the wharves. "The mob signified their satisfaction by three cheers," Drayton described.

At Steamboat Wharf, the *Pearl* crew members and the slaves were marched in a long procession, with Drayton and Sayres at the head, guarded by an armed man on each side. Thousands of residents lined the streets, shouting, "Lynch them! Lynch the damned villains!" Others in the unruly mob screamed at Drayton, "Shoot him! Shoot the hellhound!"

Fearful that crowd members would overwhelm them and take matters into their own hands, posse members put Sayres and Drayton into a carriage, and the hackman drove them to jail, where they were placed in cells as thousands of people surrounded the prison. The seventy-seven slaves were also jailed as runaways.

Drayton looked around his cell, with only its cold stone floor, a night-bucket and water can—no chair or table or stool—and felt as though he "had been a murderer" or committed some other "desperate crime." His captors refused to give him his overcoat or valise, so using his water can as a pillow, he lay down exhausted on the bare stone floor and slept.

✳ ✳ ✳

Most of the captured runaway slaves suffered a miserable fate.

After their furious owners claimed them from jail, most of them were handed over to slave traders for sale in the Deep South—the Carolinas, Alabama, Georgia, and New Orleans. One Northern newspaper reporter visited the railroad depot and spotted about fifty slaves, most shackled together, waiting to board trains. "Some . . . were weeping most bitterly," he wrote. "I learned that many families were separated. Wives were to take leave of their husbands, and husbands of their wives, children of their parents, brothers and sisters shaking hands perhaps for the last time."

After months of legal maneuvering and appeals, Drayton and Sayres were acquitted of criminal charges of larceny, but in March 1849, each was fined more than $10,000 for assisting with the escape of slaves, as well as court costs, and ordered imprisoned until the amount was paid in full. Drayton was distraught. The enormous fines, and their inability to pay them, meant they would be in jail "for life, unless the President could be induced to pardon us."

With the imprisonment of Drayton and Sayres, the *Pearl* episode, the largest attempted slave escape in U.S. history, came to a close—but only for the time being. It would have implications for the slavery debate in the nation's capital and across the land for years to come. It would affect congressional debates, slave owners, abolitionists, writers, and the U.S. presidency.

And eventually, Charles Sumner would have his say in all of it.

✳ ✳ ✳

For the time being, in June 1848, Sumner was content to express his disgust over the *Pearl* incident. "I am filled with shame at the transactions in Washington," he wrote. He was sickened that the runaway slaves were sold farther South, and while he acknowledged that Drayton and Sayres probably broke laws through their actions, he could not condemn anyone who attempted to "extricate their fellow men from unjust laws." Rather, he wondered whether Sayres and Drayton would one day be regarded as "martyrs of Liberty."

Still a private citizen, Sumner favored congressional action, demand-ing "abolition of the slave-trade in the District." The *Pearl* incident, in Sumner's view, cried out for such an "*aggressive* measure" on slavery. He also lamented the contrast between the groundswell for liberty under-way across the Atlantic while Washington, D.C., the capital seat of the United States, continued to operate under the yoke of slavery. "In Europe they *mob* for Freedom," he wrote, "in Washington for *slavery.*"

But the *Pearl* episode, he believed, was yet another occurrence that would change hearts and minds on the slavery issue and lead the way to eventual abolition. He sensed that in the summer of 1848, change was afoot. As the cry of freedom was being heard throughout Europe, Sumner observed, the *Pearl* incident had energized abolitionists and focused na-tional attention on the dreadful slave auctions in Washington, D.C.

Traditional party structures were teetering; the slavery issue threat-ened to topple them once and for all.

✳ ✳ ✳

Sumner felt that the country took a step backward in November 1848, when Cotton Whig Zachary Taylor won the presidential election easily and soft-on-slavery Michigan Democrat Lewis Cass—who opposed the Wilmot Proviso and warned against federal interference on the slavery issue—finished second. ("If the relation of master and servant may be regulated or annihilated," Cass argued during the campaign, "so may the relation of husband and wife, or parent or child.")

Sumner was appalled and disappointed with the strong showings of Cass and Taylor, while Free Soil candidate, elder statesman, and former President Martin Van Buren did not receive a single electoral vote nation-ally; but he still believed the campaign helped the party and its antislavery platform command the respect of the country. Antislavery Democrats, such as they were, abandoned Cass and rallied behind Van Buren and the Free Soil banner, likely costing the Democrat nominee the election.

"[The] public mind has been stirred on the subject of slavery to depths never before reached," Sumner said after the election. Its ideas, he pre-dicted, "will yet leaven the whole union" if only the antislavery coalition held firm.

The new year brought a whiff of change.

Sumner was encouraged when New York Whig congressman Daniel

Gott offered a motion to prohibit the slave trade in Washington, D.C. It was soundly defeated, but Sumner applauded the effort—was there any doubt that the Free Soilers had scared the Whigs into at least taking *some* action? And he was ecstatic when he received word in February 1849 that Ohio lawyer and ardent Free Soiler Salmon P. Chase was elected to the U.S. Senate, cobbling together a coalition of Free Soil supporters and antislavery Democrats in the Ohio legislature to propel him to victory. Chase's election "has given our cause so triumphant a triumph," Sumner exclaimed. "I can hardly believe it!"

Chase's success seemed to be "the beginning of the end" of slavery, Sumner said in his congratulatory letter. It would influence voters in the West and bring the antislavery cause to the heart of the national government.

Halfway through 1849, Sumner sensed that the country, perhaps the world, was beginning its shift—albeit slowly, and not yet inexorably—toward positions he held dear.

✳ ✳ ✳

This, then, was Charles Sumner in the final months of 1849: a well-traveled scholar and lawyer, whose own serious illness and the tragic death of his adored sister propelled him to seek his life's meaning on a broader humanitarian stage, unencumbered by the byzantine arcana of the legal profession; a progressive whose eyes were fully opened to the evils of slavery with the annexation of Texas and the Mexican War, convincing him to focus his efforts almost exclusively on the institution's eradication; and an uncompromising and unapologetic champion of equal rights who willingly risked friendships, personal status, party affiliation, and professional advancement to uphold his principles.

Sumner felt momentum for the cause of freedom and confidence in his abilities to lead such an effort.

"My course is taken," Sumner wrote, "and I shall pursue it without fear."

On a cold December morning in 1849, he stood outside the Massachusetts Supreme Judicial Court building, prepared to embark on his course, a journey from which he would never turn back.

✳ CHAPTER 5 ✳

A NEW DOCTRINE IS BORN

DECEMBER 4, 1849, BOSTON, MORNING

The two lawyers, one white and one black, shook hands and exchanged greetings as they approached the Supreme Judicial Courthouse, marking their status as the first interracial legal team in U.S. history. What lay ahead for Charles Sumner and Robert Morris also had historic implications; within minutes, they would present opening arguments in a case with the potential to change, in profound ways, the city, the North, and someday perhaps the entire country.

Bitter cold air swept in from the harbor as the two Boston attorneys ascended the marble stairs of the courthouse, situated on Court Street behind Old City Hall. The previous day, the first storm of the season had left the ground covered in snow. Temperatures had plunged to the single digits during the storm, while high winds had destroyed a Catholic church south of Boston, and to the north, rough seas had split a schooner into pieces near Plum Island, killing all aboard.

The whipping wind would pose no danger to the building Sumner and Morris were about to enter. As they reached the top of the stairs, they took note of the great entrance doors, solid beneath the building's wide gable, which was supported by tall Doric columns. The structure resembled an impregnable Greek temple more than an old courthouse—an edifice as imposing as the challenge the two men faced.

✳ ✳ ✳

Sumner was here at Morris's request.

The twenty-six-year-old grandson of a slave, Morris in 1847 had become the second black lawyer in America to pass the bar and the first to argue and win a case (nearly twenty-four thousand lawyers worked in the United States at the time). His achievement galvanized Boston's black community, made Morris something of a regional celebrity, and convinced black printer Benjamin Roberts to seek his representation in a case that held deeply personal meaning for the client—the right of his six-year-old daughter, Sarah, to attend a white-only grade school.

Morris lost the initial case at the county court level and asked the more experienced Sumner to assist him with the appeal before the Supreme Judicial Court of Massachusetts. When Sumner studied the facts of the case and envisioned its long-term ramifications, he agreed to work with Morris without payment. At last—a legal case that could fulfill his desire to fight for equal rights.

The thirty-eight-year-old Sumner was a natural ally for Morris. His Harvard education, his intellect, his deep knowledge of law, politics, and philosophy, his ability to employ stirring language, his advocacy for progressive causes, his willingness to fight, and, most recently, his steadfast opposition to slavery and support for equal rights all made him a strong advocate for Sarah Roberts.

It also helped that Sumner, a longtime fixture in Boston's elite circles, had lately developed a rebellious streak that set him apart and often placed him at sword's point with much of the city's old-line conservative establishment. While a large swath of Boston's elite business and cultural leaders had become increasingly uncomfortable with Sumner's radical views, his vociferous opposition to slavery endeared him to the city's black community that lived along the north slope of Beacon Hill—just blocks from Sumner—about two thousand people that formed a close-knit neighborhood known across the city as "Nigger Hill." It was not lost on Morris that Sumner found the designation abhorrent.

For the Roberts appeal, Morris and Sumner devised a strategy— Morris would lay out the facts of the case, and Sumner would argue the broader legal themes and long-term implications of the court's decision.

✳ ✳ ✳

When Sarah Roberts turned four in April 1847, her father attempted to enroll her in the school closest to their Andover Street home near Boston's North End, the Phillips School. The Boston Primary School Committee promptly denied his request in writing because Phillips was for white students only, and they refused to issue the "ticket of entrance" required for any student looking to enroll in Boston schools. Benjamin Roberts was free to enroll Sarah only in the long-established and highly respected segregated Smith School for colored children on the southeastern slope of Beacon Hill, the multiblock area that was home to about 70 percent of Boston's black population.

To get to the Smith School, Sarah had to pass by five elementary schools, including Phillips, that allowed only white students to enroll. Her father, Benjamin, recalled his own childhood experience of being forced to attend segregated schools, the shame he and his fellow black students felt that they were perceived as "inferiors and outcasts" as they walked past white-only schools and endured the stares of white children. He was determined that Sarah would not experience the same humiliation of being denied entrance to schools much closer to her home simply because of the color of her skin.

The issue had been simmering for years. A large contingent of black parents, angry at the notion of segregated schools, had engaged in a multi-year boycott of the Smith School that resulted in a 40 percent drop in attendance by 1845. Black parents either homeschooled their children or sent them to small religious-based schools that were formed in the community. At the same time, a group of eighty-five black parents, Roberts included, petitioned the Primary School Committee to abolish segregated schools, arguing that they inevitably led to a "small and despised class" of people, which, by definition, meant that the "standard of scholarship degenerates." Then, teachers and students are "soon considered and of course become an inferior class."

Segregated schools, they argued, were unlawful and insulting.

Despite the School Committee's refusal to issue Sarah a ticket of entrance for the Phillips School, Benjamin Roberts decided to force the issue and embark on what he called a "practical experiment"—to see if his daughter would truly be denied entrance because of her color. On the morning of April 15, 1847, he walked Sarah to the white-only Phillips. He was turned away by the principal, who cited his lack of the city-issued ticket—in the case of Phillips, a ticket issued only to white students. Next, Roberts escorted Sarah to another geographically close white-only school, the Otis School, and for reasons lost to history—a sympathetic principal? A bureaucratic glitch?—Sarah was admitted, and for several months she sat in a classroom side by side with white students.

But when the School Committee became aware of her attendance, it turned to the police department, which dispatched an officer to forcibly remove a weeping Sarah from class.

Outraged by Sarah's demeaning treatment, Benjamin Roberts believed he had only one recourse remaining to challenge Boston's system of segregated schools. Petitions had failed. So had boycotts.

It was time to take his "practical experiment" to the next level.

It was time to sue the city.

✳ ✳ ✳

Well before the Suffolk County Court of Common Pleas ultimately ruled against him in *Roberts v. The City of Boston* in 1848, attorney Robert Morris knew he faced an uphill climb.

Frustrated by both the unresolved issue and the affront to its power, the School Committee, whose seventy-five members included fewer than twenty integrationists, held months of public hearings in 1845 and early 1846, many of them contentious affairs, as Morris, abolitionist Wendell Phillips, and others spoke forcefully in favor of school integration. In one meeting, which lasted until past 11:00 P.M., the orations were so powerful that some observers thought the School Committee "might vote for integration that very night." But that did not occur.

Finally, one of the board's subcommittees published a lengthy report, along with its recommendation, in a June 1846 document titled *On the Petition of Sundry Colored Persons for the Abolition of the Schools for Colored Children*. The report concluded that "separate schools for colored children" were both "legal and just" and the best way to "promote the education of that class of our population." The school board's opinion: "The less the colored and white people become intermingled, the better it will be for both races."

As though to enhance the legal gravitas of the report, the committee tacked on a concurring opinion by the city attorney, solicitor Peleg W. Chandler. He agreed that the School Committee had the legal authority to establish and maintain segregated schools, specifically to "exclude white children from certain schools, and colored children from certain other schools, *when in their judgment, the best interests of such children will be promoted thereby.*"

The Boston city attorney had issued the first-ever declarative legal opinion supporting the concept of "separate but equal."

Using his opinion as a legal justification, and much to the chagrin of black parents, the citywide School Committee voted 59–16 against altering the structure of Boston's segregated schools.

✳ ✳ ✳

Boston was a city in the midst of great change—and in many ways, one of great contradictions—at the time of the Sarah Roberts case. Tolerance and bigotry, progressivism and traditionalism coexisted simultaneously in the minds and hearts of its political and business leaders.

In reality, Boston was several cities in one as 1850 approached: a city of progressive writers and thinkers, of hallowed Harvard University, of well-to-do Brahmins steeped in old money and wielding power accumulated through the generations, the vast majority white men who were classically educated, took pride in their social standing, traced their family history to Revolutionary times, traveled widely, cherished order, and contributed to churches, charities, and the arts; a city of new-money conservative and respected merchants and financiers who built their own wealth by trading with the South and with Europe and had vast influence over civic improvement and transportation projects; and a city of three groups growing rapidly outside the traditional circles of power— abolitionists, African Americans, and newly arrived Irish immigrants— who were making their voices heard.

The Brahmins and the merchants—mostly Whigs and mostly Episcopalian or Unitarian—viewed slavery as a distant issue and one that they had little control over. In polite conversation, most would denounce, at least theoretically, the institution that Massachusetts had abolished in 1783, but they had little interest in risking the national civil unrest and economic disruption they foresaw and feared if radical abolitionists had their way.

They were not opposed to equality in certain areas—in 1843, Boston had rescinded the law prohibiting interracial marriage, and "colored cars" on railroads had disappeared; blacks in Boston could vote, hold office, and testify in court. But just as a line of demarcation between blacks and whites existed in residential neighborhoods, so too had the city's power brokers insisted on separate facilities when it came to educating Boston's children. "May good men and heaven defend us from such social intercourse of the two races, as it might destroy the *usefulness of our excellent schools*," editorialized one Boston newspaper. "Give the negro his liberty, but KEEP HIM IN HIS PLACE."

✳ ✳ ✳

Part of the resistance no doubt stemmed from the major demographic changes that were afoot in Boston. Between 1845 and 1849, the city's population increased from 115,000 to 137,000; and in 1847 alone, more than 37,000 immigrants flooded Boston, three-quarters of them Irish who were fleeing the Great Famine. By 1850, 43 percent of Boston's population would be foreign born.

Boston's ruling class and its influential voices were more preoccupied by—and hostile toward—the Irish newcomers who were inundating the city than they were with assuring full equality between blacks and whites. Henry David Thoreau initially declared that the Irish were foolish, superstitious, and shiftless. Anti-Catholic newspapers predicted a surge of "popery and Romanism" in Boston, and warned readers that politically active Catholics of foreign birth would vote "precisely as their spiritual guides should dictate," accusing Catholic priests of being part of a "well-connected scheme" to bring the United States "under subjection to the Holy See."

This upheaval, caused by the influx of Irish immigrants, more strident abolitionist voices, and rebellious black parents on the school issue, created a sense of discord within the city's power establishment. Like any group fearing siege, they dug in their heels to maintain a sense of order and status quo and to hold on to the levers of power within the Boston city limits.

"The city is bigoted, narrow, provincial and selfish," Charles Sumner would soon write about Boston proper. "The [surrounding] country[side] has more the spirit of the American Revolution."

For Sumner, such a distinction at least partially explained why the nearby communities of Salem, Lowell, New Bedford, and Nantucket had already integrated their schools, while Boston stubbornly refused to do so.

✳ ✳ ✳

Without mentioning these social and demographic changes, the Boston School Committee report insisted that separate black and white schools were not only socially practical but also morally beneficial and spiritually consistent with Boston's deep Protestant religious ethos in the early to mid-nineteenth century. "The distinction [between races] is one which the Almighty has seen fit to establish, and it is founded deep in the physical, mental and moral natures of the two races," the School Committee report said. "No legislation, no social customs, can efface this distinction."

There were academic considerations, too. The committee report concluded, without providing documentary evidence, that colored children had "peculiar physical, mental, and moral structures" that required different educational treatments than whites. For example: "for those subjects which depend on memory or imitative faculties . . . the colored children will often keep pace with the white children; but, when progress comes to depend on the faculties of invention, comparison, and reasoning, they quickly fall behind."

All in all, the report stated bluntly, "the less the colored and white people become intermingled, the better it will be for both races— amalgamation is degradation."

As if such language was not dispiriting enough for black petitioners, the School Committee also chastised them for their ongoing protests against segregated schools. "We would urge the colored people and their friends to cease from these useless assaults upon the separate schools," the report admonished, "and to unite their efforts with ours, to improve them in every possible way."

Segregated schools, so long as they provided equivalent educational opportunities, offered Boston school children the best hope for a successful future.

This conclusion, the School Committee declared with emphasis, was born of a desire for its decision to be "not only *legal*, but RIGHT."

✳ ✳ ✳

From what is available in the historical record, the lower court agreed with the Boston Primary School Committee argument in its entirety. In April 1848, Morris sued, alleging that Sarah Roberts had been excluded unlawfully from the public school closest to her home and seeking six hundred dollars in damages on behalf of her father, Benjamin. Opposing

Morris in court was Peleg Chandler, who had made his opinions well known two years earlier in supporting the School Committee report.

The only surviving documentation from the initial hearing is an agreed-upon set of facts signed by Chandler and Morris; apparently the two lawyers agreed that a judgment would be entered pro forma—which meant that Morris planned to appeal if he lost, and this would expedite the process.

While the actual lower-court transcripts are lost to history, some of Morris's reasoning can be gleaned from the set of facts. Among them: that the Smith Street School was twenty-one hundred feet from Sarah's home, while the distance from her residence to the nearest primary school was nine hundred feet. And Morris apparently cited the Primary School Committee regulation that "scholars go to the schools nearest their residences" to show the conflict between the city's own language and the establishment of a single school serving black children from across the city. As for Chandler, there is little reason to think that the case he presented differed much from his concurrence with the 1846 School Committee report.

In October 1848, the trial court ruled for the City of Boston and against Sarah Roberts. Because of the pro forma agreement both parties signed beforehand, no written decision was issued by the court, though Morris was ordered to pay court costs for the suit, appraised at just over fifty dollars. As planned, Morris also filed his appeal immediately.

And he wasted no time enlisting the services of Charles Sumner.

✳ ✳ ✳

If Sumner held true to form, he likely worked late—well past midnight and possibly until 2:00 A.M.—in preparation for his December 4, 1849, appearance at the Supreme Court, then rose at 7:00 A.M. and, despite the freezing temperatures, enjoyed his daily cold-water bath and shave before breakfast.

Sumner was eager to make the case on behalf of Sarah Roberts. He would break new ground in his Roberts appeal—and urge the court to do the same—and he would do so in a powerful, wide-reaching, unprecedented, and extraordinary way. He titled his long, prepared argument "Equality Before the Law: Unconstitutionality of Separate Colored Schools in Massachusetts." It would feature the first appearance in English of the phrase "equality before the law"—translated from the French *égalité devant la loi*—and mark the first time that the concept would be introduced into American jurisprudence. This new doctrine would influence virtually every debate America held about race from then on.

Much was on the line the day Sumner and Morris entered the Supreme Judicial Court building in 1849. Sumner was staking all on an argument for which there was not yet legal precedent in the United States—the concept of equal justice under the law—and, still, he possessed full confidence that he could win the case.

Was this mere hubris on his part? Perhaps.

But over the last few years, Sumner had demonstrated his moral fearlessness, his predisposition to take risks, his willingness to trust his principles even if they took him along unconventional pathways. He proved all of this in 1845, when he declared to Boston and the rest of America his utter disdain for slavery and his unapologetic commitment to the antislavery cause; and again in 1847, when he took on the estimable Winthrop over the Mexican War vote and lost friendships because of it; and once more in 1848, when he decried the fecklessness of the Whigs and abandoned the established party entirely to become a member of the new and as-yet-untested Free Soilers.

It was his moral courage, his belief in America's promise of liberty for all, and his dedication to achieving equality between the races that would serve as the underpinning of his argument in the Sarah Roberts case and, ultimately, of his entire career in public life.

✳ CHAPTER 6 ✳

SEPARATE IS INHERENTLY UNEQUAL

Tension and drama crackled through the audience as the two lawyers entered the high-ceilinged courtroom.

Members of Boston's black community thronged the upstairs gallery and packed the floor below, hoping for a successful outcome in the fight they had been waging for several years. The large rectangular room contained a clerk's desk, the witness box, the prisoner's dock surrounded by an iron railing, and the fireplace, complete with a roaring fire on this frigid December morning.

But most imposing to the two lawyers—the first interracial legal team in U.S. history, a visible partnership that itself argued against segregation—was the high desk behind which the four justices sat, the men who would be the final arbiters of the hopes of Benjamin Roberts and thousands of free blacks in Boston and across the country.

Normally, the Massachusetts Supreme Judicial Court consisted of five justices; missing on this day was Judge Richard Fletcher, who had, before being appointed to the Supreme Court only two months earlier, ruled on a school integration case in the nearby town of Salem. Then, part of Fletcher's opinion declared that the Massachusetts constitution drew no distinction "between a colored and a white person." It is unclear whether Fletcher's absence today was because he was ill, new to the court, or believed his recent Salem ruling warranted his recusal from the *Roberts* case—what *was* clear is that Sumner and Morris were down one potentially sympathetic vote even before they started.

Fletcher's absence also meant that the opinion of one sitting judge would now carry more weight in the *Roberts* case, one judge to whom the plaintiffs' lawyers had to direct their arguments and hope to persuade—

perhaps the ablest, orneriest, longest-tenured, and most preeminent jurist in the United States.

Chief Justice Lemuel Shaw.

✳ ✳ ✳

Short, unsmiling, and with broad shoulders supporting a large head covered in a mane of usually uncombed hair, Shaw's physical countenance, courtroom presence, and legal reputation intimidated even the most experienced lawyers.

Heavy, unblinking eyes and flaring nostrils—some called his visage "frightful" or "ugly," and even charitable scribes occasionally included "homely" in their descriptions—complemented his stern demeanor.

Apocryphal or not, stories abounded about Shaw's penchant for generating fear in his courtroom, particularly among unprepared lawyers. He supposedly reduced one grizzled veteran lawyer to tears. Another attorney was seen bringing a dog into the courtroom; when a colleague asked why, the lawyer replied: "This dog's too timid—I want him to see Shaw in action so he can learn how to growl." A lawyer who appeared often before Shaw once saw an artist sculpting a lion and quipped: "Why, that's the best likeness of Chief Justice Shaw that I have ever seen."

The sixty-eight-year-old Shaw, a graduate of Harvard College, former president of the Boston Bar Association, and the father-in-law of writer Herman Melville, reveled in his reputation. The definition of a Boston power broker, he was, in fact, synonymous with the city *itself*—when Boston Town became a city in 1822, with its population of just a little over forty-three thousand people, it was Shaw who authored the city charter. His influence went beyond legal circles and reached high and deep into Boston's political power structure, and even his critics—reticent though they were to speak publicly—found it hard to question his probity and integrity.

But it was in the legal arena where he had gained national respect. Shaw, who always did his homework, had sharp analytical skills that allowed him to drill deftly to the heart of the matter. For nearly two decades—a third was yet to come—he had served as chief justice of the Massachusetts Supreme Judicial Court, and he didn't just lead it, he dominated it in a way that few have in the history of American jurisprudence. In all but three of the fifty constitutional decisions in his career, Shaw spoke for a unanimous court, surpassing the record of the legendary John Marshall. And in a total of twenty-two hundred opinions in which he participated, Lemuel Shaw wrote in dissent only once.

The unalterable fact was, as Lemuel Shaw went, so went the Massachusetts Supreme Judicial Court. And today, so would go the *Roberts* case.

Shaw knew it, his fellow justices knew it, the black spectators who packed the gallery knew it. All of Boston knew it.

So did Robert Morris as he sat down after outlining the facts in his case.

And—as he rose to his full six-foot-four-inch height, laid his lengthy, handwritten legal argument on the desk before him, and prepared to address the court on the broad legal themes of the *Roberts* case—Charles Sumner knew it, too.

✳ ✳ ✳

Unfortunately for Sumner, he had a not-so-favorable history with Shaw.

Sumner's cranky battles with old-line Boston Whigs during the Robert Winthrop and Mexican War controversies had once cost him a coveted professorship at Harvard Law School. Shaw, who carried enormous influence with Harvard and had not supported Sumner's appointment, later attributed the snub to the fact that Sumner "had not . . . rendered himself and his services acceptable to the students" in trial teaching assignments at the school. But this appeared to be academic code language. The previous holder of the professorship pointed out another reason Shaw and the Harvard College Corporation were reluctant to offer the position to Sumner: his radical politics and combative demeanor. It was all too much for the conservative Harvard College Corporation, which, in the words of one Harvard insider, "considered Sumner in the law school as unsuitable as a bull in a China-shop."

In a small city like Boston, whose power was concentrated in the hands of a few, where word-of-mouth news spread rapidly in drawing rooms and men's clubs, Sumner would have at least gotten wind, and perhaps even confirmed outright, that Shaw—a venerable, conservative, and influential Whig—not only disapproved of his politics but was also a leading

voice in sabotaging his chances for appointment to the law school position at Harvard.

✳ ✳ ✳

If Sumner was thinking about this unfortunate history with Shaw, he hid
it well. He stood tall before the packed courtroom and proceeded to deliver one of the most wide-ranging and memorable arguments in American legal history. It would become the foundation upon which nearly all
future arguments against inequality, even racism, would rest.

He began by framing for the justices *why* they were gathered on
this morning, why their courtroom was full, and what was at stake. He
opened with the central question: "Can any discrimination on account
of race or color be made among children entitled to the benefit of our
Common [public] Schools under the Constitution and the Laws of Massachusetts?"

With Justice Shaw already taking notes, Sumner said the key to answering this question was not to consider whether Boston School Board
members had the power under Massachusetts law to *integrate* schools but
whether they had the power "to *exclude* colored children" from schools
and compel them to find education at separate schools "at distances from
their homes less convenient than schools open to white children."

By all that was legal, moral, and constitutional, Sumner argued, they
did not.

Sumner faced an uphill battle and he knew it. There was no Fourteenth
Amendment yet (though much of Sumner's underlying rationale in *Roberts* would find its way into it years later), so the concept of "equality before the law" would be more of a moral and philosophical argument than
a legal one. Shaw was a strict constructionist who believed in a more literal interpretation of the statute books and the Constitution; in one decision, he had dismissed the ethereal concept of "natural justice" in favor
of obedience to the law. Would Sumner's argument, which relied on the
virtues of natural justice, have any chance?

As if anticipating Shaw's silent objection, Sumner next sought to
ground his remarks in a more constructionist fashion. "Of equality I
shall speak, not only as a *sentiment*, but as a principle embodied in the
Constitution of Massachusetts," he said. Ratified in 1780, the state's constitution reinforced the essential truths articulated in the Declaration of

Independence four years earlier, but in a slightly different form: "All men are born free and equal, and have certain natural, essential, and unalienable rights."

Sumner argued that requiring black students to attend separate schools violated the state constitution in two ways: first, by subjecting these students to "inconvenience inconsistent with the requirements of equality," and second, by establishing an odious "system of caste . . . generally used to designate any hereditary distinction, particularly of race," which was in direct violation of both the state and the U.S. Constitution.

"Caste and equality are contradictory," Sumner reasoned in one of his most memorable arguments. "They mutually exclude each other. Where Caste is, there cannot be Equality. Where Equality is, there cannot be Caste."

Sumner pointed out that U.S. law and tradition reviled nobility of all kinds—"but *here* is a nobility of the skin"—and abjured all hereditary distinctions—"but *here* is an hereditary distinction, founded not on the *merit* of the ancestor, but on his *color*."

School segregation, he said, was Boston's own "peculiar institution," in the same way that slavery was the South's.

※ ※ ※

Was Sarah Roberts among the members of the courtroom crowd that morning?

The historical record is silent on this, but based on how Sumner referred to her in his appeal to the justices, it is likely that she was present with her parents. "This little child asks at your hands her *personal rights*," Sumner implored the judges, and, by so doing, "she calls upon you to decide a question which concerns the rights of other colored children."

On one side of the issue, arrayed against Sarah, was the great wealth and influence of the City of Boston. "On the other is a little child," Sumner said, "of degraded color, of humble parents, still within the period of natural infancy," but part of a family that had fought segregation for years, a spirit that had helped her to become "strong from her very weakness."

Sumner's legal argument on behalf of Sarah centered on the Massachusetts constitution's mandate that every man, without regard to race, be treated equally before the law. "He is not poor, or weak, or humble, or black," Sumner argued, "not Caucasian, nor Jew, nor Indian, nor Ethiopian—nor

French, nor German, nor English, nor Irish; he is a Man—the equal of all his fellow men." No person could be created or born with privileges not enjoyed equally by all, nor could any institution be established that recognized distinction of birth. "We are brought back to one single proposition," he said, "*the equality of men before the law.*"

Sumner contended that the Boston School Committee had no power to exclude children from certain schools because of race, because the committee "cannot brand a whole race with the stigma of inferiority and degradation." To allow the continuance of that power "would place the Committee above the Constitution . . . to draw a *fatal circle*, within which the Constitution cannot enter; nay, where the very Bill of Rights shall become a dead letter." Thus, it was the duty of the court to set aside this unjust bylaw and forever end years of fighting over this topic.

Sumner's argument to this point, his unwavering conviction that "equality before the law" was both a natural right and one enshrined in the Massachusetts constitution and gleaned from the Declaration of Independence, was extraordinary on its own in 1849. These words would have enormous and far-reaching implications.

But he wasn't finished.

❋ ❋ ❋

What of the argument by some, including the Boston School Committee, that segregated schools offered *equivalent* educations to their students so long as both black and white schools were managed, operated, and funded in similar ways? Sumner sought to preempt any legal argument the justices—specifically Shaw, who had once served on the School Committee—might have been contemplating.

It was during this portion of Charles Sumner's case that we might imagine him, standing even taller before Shaw and the other justices, raising his voice, gesticulating with force, exuding his passion as he challenged the legal status quo and broke new ground in American law and race relations. Dismissing all precedent, Charles Sumner boiled his argument down to one simple concept that would not become codified into U.S. lawbooks for more than a century after he articulated it:

Separate schools for white and black children were not only illegal but—contrary to the School Committee's central thesis that they provided equivalent educations for both races—also *inherently unequal.*

He started with the practical. Sarah Roberts had to walk more than twenty-one hundred feet to attend the nearest black school, passing five white-only schools along the way, while the nearest white-only primary school was only nine hundred feet from her home. The long trip was "a daily tax upon the time and strength" of Sarah and other Black children that white children were not forced to endure.

But Sumner had much more.

Separate schools, he argued, inherently hurt and demoralized an entire race of students in ways difficult to measure in the moment but that were as clear to him as cold water in a mountain stream. Sumner began the most masterful and novel phase of his argument with what he called the "disastrous consequences" of the Boston School Committee's power to establish separate schools.

If the board could distribute children into different schools according to race, then what could stop them from creating different schools based on "mere discretion?" Could the School Committee establish separate *public* schools for people of Irish or German heritage? Could they separate Catholics from Protestants? Would not the School Committee have the power to create separate public schools for the rich, so "they may not be offended by the humble garments of the poor?" Or perhaps "exclude the children of mechanics and send them to separate schools?"

The court would surely and justly rule any of these mandates illegal, Sumner said, and also immoral, *regardless of the quality of any of the separate schools*. The fact was, such "compulsory segregation from the mass of citizens is of itself an *inequality* which we condemn . . . it is a mockery to call it an equivalent."

This could be illustrated more practically, he said, if the judges considered that throughout the educational system of the Commonwealth, all other discrimination *already* was illegal. A colored man could serve as governor of Massachusetts, which empowered him to select the Board of Education; or as lieutenant governor, which entitled him to serve as an *ex officio* member of the School Board; or as secretary of the board; or as a member of any School Committee in the state. He could vote for School Committee members and teach in the state's common schools. "Thus, in every department connected with our Common Schools, throughout the whole hierarchy . . . there is no distinction of color known to the law," Sumner argued. "It is when we reach the last stage of all—the children themselves—that the beautiful character of the system is changed to the deformity of Caste."

The effect of this discrimination on black students was devastating, Sumner said. It deprived them of "healthful animating influences" that would benefit them if they studied with white children. It also "adds to their discouragements. It widens their separation from the community, and postpones that great day of reconciliation [between the races] which is sure to come." Segregated schools diminished the whole system of public schools, too, which was designed "to furnish an equal amount of knowledge to all."

The law, he said, "contemplates not only that all shall be taught, but that *all* shall be taught *together*."

✳ ✳ ✳

Finally, employing language never before used in an American courtroom, and intended as much for the public and posterity as for the judges themselves, Sumner implicitly asked the court to rise above its role as a cold arbiter of laws and regulations by remembering that "the principles of morals and natural justice lie at the foundation of *all* jurisdiction."

He declared that segregated schools ultimately harmed society by preventing the "intimate communion" between races and classes that helped to bridge gaps, promote understanding, and convince enemies to become friends. "The separation of schools, far from being for the *benefit* of both races, is an *injury* to both," he argued. "It tends to create a feeling of degradation in the blacks, and of prejudice and uncharitableness in the whites."

Such feelings were poisonous to children, adults, and society. "Prejudice is the child of ignorance," Sumner told the justices and the packed courtroom. "It is sure to prevail where people do not know each other." Conversely, he added: "Society and intercourse are means established by Providence for human improvement." The system of segregated schools in Boston prevented this "intimate communion" during a child's most formative years, and therefore, Sumner said, "*directly interferes with the laws of God.*"

Bold, brilliant, unprecedented—all describe Charles Sumner's extraordinary argument before the prickly Shaw, who had spent years building a celebrated and respected legal career by arriving at decisions based on past legal precedent and the precise meaning of words on the page.

Which is why Charles Sumner's appeal to the judges to consider a higher purpose as they deliberated was also downright risky.

✳ ✳ ✳

After two hours of intense argument, Sumner reached his closing.

The court, he said, had a profound and sacred duty to finish a job. Massachusetts had already abolished laws prohibiting marriages between blacks and whites, eliminated segregated railroad cars, and of course, most significantly of all, banished slavery from the Commonwealth. Now, Sumner demanded, "I call upon you to *obliterate the last of its [slavery's] footprints.*"

Comparing the evils of segregated schools to a form of slavery seemed likely to offend Shaw and his justices, but Sumner suggested that both were symbols of massive abridgments of freedom that required remedy. Surely, the judges could see that *equality of men before the law* stood as the "mighty guardian of colored children in this case." Surely, deciding in favor of Sarah was consistent with the Commonwealth's pledge of "frowning upon every privilege of birth, every distinction of race, every institution of Caste."

Ending segregated schools in Massachusetts would send a message to both free and slave states. "Slavery in one of its enormities *is now before you for judgment,*" he said to the justices. "Do not hesitate to strike it. Let the blow fall which shall end its domination here in Massachusetts."

By ruling in favor of Sarah Roberts, by abolishing segregated schools, Shaw's court would forever take its place on the right side of history, Sumner predicted in a final appeal to the justices before him. "Your judgement will become a sacred landmark, not in jurisprudence only, but in the history of Freedom," Sumner concluded.

Drained, and with little sense of how Shaw and his fellow judges had received his arguments, Sumner thanked the court and took his seat next to Morris.

✳ ✳ ✳

In the hours and days following the dramatic court appearance, Sumner felt a sense of unease settle over him. He sent his argument to his brother, along with a note: "I could make it much better." Soon, though, word began circulating about Sumner's powerful argument, and the widespread praise he received buoyed him and caused him to think much differently about his performance.

One Boston newspaper devoted almost its entire front page to the *Roberts* case, publishing Sumner's "clear and convincing" argument in its entirety.

A confident Salmon Chase, Free Soil U.S. senator from Ohio, suggested with enthusiasm that Sumner's argument would carry the day and recommended publishing the remarks so that his message could be widely circulated *before* the court issued its ruling. Benjamin Roberts agreed, and within ten days of Sumner's argument on behalf of his daughter, he printed it in pamphlet form and distributed it to antislavery offices and black social clubs around the city. Black abolitionist William Cooper Nell, a resident of Beacon Hill and one of the community's most respected and influential leaders, told Sumner that "[black Bostonians] repose confidence in you and are constantly praying for a successful *result* of your labors."

William Lloyd Garrison, Boston's most famous abolitionist at the time, who called Sumner's argument "luminous and profound," printed it over several issues in the abolitionist *Liberator*. Garrison predicted—prophetically it turned out—that Sumner's ideas would not be a matter of "temporary local interest" but would be part of any antislavery and equality discussion in other states for years to come.

The opinionated Garrison added one final thought on the upcoming court decision, a sentiment consistent with the confidence of Chase and the hopes of Sumner, Benjamin Roberts, and the entire Boston black community:

"There can be *no doubt*, it seems to us, that it will be in favor of the plaintiff, and therefore against an odious 'complexion caste.'"

✳ CHAPTER 7 ✳

"TRUTH IN THE END MUST PREVAIL"

A full four months would pass until the Supreme Court of Massachusetts finally issued its decision on the *Roberts* case on April 4, 1850.

The court had been busy—in addition to *Roberts*, justices were enmeshed in a case that had captured the world's imagination, generated unprecedented publicity, and placed Shaw, especially, in the public spotlight.

On the Friday before Thanksgiving, November 23, 1849, Dr. George Parkman, a benefactor of Harvard and one of the richest men in Boston, left his home around noon and was last seen entering the Harvard Medical College. His apparent goal: to collect on some long-overdue notes from his Harvard classmate and friend of fifty years, Dr. John Webster. In thirty years, Parkman had never failed to come home for his 2:00 P.M. lunch—"dinner," as it was called then—but in this case, his wife sat up all night awaiting his return before calling police to say her husband had disappeared.

A week later, after a frantic citywide search that involved authorities and private citizens, police discovered Parkman's dismembered body in the vaults near Webster's offices at Harvard Medical. Webster was arrested for the gruesome crime.

Webster's sensational trial, with Lemuel Shaw presiding (capital cases in Massachusetts were heard by the Supreme Judicial Court), began on March 19, 1850, and over the next twelve days, Boston police estimated that some sixty thousand people filed through the courthouse to view a portion of the proceedings. Journalists from around the country and the world covered the trial—which introduced the first use of forensic evidence in American history—and even Sumner was caught up in the excitement. "There seems to be very little doubt in the public mind that he [Webster] is guilty," he wrote to his brother George. "Many doubt whether he will be convicted."

The public was correct about Webster's guilt, and wrong to doubt the jury. On March 30, Webster was found guilty of murder, and on April 1, before a packed courtroom, Shaw sentenced him to hang for his crime.

Finally, days later, with the Webster-Parkman case behind him, Shaw found time to issue the court's written ruling in *Roberts*.

✳ ✳ ✳

Sumner's hopes, and those of Benjamin Roberts and Boston's black community, were dashed by Shaw's court.

The devastating judgment against Sarah Roberts began with one sentence that left no doubt about the court's position:

> The general school committee of the city of Boston has power, under the constitution and laws of this Commonwealth, to make provisions for the instruction of colored children, in separate schools established exclusively for them, and to prohibit their attendance upon other schools.

The Massachusetts Supreme Court had, unanimously and without ambiguity, ended any hope of Sarah Roberts attending an integrated school in Boston in the fall of 1850.

Unusually magnanimous in his assessment of Sumner's argument, Shaw complimented the "learned and eloquent advocate" of the plaintiff for advancing the principle that, according to the constitution and laws of Massachusetts, "all persons without distinction of age or sex, birth or color, origin or condition, are equal before the law." As a broad general principle, Shaw conceded, Sumner's treatise was "perfectly sound" and belonged in a "declaration of rights." The principle not only found expression in the constitution; it "pervades and animates the whole spirit of our constitution of free government."

The issue became clouded, Shaw contended, when this "great principle" was applied to the "actual and various conditions of persons in society." There was no one-size-fits-all, Shaw wrote. For example, the theory would not "warrant the assertion that men and women are legally clothed with the same civil and political powers," or that "children and adults are legally to . . . be subject to the same treatment." Laws governed each of these circumstances. The equality-before-the-law principle warranted only that the rights of all, as they were "regulated by law," were equally entitled to the "protection of the law for their maintenance and security."

Shaw conceded that "colored persons, the descendants of Africans" were entitled by Massachusetts law to equal rights—the only question for the court to settle was whether separate schools *violated* any of those rights.

The court's view was that they did not.

* * *

The legislature, Shaw continued, had vested sole power in the School Committee to "arrange, classify, and distribute pupils in such a manner as they think best adapted to their general proficiency and welfare," and so long as the committee provided an equal education to all students, the court had little business deciding how those students should be physically housed.

"If they should judge it expedient to have a grade of schools for children from seven to ten, and another for those ten to fourteen," Shaw argued, it was in the committee's authority to establish such schools. Similarly, the School Committee would have the power to establish separate schools for males and females, or to establish special schools for "poor and neglected children" who, due to their circumstances, had fallen behind in their learning and needed specialized instruction.

Thus, it stood to reason, if the School Committee were legally entitled to establish schools according to age, gender, and student achievement levels—and the court believed the committee *was* so empowered—it also had the legal authority to organize schools according to students' color, so long as the power was *reasonably* exercised, "without being abused or perverted."

Shaw saw no violation of the principle of equality with segregated schools; instead, the court believed the committee's decision was based on "the honest result of their experience and judgment." Sumner's charge that the maintenance of separate schools, in and of themselves, tended to "deepen and perpetuate the odious distinction of caste, founded in a deep-rooted prejudice in public opinion," was, in Shaw's view, beyond the purview of his court or any court. "This prejudice, if it exists, *is not created by law,"* Shaw wrote in what would become an oft-quoted passage, "and probably cannot be changed by law."

Further, the court heard no evidence beyond Sumner's impassioned argument that compelling white and colored children to attend the same schools would *reduce* prejudice in the community. In any case, according to laws passed by the legislature, such a decision, while fair grounds for debate, belonged in the hands of the School Committee.

In short, the court ruled that Sarah Roberts had not been "unlawfully excluded from public instruction." Therefore, she was not entitled to sue for damages under the Act of 1845.

As for the increased distance to which Sarah Roberts was obliged to travel from her home to the colored school, the court did not find it unreasonable or illegal.

✱ ✱ ✱

In his opinion in the *Roberts* case, one of the most influential of the antebellum period, Chief Justice Lemuel Shaw introduced into American jurisprudence the soundness of the "separate but equal" doctrine as a constitutional justification for racial segregation in public schools—and in many other areas as well.

Had he simply dismissed Roberts's appeal, Shaw's decision would have had limited, even minimal, implications. But by conceding Sumner's contention that "equal protection under the law" was a bedrock constitutional principle, and at the same time denying any constitutional requirement against separating the races, Shaw ensured that the "separate but equal" doctrine would long outlive him—and become one of the most vital and precedent-setting legal concepts ever articulated.

In the decades that followed, courts in New York, Arkansas, Missouri, Louisiana, West Virginia, Kansas, South Carolina, Oregon, California, and Nevada cited Shaw's decision in the *Roberts* appeal to uphold segregated schools. The Shaw decision was used successfully by judges and states that sought to impose segregation even after the Fourteenth Amendment to the Constitution—passed in 1868, nearly twenty years after *Roberts*—guaranteed "equal protection of the laws."

And the impact of Shaw's opinion went beyond schools. The concept of "separate but equal" across the board was codified by the U.S. Supreme Court in 1896 in the landmark *Plessy v. Ferguson* case, which carried the force of national law for nearly sixty years and established the foundation upon which many discriminatory Jim Crow laws were based. Homer Plessy had challenged Louisiana's "Separate Car Act," under which he had been arrested for refusing to vacate the "whites only" car of a Louisiana train. Plessy argued that the separate railcars violated the Equal Protection Clause of the Fourteenth Amendment. The court disagreed, reverting to Shaw's opinion in *Roberts* as a leading precedent for the validity of state legislation that required segregation of the races.

Such segregation laws, the Supreme Court ruled while referencing Shaw's opinion, "do not necessarily imply the inferiority of either race to the other."

* * *

Much of Boston's traditional Whig and merchant class agreed with Shaw's decision in 1850, but Sumner was obviously disappointed and resentful, not only of Shaw's failure to consider broadly the "equality under the law" argument but also for placing the court's imprimatur on the "separate but equal" doctrine.

The day after the court ruling, he admitted: "I lament this very much. Is everything going against us?" Later, still rankled by the loss, he returned the books that he had used to research the case—"as you have probably seen—unsuccessfully"—to his friend John Jay. He wrote: "I am sure that the court, in their opinion, have not answered my argument." Sumner predicted that within ten years, the legal profession and society at large would repudiate Shaw and agree instead with his argument on the unconstitutionality and moral shortfalls of "separate but equal" schools.

He would be proven right in Boston at least. In 1855, pressured by black and white abolitionists furious over a draconian national Fugitive Slave Law and inspired by a speaking tour and petition drive by Sarah's father, Benjamin Roberts, the Massachusetts legislature passed a law decreeing that throughout the common schools of the state, "no distinction shall be made on account of the race, color, or religious opinions of the applicant or scholar."

Nationally, it would take the country 105 years to follow Charles Sumner's lead.

* * *

In 1954, eighty years after Sumner's death, a young African American lawyer named Thurgood Marshall, seeking to overturn *Plessy v. Ferguson*, argued before the Supreme Court that the segregated school system in Topeka, Kansas, was unconstitutional. Marshall found inspiration for his *Brown v. Board of Education* argument in Charles Sumner's groundbreaking 1849 argument in the Sarah Roberts case.

The twentieth-century Supreme Court agreed with Marshall's argument, and in its decision in *Brown* asked the critical question: "Does segregation of children in public schools solely on the basis of race, even though the physical facilities and other 'tangible' factors may be equal, deprive children of the minority group of equal educational opportunities?"

The court issued its answer in economical language that reverberated across the land:

"We believe that it does."

And then, echoing and vindicating Charles Sumner from a century earlier, the 1954 Supreme Court decision finally changed law and history yet again by declaring:

"Separate educational facilities are inherently unequal."

✳ ✳ ✳

Many years after the *Roberts* appeal, one modern legal scholar said that Sumner laid out a case "so comprehensive that the arguments of the next hundred years would not add significantly to the themes he developed."

This was no overstatement.

Sumner's stirring argument was the first great charter drawn up for the entitlement of blacks to equal education—yet it was far more than that. The phrase *equality before the law* had entered into the American lexicon and, for the first time, offered a heretofore unimagined promise of equality for all citizens in every walk of life.

For the thirty-nine-year-old Sumner, the *Roberts* argument marked the tangible beginning of what one good friend called "his warfare on caste" and his unwavering and persistent lifelong advocacy for civil and political rights for all, irrespective of race or any other condition.

✳ ✳ ✳

With the exhausting and groundbreaking *Roberts* argument behind him, Charles Sumner wrote two letters in the first half of 1850 that offer a glimpse into his state of mind.

In January, while awaiting the court's decision in *Roberts*, Sumner lamented to Salmon Chase: "If I did not believe that Truth in the end must prevail, I should be disposed at the present moment to despair of our cause."

Then in May, dejected about Shaw's decision, Sumner complained to John Jay: "I am sick at heart when I observe the apostacies to Freedom." The quality lacking most in public officials, he told Jay, was "*backbone . . . moral firmness*—without which they yield to the pressures of interest, of party, of fashion, of public opinion."

In both letters, Charles Sumner was referring to more than the *Roberts* case.

Lemuel Shaw's ruling against him was only one disappointment Charles Sumner faced in 1850.

What discouraged him more had even greater implications for the nation's future.

PART TWO

UNSTOPPABLE PERIL

SOUTHERN CHIVALRY — ARGUMENT versus CLUB'S.

CHAPTER 8

PRESERVE THE UNION AT ANY COST?

Though he was a student of history and understood how discrete occurrences often fused to affect people and nations, Charles Sumner could never have dreamed that three events would intertwine to launch his political career and catapult him to national prominence—the discovery of gold in California in 1848; the controversial response to it in 1850 by the incumbent U.S. senator from Massachusetts, Daniel Webster; and, in 1851, the capture of a runaway slave in Boston.

If the Texas annexation and the Mexican War angered Sumner and exacerbated sectional tensions in the 1840s, these three stunning events sent shockwaves across Massachusetts and the country, pushed the political mainstream closer to Charles Sumner's point of view, and cleared the way for the Massachusetts legislature to elect a man to the U.S. Senate who had never before held political office.

The January 1848 discovery of gold at Sutter's Mill in northern California provided the catalyst for all of it.

* * *

The California Gold Rush, one of the seminal events in American history and second only to the Civil War in significance during the tempestuous nineteenth century, attracted tens of thousands of intrepid fortune hunters from Europe, Asia, Australia, South America, and every part of the United States to seek riches.

Delirious with gold fever, which conjured up visions of indescribable riches, men and women alike risked everything, depleted their savings, quit their jobs, jeopardized their children's safety, and endured injury and disease to reach the California promised land. Thousands who left their old lives behind made the harrowing journey by ship over treacherous seas;

thousands more embarked on the grueling overland journey across the American continent. They fought against starvation, fever, Indian and white raiding parties, fear, despair, loneliness, and the second-guessing that accompanied hundreds or thousands of miles of emptiness and uncertainty—all to reach California's hailed rivers of gold.

Those who faced and overcame enormous odds on their trek and populated California in two short years tended to possess self-reliance, courage, determination, a deep reservoir of optimism, and perhaps a measure of recklessness and rebelliousness—qualities that influenced their politics. They moved quickly and decisively, essentially skipping the stage of requesting Congress to admit California as a territory; instead, they ratified a governing constitution in November 1849 and petitioned Congress for statehood in early 1850.

But it was at this point that California's momentum slowed. Its approved constitution sent ripples of controversy across the continent. Voters in the land of gold had adopted a governing document that forbade slavery. Some of the reasons were geographic and based on population—like many states that had entered the union since the original thirteen, California did not contain the large farms or plantations that would make slavery economically viable, plus the region's black population was small. Other reasons were philosophical; those who ventured to California were free spirits, entrepreneurs, and live-and-let-live adventurers. The very fact that they had traveled so far under onerous conditions to reach America's West Coast, that they had pursued a dream that some viewed as quixotic at best, was a testament to their love and desire for freedom of movement. The nature of their personal constitutions made them averse to embracing slavery in their state constitution.

It was no great surprise that California was seeking admittance to the union as a free state.

* * *

By itself, California's admittance as a free state was objectionable enough to the South, but the impact was exacerbated by simple mathematics.

As Congress considered California's request, the American union consisted of thirty states—fifteen slave and fifteen free—a delicate balance that both sides had worked to achieve, a fragile coexistence that had lasted for decades. If and when California joined the union as the thirty-first state, Northern abolitionists and even moderate antislavery elements would rejoice, believing, probably correctly so, that slavery's future was doomed, that the newly acquired territories of New Mexico and Utah would follow suit, that Southern power would become irreparably weakened, that slave owners would become further isolated and vilified, and that the peculiar institution, deprived of oxygen and unable to spread further, would wither and die.

Southerners believed almost all of the same things, which meant they viewed California's admittance with a sense of foreboding and outrage.

Whatever Congress did with California's petition would have profound consequences, North and South.

How could the country survive?

With the stakes so high, the nation looked, as it often did in this period, to the Senate—which often provided leadership on great issues during the antebellum era prior to the strong presidency—and three men in particular, for answers: Henry Clay of Kentucky, the Great Compromiser, known for his temperate and judicious reasoning and uncanny knack of weaving together disparate coalitions to fashion legislation; South Carolina's John C. Calhoun, the ancient giant of the South, physically weakened but still formidable, a fierce sectionalist who possessed a deep intellect and an enduring faith in the Constitution, surpassed only by his bone-deep loyalty to the Southern cause and unshakable belief in slavery; and Daniel Webster of Massachusetts—whose actions would draw the greatest interest from Charles Sumner and other Boston residents—a powerful and confident politician, a dealmaker whose oratorical skills, arrogance, and legislative acumen made him an implacable ally and a dangerous foe.

These three Senate icons had worked together before to achieve compromise on sectional differences, and though aging (all would be dead within two years), they commanded the respect of their colleagues and their constituents. Their reputations helped them to transcend politics and assume the role of statesmen who could navigate the California controversy and its inevitable impact on the nation's most divisive issue: slavery.

Clay, Calhoun, and especially Webster would touch off a firestorm when they fashioned and endorsed—albeit Calhoun with great reluctance—what would become known as the Compromise of 1850.

✳ ✳ ✳

The legislation was Clay's brainchild, but Webster assumed the role of political whip—before the term became part of the Washington vernacular—who twisted arms and brokered deals in his effort to build support for the controversial measure.

The proposed bill had many tentacles. Among them: admitting California as a free state; allowing the newly acquired territories of Utah and New Mexico to decide for themselves whether to permit slavery or not; banning slave trading—but not slavery itself—in Washington, D.C., and stipulating that slavery could be abolished in the nation's capital only if its residents and the State of Maryland approved and its slave owners were compensated for their slaves; and prohibiting Congress from interfering with the slave trade within or between states.

As important as these components were, though, they paled in comparison to the most controversial element of the proposed compromise, the linchpin seen as the counterweight to the decision to admit California as a free state, the language that would most placate the South, stifle the whispers of secession, and perhaps hold the union together.

Southern slave owners demanded it, and Northern abolitionists dreaded it—a harsher and more stringent Fugitive Slave Law.

✳ ✳ ✳

"I wish to speak today not as a Massachusetts man, not as a northern man, but as an American, and a member of the Senate," Daniel Webster began his soon-to-be-historic March 7, 1850, speech in support of the Compromise on the Senate floor before a hushed chamber.

Webster, who loved the union as much as any man, believed the Compromise would preserve it and agreed to support the measure regardless of the consequences he might face in the North. Above all, he thought, the Compromise's most controversial section—the Fugitive Slave Law—might succeed in holding together a nation that was fraying at the seams. Fully aware that he would anger many Northerners and that his hopes for a future presidential run could evaporate, Webster believed that preserving the union outweighed any sectional loyalties.

Webster realized that the law mandated harsh and summary enforcement over civil liberties, but he understood that its very strictness was the only way to ensure Southern support; even the most fervent proslavery lawmakers would recognize the new bill's good-faith concessions to Southern interests.

The proposed law was heavily slanted toward the interests of slave owners. It would allow a slave owner or his agent to reclaim a runaway fugitive slave by securing a warrant beforehand or arresting the runaway on the spot. It mandated that the Northern jurisdiction to which a slave escaped employ the full force of its law enforcement and legal machinery to ensure the runaway's return to bondage. The case for returning a slave to his master would be heard by a federal judge or a court-appointed federal commissioner, who would be paid ten dollars if the certificate of removal were issued (that is, returning a runaway slave to his or her master), but only five dollars if the claim was denied and the runaway was allowed to remain free. Abolitionists, of course, decried this measure as virtually bribing the commissioner to return an individual to bondage.

Further, no jury could be called during the court proceedings, and—in one of the proposed bill's most astonishing and offensive sections— testimony from the fugitive slave was prohibited. Judges would never hear a slave tell stories of beatings or other mistreatment that may have prompted their decision to run. Another provision prohibited the appeal of a commissioner's decision and forbade other courts and magistrates from issuing temporary injunctions that would delay a slave's return to bondage.

Finally, the law called for stiff penalties—a $1,000 fine and up to six months in jail—for aiding a fugitive or interfering with his or her return to slavery, a component that chilled and infuriated abolitionists.

All of this Webster endorsed in his momentous "Seventh of March" speech, much to the surprise and chagrin of most Massachusetts residents, not least Charles Sumner.

✳ ✳ ✳

"I might call him Judas Iscariot or Benedict Arnold," Charles Sumner exclaimed of Daniel Webster days after the March 7 speech.

An indignant Sumner had plenty to be angry about as he picked his way through Webster's remarks. The legendary and aging Webster had decided to toss political diplomacy to the wind by proudly going on the offensive in the most offensive way, instigating and inviting rebuttal attacks from abolitionists as he stood as defiantly as a man in a field shaking his fist at an unrelenting swarm of wasps.

Webster blasted abolitionists, accused them of being enemies of the union and of society, denounced antislavery efforts as "mad, theoretic, fanatical, and fantastical," leading away "silly women and sillier men." At one time Webster had viewed slavery as a great moral and social evil, but now he appeared to contemplate it almost with indifference, viewing its abolition as a quixotic dream and diminishing its opponents merely as "a race of agitators" willing to derail a compromise that could save the very country.

Webster shocked his Massachusetts constituents by sneering at abolitionist societies in his own state and across the North. "I do not think them useful," he said. "I think their operations for the last twenty years have produced nothing good or valuable." Employing a coarseness in language antithetical to his reputation as a seasoned diplomat, Webster ridiculed, both during and after the speech, what he perceived as excessive sanctimony by abolitionists, especially those in Massachusetts, thereby reversing years of his peaceful coexistence with the state's most fervent antislavery coalition.

Webster contended that the *result* of radical abolitionism was contrary to its *intent*. Because of abolitionists' recklessness, "the bonds of the slaves were [now] bound more firmly than before" by Southerners who feared a total upheaval to their way of life. In essence, Webster argued, the unrelenting and nonnegotiable calls for immediate, total, and uncompensated manumission had hurt slaves more than helped them.

Webster contended that the new Fugitive Slave Law was necessary because Northern legislatures and individuals had shown a "disinclination to perform fully their constitutional duties" to uphold the law and return slaves who escaped into free states. "In *that* respect," he said, "it is my judgment that the South is right and the North is wrong."

✳ ✳ ✳

Abolitionists could scarcely believe the forcefulness and tenor of Webster's argument.

Had he lost his mind?

Webster sounded more like a Southern slaveholder than a senator representing one of the most antislavery states in the union, but for him, the practical preservation of the country, and the Constitution that governed it, outweighed any moral objections to slavery. If a stringent Fugitive Slave Law mollified Southerners, reinforced constitutional language that already required the return of escaped slaves, and quashed discussion of secession, Webster would fight for it to his last breath.

Only a law with the sharpest teeth could stave off the worst.

If coexistence with slave owners and slavery was the price to pay to keep the union intact, so be it.

✳ ✳ ✳

For weeks, Webster's Seventh of March speech was the topic of conversation on street corners and in taverns, in smoking rooms and social clubs, in cities and across the countryside.

Furious abolitionists and other antislavery groups vilified Webster with the venom reserved for traitors and turncoats. Like Sumner, Walt Whitman compared Webster to Judas. Ralph Waldo Emerson spat: "The word *liberty* in the mouth of Mr. Webster sounds like the word *love* in the mouth of a courtesan." Charles Sumner believed Webster's support of the Fugitive Slave Law was an "elaborate treason," and the man himself "a traitor to a holy cause."

Still, Sumner saw some good coming out of the speech. He believed that Webster's intemperate support for the Fugitive Slave Law represented a watershed moment that would benefit the antislavery cause, bolster Free Soilers' political fortunes, and ultimately hasten the demise of the evil institution.

Since the Missouri Compromise of 1820, Congress had cobbled together a series of convoluted agreements—some legislative and some informal—to maintain the precarious sectional truce on the slavery issue. The South was often the aggressor in these accords, seeking not only to maintain but also to expand slavery's influence and its own economic and political power. For the most part, the North, whose economy benefitted from cheap slave labor, was content to deal with slavery by either grudgingly accepting it, tepidly condemning it, or ignoring it outright—whichever approach was most likely at the time to serve as a steam-release valve to prevent the issue from boiling over. In short, for thirty years, both spoken and unspoken congressional ground rules dictated the tone and tenor of debate, but always with an eye toward the status quo, designed to reduce the potential for sectional conflict.

In Sumner's view, the new Fugitive Slave Law could change all of that and finally provide an opening for drastic change.

It was one thing for Northerners to consider slavery in the abstract, a system that occurred hundreds of miles away with little direct connection to their daily lives. It would be another matter entirely, Sumner surmised (correctly, it would turn out), once Northerners were confronted with slavery's evils in their own backyard—forced to capture, imprison, degrade, and return runaway slaves to bondage. The very notion of the federal government requiring the suppression of freedom in free states might speak louder and send a more powerful message on the moral repugnancy of slavery than an endless litany of abolitionist speeches.

✳ ✳ ✳

As the first half of 1850 drew to a close, Charles Sumner felt he was being tested.

His loss in the *Roberts* case, Webster's stunning and unexpected betrayal, Sumner's fearful expectations that the disastrous Compromise of 1850 would pass the Senate and the House, his disappointment in the lack of backbone shown by Boston's "Webster Whigs," who refused to stand strong against slavery—all of these left Sumner feeling disoriented and untethered by late June. He never questioned his convictions but perhaps second-guessed the benefit of standing up for them at any cost.

"I am alone, quite alone," he wrote to a friend on June 25. "More and more so, every day."

Just a few weeks later, a family tragedy would deepen Sumner's loneliness and his feeling that, in 1850 at least, the fates were arrayed against him.

On July 19, his twenty-six-year-old brother Horace died at sea off Fire Island, New York, when his ship, the *Elizabeth*, foundered in the midst of a gale-force storm on a return voyage from Italy, struck a sandbar several hundred yards from shore, and was torn apart by massive waves.

Now thirty-nine, Sumner had lost his father and four of his siblings, and again, he struggled to convey his grief (with Mary's case being the one exception). He wrote of Horace's death with a sense of detachment, almost as if his brother were a stranger: "All who knew him speak warmly of his gentle, loving, and utterly unselfish nature," he observed in a stilted summary.

Sumner was brilliant of mind, worldly in perspective, commanding in oratory, deft in debate, and a master of the written word—but personal relationships continued to vex him.

* * *

While Charles Sumner contemplated the cataclysmic storm that took his brother's life, a political tempest swept across Washington, D.C., and Massachusetts and further influenced the impact that Daniel Webster's speech would have on Sumner's future.

Debate on the Compromise of 1850 continued throughout the summer, but the die was cast with the March 7 speech, and, with Webster and other leading Northern Cotton Whigs fully behind the deal, it was clear the controversial measure was on its way to passage. Proponents of the Compromise were further buoyed after President Zachary Taylor died from typhoid fever on July 9 and Millard Fillmore, who had already expressed support for the bill, ascended to the presidency.

Ironically, despite a final speech in support of the measure on July 17, Webster, the Compromise's most articulate and passionate defender, would not cast a final vote on its passage in early September. President Fillmore chose Webster as his secretary of state—Sumner had long predicted that Webster had his sights on the office—meaning the powerful senator would have to resign his Senate seat. Massachusetts governor George N. Briggs appointed none other than Sumner's nemesis, Congressman Robert Winthrop, as a placeholder to serve the remainder of Webster's term, which would expire in 1851.

In the eyes of the state's abolitionists and Free Soilers, who were already rallying around a potential Charles Sumner candidacy for Webster's senate seat, Winthrop and Webster were interchangeable Whigs who were hopelessly out of touch with the growing antislavery sentiments in Massachusetts, especially from residents outside of the Boston city limits.

On September 18, 1850, President Fillmore signed the Compromise of 1850, and thus the new Fugitive Slave Act, into law. On October 2, Secretary of State Daniel Webster wrote: "We have now gone through the most important crisis that has occurred since the foundation of this government—whatever party may prevail, hereafter, the Union stands firm!"

It was one of the great miscalculations in American history.

CHAPTER 9

"YOU HAVE WHIPPED WEBSTER!"

harles Sumner spent the late summer and fall of 1850 alternatively insisting that he had no desire to become a senator and working behind
the scenes to enhance the likelihood that it would happen.

Shy by nature, Sumner was fiercely protective of his privacy and genuinely angst-ridden about the notion of entering the public arena—he certainly protested too much as he repeated his disdain for politics—but at
the same time, he recognized the value of rowing toward his destination
with "muffled oars," in the words of one historian, to catch his opponents
by surprise.

In public and even in private letters to friends, he adopted a nuanced,
even coy, position about the political crosscurrents swirling and shifting
around the Webster-less Senate seat, somewhere between cool reserve,
even bored indifference, on the one hand, and, on the other, a concession
that if a groundswell of support "for the cause" swept him along with it,
he might be forced to serve almost in spite of himself.

"I do not desire to be Senator, I would not move across the room to
take the post," he wrote. "It must seek me—and . . . if it finds me, it will
find an absolutely independent man, without any pledge or promise."

On a long August evening on a Swampscott beach, Sumner's friend,
poet John Greenleaf Whittier, convinced him to accept a Senate nomination if Free Soilers and moderate Democrats—whose support for slavery
was lukewarm at best—could form a coalition to upset the Whigs. At
first, Sumner was reluctant, but he listened to Whittier's arguments and
finally consented to serve—if duty called. "He really did not want the
office," Whittier would write later of the agreement the two men reached
on the beach. "But we forced it upon him."

But whether he would be "called" remained doubtful. Sumner's criticism of Webster and the Fugitive Slave Law and the growing rift between Whigs and Free Soilers had produced such tension that personal and political lines had blurred; so much so, Sumner said, that more than a few Boston Whigs who would have normally expressed their condolences for the loss of his brother now "avert their faces from me."

Still, such treatment did not stop Sumner.

✻ ✻ ✻

Webster was gone from the Senate, but the upcoming state election—which would, in turn, influence whom the state legislature would select for U.S. senator to replace Webster—was shaping up as a battle between those who opposed the Compromise of 1850, regardless of party, and Cotton Whigs, whom Sumner now ridiculed as "*Compromise* Whigs." Out of devotion to Webster, they had become timid "professors of compromise" by supporting, in the Fugitive Slave Law, a "hideous, Heaven-defying bill."

Webster was furious at Sumner's public statements, and at anyone who repudiated the Compromise in any way. He had tied himself to the legislation as a means to preserve the union and viewed any pushback as bordering on national apostasy. Forgotten—by him, if no one else—were his long-held, crisply crafted antislavery positions; now, his blind spot when it came to the Fugitive Slave Law was seen as an unfathomable and unforgivable betrayal by Sumner, Free Soilers, and Conscience Whigs.

Free Soilers held their state convention in Boston on October 3, which Charles Sumner attended as a delegate; virtually all speeches and resolutions denounced the Compromise of 1850 and the Fugitive Slave Act. Speakers repeatedly excoriated Webster with phrases such as "Traitor to Liberty," "Benedict Arnold," and "Lucifer fallen." Most remarkable about the speeches were that most were not passionate outbursts but the words of men who had thought carefully about their remarks and were willing to stand behind them. In their eyes, Webster's fall from grace was rapid and bottomless; the Fugitive Slave Act he had helped spawn and now vigorously supported was a humanitarian disaster and a blight on a nation conceived in liberty.

Then, on November 6, days before the state election, Sumner had the opportunity to address a huge audience at Faneuil Hall in support of the Free Soil Party's slate of candidates.

He did not disappoint.

✳ ✳ ✳

Later, several of Sumner's contemporaries said his November 6 speech was the oratory that made him senator. Before hundreds of Free Soilers who greeted him with a raucous welcome, Sumner declared that the Fugitive Slave Law was unconstitutional on its face, that the people had a duty to resist this "legalized outrage," much as their Revolutionary ancestors had risen up against the Stamp Act. He refused to even call it a "law," which cloaked it with false legitimacy, instead insisting on calling it a "bill."

Interrupted at the end of nearly every sentence with cheers and applause, Sumner attacked the law and its authors—Clay and Webster primarily—who had, he argued, passed into the "immortal catalogue of national crimes," drawing with them the President of the United States, Millard Fillmore, who had signed the bill. Using his most vitriolic language against the President, Sumner spat that Fillmore's signature forevermore left him languishing in the depths of infamy: "Better for him had he never been born! Better for his memory, and for the good name of his children, had he never been President!" Other presidents might be forgotten, Sumner said, "but the name signed to the Fugitive Slave bill can *never* be forgotten."

Sumner's goal was to create such a groundswell against the bill as to render its enforcement impossible. He called on the people of Massachusetts to fight slave-hunters every step of the way, even preventing them from setting foot in the Commonwealth. And if by some chance a slave-hunter arrived on Boston streets, Sumner advocated no violence but urged his fellow citizens to shun him, to turn their backs on him. Any slave-hunter should be treated as a pariah and an outcast, and the public should know of his crimes.

As for Southern Democrats, moderate Whigs, and Washington insiders who contended that the slavery question was "settled," that both Northern and Southern interests were best served by maintaining the status quo, Sumner told the crowd that such claims contravened the very meaning of a free and open society: "*Nothing can be 'settled' which is not right*. Nothing can be 'settled' which is against freedom. Nothing can be 'settled' which is against divine law."

Launching an argument that he would continue to make throughout the fall, Sumner called for slavery to be abolished "within the sphere of the national government," which included inside the confines of the District of Columbia, on the high seas and the waterways that crisscrossed the American continent, and in the territories. He also called for the elimination of the domestic slave trade in which slaves from one state were sold to owners in another. A stalwart constitutionalist, Sumner acknowledged that the federal government currently lacked authority to reach into individual states to end slavery, but by making "slavery sectional and freedom national"—the opposite of the current state of affairs—he was convinced that slavery would be removed from the "vortex of national politics" and begin to die of its own accord within state borders.

The bold nature of Sumner's language and ideas, his willingness to challenge Webster and the establishment Whigs with a direct assault, and the undeniable courage of his antislavery convictions—all of these provided Free Soilers, most of whom were former Conscience Whigs, with a champion around whom to rally. Should their coalition with moderate Democrats prevail in the state election, they had no doubt about whom they would nominate as their candidate for U.S. senator from Massachusetts.

✳ ✳ ✳

Prevail they did. The Massachusetts state election was no contest.

The successful Democrat and Free Soiler coalition secured a considerable majority in both houses of the legislature; what's more, people from across the state turned their backs on the Whigs. Twenty-one Free Soil and Democratic senators were elected statewide compared with only eleven Whigs; in the House, Free Soilers and Democrats won 220 seats compared with 176 for the Whigs.

The results, based on handshake agreements between Free Soil and Democratic party leaders, all but ensured the next U.S. senator from Massachusetts would be a member of the Free Soil Party. Even the most optimistic anti-Whig, antislavery voices were stunned by the outcome. Massachusetts for years had been one of the most steadfast Whig states in the union, but no longer. The Whig demise had happened with lightning speed. "In Massachusetts, the Whigs are prostrate," Sumner wrote with glee to his brother George. "They are in a minority from which they cannot recover."

One Sumner supporter said it best when he wrote to congratulate him on the Free Soiler performance: "You have whipped Webster!"

On the morning after the election, a supporter left a memorandum in Sumner's office announcing the final results, and scrawled a note at the bottom that left no doubt of whom the party would nominate for U.S. senator:

"You are bound for Washington!"

* * *

Sixteen years after he had seen his first slaves, five years since he had made his fiery first antislavery oration, and six months after the Massachusetts Supreme Court had rejected his eloquent "equality before the law" argument in the *Roberts* case, Charles Sumner found himself the living embodiment of the most fervent hopes and aspirations of the Massachusetts abolitionist movement, and all else who opposed the further extension of slavery.

He was a symbol and the architect, in the state and beyond its borders, of a new way of looking at slavery, at least in the North.

Sumner had turned the abolitionist argument on its head. The Declaration of Independence and the Constitution should not be *rejected* because they explicitly did not prohibit slavery, they should be *embraced* because their indisputable messages of freedom obliterated the very notion of slavery. Sumner's framing had moved the radical abolitionist movement nearer to the mainstream (with still a long way to go) and caused those who were ambivalent or agnostic about slavery to take a fresh look at the issue.

An antislavery position was no longer an *anti-American* position, as the abolition movement was often portrayed with its initial calls for rejecting the Constitution. Such an extreme view too often provided fodder for opponents who sought to ridicule the movement and relegate it to the radical fringe.

In his youthful days, Sumner himself had once called for "abolish[ing] the Constitution because of the slavery question," but as he wrote and thought further about the issue, his thinking evolved and had come full circle.

Now, Sumner believed that those who revered the country's founding documents—people precisely like him, in fact—could feel comfortable that demanding slavery's demise represented the loftiest ideals of the American founding promise of freedom and equality.

If you loved America, Sumner insisted, then you *must* hate slavery.

✻ ✻ ✻

With such a fresh perspective, antislavery voices sensed that a Sumner Senate candidacy could finally make a difference, could catalyze action on an issue that had been debated over and over again for decades, with barely any incremental progress to show for the effort. "Many eyes—yes, many hearts—now turn towards the defender of peace, of freedom . . . in a word, of human progress," declared Sumner's friend and future biographer Edward L. Pierce just days after the November election, expressing sentiments of many who wrote to Sumner.

This was heady stuff for Sumner, and he was unsure how to respond to the groundswell of support. He vacillated between cautious enthusiasm in favor of accepting the candidacy to outright gloom were he ever to win election. He had never imagined himself a member of the U.S. Senate, but he understood fully the maelstrom into which he'd be heading. If he agreed to become a candidate, he would have to "renounce quiet and repose forever; my life would be in public affairs. I cannot contemplate this without repugnance."

Yet, he observed within the same letter, would not his selection as a U.S. Senate candidate be "a vindication of me against the attacks to which . . . I have been exposed?"

In one form or another, in one letter after another, Charles Sumner swung back and forth between his private aspirations and his public duty.

And because of this ongoing struggle and indecision, Sumner wondered, would not Free Soil members of the legislature be better off simply nominating someone else?

✻ ✻ ✻

The immediate answer to Sumner's question, particularly in this era before senators were elected directly by the people, depended on party affiliation.

The Free Soilers answered with a resounding "no." They overwhelmingly nominated Sumner for the U.S. Senate (one contemporaneous source said the vote was 82–0 in his favor; another tallied it as 84–1).

When Sumner's name was presented to the Democrats—their anti-Whig feelings and their Free Soil coalition notwithstanding—there was some reluctance to accept him, some dealmaking, some jockeying for position. But in the end, only five Democrats dissented from joining their Free Soil counterparts. Despite their strong differences with the Free Soilers on abolitionism, most moderate Democrats favored the coalition as "the only means available to break down a dynasty of wealth and aristocracy [the Cotton Whigs], such as existed no where else in the country." Despite his strident antislavery voice, Sumner was palatable enough to many of these Democrats because he was sound on "*all the great measures of Democracy, from Jefferson's time downward.*" They did not like Sumner's "red-hot abolitionism," but they despised the Webster Cotton Whigs more; hence their coalition with Free Soilers, the strangest of bedfellows.

Old-line Cotton Whigs—enthusiastic supporters of Webster—unenthusiastically nominated Robert Winthrop, who had been keeping Webster's seat warm since his temporary gubernatorial appointment. Many felt Winthrop had not supported the Compromise of 1850 with enough vigor; others felt some of his public positions on slavery indicated that he was "badly tinged" with abolitionism. A few of these party stalwarts actually preferred Sumner "on the desperate grounds of *the worse, the better.*"

Webster Cotton Whigs also denounced what they called the unholy alliance of Free Soilers and Democrats who were supporting Sumner as a "combination of opposing elements like oil and water," with no principle in common "but the spoils of office." The *Boston Advertiser* declared that the most "dishonorable, disgraceful, and immoral means" were in play to select Sumner as senator. If he were elected, the paper said, it would only be because he was "ignobly shuffled through the forms of an election, by the machinery of a political gaming table."

Among the general public, while those with Free Soil sympathies represented a sizable minority within the city, Boston was primarily a Whig and Democratic stronghold. Most Free Soil support came from the surrounding towns and the Massachusetts countryside.

In the midst of this political swirl, the Massachusetts House designated January 14, 1851, for members to elect a senator to replace Webster, one of the most eagerly awaited elections in state history.

✻ ✻ ✻

When the dust cleared, Sumner was five votes short of the simple House majority required for victory; several Democrats still balked at supporting him and simply refused to cast ballots, arguing that his antislavery position constituted both abolitionism and "disunionism." (The Massachusetts Senate elected Sumner handily on January 22.)

The House's failure to select a senator on its first ballot touched off a fiery two-month marathon, with bitter debate and intense maneuvering on both sides. Whig newspapers called on Sumner to retract his pre-election remarks about Webster and Fillmore, and when he refused, they called him a traitor. Dissenting Democrats asked for assurances from Sumner that he would not "agitate" the slavery question in the Senate, which he steadfastly refused to provide. "There were . . . uneasy stomachs at the chances of my success," Sumner observed. Free Soilers rallied public opinion, hoping citizens could persuade on-the-fence legislators by publishing glowing articles about Sumner's intellect, his reverence for the Declaration and the Constitution, and his love for the union.

In late February, Sumner, still short of the votes needed to secure election, offered to withdraw his name in favor of a more traditional candidate. But Free Soilers again stood resolute behind him—both inside and outside the legislature. "You must be the hero of this war to the end," one wrote, "the conquering hero." On March 17, Free Soilers declared that they would present no other candidate as an alternative to Sumner, and a Free Soil newspaper reprinted Sumner's Faneuil Hall speech as the governing doctrine of the party.

Still, by April 1851, despite their unwillingness to waver, some Free Soilers were growing weary of the logjam and many vocal party members expressed only faint hope for Sumner's success. They had failed to rally additional votes for him—recalcitrant Democrats still viewed him as too much of an agitator on the slavery question—and now it seemed the Webster Whigs were content to outwait or end-run them, to create enough doubt about Sumner's viability that the stalemate would calcify and eventually, out of sheer weariness, enough Democrat votes would shift from the beleaguered Sumner to the safer Winthrop.

The strategy might well have succeeded if not for the arrival in Boston of a slave-hunter from Georgia.

CHAPTER 10

A FUGITIVE SLAVE RETURNED, A NEW SENATOR ELECTED

On the morning of April 3, 1851, Georgia slave-hunter John Bacon walked into the Boston courthouse and secured a warrant for the arrest of twenty-three-year-old Thomas Sims, a runaway slave from Savannah, Georgia.

Using the tough Fugitive Slave Law passed as part of the Compromise of 1850 as his legal justification, Bacon demanded that Boston city authorities find and capture Sims and return him to his rightful owner— rice planter James Potter, who lived about ten miles from Savannah.

Sims, a talented bricklayer who had resided with his mother and sister in Georgia, was often hired out by Potter for contract work, and the slave was forced to turn over his wages to Potter each month. Sims had been Potter's property for fifteen years—since he was a child—and finally saw his opportunity to escape. Days before he did, Sims approached a crew member of the *M&JC Gilmore*, a brig moored in Savannah harbor, and asked whether the vessel needed a cook. He was told no and ordered off the ship. Sims complied, but he had seen enough of the ship and the surrounding docks to formulate a plan. When the brig left Savannah for Boston on February 22, Sims stowed away.

For two weeks during the ship's wintry northward voyage, he escaped detection, avoiding the crew, foraging for food, and providing for himself. Then, with Boston's lights in sight, the brig's mate discovered the stowaway, and the Georgia captain ordered Sims locked in a cabin while the ship lay anchored outside Boston Harbor.

But the crew failed to take his pocketknife, and on the night of March 6, Sims jimmied the lock, lowered one of the brig's lifeboats, and rowed toward freedom. He landed in South Boston and, according to one newspaper account, "took lodging in a colored seaman's boardinghouse." Despite the looming presence of the Fugitive Slave Law, "while in the city, [he] made no effort to conceal himself."

Even this lack of caution might not have led to Sims's capture if he hadn't made a grave mistake.

Destitute for funds after a few weeks in Boston, Sims wired his mother in Savannah asking for money, and the telegram included his return address. Somehow—perhaps through an observant telegraph operator or simply word-of-mouth gossip—Sims's message, and his whereabouts, became known. Potter, the rice planter who owned Sims, first dispatched slave-hunter Bacon to visit the slave's mother. When Bacon did so, he reported that Sims's mother begged him, "whether her son was in a free state or a slave state, for God's sake to bring him back again."

Potter wasted no time ordering Bacon to Boston, and Bacon was equally efficient in securing his arrest warrant for Sims on April 3.

The Boston police moved just as swiftly. That evening—with the next House vote for the Senate set for twenty days later—Boston police cornered Sims on a downtown street and arrested him as a fugitive slave. Sims fought hard, stabbing officer Asa Butman in the thigh with a pocketknife, snapping the knife in two. Police overpowered Sims, tossed him into a carriage, and drove him to the courthouse where he was imprisoned.

Witnesses heard him cry, "I'm in the hands of kidnappers!"

✳ ✳ ✳

Boston abolitionists met at the courthouse in Court Square the next morning to protest Sims's detention. The previous night, while Boston slept, City Marshal (the equivalent of a police chief) Francis Tukey had ordered the building encircled with chains and directed hundreds of Boston police and armed federal guards to surround the courthouse.

Only authorized people could get within ten feet of the courthouse entrance. Harvard librarian and abolitionist sympathizer John Langdon Sibley bemoaned the fact that the state's chief justice, Lemuel Shaw, "had to crawl under chains to get to his own court room!" Inside the courthouse, the handful of lawyers who had ventured upstairs reported that the third-floor room in which Sims was held was guarded by at least twenty police officers.

By Saturday, April 5, abolitionists had been joined by curiosity seekers and other concerned Boston residents, creating a huge crowd milling outside the building to get a glimpse of the principals in the proceedings or glean some information about the outcome of legal maneuverings. An irate Henry Wadsworth Longfellow wrote incredulously in his journal: "Troops under arms in Boston; the court house guarded; the Chief Justice of the Supreme Court forced to stoop under chains to enter the temple of Justice!"

* * *

In the days following, volunteer attorneys for Sims, including Sumner, tried every conceivable method to interrupt or halt the proceedings against him. They attacked the constitutionality of the Fugitive Slave Law and petitioned Lemuel Shaw for a writ of habeas corpus, requesting that Sims be allowed to call witnesses in his own defense to prove he was a "free colored man" and not a slave. Shaw declined on the grounds that he had little jurisdiction to interfere in federal law.

To Sumner's dismay, the chief justice also upheld the constitutionality of the Fugitive Slave Law, pointing out that the initiative was an "essential element" in the formation of the nation when it was passed nearly sixty years earlier. The fact that Congress had sharpened and toughened the law as part of the Compromise of 1850 was hardly grounds to rule it unconstitutional. Abolitionist Theodore Parker promptly lost all sympathy for Shaw's forced crawl under the courthouse chains, announcing that once the chief justice upheld the Fugitive Slave Law, he "spit in the face of Massachusetts."

With their legal options running out, abolitionists devised a plan to break Sims out of jail by having him jump from his open third-floor window to mattresses below. But the idea was foiled when a betrayer notified officials of the plot; on the day the breakout was planned, guards fitted iron bars across the window of Sims's cell.

The huge law enforcement presence in Boston in the Sims case came after the city's abolitionists had helped three runaway slaves escape hunters—William and Ellen Craft in October of 1850, and Shadrach Minkins in February 1851. President Millard Fillmore's administration indicted eight men for violating the Fugitive Slave Law and abetting Minkins. Divided juries failed to convict them, but to prevent a repeat of the Minkins affair, Fillmore authorized the use of federal troops to quell any future agitation in Boston. An example needed to be set.

On Friday, April 11, a mere eight days after Sims was captured, the court issued a certificate attesting that he was indeed the property of James Porter and identified him as "a chattel personal to all interests, uses, and purposes whatsoever." Abolitionists pledged to Bacon to raise $1,800—Sims's estimated value—to buy the runaway's freedom, but Bacon said Potter was unwilling to sell his slave at any cost.

The legal proceedings were over.

With his fate sealed, Thomas Sims exclaimed to his counsel: "I will *not* go back to slavery. Give me a knife, and when the Commissioner declares me a slave, I will stab myself in the heart and die before his eyes! I will not be a slave."

⁂

On Saturday, April 12, 1851, Thomas Sims ran out of time.

In the damp early morning darkness, Boston police and federal troops mustered by the weak light of a single gas lamp. It was just after 3:00 A.M., and more than one hundred police officers, armed with double-edged Roman swords, plus another one hundred volunteers armed with clubs and hooks, drilled for more than an hour, their heavy boots clomping on the dirt-packed street. The men established a two-level "hollow-square" formation, one inside the other, with an open middle. Police officers manned the inner square—they would be closest to the prisoner—and the volunteers formed the outer square. Word spread that Sims's departure was at hand, and by 4:00 A.M., nearly two hundred horrified abolitionists looked on as the drilling continued.

At 4:15, "after the moon had gone down, in the darkest hour before daybreak," the officers and volunteers assembled and marched in formation to the east door of the courthouse. There, they were joined by an additional one hundred armed officers, who formed another double file around the hollow square. The main doors of the courthouse opened, and Sims appeared, tears streaming down his face, "but . . . his small dark frame erect," one abolitionist described.

Police escorted the prisoner to the center of the square. On Tukey's command of "March!" the three hundred guards who surrounded Sims began their slow tramp toward the dock, forcing the runaway to keep time with them.

Abolitionists preceded them, followed them, and flanked them as the guards continued their relentless march down State Street, forcing the despondent and reluctant Sims to keep up with them. The antislavery observers hissed and shouted "Shame!" and "Infamy!" but made no attempt to stop the march. The procession finally arrived at Long Wharf, near the site of the Boston Tea Party, where colonists had once famously protested oppression—the irony of which was not lost upon the abolitionists. The brig *Acorn*, its sails unfurled, was ready for sea, prepared to transport its human cargo to Georgia.

The armed police surrounding Sims marched close to the vessel, and one section broke ranks momentarily, like a door swinging open, to deliver its prisoner to a contingent of guards waiting on board. As Sims reached the *Acorn*'s deck, a man standing on the wharf cried out, "Sims, preach liberty to the slaves!" With his last words, Sims offered a sharp rebuke to his captors: "And is *this* Massachusetts liberty?"

He was ushered below immediately, and within two minutes, at just after 5:00 A.M., the *Acorn* was moving. As the vessel cleared the dock, the stunned spectators listened in solemn silence to the Reverend Daniel Foster, who asked them to kneel and pray for "the poor brother who is carried by force to the land of whips and chains."

Boston, the birthplace of the struggle for America's liberty seventy-five years earlier, had sent its first free man back to slavery.

✳ ✳ ✳

The momentous occasion produced a cacophony of emotional reactions, in Boston, Massachusetts, and across the country. There was no one-size-fits-all response to the Sims episode, and the case provides an illuminating lens through which to view the mood of the nation.

Boston-area abolitionists were distraught and embarrassed. "Shame on my country! Shame on Boston!" wrote Harvard's Sibley in his April 12 diary entry. An antislavery newspaper labeled the Sims affair the "darkest and most disgraceful crime that ever has been perpetuated" in Boston's history. Abolitionist preachers declared a day of fasting.

But most Boston establishment newspapers and Cotton Whigs applauded the city's law enforcement apparatus for its efforts in returning Sims and abiding by the Fugitive Slave Law. The *Boston Herald* expected the South to now "please accord us all the credit which is due."

Some Southern papers granted the *Herald*'s wish, but the favorable reaction was far from unanimous. One Georgia editorial agreed that Boston deserved credit for complying with the Fugitive Slave Law, but another reprimanded the city's authorities for taking a whole week to return Sims to his rightful owner. The proslavery *Louisville Journal*, employing language with which some militant Boston antislavery men would agree, ridiculed the cowardice of abolitionists, who at the crucial moment—when Sims was hustled aboard the *Acorn* for the return trip to Georgia—had lost their courage and turned to prayer rather than taking up arms.

Elsewhere in the nation, there was much rejoicing at the vindication of the Compromise of 1850. Daniel Webster wrote President Fillmore, arguing that the next step was to discredit some of the "insane" abolitionists.

Fillmore replied by congratulating Boston on a "triumph of law. . . . She has done nobly."

✹ ✹ ✹

For the purposes of the nail-biting fight for the U.S. Senate seat from Massachusetts, still stalemated, the most important response to the Sims affair was that of moderate Democrats outside of Boston. These were citizens, journalists, and legislators who viewed slavery as beyond their control, part of the fabric of Southern plantation life, but not something that affected their daily lives or their families' economic well-being. To this group, many of whom felt pride in the liberty-based historic legacy of their state—especially during the American Revolution—the arrest, imprisonment, and, especially, return to bondage of Sims elicited deep sadness and unease.

They wondered: Was a Fugitive Slave Law that mandated the merciless re-enslavement of a runaway necessary to preserve the union?

Sumner, who alternated between tears and rage over the Sims case, recognized that a shift was taking place—moderates found themselves agreeing with abolitionists about the unjustness of the Georgia slave's fate. And that unlikely alliance was strengthened when Massachusetts received word on April 19, one week after Sims had left Boston, that upon his arrival in Savannah he'd been whipped in the public square for his "crime" of escaping the shackles of slavery. The punishment, thirty-nine lashes across his bare back, was followed by three months in prison. When the prison doctor told Potter that Sims would die if he remained incarcerated much longer, Potter had him released and brought into the Savannah countryside to recover. Unwilling to risk another Sims escape attempt, Potter sold him to a new owner in Charleston, South Carolina, who soon resold him—touting his skills as "an expert bricklayer" to a Louisiana slave broker.

Sims would eventually escape in 1863 during the Civil War and make his way back to Boston, a city in which he had made "dear friends . . . whose hearts bled with sorrow when I was sent away from that city." City authorities might have conspired to send Sims back to bondage, but Sims said ordinary Bostonians showed him respect and understanding—"I am under a thousand obligations to them, for their kindness to me in the hours of my deepest distress."

Many Massachusetts moderates were disgusted that Boston's actions played such an active role in Sims's horrific punishment.

"My appeal is to these people," Sumner wrote, "and my hope is to create in Massachusetts such a public opinion as will render the [Fugitive Slave] law a dead letter." Once again, perhaps a measure of good could be extracted from an act of evil. The Sims episode, he concluded, had given Massachusetts and the other free states "a sphere of discussion which they would otherwise have missed."

✳ ✳ ✳

On April 24, the Massachusetts House of Representatives finally spoke on the battle for U.S. senator, and its voice was heard across the land.

Yet, even with the Sims episode fresh in legislators' minds, the Senate race was decided by a razor-thin margin. On the House's first-ballot vote on April 24—the twenty-fifth overall over a four-month period—Sumner picked up a few votes but remained two votes short of a majority. Then, Boston Whig Sidney Bartlett, in an apparent attempt to give Democrats an opportunity to vote secretly *against* Sumner, proposed that ballots should be cast in writing and enclosed in envelopes, which would then be opened by the Speaker who would announce the results. The motion was approved.

On the next House ballot, the twenty-sixth, Sumner received 193 votes, the exact number he needed to secure the Senate seat. Two votes had shifted in his *favor* during the secret ballot. No one could say for sure whether additional Democrats cast ballots for Sumner or—even more alarming to the Whig establishment—whether a Whig or two had crossed over and voted for the fanatical antislavery candidate.

Regardless, it was official: political novice Charles Sumner would fill the vacancy in the U.S. Senate left by the legendary Daniel Webster.

✳ ✳ ✳

It was a stunning choice by the Massachusetts legislature, one that would have been inconceivable only a year earlier, prior to Webster's March 7, 1850, speech and the passage of the Fugitive Slave Law, prior to California's admission in September, and, most especially, prior to the Sims debacle—the runaway's capture, return, and punishment were enough to swing the vote toward Sumner. "The election of Sumner . . . practically followed from it [Sims's misfortune]," wrote minister and militant abolitionist Thomas Wentworth Higginson, who celebrated Sumner's win as a glorious and portentous first step in the eventual erosion of the slaveholders' grip on the national government.

The ironies of Sumner's election to the six-year term were layered upon each other and impossible to miss by the people of Massachusetts or the nation.

Webster, whose unabashed support for the Fugitive Slave Act diminished his stature in Massachusetts, would be succeeded by Sumner, whose rock-ribbed opposition to the same law elevated his. In addition, Webster, who believed the Fugitive Slave Act would still the nation's turbulent waters, had been replaced by Sumner, who believed the Compromise would roil the sensibilities of even the most ambivalent Northerner and generate a groundswell that would ultimately lead to the rejection of slavery. Finally, Webster, the ultimate compromiser, had been succeeded by Sumner, who, especially on the subject of slavery, believed compromise was a euphemism for weakness.

Abolitionists and Free Soilers were jubilant over Sumner's improbable victory; many said it was the happiest moment of their lives. On the night of Sumner's election, and on several succeeding nights, they celebrated with bonfires, bell ringing, cannon fire, and public speeches. As word spread of Sumner's victory, nearly ten thousand people—about 10 percent of Boston's population—gathered near the antislavery *Common-wealth* newspaper office, which displayed red, white, and blue bunting from its location on the corner of Washington and State streets; later in the night, staffers fired rockets into the sky.

✳ ✳ ✳

Meanwhile, the new U.S. senator-elect felt more dread than elation, though he avoided sharing his feelings. Sumner heard the news of his election around 3:00 P.M. on April 24, while he was visiting the home of Charles Francis Adams at 57 Mount Vernon Street, a one-minute walk from the statehouse. Adams's son Henry, who had been monitoring the situation in the House chamber, reported the results of the vote, and the family congratulated Sumner, who remained placid when he heard the news and unflappable as he shook hands. "He received the news of his success with as perfect calmness and absence of any . . . excitement as was possible," recounted Adams's other son, Charles Francis, Jr.

Sumner decided to spend the night of his election, and the next several nights, at Longfellow's house in Cambridge, where he attempted to adjust to his victory and new status but was gripped by a sense of fear and morbidity. Longfellow observed in his diary on April 25, capturing Sumner's trepidation about prevailing in the Senate race: "The papers are all ringing with Sumner, Sumner! And the guns are thundering out their triumph; meanwhile the hero of the strife is sitting quietly here, more saddened than exalted."

A few days after his election, Sumner confided to his brother George that the joyful celebrations across the state left him fearful that he could not meet the expectations others had of him. To a friend, Sumner shared his insecurities and doubts about his fitness for the job. Would he be able to fulfill the solemn trust others had placed in him?

Now that he had been elected to an office from where he could make a practical, if not immediate, difference on the great issue of his time, Sumner seemed frightened of the lofty antislavery goals his supporters expected him to achieve and wary of the public arena in which he would be fighting for them. "At this moment," he wrote to George immediately after his victory, "could another person faithful to our cause be chosen in my place, I would resign."

To a friend, he stated it more simply:

"I do not wish to be a politician."

✸ ✸ ✸

It did not help Sumner's mood that scowling Webster Whigs, apoplectic over his election, expressed their views with relentless public fury. "They hated Sumner as few men have been hated," Edward L. Pierce wrote, "and he was now to fill the high place which their idol had filled so long." Sumner supporter Edmund Quincy was equally blunt as he described the reactions of angry Boston merchants and business leaders to Sumner's election: "If you could have heard the swearing, your hair would have stood on end."

Furious Whigs did more than curse. The day after the election, Whig-sympathizing men, women, and children wore black crepe armbands on their sleeves to mark the death of "pure government" in Massachusetts. Webster himself announced that he was "grieved and mortified" by the results, and one Whig newspaper decried Sumner's election as the "blackest of frauds."

Though hurt by the anger he faced from traditional Whigs on the streets of Boston, Sumner assessed that the city's "State Street set" was either willfully ignoring the changes in attitudes toward slavery that were occurring statewide or frightened about what a "Senator Sumner" term likely meant for their already waning power.

"For the first time they are represented in the Senate by one over whom they have no influence, who is entirely independent," he declared.

✸ ✸ ✸

As much as the bitter Whig response may have unnerved him, Sumner was buoyed by warm wishes from outside Massachusetts, across the country and across the Atlantic. These correspondents sensed that *something* had changed—and that something *would* change in Washington, D.C.—and they, and thousands of others, saw in Sumner's election "deep and unexpected happiness," in the words of one Brooklyn writer. Sumner's English friends also sent congratulations, most citing Sumner's courage, intellect, and ideals as the attributes needed to change the American government's view on slavery.

For his part, Sumner did his best to temper the unrealistic expectations so many had of him. In his acceptance letter to the legislature, Sumner reminded the body that "for the first time in my life, I am called to political office," and that such an honor came to him "unsought and undesired." He reiterated his support of the Constitution and opposed sectionalism in any form; as such, while he personally desired an end to slavery, he recognized that, at this point in the nation's history, Congress had no authority to mandate freedom in individual states. He would also be only one of three Free Soil senators in the upper chamber.

Still, he meant to fight against unconstitutional efforts by the South to "carry the *sectional* evil of slavery into the Free States," or into areas under the federal government's jurisdiction—territories, waterways, and Washington, D.C.—and to battle with all of his strength and conviction against the outrage that was the Fugitive Slave Law. Hearts and minds needed to be changed before laws promoting full-fledged freedom could become palatable to the majority of Congress, and the concept of freedom for all men would require time to take hold. He would bide his time—as a "stranger to the Senate," he considered it his "first duty to understand the body . . . before rushing into its contests."

Boston abolitionists were unhappy with Sumner's cautious acceptance letter and the tempered course of action he laid out. They'd been expecting immediate and zealous antislavery thunder and lightning to boom and crackle across the land, to shake slaveholders and their Northern supporters from their complacency; yet, Sumner was now promising that he would adopt a soft-rain approach to nurture the idea of freedom and help it grow by cultivating allies and converting them to his cause.

Sumner assured his brother George that once he was seated in the Senate, patience would help him, the Free Soilers, and all who cherished freedom to achieve their goals. A few months of becoming familiar with the Senate's machinations would not hurt the cause.

"Our ultimate triumph is none the less certain," he predicted to George.

CHAPTER 11

"SLAVERY IS THE SOURCE OF ALL MEANNESS HERE"

Forty-year-old Charles Sumner wept three times before leaving Boston for Washington on November 25, 1851, to begin his journey as an elected official—first when he said good-bye to his mother and his sister Julia at the family home on Beacon Hill; then when he bid farewell to the Longfellows; and, finally, when he parted with his friend Samuel Gridley Howe. As difficult as it was for him to form close attachments, he shared real affection with this small group.

He arrived at his Washington, D.C., ground-floor lodgings, located on New York Avenue between Fifteenth and Sixteenth Streets, and spent his first days in Washington reading and preparing for the December 1 opening session of the Thirty-Second Congress.

He fretted about what lay ahead, questioned what influence he could have in a body about whose workings he knew virtually nothing, pondered how to avoid disappointing even his strongest supporters with his cautious wait-and-see approach on the slavery issue, and wondered how he would react in close proximity to his new slaveholding colleagues—a much different dynamic than criticizing them from five hundred miles away.

As his first day as a U.S. senator approached, Sumner predicted to Longfellow that he faced tumult ahead. "Those calm days and nights [we shared] of overflowing communion are gone," he wrote to his dearest friend.

✳ ✳ ✳

With Free Soilers so few in number, they had no section of their own—their seats were located on the Democratic side of the chamber, though Sumner's seat was directly in front of fellow party member Salmon P.

Chase of Ohio, whom Sumner found "a tower of strength." In a footnote that would one day become laced with both sectional and national irony, Sumner's seat was previously occupied by Jefferson Davis of Mississippi, who had resigned from the Senate a month earlier to run for Governor of his state—and it was located in close proximity to chairs occupied by proslavery titans James Mason of Virginia and Andrew Butler of South Carolina.

And there was more irony: On the day Sumner took his seat, Senator Henry Clay, architect of the Compromise of 1850, sat in *his* chair for the final time. Enfeebled by age and illness, Clay tottered into the chamber, spoke twice on procedural matters, and left the Capitol never to return (he would be dead in six months). The Great Compromiser was leaving, even as Sumner, who would entertain no compromise on the slavery issue, was entering the Senate chamber.

In his first weeks, Sumner felt off-balance in his new career.

It didn't help that he, Chase, and Free Soiler John P. Hale of New Hampshire were men without a home in the Senate, on the outside looking in at Southerners who unquestioningly supported slavery and slaveholding interests, and at Northern Whigs and Democrats who welcomed any compromise on the slavery question so long as it maintained the fragile peace and was deemed essential to party success. Senate leadership assigned Sumner to two lackluster committees—one on Revolutionary War compensation and the other on roads and canals—presumably where he could do the least damage as an antislavery agitator.

Southern Democrats devoted to slavery, including Butler, Mason, and Mississippi's Henry Foote, did not avoid him—in fact, because of Sumner's intellect and classical training, they conversed with him cordially on nonslavery matters such as literature and philosophy. Butler even asked him to verify classical quotes that he would insert into his speeches. Sumner conceded—or condescended—that Butler, "had he been a citizen of New England . . . would have been a scholar, or at least, a well educated man."

But Sumner noted that his enormous differences with them on the most important issue facing the nation always lurked beneath the polite surface.

"Slavery is the source of all meanness here, from national honesty down to tobacco-spitting," he explained to Howe.

✳ ✳ ✳

As the calendar flipped to 1852, Sumner was determined to establish his credibility as a serious senator, a statesman who could speak intelligently on all issues that came before the body, not just the slavery question. Only this approach, he believed, would make his voice *more* effective when he eventually rose to condemn the Fugitive Slave Law.

Again, Free Soilers at home condemned this cautious strategy, and Whigs taunted him for it, but Sumner stayed the course and explained his rationale in letters to Howe. "My position here is *peculiar*," he emphasized. "The prejudices against me before I came, not only here but throughout the country, were enormous." Through a series of what Sumner labeled as "forgeries and misrepresentations" of his position, he was "held up as a man incapable of public business, of one idea, a fanatic." He was determined to correct this erroneous impression "*as a first condition of my usefulness*, and to my final influence on our cause."

Thus, he engaged in Senate debates on a series of issues that Free Soilers viewed as mundane: to grant land to the State of Iowa to build additional railroads within its limits; to raise the pay of enlisted men in the Navy; to reduce the cost of transatlantic postage rates; and to review and revise public statutes by simplifying their language. All of this pedestrian work, he assured Howe, helped "overturn a mountain of prejudice" against him and would help him "secure a hearing" when he decided to speak his heart on slavery, and especially on the evils of the Fugitive Slave bill.

As for impatient Free Soilers and abolitionists from his home state, Sumner suggested that Howe offer a simple answer to any who questioned the new senator's course of action:

"You can say that I have always known when to speak," Sumner said, "and that I shall speak at the proper time."

Abolitionists believed that the "proper time" for Sumner to speak against slavery and the Fugitive Slave Law was when they handed him what they believed was the perfect issue—a petition demanding the release from prison of sea captains Daniel Drayton and Edward Sayres, who had spearheaded the failed slave escape attempt aboard the *Pearl* in 1848.

✳ ✳ ✳

Both men had spent more than four years in jail for their inability to pay the fines imposed by the court, and their incarceration had elicited sympathy from Northern abolitionists, who viewed it as a terrible mis-carriage of justice. Leading abolitionists, represented by the eloquent Wendell Phillips, forwarded the petition to Sumner for presentation to the Senate. They expected Sumner to make his voice heard immediately, as much for the antislavery cause as for the benefit of Drayton and Sayres.

But Sumner decided on a different course. He was not a natural politician, but his cautious approach had allowed him to build up some political capital, and his time fraternizing with Southern senators had taught him something about political personalities.

He was certain that any attention-seeking theatrics on Drayton and Sayres would backfire in the Senate and instead embolden slaveholding senators to resist the release of the *Pearl* captains. Additionally, because President Millard Fillmore would be seeking the 1852 presidential nomination at the Whig convention in June, a confrontational public demand to free Sayres and Drayton would almost require the President to deny a request for a pardon of the two men (which, Sumner believed, was their best chance of release) for fear of alienating Northern Democrats and other moderates.

Sumner's plan was to withhold the petition and work behind the scenes—vigorously and effectively, but quietly. His goal was not to engage in a public spectacle merely to portray Sayres and Drayton as symbolic victims of slaveholders but to actually secure freedom for the two seamen. Sumner consulted with close friends and secretly visited Drayton in prison. He informed the captain, according to Drayton's recollection, that his release from prison would be accomplished "not by agitating the matter in the Senate, but by private appeals to the equity and conscience of the President." Drayton agreed and concurred with Sumner that his interests "ought [not] be sacrificed for the opportunity to make an antislavery speech."

With Drayton's blessing, Sumner appealed to President Fillmore, who, despite the vituperative language Sumner had used against him when Fillmore signed the Fugitive Slave Law, agreed to hear him out on the merits of the argument. Afterward, he asked Sumner to prepare a legal opinion on whether the President had a right to pardon the two men in this case. While the slave escape had taken place on federal land (Washington, D.C.), Drayton and Sayres had been convicted and imprisoned only on charges of failure to pay their fines—was that a gray area into which the President could legally tread? Could he not only free them but forgive their unpaid fines? Sumner submitted his opinion to Fillmore and the attorney general on May 14, entitled "The Pardoning Power of the President." In short, Sumner argued, both common law and legal precedent suggested that Fillmore's power to pardon Drayton and Sayres was constitutionally appropriate.

Meanwhile, Sumner was in close touch with author, nurse, and reformer Dorothea Dix, who had a personal relationship with President Fillmore. Dix and Fillmore had corresponded regularly after meeting in the spring of 1850. Sumner urged Dix to "take advantage of the familiar access . . . and plead their [Sayres and Drayton's] case with him and his family."

As summer 1852 approached, political novice Charles Sumner moved with deftness and purpose to achieve justice for the men who had nearly pulled off the largest slave escape in American history.

✳ ✳ ✳

But because he worked under the cloak of secrecy ("I mention these things to *your private ear*," he impressed upon his abolitionist friend, Henry Wilson, president of the Massachusetts Senate), Sumner received intense criticism from abolitionists and Free Soilers in his home state for his failure to take the *Pearl* prisoner case to the Senate floor.

The often-grandstanding William Lloyd Garrison, especially, showed Sumner no mercy, declaring that his actions were inexplicable, and at one antislavery meeting, he succeeded in passing a vote of censure against Sumner. He followed it up with an editorial in the *Liberator* entitled "Inquiry after a Back-Bone," slamming Sumner for his silence on the slavery issue after more than four months in the Senate and accusing him of fumbling the opportunity that had been handed to him with the petition to free Sayres and Drayton.

Sumner wrote that he demonstrated "*backbone* in resisting the pressure even of friends." Had he grandstanded, or even "uttered a word" for Drayton and Sayres on the Senate floor, he "should have dealt a blow at them." He believed firmly that the public presentation of a petition to the Senate "would do more harm than good" for Sayres and Drayton by backing Fillmore into a corner.

✳ ✳ ✳

Things finally moved in Sumner's direction in June, when the Whigs nominated General Winfield Scott, and not Millard Fillmore, as their presidential candidate. Influenced by Sumner's legal brief, sensitive to the pleas of Dorothea Dix, and now freed from the constraining optics and politics of a presidential campaign, Millard Fillmore finally issued a full pardon for Drayton and Sayres on August 11, 1852. The President had given Sumner a heads-up two days earlier and suggested that the senator inform the prisoners of their impending freedom, which Sumner did.

Fearful that Southerners would attempt to re-arrest Drayton and Sayres upon their release, Sumner rushed to the D.C. prison, and once the pardon arrived at 5:00 P.M., silently escorted the two *Pearl* captains to a waiting carriage, where an armed friend of Sumner's would escort them northward. Sumner wished the freed prisoners Godspeed, and after the men ate supper at the nearby home of a sympathetic abolitionist, the carriage driver persevered through a night of torrential rain and lightning storms to get the two free seamen to Baltimore by dawn. From there, Sayres slipped into Philadelphia, and Drayton boarded a train for Harrisburg, experiencing immense satisfaction "as the cars crossed the line from Maryland into Pennsylvania."

Back in Washington, Sumner, too, felt relief, satisfaction, even joy. He had devised the plan himself, kept it under wraps from even his closest allies and sympathizers, and managed to strike a blow against slave owners—most of whom still despised Sayres and Drayton—by spiriting away the two high-profile prisoners from right under their noses. Wendell Phillips, critical of Sumner only weeks earlier, now congratulated him, admitting: "You have *earned* your honors."

Sumner felt vindicated against the barrage of criticism leveled against him—that he lacked backbone, that he kowtowed to Southern slave owners, that he was a "dough-face" who feared confrontation and thus had become lost in a "dismal Sahara of silence."

The liberty of Drayton and Sayres had proven all his critics wrong.

"Here ends one of the miserable charges against me," Sumner wrote to Theodore Parker. "The others will end soon."

CHAPTER 12

THE FUGITIVE SLAVE LAW ASSAILED

You must *not* let the session close without speaking," wrote Free Soiler Henry Wilson to Sumner on March 9, 1852, about the new senator's opposition to the Fugitive Slave Law. "Should you do so, you would be openly denounced by nine-tenths of our people."

It was not just a matter of principle for these people, Wilson said, but of their day-to-day existence and reputation as they went about their business and social interactions. As president of the Massachusetts Senate, Wilson was more responsible than any other single person for Charles Sumner's election—his words carried weight, his on-the-ground knowledge of Sumner's Massachusetts constituents even more so.

Sumner's work to free Drayton and Sayres had not spared him from the increasing impatience and criticism of friends who felt he had misplayed the opportunity to speak against the Fugitive Slave Law, leading to Wilson's advice that he'd better speak up before the end of session. "Almost seven months has he sat in the U.S. Senate, yet not a syllable has he uttered against that [Fugitive Slave] Bill," said one Boston abolitionist newspaper in August, "though men, women, and children are hunted daily and ruthlessly shot down or dragged back to bondage." Reverend Theodore Parker warned that Sumner was in "imminent deadly peril" from impatient abolitionists at home and concluded that "if he does not speak, then he is *dead—dead—dead*!"

✳ ✳ ✳

After months of biding his time, Sumner was ready to speak against the Fugitive Slave Law but found it difficult to find an opportunity within the Senate rules, which restricted debate to topics at hand—and the only time the subject of slavery had come before the Senate was months earlier, when both Democrats and Whigs, in the spring of 1852, adopted platforms *condemning further agitation* on the slavery issue before the presidential election. Sumner nonetheless assured his supporters in letters that the subject of slavery was "always in my mind and heart," and he worked on writing and memorizing a speech on the subject, which he entitled "Freedom National; Slavery Sectional," throughout the summer.

Finally, on July 27, with Wilson's admonition from months earlier in mind, under constant pressure from his constituents, and worried as the session was winding down, Sumner decided it was time to ignore Senate rules. He stood and made a stand-alone motion to repeal the Fugitive Slave Law, and the next day, asked consent to speak on the motion, a request that required a vote but was usually extended to senators as a matter of courtesy.

Not in this case.

Sumner's colleagues denied his request to speak on the issue by a vote of thirty-two to ten. It was an embarrassing defeat on a routine procedural vote that left Sumner "mortified and dejected." Some Southerners warned that Sumner's motion was "equivalent to . . . a resolution to dissolve the Union." Senator Butler said Sumner was looking for a pretense to "wash deeper and deeper the channel through which flow the angry waters of agitation." Some Northerners who voted "no" assured Sumner afterward that they sympathized with his desire to speak, but their hands were tied by the party platforms prohibiting agitation against slavery.

After the rejection, influential Virginia senator James Mason, who voted "no" and whose clout unofficially controlled the votes of numerous Southern colleagues, told Sumner: "You may speak *next* term." Mason knew any attempt by Sumner to again put forth a stand-alone motion would suffer the same fate. When Sumner responded that he must speak in the current term, and that Mason had no authority to prevent him from doing so, Mason snapped back: "By God, you shan't."

But Sumner believed he had one more card in his deck before the scheduled end of the session on August 31. And ironically, it was another slaveholding Virginian senator who gave him the opening to play it.

✳ ✳ ✳

As he had during the Drayton-Sayres affair, he proceeded with cloak-and-dagger secrecy.

Sumner confidentially informed E. L. Pierce that he planned to speak on the Fugitive Slave Law during the Senate's discussion on the budget appropriation bill—to enforce the law required funding, which would provide him with the opening he needed—and this was the last major item the upper chamber would discuss before adjournment. "*Do not* let this be known publicly," he warned Pierce.

To allay any Southern suspicions on the day he made his move, Sumner cleared off all papers from his desk and offered no hint that his lengthy antislavery speech lay in his top drawer. Sumner planned to offer an amendment to the budget bill demanding that no money be appropriated to enforce the Fugitive Slave Law. At that moment he would be heard, "not as a favor, but as a right."

The Senate began debate on the budget on August 19, but it was not until August 26 that Sumner got his chance. Virginia senator Robert Hunter, on behalf of the committee shepherding the bill through the Senate, put forth an amendment for paying "the extraordinary expenses incurred by ministerial officers executing the law." Though no particular law was mentioned, senators knew the language was intended to cover expenses incurred in the enforcement of the Fugitive Slave Law. Just to be sure, Sumner also consulted with the Senate's auditor to confirm the purpose of Hunter's amendment.

It was the opportunity he'd been waiting for. To Hunter's amendment, he offered a startling one of his own: "provided, that no such allowance shall be authorized for any expenses incurred in executing the Act of September 18, 1850, for the surrender of fugitives from service or labor, *which said Act is hereby repealed.*"

Without hesitation, he seized the floor and with it history by delivering what would be the first major antislavery speech ever made in the U.S. Senate.

✳ ✳ ✳

For nearly four hours Sumner addressed the body from memory.

Slavery, he told them, was a deviant sectional institution, while freedom was virtuous and national in scope.

At the same time, he demonstrated with ample evidence what he had been preaching for months—that a deep antislavery philosophy wove through the tapestry of the country's founding and was incorporated within the Constitution; indeed, opposition to slavery epitomized the very heart and soul of America's promise.

During the course of his remarkable and groundbreaking "Freedom National; Slavery Sectional" speech, Sumner also established the foundation for the antislavery and equal rights views he would articulate in the years to come.

He began by ridiculing the notion that the Compromise of 1850 had settled the question of slavery, criticizing the cozy agreement by Northern and Southern lawmakers that placed the topic of slavery off-limits in Congress. Such a grievous trampling on the right to free speech was an outrage, he said, one that he protested with his entire being. The prohibition against discussing slavery was "impotent and tyrannical"—whether or not slavery was discussed on the floor of Congress, it was a topic discussed everywhere else in the nation, "wherever two or three are gathered together."

Sumner set out to achieve a *radical* end—the destruction of the Fugitive Slave Law, and perhaps the first step in the eradication of slavery itself—by employing *conservative* means. To accomplish this objective, he argued against the general federal protection of slavery and the specific outrage of the Fugitive Slave Law. He put forth the case that supporters of the Compromise of 1850, who most often saw themselves as conservative unionists, were actually radical sectionalists, while antislavery so-called "radicals," portrayed as sectional agitators, were the true unionists.

As his voice rang across the Senate chamber, spectators began to crowd the gallery to hear the new senator from Massachusetts. Many House members made their way into the Senate, and Daniel Webster, within two months of his death, also came to listen.

Sumner would later crow that he, not the aging secretary of state, was now the spokesman for Massachusetts.

✳ ✳ ✳

During the first ninety minutes of his speech, Sumner once again argued that the United States, as a country, was born in an atmosphere of freedom for all men—it was only "the imbecility of Southern states" that condoned slavery—and that the notion of slavery as a national institution was anathema to the very precepts of the nation's origins.

While compromise with slave states was necessary to make possible the adoption of the Constitution—one reason the new document did not explicitly *prohibit* slavery outright—its very ratification without mention of slavery was proof of the Founders' intent to create a federal framework based on freedom.

He pointed out that many Founders and Framers, including James Madison, Roger Sherman, Elbridge Gerry, and Benjamin Franklin, were on record opposing slavery's enshrinement anywhere in the Constitution. Even Founders who were slaveholders in their individual states understood fully the unreconcilable contradiction of their individual situations and the birth of a new nation grounded in freedom and equality. These men—Washington for example, who wrote numerous times about the injustices of slavery and ordered his slaves freed upon his death— were, at the same time, reluctant slaveholders *personally* and national "abolitionists" *philosophically*.

They generally favored an end to slavery, Sumner contended, but were willing to forego the immediate (and unwinnable) fight with ardent slave owners for the sake of forming a new government, whose national liberty-infused character would force slavery's demise within two decades—around the time, 1808, when the Constitution obliquely suggested an end to the international slave trade.

✳ ✳ ✳

Evidence that the Founders hoped to create a national framework unencumbered by slavery was clear, if imperfect, Sumner argued: freedom was the bedrock principle of virtually all of America's founding documents, which were *federal*—national—in nature.

The Declaration of Independence guaranteed that "all men were created equal" and ensured the right of "life, *liberty*, and the pursuit of happiness" for all. The Northwest Ordinance, in which the Founders excluded slavery from all the western territories then owned by the federal government, was another example of their devotion to liberty and hope for a slave-free future on the American continent. And, of course, the Constitution, whose preamble pledged to "establish justice . . . and secure the blessings of liberty" for all citizens, whose Fourth Article required the United States to guarantee a "republican form of government" to all, and whose text omitted the word "slavery" and "slave" entirely, attested to the fact that the country's overarching governing document *defaulted* to freedom, not slavery.

In fact, this last point was most critical, Sumner argued. For slavery to be considered "national" in scope, it would require that the Constitution contain affirmative, unequivocal language that endorsed, sanctioned, or mandated it. Yet, in the same way that the Constitution "contains no power to make a King," it also contained no power "to make a slave or hunt a slave." The Constitution describes a government with limited powers, and it "has no power which is not delegated."

To find support for slavery in the Constitution was a fool's errand, Sumner said, because it simply did not exist, and no one could "infer, suppose, conjecture, surmise, fancy, guess, or presume that Slavery can have any sanction in words which do not plainly and unequivocally declare it."

And because no such words existed in the federal Constitution, Sumner said, no justification could be found *anywhere* for slavery on a national level.

✳ ✳ ✳

Therefore, Congress lacked authority to *establish* slavery within its purview, in the same way Southerners argued it had no authority to impose laws in individual states to *eliminate* slavery. Here, with decided brilliance, Sumner used the argument of slaveholders against them.

"When Washington took his first oath, nowhere within the *national territory* covered a single slave," Sumner declared. The outsized influence of slaveholders had caused the nation to backslide on its promise of freedom and equality, and the Fugitive Slave Law was the latest outrageous violation of the Constitution's pledge to form a more perfect union. But now, the Senate had the opportunity to revisit the entire slavery issue and reinstitute the principles that were in place during Washington's time.

Sumner enumerated what this would mean:

"In all national territories, Slavery will be impossible.

"On the high seas, under the national flag, Slavery will be impossible.

"In the District of Columbia, Slavery will instantly cease.

"Inspired by these principles, Congress can give no sanction to Slavery by the admission of new Slave States.

"Nowhere under the Constitution, can the nation, by legislation or otherwise, support Slavery, hunt slaves, or hold property in man."

Banishing slavery everywhere under federal jurisdiction would mean that "it will cease to vex our national politics," Sumner maintained. "It will no longer engender national animosities when it no longer demands national support."

Abolishing the Fugitive Slave Law was the critical first step.

✳ ✳ ✳

The law was the most egregious example, a "monstrous act," of the national government's overreach, Sumner argued. If the Constitution provided no protection for slavery in any federal jurisdiction—and he had made the case that it did not—it most certainly did not allow authorities from slave states, in the form of slave-hunters, to "stretch their arms" into free states to enforce laws.

Worse, the Fugitive Slave Law required states that abhorred slavery to enter into an unholy alliance with slave owners by marshaling their law enforcement and legal machinery against runaway slaves, thereby making free states complicit, against their will, in returning escapees to bondage—a clear violation of the Tenth Amendment, which reserves for the people and the states all power that is not specifically delegated to the federal government.

The dastardly law also violated many other constitutional rights, Sumner argued: it did not allow escaped slaves a trial, only a summary proceeding before a magistrate; it did not allow slaves to cross-examine slave-hunters, slave owners, or law enforcement personnel; it took away the Eighth Amendment right of trial by jury; it bribed commissioners to "pronounce against freedom" by offering a ten-dollar reward if they doomed runaways back to slavery and only five dollars if the slave were allowed to go free. Sumner even argued with passion that the Fugitive Slave Law violated the First Amendment right to the free exercise of religion by imposing penalties on "faithful men and women" whose religious beliefs would otherwise compel them to offer aid to fugitive slaves.

As he reached his rousing conclusion, Sumner contended that the Fugitive Slave Law—the "act" as he called it repeatedly—not only violated the Constitution and shocked the public conscience but also "offend[ed] against Divine Law." How else to describe legislation that required good citizens to engage in the capture of "shivering fugitives, guilty of no crime, pursued, hunted down like beasts, while [they] pray for Christian help and deliverance?"

The Fugitive Slave Law was a despotic mandate, a perversion, and it should fill God-fearing people with horror, Sumner said. God's law and the Constitution made him "bound to disobey this Act," regardless of the consequences.

He concluded by urging his fellow senators: "Repeal this enactment— Let its terrors no longer rage through the land."

When Sumner took his seat, amid tumultuous applause from spectators who had given him their unbroken attention throughout the long speech, many in the citizens' gallery—men and women alike—were reduced to tears.

✳ ✳ ✳

But most senators were not so moved. In the debate that followed his proposed amendment, Northerners and Southerners rejected Sumner's speech out of hand; in light of the agreement the Senate had made not to "agitate" the slavery question, many were irate that he had even broached the topic.

Senator John Weller of California said that while Sumner's speech was eloquent, he saw no purpose to it unless it was to incite riots in Northern states. He would hold Sumner responsible for any law-enforcement blood spilled in the process of executing the Fugitive Slave Law. Stephen Douglas of Illinois complained that Sumner's attack on the law was an assault on the Constitution, whose language did not prohibit slavery. Iowa Democrat Augustus C. Dodge was fearful that Sumner would next try "to introduce black-skinned, flat-nosed, and woolly-headed senators and representatives" to Congress.

And those were reactions from the *free states*.

Slave-state senators were also disdainful. In a long formal reply, George Edmund Badger of North Carolina, a lawyer by training, upbraided Sumner for delaying for eight months the "tirade of abuse" for which he had planned from his first day in the Senate. Alabama's Jeremiah Clemens urged his colleagues to ignore Sumner's remarks. "The ravings of a maniac may sometimes be dangerous," he said, "but the barking of a puppy never did any harm."

Other Southerners ridiculed Sumner's argument, perceiving the speech as superfluous to the business of the Senate, and said his remarks bordered on treason.

It was best to ignore him, to treat him as an outcast.

✳ ✳ ✳

Debate continued until nearly 7:00 P.M., and restless senators milled about, left the room from time to time, and huddled in small groups. Finally, Senator Hunter convinced the chair to end debate and call the roll.

Sumner's motion to repeal the Fugitive Slave Law was defeated 47–4. He was supported only by the two Free Soil senators, Salmon Chase of Ohio and John Hale of New Hampshire, and by Chase's Ohio colleague, antislavery Whig and Senate newcomer Benjamin Wade. Hale told the Senate that Sumner's speech had placed him "as far ahead of any living American orator as freedom is ahead of slavery."

It was a shattering defeat for Sumner, perhaps more brutal than he could have imagined. Just as crushing was his lack of support from New England and other Northern colleagues, some of whom professed antislavery sentiments but refused to support a measure that violated the Senate agreement, especially this close to the election, or take on a fight they believed could shred the union.

Though he was discouraged and humiliated, Sumner was undeterred. He had kept his promise, and in his first session—and for the first time ever—antislavery fire and brimstone rained upon the Senate, in the middle of the nation's capital.

He had, in a more thorough and effective way than anyone ever before, set down the intellectual underpinnings that proved America's founding tradition had its roots in antislavery dogma; and had credibly argued that the Constitution's omission of slavery left no legal avenue for the federal government to support it, condone it, accept it, or mandate it.

The Fugitive Slave Law had no legal authority from which to draw its power, and no one had convinced him otherwise.

✴ ✴ ✴

If Sumner's speech hadn't been enough to convince most of his colleagues, it would have a dramatic impact on society at large. The talk of the town in Washington for weeks, it also drove conversations in the North, the South, and in Europe; a cleansing on the topic of slavery had occurred—the gentlemanly niceties between North and South were beginning to erode.

Despite their criticisms and contemptuous sneers at Sumner's argument, Southern proslavery senators, especially, had no real answer to his unprecedented and all-encompassing treatise on the unconstitutionality of slavery in federal jurisdictions, and on the Fugitive Slave Law in particular.

From the moment Sumner finished speaking, slavery's partisans recognized a new power in the Senate and in the country. His tenacity, fearlessness, and honesty unsettled and troubled Southerners. Sumner had demonstrated that he couldn't be bullied or bribed into changing his views. A Kentucky congressman said the South believed Sumner was the only Northern man who would "never under any circumstances swerve from his position." Blatant politicking and backroom dealmaking were simply not part of his makeup. Unlike other Northern senators who muttered privately about the evils of slavery but remained silent on the Senate floor for fear of antagonizing slaveholders, Sumner spoke his mind with no hesitancy and complete honesty.

He was single-minded and indefatigable on the slavery issue. Such qualities were dangerous to the entire slaveholding apparatus and made Charles Sumner more than a political target—they turned him into a feared enemy.

✳ ✳ ✳

Antislavery reformers were jubilant with Sumner's speech, and praise poured in from the North and across the Atlantic. A writer from England "wept with joy" when he read Sumner's "magnificent" speech; one Cincinnati jurist believed Sumner's view of the unconstitutionality of slavery was the view "of all candid men, and even of the Southerners," if they cared to admit it.

Literary luminaries also weighed in. The Fugitive Slave Law, and Sumner's powerful opposition to it, had mobilized Boston's influential writing community, those whose works had led to the city's designation as the Athens of America a decade earlier. Emerson, Thoreau, Longfellow, Melville, Nathaniel Hawthorne, Amos Bronson Alcott (and later, his daughter, Louisa May) all spoke and wrote against slavery, their words ringing across the nation and the world.

Yet, Sumner's most significant and noteworthy literary bedfellow was not a writer but a publisher. John P. Jewett, an abolitionist and the head of a prestigious Boston publishing house that bore his name, decided to take a chance on an author whose antislavery fiction had been serialized in a weekly Washington paper. In late March 1852, as Charles Sumner sought an opening to speak on the Fugitive Slave Law, Jewett published Harriet Beecher Stowe's *Uncle Tom's Cabin* in book form.

Stowe had applied to several Boston publishers who were hesitant to publish the controversial work, which they considered a "dangerous anti-slavery production." To Jewett, the antislavery content of the book only made him all the more anxious to publish it. "My wife, on whose judgment I had frequent occasions to rely . . . declared that 'Uncle Tom' would make a book that would sell largely," Jewett recounted.

But in her wildest dreams, Mrs. Jewett could not have anticipated its impact.

❋ ❋ ❋

Within two days of its publication, *Uncle Tom's Cabin* had sold five thousand copies, by the end of the week that number had doubled, and by the end of the year it would sell more than three hundred thousand copies. "So large were the orders for the book, that from the day I first began to print it the eight presses never stopped, day or night, save Sundays, for six months," Jewett recounted, "and even *then* there were complaints that the volumes did not appear fast enough."

Stowe's evocative writing style, sympathetic characters, and almost religious attack on the institution of slavery moved readers in a way nothing else had. Its impact on the general public's view on slavery was incalculable. The popularity of the novel "finally took the sting of fanaticism out of abolitionists," wrote astute author Henry Mayer, and gave "weight to the idea of emancipation as a moral and historical inevitability."

Charles Sumner, who was determined to make emancipation a legal and political inevitability as well, recognized the importance of the novel to affect the culture, and also that the impact of his anti–Fugitive Slave Law speech was heightened by the book's rousing success.

"I rejoice in your devotion to the cause," he wrote to Harriet Beecher Stowe in November 1852, "and the great work you are doing."

✳ CHAPTER 13 ✳

KANSAS AND NEBRASKA—
"AT THE VERY GRAVE OF FREEDOM"

WINTER, SPRING 1854

Along with the scorn of many of his colleagues, Charles Sumner began to receive threats of "murderous violence" from Southern citizens in June of 1854.

If the death threats bothered him, he did not let it show. "The threats to put a bullet through my head and hang me—and mob me—have been frequent," Sumner confessed to Theodore Parker on June 12. "I have always said: 'let them come: they will find me at my post.'"

Many of Sumner's utterances, public or private, since his Fugitive Slave Law speech nearly two years earlier could have prompted such threats, but Sumner's letter to Parker referred specifically to the senator's fervent and vociferous opposition to a shocking piece of legislation known as the Kansas-Nebraska Act, which repealed the Missouri Compromise of 1820 and cleared the way for slavery's extension into the western territories. For months Sumner had railed against it, and a recent May 25 midnight speech was his final unsuccessful attempt to kill the measure. He viewed the odious law as the third unacceptable sin of slaveholders hoping to expand their power, behind the admittance of Texas as a slave state in 1845 and the barbaric Fugitive Slave Law.

What made the Kansas-Nebraska Act even more distasteful was that, like the Fugitive Slave Law, it was conceived of, fashioned, promoted, and shepherded through Congress by an influential and powerful Northern senator—in this case, Illinois Democrat Stephen Douglas. It was then signed into law by President Franklin Pierce, a New Hampshire Democrat who made it clear in his inaugural address that he believed slavery was permitted under the Constitution.

Pierce fervently hoped that the slavery issue was "at rest" and that "no sectional ambitions or fanatical excitement may again threaten durability of our institutions."

He failed to observe the irony that his own signing pen had dashed any such hopes.

✳ ✳ ✳

Sumner had endured a series of political disappointments since his triumphant speech against the Fugitive Slave Law: Pierce's election in 1852; the Whigs' return to power in Massachusetts; the subsequent decline in Free Soil membership after their battle against the Whigs (both parties would disappear within a year); a general apathy on the slavery question in Massachusetts and Washington; a taunting call by Whig newspapers for Sumner to resign due to a lack of popular support; and a corresponding call by Garrisonian abolitionists to step down after his "Freedom National" speech vigorously *defended* the Constitution—"Webster's fall was not so deplorable as that of Charles Sumner's," one antislavery society member said (Webster had died on October 24, 1852).

To Sumner's chagrin, he and Chase were the only two Free Soil senators when the Thirty-Third Congress opened its session on December 5, 1853 (Hale had been succeeded by a Democrat), and a frustrated Sumner was again relegated to minor committees. Rumors—false ones—circulated of his impending resignation.

He was saddened and perplexed that the Senate and the country seemed to have lost interest in banning slavery. "This Congress is the worst—or rather promises to be the worst—since the Constitution was adopted," Sumner wrote in December 1853; "it is the 'Devil's Own.'"

As the new year approached, the congressional session promised little beyond the prosaic and uneventful. Nothing presaged the great struggle ahead that would reignite the flame of Charles Sumner's passion, reestablish permanently his national influence, and make 1854 one of the most remarkable years in the country's history.

✳ ✳ ✳

Unyielding and smart, like Charles Sumner, and—unlike him—breathtakingly ambitious, forty-one-year-old Democratic Illinois senator Stephen Douglas had designs on the presidency as 1854 commenced. The "Little Giant"—so-called because his five-foot, four-inch height belied his towering political stature—knew well that he would need widespread support from Southern party members to even have a chance to achieve such a goal. It didn't help that he sought a northern route for an envisioned transcontinental railroad that would link the country's Midwest with the West and become a connection for Eastern goods to reach across the continent. Douglas wanted the eastern terminus of the proposed railroad in Chicago, in his free home state, while most Southerners favored St. Louis, located in the slave state of Missouri, as the easternmost point. He needed to change Southern minds.

To satisfy both political ends, Douglas, chairman of the Senate Committee on Territories, offered tribute to the South by maneuvering deftly behind the scenes with members of the slaveholding coalition to hatch an audacious South-friendly scheme for organizing the territories of Kansas and Nebraska. He believed his timing was favorable, too, now that Franklin Pierce, sympathizer to slaveholders, was ensconced in the White House.

Douglas never imagined the fury he would unleash.

His radical legislation repealed the portion of the Missouri Compromise of 1820 that forbade slavery in the former Louisiana Territory north of the 36° 30' latitude parallel, except within the boundaries of the then newly admitted state of Missouri (with Missouri entering the Union as a slave state in 1820, Congress, to maintain a balance, designated a large northern section of Massachusetts as a new free state, Maine).

Instead, the new Kansas-Nebraska Act, as conceived by Douglas, proposed that the future of slavery in those territories would be decided by the popular vote of residents. While Douglas knew the legislation would spark acrimonious debate, he did have convictions beyond the purely political in mind when he proposed its passage. He believed strongly in the principle of popular sovereignty (self-rule by the citizenry), and he predicted that the residents of Kansas would choose to prohibit slavery, even if they had a right to allow it (Nebraska was probably too far north to make slavery economical). Douglas insisted that allowing Kansans

and Nebraskans to vote on slavery was no different than what California
had done when it petitioned Congress for admittance as a free state in
1850.

But the savvy politician had badly miscalculated.

✳ ✳ ✳

The North was incensed, believing the Douglas-sponsored legislation
recklessly and unnecessarily destroyed the delicate compromises on
slavery that had existed since the nation's founding, and worse, opened
vast new territories to slavery's expansion. Not even the irrepressible and
defiant Calhoun, slavery's most ferocious guardian, or the proslavery
Democratic senator from Missouri, David Atchison, had contemplated
overturning the more than three-decade-old Missouri Compromise.

When Douglas introduced his bill, it reignited antislavery sentiments
in the North—the apathy about the slavery issue that Sumner feared disappeared virtually overnight. The bill's opponents held raucous public
protest meetings throughout the North—three thousand attended one
in Boston's Faneuil Hall, and more than five thousand gathered in New
York's City Hall Park. An outraged Northern press vilified Douglas, some
sounding the alarm even before the bill was printed by the Senate to begin debate. Influential Northern clergy were unified in their exhortations
against the bill.

Douglas was distressed by the explosive hostility across the North. At
mass meetings and rallies, speakers urged his removal from office, and
in several places he was hanged in effigy. Never one to resist the pull of
gallows humor—in this case, literally—the self-aware Douglas half joked
and half lamented that, during debate on the bill, he could have traveled
the entire route between Washington, D.C., and his home in Illinois by
the light of his own burning effigies.

Unsurprisingly, Charles Sumner was not laughing.

To Sumner, Douglas's actions were not simply unforgivable from a
moral standpoint, they were so politically risky as to be illogical; he predicted that the Illinois senator would suffer regardless of the outcome of
the Kansas-Nebraska Act. "If he does *not* succeed in his plot, he will be
kicked by the South," Sumner wrote in late January; "if he *does*, his brains
will be dashed out [by] the North."

Sumner delivered his first speech against the act on February 21, in which he reiterated his themes of freedom being a national concept, urged his fellow senators not to tamper with the longstanding Missouri Compromise, and scoffed at the notion that a popular sovereignty bill permitting slavery could be essential to self-government. "It is like saying *two* and *two* make *three*, if [in] the name of liberty, you open the door to slavery," he said.

Sumner's comments held little sway over a Senate still beholden to slaveholders. Just before 5:00 A.M. on March 4, after a seventeen-hour continuous session, the Kansas-Nebraska Act passed the Senate by a vote of 37–14—a coalition of Southern Democrats, Southern Whigs, and Northern Democrats loyal to Douglas came together to assure the bill's passage. All Northern Whigs, two Southern Whigs, and a handful of Northern Democrats joined Sumner and Chase in opposition. "The North, through this [Pierce] administration, is delivered bound, hand and foot, to the South," Sumner wrote.

But as long as Massachusetts was behind him, he would fight on.

The state delivered him a resounding message almost immediately. Two days after Sumner's speech, Massachusetts Whigs *and* ardent antislavery forces—political oil and water—met at Faneuil Hall, and while the two groups did not mingle physically, they came together as a single mind to express a unified opinion: the Kansas-Nebraska bill was an abomination.

One Whig speaker after another suggested they had been duped by slaveholders, and that they had paid too high a price for surrendering to the Compromise of 1850 four years earlier. Even Whig newspapers, allies to the Boston merchants and always reluctant to discuss the evils of slavery, published pieces denouncing the act as an overreach by the slaveocracy. Free Soilers beamed with satisfaction as they saw their old adversaries, the Webster Whigs, confessing to the failures of the Compromise and repeating the claims of Free Soilers whom they once denounced as unpatriotic and treasonable.

Antislavery men walked "with heads erect" on Boston streets, meeting dozens of Whigs who greeted them with the salutation "'You were right,'" one writer observed, "where before they had encountered only averted faces."

✳ ✳ ✳

After the Kansas-Nebraska bill was debated and slightly amended in the House, it returned for final passage to the Senate, where Sumner made the most of another opportunity, if in vain, to flay Douglas's proposal.

The Senate passed the amended Kansas-Nebraska Act just before midnight 35–13, the vote breaking along similar lines as on March 4. Sumner spoke shortly after the vote—"this dark midnight hour," he called it—before jam-packed galleries despite the time. He found renewed hope in what he believed would be an "awakened" North, welcomed Northern agitation, and forewarned of, and even encouraged, future "civil strife and feud" once Kansas-Nebraska was signed into law.

Predicting dire consequences from the bill as the nation stood "at the very grave of freedom in Nebraska and Kansas," Sumner nonetheless recognized that it had set up a grand showdown between freedom's good and slavery's evils, describing the Kansas-Nebraska bill as "at once the *worst and best* which Congress ever acted."

It was the worst for obvious reasons—it provided slave owners with yet another victory by making slavery possible in an immense territory of the American continent that exceed the combined area, in square miles, of France, Spain, and Italy. But, Sumner added, just as important and just as undeniably, "it is the best bill . . . for it . . . annuls past compromises with slavery and makes all future compromises impossible." Therefore, he declared, "it puts Freedom and Slavery face to face, and bids them both grapple. Who can doubt the result?"

Thus, Sumner said as the clock ticked into the early morning hours, Kansas-Nebraska filled him with mixed feelings: "Sorrowfully I bend before the wrong you commit—joyfully I welcome the promise of the future."

The day after Sumner's speech, a celebrated and ugly episode in Boston would solidify Northern sentiment that slave owners had gone too far and convince Southerners that Charles Sumner was downright dangerous. Three years after the Thomas Sims case, Boston, unbelievably, was about to send its second runaway slave back to bondage.

But this time, infuriated Bostonians did more than howl in protest.

✻ ✻ ✻

The youngest of thirteen children who was born into slavery in Virginia in 1834—the same year Charles Sumner had seen his first slaves en route to Washington, D.C.—runaway Anthony Burns was arrested in Boston on May 24, 1854, on an escape warrant. Burns ran away shortly after the financially strapped widow of his former owner sold five of Burns's siblings and hired out Burns and his other brothers and sister for additional income. Burns stowed away on a ship and arrived in Boston in March. He was captured one week before his twentieth birthday.

Burns's incarceration occurred during debate of the Kansas-Nebraska Act, "at the most combustible moment imaginable," in the words of one historian.

On the evening of May 26, approximately eighteen hours after Sumner's midnight speech in Washington, militant Boston abolitionist Thomas Wentworth Higginson led a group of rioters, armed with axes, on a courthouse assault to free Burns. "We hammered away at the southwest door . . . before it began to give way," he wrote. A few men squeezed inside and were met by a half dozen policemen wielding clubs, "driving us to the wall and hammering away at our heads."

Suddenly, a pistol shot was fired—it was impossible to say by whom— and a twenty-four-year-old guard named James Batchelder was killed. The effort to free Burns failed.

Southerners and other Sumner enemies responded by blaming his speech for inciting the riot, and for Batchelder's homicide, ignoring the fact that telegraphic reports of his speech did not reach Boston until the day *after* the Burns riot. The *Washington Star* accused Sumner of "counseling treason" against the country's laws and inciting "the ignorant to bloodshed and murder."

New Englanders were having none of it. The timing of events—the seizure of Burns, the alliance that successfully repealed the Missouri Compromise, and the attempt to intimidate Sumner—had unified them.

It was no great surprise when Henry David Thoreau praised Higginson, calling him the "only Harvard Phi Beta Kappa, Unitarian Minister, and master of seven languages who has led a storming party against a federal bastion with a battering ram in his hands."

But it *was* notable when heretofore anti-abolitionist merchant and Boston Whig George Livermore wrote to Sumner: "Let the minions of the Administration and of the slaveocracy harm *one hair of your head*, and they will raise a whirlwind which will sweep them to destruction."

✳ ✳ ✳

Sumner was bolstered by the support of his Massachusetts constituents, remained defiant in the face of negative newspaper coverage, and stood fearless in the wake of intimidation.

Despite renewed death threats and pleas from friends to be on his guard, or even to leave Washington, he did not deviate from his usual routine and always walked unarmed from his lodgings along Pennsylvania Avenue to the Capitol. One evening at the restaurant where he often dined, several Southerners insulted him but attempted no physical attack. To friends who urged him to take precautions, Sumner replied: "I am here to do my duty and shall continue to do it without regard to personal consequences."

The degree to which the Boston public had moved in Sumner's direction became clear on June 2, 1854, when Burns was marched down State Street to the docks in a route eerily similar to the one Thomas Sims had followed three years earlier.

In an unprecedented scene in Boston, more than fifty thousand residents thronged the streets and rooftops to protest Burns's return to slavery. As Burns marched toward Long Wharf, surrounded by one thousand U.S. soldiers and militiamen, the Brattle Street Church bell tolled, and the crowd booed, hissed, cursed, and cried, "Kidnappers, Kidnappers!" Black bunting draped office buildings in Boston's mercantile and financial districts, and the accompanying symbolic props were telling. From one building, a coffin was suspended with the word "Liberty" emblazoned on its side; at the Mercantile Exchange, a petition calling for repeal of the Fugitive Slave Law was signed by many of Boston's commercial elite, proving that, as abolitionist Theodore Parker concluded, "the most solid men of Boston . . . are fast falling into the ranks of freedom."

Many Webster Whigs, among the strongest pro-union voices in the country, felt betrayed by the South. The Fugitive Slave Law was unsettling enough; now, the repeal of the Missouri Compromise had broken the bonds linking conservatism to slavery and turned the tide against slavery's further extension.

Influential merchant Amos Lawrence colorfully assessed the changes in attitude brought about by Kansas-Nebraska and the Burns episode:

"We went to bed one night, old fashioned, conservative, compromise Union Whigs, and waked up stark mad Abolitionists!"

✳ ✳ ✳

"I find myself a popular man," Charles Sumner wrote upon his return to Boston in the late summer of 1854. "If my election to the Senate were now pending before the million [*sic*] of educated people whom I now represent, I should be returned without any opposition."

He had battled hard throughout the final debate on the Kansas-Nebraska bill, and in June he launched into a fresh and fierce debate on slavery when he presented the petition of three thousand Massachusetts citizens calling for repeal of the Fugitive Slave Law. He reiterated that he would never support the law, again prompting Southern shouts that he refused to uphold the Constitution. "I recognize no obligation in the Constitution of the United States to bind me to help to reduce a man to slavery," he retorted during debate.

Southerners engaged in an all-out assault on Sumner's position. They labeled him a fanatic, a charge he welcomed, pointing out that Bostonians were familiar with the label and often wore it as a badge of honor. "It is the same which opposed the Tea-tax," he asserted, "it is the fanaticism which finally triumphed on Bunker Hill."

During debate over the Massachusetts petition, Sumner spoke in bitter personal language, intending from the outset to be "as severe as the overseer's lash." Gone was the mutual courtesy he had exhibited toward Southern senators, gone was his scrupulous observance of Senate decorum.

"From the Kansas and Nebraska bill came forth a demon," he declared.

✳ ✳ ✳

Sumner attained new stature during the summer of 1854, and he returned to Massachusetts with renewed purpose. His position at home, within the Senate, and across the nation was dramatically strengthened. He became a magnet for Southern vituperation, and in so doing, proved to his supporters that he was more than an intellectual; the public admired his fearless and defiant spirit with which he confronted slaveholding senators and sympathizers. He could stand rock solid against criticism, even when vastly outnumbered, where lesser men may have withered.

In short, he would fight.

Perhaps more than ever before or after, the slavery battles in the spring and summer of 1854 represented Sumner's most triumphant hours in the Senate. He received hundreds of letters in the weeks to follow, sometimes as many as fifty a day, expressing admiration and respect for his arguments, self-restraint, and imperturbable dignity against his Senate assailants.

New England families gathered around their firesides to read and listen to his speeches. Clergymen, in their sermons and their newspaper columns and letters, commended him for his courage and perseverance. When Frances Seward, wife of New York senator William Seward, wrote to Sumner that his speeches during the final passage of the Kansas-Nebraska bill had filled her with "tears of gratitude that so much ability and eloquence were devoted to the advancement of truth and freedom," she was expressing sentiments held by thousands across the North.

More than anything, the events of 1854 had turned Northerners of all political persuasions against the Fugitive Slave Law. As one observer noted, "the return of fugitive slaves had become revolting to the moral sense of the free States."

✳ ✳ ✳

SEPTEMBER 7, 1854, WORCESTER, MASSACHUSETTS

The crowd of several thousand murmured at first, then craned their necks as one, searching for Charles Sumner and then, finally, spotting him as he made his way into the great hall. Suddenly, the immense audience rose in unison, stomped their feet, and cheered wildly—"Sumner! Sumner! Sumner!" they roared—as the tall senator passed by on his way to the speaker's platform. The thunderous ovation continued for several minutes as men waved their hats frantically, whooped, and thrust their fists skyward.

They had come specifically to see Sumner, to hear his voice, to let him know they appreciated his toughness, and attendees swore later that never had a crowd delivered such an enthusiastic response to a public speaker. Never either, in the words of one writer on the scene, had Sumner "been so near the heart of Massachusetts as then."

The occasion was the nominating convention of the new Republican Party—a patchwork antislavery coalition of former Free Soilers, Whigs, and even some Democrats—whose Massachusetts leaders begged Sumner to attend to ensure a large, boisterous, and enthusiastic audience.

Sumner stepped to the rostrum, and the cheers and shouts grew louder. He raised his hands and waited for the furor to subside before speaking. And when he did, the crowd responded. Sumner's voice was powerful in volume, earnest in pitch, and indignant in tone. He had two objectives for the speech—to "vindicate the necessity of the Republican Party," and to destroy the Fugitive Slave Law operation in Massachusetts.

His ninety-minute speech was interrupted every few moments—and in some parts at the end of each sentence—by loud and prolonged applause from the appreciative audience.

Sumner blasted the national proslavery administration, branded the Kansas-Nebraska Act an atrocity, and said federal authorities had shamelessly run roughshod over the law, and over Boston, in the Burns case. He viewed this new, principled Republican Party, fledgling though it was, as the only antidote to the slave power, arguing that neither Democrats nor Whigs could effectively carry on the fight. The Whigs were split irreparably over the slavery question, and the Democrats had maintained commercial and policy alliances with slaveholders for so long that it was fanciful and naïve to expect them to bite the hand that fed their political interests.

The Republicans were the nation's best hope—maybe its only hope—to end the scourge of slavery, and what the party lacked in numbers and political clout it made up for in enthusiasm and vision.

✳ ✳ ✳

Sumner had returned home from Washington "full of fight on the slavery question" and rejoiced after the response he received in Worcester.

His popularity had grown so much that journalists, even unfriendly ones, could not afford to ignore him. One newspaper, the *Traveller*, hired a special train from Worcester so it could publish Sumner's speech for its Boston readers, forty miles away, the same afternoon in advance of its rivals. Even the most ardent Whig journals acknowledged Sumner's impact on the audience. Sumner noticed it, too. "The change towards me is rather with the great bulk of the *people* than with the old *leaders*," Sumner observed with satisfaction. "It is apparent wherever I go—in the streets and also in the newspapers. No papers in Massachusetts now mention my name except with kind words."

After the Worcester response, the Massachusetts Republican state committee distributed Sumner's speech widely in pamphlet edition. He instantly became the new party's public face. Sumner would eventually and almost single-handedly be responsible for the meteoric growth of the Republicans on a national scale, though, as the calendar turned to 1855, neither he nor anyone else could ever have imagined how.

For the rest of the year and into 1856, the great slavery debate shifted away from Massachusetts, away from Washington, D.C., and the plantations and capitals of the Deep South.

Instead, thousands of eyes were cast westward.

Assaults, barbarity, crime, mayhem, and sectional strife were sweeping the Great Plains.

Kansas was bleeding.

CHAPTER 14

BLEEDING KANSAS

My dear sir—help us," despondent Kansas resident Hannah Ropes wrote to Charles Sumner on January 22, 1856. "Where should the weak flee if not to strong heads and hands like yours?"

Kansas was suffering through a punishing winter and a desperate war for its soul. Heavy snow blanketed the prairie, knifing winds ripped across the plains, and temperatures plunged to thirty degrees below zero. All of this threatened "total destruction," Ropes wrote, but she was more frightened by the storm of wanton violence perpetrated by proslavery forces—lawlessness that caused "the most heroic hearts among us [to] cower."

For nearly two years, since the passage of Kansas-Nebraska, violence had rocked the territory, and because of its geography and potential ability to support slavery—its soil and weather were not conducive to producing cotton but would allow for the growth of hemp and tobacco—Kansas became the center of the sectional storm, a battleground between stalwart proslavery and fervent antislavery forces, and the symbol of the country's very future.

Its fate and Charles Sumner's would soon be intertwined.

* * *

The South, desperate to extend slavery, still smarting about the admittance of California as a free state, and fearful that a free state on the western border of slave-state Missouri would harbor escaped slaves, was intent on doing almost anything to make Kansas a slaveholding state. A Missouri newspaper warned that failure could mean "abolitionists would settle in Kansas and run off with our slaves."

Those fears were not unfounded.

The Massachusetts legislature had chartered the New England Emigrant Aid Company, which was established to send settlers with antislavery sentiments into the Kansas territory to secure its admission to the union as a free state. Upon their arrival in Kansas, company volunteers established residences; built homes, schools, and mills; cleared land and planted crops; and secured reduced transportation fares for other emigrants traveling West.

Residents of the slaveholding South, and Missouri in particular, were outraged by what they perceived as long-distance interference by the North. Missouri senator David Atchison urged his constituents to cross his state's western border and engage in illegal interstate voting. He said it was the most effective way slavery proponents could counteract antislavery emissaries, "fanatics and demagogues," who had arrived in Kansas from the East and were pouring money into an effort to "abolitionize Kansas."

Atchison said he could send as many as five thousand men to cross the border into Kansas, "enough to kill every God-damned abolitionist in the territory."

✳ ✳ ✳

Nor would Missouri provide the only proslavery firepower.

Atchison also sent out appeals to other slave owners to relocate their slaves to Kansas and urged armed men from the slave states to travel to the territory and fight for slavery.

Troops arrived from Alabama, South Carolina, Georgia, Mississippi, and Tennessee. The *Montgomery (AL) Journal* noted that the South "stood ready at any moment to supply any balance of voters which may be necessary." Southern women sold their jewels to help fund the cause, and several Southern railroads offered free passage to those willing to travel to Kansas. A proslavery committee in Abbeville, South Carolina, offered two hundred dollars to every "suitable person" who would emigrate to the divided territory.

The roiling on the plains reached a climax on May 30, 1855, when Kansas held its territorial elections. Emboldened by the rhetoric of their elected officials and supported by like-minded people across the South, proslavery Missourians by the thousands, armed and ready for violence, crossed the border. Although only fifteen hundred men were registered to vote in Kansas, more than six thousand ballots were cast, many of them by proslavery "border ruffians" from adjacent Missouri who flooded into Kansas to vote. They terrorized the few polling officials who dared try to stop the outrage and elected a rogue proslavery legislature that passed stringent laws protecting slavery in Kansas.

Known as the "black laws," they blatantly disregarded the Constitution and the Bill of Rights and were among the most egregious violations of civil rights in American history. They mandated severe punishment for antislavery activity: two to five years of hard labor for anyone possessing an abolitionist publication; five years of hard labor for authors or publishers of antislavery writings. The laws also mandated the death penalty for anyone fomenting slave revolts.

The black laws proved so extreme as to be virtually unenforceable, but they created an atmosphere of brutality and mayhem. Antislavery settler E. P. Brown was attacked by a crowd of border ruffians near Leavenworth, hacked with knives and a hatchet, and left at his cabin door. He died in his wife's arms. Proslavery men shaved the head of, then tarred and feathered, a Leavenworth lawyer who had spoken out against election fraud; later they shot him dead in his home. Thomas Barber, a free-state Kansan who lived ten miles outside of Lawrence, bled to death after he and his brothers were attacked and shot by a band of fifteen proslavery Missourians.

In her letter to Sumner, Kansas resident Lydia Hall described the impact of the violence: "The cowardly murders . . . and the thousand nameless indignities offered in the same spirit, burnt deep into the hearts of our people."

✳ ✳ ✳

In August 1855, Kansas Free Soilers and abolitionists organized their own Free-State convention to challenge the bogus legislature. A month later they selected antislavery candidates, voted to oppose the black laws, and formed a committee for counting votes during elections. The convention passed a resolution stating that the antislavery coalition would resist, with force if necessary, the "tyrannical enactments" of the proslavery legislature.

Free Soilers drew up a constitution that prohibited slavery in Kansas and submitted it to the territory's voters, who approved it by an overwhelming majority. The Topeka Free Soil government then asked Congress to admit Kansas as a free state.

Kansas now had two competing legislatures: one allowing slavery, the other prohibiting it. President Franklin Pierce threw his support behind the proslavery legislature and asked Congress to admit Kansas as a slave state. Advocates of slavery were exultant and opponents mortified. "We hear that Franklin Pierce means to crush the men of Kansas," said militant abolitionist John Brown, who had arrived in Kansas during the peak of the violence. "I do not know how well he may succeed—but I think he may find his hands full before it is over."

Throughout the winter months of late 1855 and early 1856, despite frigid temperatures and brutal storms, antislavery men posted sentries in Lawrence to stand guard against possible attacks. The miserable weather temporarily dissuaded wide-scale bloodshed, but with spring approaching, Kansas Free Soilers expected fresh outbreaks of violence and additional armed incursions from the western counties of Missouri.

"We are expecting open warfare, eventually," Lydia Hall predicted to Charles Sumner.

✳ ✳ ✳

As if on cue, as the weather warmed, violence ensued across eastern Kansas territory, with shootings and hangings of antislavery men by proslavery forces. George Washington Brown, editor of the *Herald of Freedom* newspaper, was one of seven free-state leaders arrested in the spring of 1856, charged with high treason, and held prisoner by federal troops near Lecompton.

Proslavery leaders viewed Lawrence, the "free-state" capital, as a viper's nest of traitors, and their claims were bolstered when a judge, responding to President Pierce's proslavery stance, ordered a grand jury to indict members of the Free Soil legislature for treason. A federal marshal claimed that rebels in Lawrence had interfered with the execution of the indictments. He called for "law-abiding citizens of the territory" to assemble for an all-out attack on the town.

"My heart is sick," Charles Sumner despaired to a fellow abolitionist as the Senate began its debate over Kansas in March 1856.

For months in early 1856, Sumner's mail was full of urgent letters about the ominous developments in Kansas, as antislavery settlers asked his help in recognizing the free-state government. Hannah Ropes was not alone—hundreds of others viewed Sumner as their savior. From these correspondents, Sumner formed the opinion that the brutal and repressive proslavery government had been set up in Kansas with the disgusting endorsement of President Pierce. Sumner feared for the safety of the Free Soilers, and for the future of the country.

Once again, he was appalled at a federal government's predisposition to slavery. He also despaired that the turn of events in Kansas and the proslavery sentiments expressed in Washington had demoralized anti-slavery forces in Congress. "In the House, we are weak, in the Senate powerless," he wrote.

He summed up his feelings about Washington's role in the Kansas debate to a fellow abolitionist: "Truly—truly—this is a Godless place."

Events in Kansas, he concluded, had caused the country to "shake with the first throes of civil war."

✳ ✳ ✳

For Sumner, the violence on the prairie and in the towns of Kansas epitomized the monumental clash of differences between North and South; the geographic center of the American continent represented the center of the country's bitter debate over slavery.

He knew hours of exhausting debate lay ahead.

"You will hear nothing but Kansas from this time *forever*," he communicated to his friend and Boston abolitionist Theodore Parker. He was confident Kansas would eventually be a free state, but he expected the upcoming passion play in Washington to produce debate in which "truth will be mocked and reviled."

In his view, the perversion of truth started almost immediately after the Thirty-Fourth Congress began debate. Rather than Congress offering relief to Kansas settlers for the outrages taking place in the territory, Southern fire-eaters (by this point, the Northern term for proslavery extremists) and Northern Democrats had outflanked antislavery lawmakers by focusing the early debate on a narrow critique of the Massachusetts Emigrant Aid Society's efforts to send aid to Kansas—was the company interfering unjustly in territorial affairs? If so, what should Congress do?

Senator Stephen Douglas heavily influenced an *Affairs of Kansas* report issued on March 12, which devoted several pages to criticism of the Emigrant Aid Company for interfering in the internal affairs of Kansas and escalating the level of violence in the territory.

Sumner ridiculed the report, recognizing the document as an extension of what he believed was Douglas's misguided thinking when he put forth the Kansas-Nebraska Act. By emphasizing the Emigrant Aid Company's role in Kansas, the Senate report served as a distraction from the larger issue, what Sumner viewed as a typical sleight of hand by slaveholders to focus on small details to obscure the larger view of slavery's impact. He argued that the slave oligarchy would stoop to anything and stop at nothing to win the fight to admit Kansas to the union as a slave state.

He implored Northerners to settle their past differences and rally together to prevent such an atrocity. *"Union to save Kansas and Union to save ourselves*, should be the watchword," he implored.

✳ ✳ ✳

He was prone to hyperbole, but Sumner's assessment of the South's goals for Kansas was no exaggeration.

Still stung by the admission of California as a free state in 1850 but buoyed by the Kansas-Nebraska Act and President Pierce's support of slavery in Kansas, the South viewed any attempt to prevent slavery in the new territory as a direct assault on the region and its way of life. Emotions ran deep. Southerners warned that any decision in favor of antislavery forces would anger Southern voters and mean the defeat of Democrats in the 1856 November elections. One Georgia man warned his senator that if Kansas came into the union as a free state, Southern masses would turn on their leaders in fury.

As Congress readied to debate Kansas, two dire warnings were issued by South Carolina lawmakers Congressman Preston Brooks and Senator Andrew Butler. They represented the South's most ardently proslavery state (South Carolina candidates were *required* to own at least ten slaves to run for Congress).

Brooks wrote a letter to a newspaper in which he argued that if Kansas were to become free, the value of slaves in adjacent Missouri would drop by 50 percent, and "so with Arkansas; so with upper Texas." This would occur for two reasons: first, it would be easier for slaves in those states

to escape to Kansas due to the vastness and isolated areas of the territory; and second, "abolitionism will become the prevailing sentiment" in
counties bordering Kansas. But his larger argument was far more solemn
and momentous: "The admission of Kansas into the Union as a slave
state is now *a point of honor* with the South—it is my deliberate conviction that the fate of the South is to be decided with the Kansas issue."

Senator Butler, Brooks's second cousin, warned that "one drop of
blood shed in civil strife" in Kansas territory "may not only dissolve the
Union, but may do worse."

❋ ❋ ❋

In late March 1856, Sumner concluded that the best way he could help
Kansas—"that distant plundered territory"—was to deliver a major oration against both the Southern fire-eaters and the Northern Democrats,
the latter led by Douglas, whose ill-conceived legislation had directly
caused the violence in Kansas.

With the encouragement of antislavery allies who had clamored for
Sumner to make his voice heard in the midst of the country's grandest
debate, Sumner plunged into preparing his speech with a near-religious
fervor. In this speech, he would exchange the cloak of antislavery crusader for the mantle of freedom's messiah. He assured Theodore Parker
that he would "use plain words" in his remarks but boasted—perhaps
signaling the invective that would be contained in those words—that he
intended "to pronounce the most thorough philippic ever uttered in a
Legislative body."

Sumner promised to "expose this whole crime at length," and vowed
to do so "without sparing language."

It was a vow that would lead to terrible consequences for him.

CHAPTER 15

"THE CRIME AGAINST KANSAS"

All that was missing when Charles Sumner entered the Senate chamber on May 19, 1856, was a fanfare of trumpets.

The sweaty, jammed chamber thrummed with tension, suffocating heat, and the expectant murmur of nervous lawmakers, but of all the indicators that big events were afoot, the most stunning was the number of women present. "Even the Ladies Gallery was *full to overflowing*," one New York scribe reported. Normally, the women's section stood empty or contained a mere handful of occupants. This day, though, with dresses clinging and hand-fans waggling in the stiflingly close quarters, where temperatures reached ninety degrees, women jostled for position and craned their necks for a better view of the drama. Their trip into the chamber had not been easy: they had gathered up their long dresses and slogged through thick mud on the streets outside, avoided squealing pigs that ran wild along Pennsylvania Avenue, and covered their mouths with lacy handkerchiefs as they high-stepped through the dust-choked construction area, part of the Capitol's renovations.

But it was worth it to secure a spot in the Senate chamber on a potentially historic day.

✳ ✳ ✳

The import and energy of the women's presence eclipsed several other telltale signs that something special was in store: dozens of eminent statesmen, former politicians, and ordinary citizens clogged the aisles and doorways and anterooms; many members of the House of Representatives, including South Carolina's Preston Brooks and Laurence Keitt, had ventured to the Senate chamber to witness the moment; Southern delegates, en route to the Democratic National Convention in Cincinnati, detoured to the nation's capital to observe the day's events; every journalist's chair was filled, and virtually every senator was uncharacteristically seated at the session's outset, awaiting the words of a colleague.

For Sumner, all of it—the huge crowd, the intense heat, the grand stage, the sectional tension, the magnitude of the moment, the nation's eyes upon him—lent a drama that suited his irresistible desire to preach to the masses in the name of their enlightenment.

He felt the occasion was "the greatest . . . that has ever occurred in our history," a categorization that presumably referred to the future of slavery, and the events swirling in Kansas, but also served as a less than subtle reference that *he,* and not someone less able, would be addressing these issues.

✷ ✷ ✷

As always, he was prepared. Sumner had laboriously written out his speech, which, in printed form, spanned 112 pages; his remarks were being set in type elsewhere even as he approached the rostrum, and printed copies would be available in a couple of days. As was his custom, he committed the speech to memory, practicing for hours on end, including in front of New York senator William Seward and his wife, Frances, so he could test his remarks before a live audience.

Sumner planned all along to pepper his antislavery arguments with personal attacks to call attention to larger themes. He believed it was necessary to "say something of a general character [about his political opponents], *not belonging to the argument,* in response to senators who have raised themselves to eminence on this floor in championship of human wrongs." Even as Sumner gained political experience, his need to moralize and render judgment antagonized the South and even irritated many of his Northern colleagues who otherwise might have been sympathetic to his message. Historian Allan Nevins would write years later that, by the spring of 1856, Sumner's sanctimonious demeanor had cloaked him with the unofficial—the South would say befitting—title of "the best-hated man in the Chamber."

Aware of her friend's reputation, Frances Seward strongly advised Sumner to remove the stinging personal attacks he had included in the speech; her husband also disapproved of the "gratuitous assault against the honor of South Carolina." Sumner ignored them both—he had promised "unsparing language," and he would deliver.

Violence on the plains, high drama in Washington, unprecedented acrimony between North and South, expectations across the nation, the debate on the future of Kansas; it was upon this canvas that Sumner would apply his broad and slashing brushstrokes in the biggest speech of his career, designed to shock the conscience of the Senate and reset to true north the moral compass of America.

At one o'clock in the afternoon, in a thronged and sweltering Senate chamber, Charles Sumner of Massachusetts rose to denounce and demand redress for "The Crime Against Kansas."

✳ ✳ ✳

A crime has been committed," he began, "which is without example in the records of the past. . . . It is the rape of a virgin territory, compelling it to the hateful embrace of slavery."

Senators listened intently as Sumner promised to strip bare the proslavery conspiracy against Kansas in all its brutality, without, in the words of one correspondent, "a single rag, or fig-leaf, to cover its vileness." Sumner's speech would span a total of five hours over two days—three hours on the first day—and one New York antislavery correspondent described him as "animated and glowing throughout, hurling defiance among the opposition, and bravely denouncing the Kansas swindle from first to last."

Sumner charged that the violence perpetuated by proslavery forces in Kansas had forced the citizens of Lawrence to arm themselves before they slept, and despite the bitter winter, deploy "sentinels" to keep watch during frozen nights against surprise attacks. "Murder has stalked—assassination has skulked the tall grass of the prairie," he said. Worse, this violence was originating outside of Kansas, carried out by men who relied on brute force to accomplish their lawless ends because they could not achieve their goals peaceably.

The Kansas violence had brought the entire nation to the brink, Sumner contended. Kansas threatened a United States that already "palpitates with the mutterings of civil war."

Sumner outlined the four "crimes against Kansas" and the four apologies offered by their perpetrators. The first crime was the passage of the

Kansas-Nebraska Act; second was President Pierce's decision to appoint a territorial official in Kansas who enforced the "tyrannical usurpation" of freedom by Southern slave mongers; third was the intimidation of antislavery northerners who traveled to Kansas; and fourth was the use of violence against antislavery advocates already living in the territory.

For each of these crimes, Sumner ridiculed the "apologies" offered by proslavery advocates, the most egregious of these the "Apology Imbecile," a fileting of President Pierce's contention that he had no power to intervene in Kansas. Sumner maintained that this presidential abdication of responsibility encouraged border ruffians from Missouri to cross into the territory to commit violence. On the second day of the speech, Sumner spoke for an additional two hours on the four "remedies" available to stop the violence in Kansas, among them the "Remedy of Justice and Peace" to reverse the outrage against the territory—which was for the Senate to wield the "angelic power" of freedom and admit Kansas immediately as a free state.

If "The Crime Against Kansas" had contained nothing more, history would have regarded the speech as powerful, even noteworthy, but certainly not transformational or even controversial for its time. But Sumner did not stop with a recitation of the issues in Kansas and their possible resolution. He had promised to go much further, to get more personal, to generate as much shock and impact as possible.

And he did.

✳ ✳ ✳

Sumner chose as his primary Senate villain Andrew Butler of Carolina, though he also singled out for criticism Virginia's James Mason, primary architect of the Fugitive Slave Law, and Northerner Stephen Douglas, author of the Kansas-Nebraska Act.

He reserved his most vicious and insulting verbal attacks for the man least able to fight back—the elderly, ailing, absent Butler—and for the state from which he hailed, South Carolina. On the first day of the speech, Monday, he berated Butler in a highly charged passage that would produce one of the speech's most referenced and famous lines.

Sumner compared Butler to Cervantes's fictional character Don Quixote (Sumner had borrowed *Don Quixote* from the library to prepare his speech), a man who believed himself to be a chivalrous knight but who was actually deluding himself—a true knight who practiced genuine chivalry would have resisted the temptation of slavery. In perhaps his speech's most provocative passage, Sumner charged that Butler "has chosen a mistress to whom he has made vows, and who, though ugly to others, is always lovely to him; though polluted in the sight of the world, is chaste in his sight—I mean the harlot, Slavery."

At that moment, Douglas, pacing at the back of the Senate chamber, later recalled saying to himself, "That damn fool will get himself killed by another damned fool."

South Carolina congressman Preston Brooks was in the Senate chamber for some of Sumner's speech on that first day and was deeply offended to hear Butler, his second cousin, referred to in such baldly disrespectful terms.

In fact, Sumner's repeated sexual references in the speech, his use of words like "harlot," "virgin," and "rape," were particularly galling to Southern slaveholders who repeatedly chafed at stubborn rumors (many proven true) that some engaged in sexual relations with their slaves.

Sumner's choice of language, no accident, was designed to cut to the quick.

✼ ✼ ✼

Brooks was not in the Senate chamber for Sumner's second-day attacks against Butler and South Carolina, utterances that were not as inflammatory as his "harlot" remark but were in some ways more personally cruel, biting, and—Southerners would later claim—cowardly, because they were directed against a defenseless opponent.

Senator Butler had suffered a stroke, causing a slight facial paralysis that slurred his speech. Sumner ridiculed his condition, describing Butler as arguing against the admission of Kansas as a free state "with incoherent phrases [that] discharge the loose expectorate of his speech." Besides discharging annoying spittle when he spoke, a mocking Sumner told a shocked Senate chamber, Butler's affliction served as the perfect metaphor for his buffoonery. The South Carolinian "touches nothing which he does not disfigure with error," Sumner said, a clear reference to Butler's drooping face after the stroke. And in an outrageous conclusion to his insults, Sumner referred to both Butler's physical struggle to speak and the bankrupt content of his ideas when he declared, with double meaning, that Andrew Butler "cannot open his mouth but out there flies a blunder."

Sumner also targeted Butler's reliance on the "shameful imbecility of slavery" and ridiculed him for his past questioning of the value and contributions of Kansas territory when his own state had so much about which to be ashamed. He labeled as "madness" Butler's previous attempts to diminish Kansas by comparing it to South Carolina. "In the one is the long wail of slavery," Sumner said, "in the other, the hymn of freedom."

As the clock approached three in the afternoon, after five hours of oration over two days, a drained Sumner begged his fellow senators to admit Kansas as a free state, "in Christian sympathy for the slave . . . in the name of the Constitution . . . and, in the name of the Heavenly Father, in whose service is perfect Freedom."

✳ ✳ ✳

When Sumner finally sat down, the storm broke forth in the stunned Senate—and it was mostly from Northerners, who believed Sumner had gone too far.

Michigan's Lewis Cass, the dean of the Senate and the man who formally presented Sumner to his colleagues for his swearing-in ceremony in 1851, declared to his colleagues that Sumner's speech was "the most un-American and unpatriotic that ever grated on the ears of the members of this high body." Stephen Douglas and Sumner engaged in a shouting match on the Senate floor. Douglas wondered if Sumner's goal was to "provoke some of us to kick him as we would a dog in the street, that he may get sympathy upon the just chastisement." Sumner retorted that Douglas "fills the Senate with his offensive odor."

As remarks wound down late in the afternoon of May 20, a handful of Sumner's allies gathered around him and congratulated him for taking the fight to his opponents; one newspaper correspondent in attendance later called Sumner's remarks "majestic, elegant, and crushing." But amid their praise, Sumner's Republican colleagues also feared for his safety, especially troubled that Douglas's reference to kicking Sumner "as we would a dog in the street" could provoke violence. Henry Wilson of Massachusetts and Ohio's Ben Wade insisted that they accompany Sumner home.

He dismissed the idea: "None of that, Wilson," and shooed both men away.

Then Charles Sumner slipped out a side door of the Capitol and walked alone to his lodgings.

✳ ✳ ✳

Beyond the walls of the Senate chamber, reactions to Sumner's speech began almost immediately, with equal intensity on both sides of the Mason-Dixon Line.

Northern abolitionists were thrilled that Sumner had finally spoken out forcefully against the deteriorating situation in Kansas and slavery in general. Proslavery Southerners concluded that Sumner's extreme views and his personal attacks, especially against Butler, were yet further examples of the radical, destructive, and uncompromising beliefs of abolitionists—evidence of their desire to obliterate the Southern way of life. Most political moderates, Northerners and Southerners alike, expressed dismay at Sumner's harsh tone, claiming that the Massachusetts senator had rudely overstepped on the subject of slavery, sensing also that recriminations were likely.

Sumner's speech was printed at once in leading newspapers in many Northern cities, and large pamphlet editions were soon made available in New York, Boston, San Francisco, and Washington, D.C.—more than one million copies of *The Crime Against Kansas* would be distributed within a couple of months. Sumner himself picked up the final copies of the speech from the printer on May 21, one day after he had concluded his five-hour oration.

On street corners and in taverns, homes, shops, and offices across Washington—a city filled with proslavery interests—Southerners seethed at Sumner's insults and discussed retaliation. They denounced Sumner, with South Carolina congressman Preston Brooks taking Sumner's caustic words as a personal affront to his family, his region, and his manhood. To Brooks, part of a new breed of young Southern lawmakers who fiercely and unapologetically defended their region's way of life, Sumner represented a dangerous group of Radical Republicans who threatened the South, its sense of order, and its cherished institution.

Sumner's calls for an end to slavery in the territories, and worse, his demands for the nation to condemn slavery in all forms, posed a grave danger to the Southern economy and the region's autonomy. If a man could be forced by the federal government to surrender his property—human or otherwise—then such a government, and its representatives who advocated this abuse of power, must be stopped.

✳ ✳ ✳

In the thirty-six hours after Sumner's speech, Preston Brooks was tormented by proslavery Southerners everywhere he turned. "He could not go into a parlor, or drawing-room, or to a dinner party, where he did not find an implied reproach that there was an unmanly submission to an insult to his State and his countrymen," Senator Andrew Butler revealed after he returned to the Senate. "It was hard for any man, much less a man of his temperament, to bear this."

As Brooks bristled under these reproaches, he considered his options.

Though Sumner's remarks were slanderous, legal action was out of the question. No Southern gentleman considered a lawsuit the proper redress for a slur upon his good name or that of a family member.

According to the normal code of Southern chivalry, Senator Butler would be obliged to flog Sumner—but Brooks's elder cousin was now sixty years old and infirm, and the six-foot, four-inch, broad-shouldered Sumner was a physically large and powerful man.

Nor would Brooks challenging Sumner to a duel be an appropriate remedy; duels were fought only between gentlemen of honor, and Brooks could never confer such status upon the deplorable Sumner.

Finally, after two sleepless nights, Preston Brooks made his decision.

✳ CHAPTER 16 ✳

BLEEDING SUMNER

WEDNESDAY MORNING, MAY 21, 1856

Preston Brooks and his friend, Virginia representative Henry Edmundson, sat on a bench in the blistering heat near the walkway leading from Pennsylvania Avenue and the Capitol and awaited Charles Sumner's arrival. After fifteen minutes and no sign of the Massachusetts senator, the two Southern congressmen concluded that either they had missed their quarry or Sumner was not going to show.

Much to Brooks's frustration, he and Edmundson made their way to the House chamber to participate in the session.

That same afternoon, Brooks read the full text of Sumner's "The Crime Against Kansas" speech, which stoked his rage anew. That evening, he told his close allies from South Carolina, Representatives Laurence M. Keitt and James L. Orr, that he planned to "disgrace" Sumner with a "flagellation," though he stated neither the time nor the place.

Edmundson reminded Brooks of persistent rumors that Sumner had armed himself in anticipation of an attack and asked Brooks what preparations he had made for such an occurrence.

Brooks shrugged and replied: "I have nothing but my cane."

✳ ✳ ✳

THURSDAY MORNING, MAY 22, 1856

On the day he would unknowingly alter the course of American history, South Carolina congressman Preston Brooks awakened early after barely sleeping, still smoldering from the repeated insults in Charles Sumner's speech, angry that Sumner had escaped his wrath the previous day.

He left his lodgings carrying his cane made of gutta percha—a material similar to hard rubber—and met Edmundson again, this time at the western end of the Capitol. The location provided him with a wide view of the approach Sumner was likely to take.

Brooks intended to assault Sumner there if the senator walked to work; if he came by carriage, Brooks planned to cut through the Capitol grounds, run up a series of stairs, and intercept Sumner behind the building where the carriages stopped. Edmundson advised against the latter plan, insisting that Brooks would become fatigued climbing so many stairs and would thus be physically incapable of overpowering the larger, stronger Sumner.

Perhaps Brooks agreed with Edmundson's logic, perhaps he was miffed that his colleague put so little faith in his physical abilities. In any case, minutes after Edmundson's warning, he and Brooks walked toward the Capitol. When the two arrived at the door leading to the rotunda, Brooks abruptly headed toward the Senate chamber. Edmundson turned toward the House, but shortly thereafter, once the House had adjourned, made his way to the Senate—both houses of Congress had planned to adjourn early to mourn the recent death of a representative from Missouri, and the House broke session first.

Edmundson said he wanted to hear the remaining Senate eulogies for the Missouri congressman, but he also admitted that he expected an "interview" to take place between Brooks and Sumner, and "perhaps that influenced me in remaining longer in and near the Senate Chamber than I otherwise should have done."

Brooks confirmed to Edmundson that he planned to punish Sumner. The Massachusetts senator had deliberately attacked and provoked Senator Andrew Butler and South Carolina, and Brooks "would not feel that he was representing his State properly" if he let the insults stand. He asked Edmundson to accompany him as a witness—but to take no part in the confrontation. "Sumner may have friends with him, and I want a friend of mine to be with me to do me justice," Brooks said.

But Brooks insisted he would act alone.

"I felt it to be my duty to relieve [Senator Andrew] Butler and avenge the insult to my State," he said.

The Senate adjourned at 12:45 P.M.

Brooks and Edmundson entered the chamber.

✳ ✳ ✳

An hour later, Brooks was squirming in his seat in the Senate chamber and silently cursing the woman who stood a few feet from him chatting with the sergeant at arms. Agitated and sleep-deprived, Brooks was out of patience.

He needed the woman to leave—now.

He could hardly carry out his mission to avenge his kin, and his region, in the presence of a lady. It would violate the code of honor he lived by as a Southern gentleman.

He had tried once, but failed, to get the sergeant at arms to remove the woman.

Seated in the back row of the chamber with Edmundson, Brooks seethed, but was at least thankful his moment was near. During his lifetime, Brooks had been seriously wounded in a duel, contracted and recovered from typhoid fever, lost a brother in action during the Mexican War, buried his first wife, and watched his three-year-old daughter die from illness—yet in some ways, the days and hours after Charles Sumner's speech were the longest and most trying of his life.

Now, as he sat in the Senate chamber, Brooks was even more furious. He knew from the conversation around him that Sumner was signing copies of *The Crime Against Kansas* to mail to constituents—"franking," the practice was called. It wasn't bad enough that Sumner had crossed the line with his five-hour oratory in front of the Senate, which had been picked up by every newspaper in the country. Now Sumner had the temerity to disseminate his radical and nonsensical views even further!

Brooks fixed his eyes on Sumner—other senators milled about, but Brooks paid them no notice. He considered sending a note to Sumner, asking the Massachusetts senator to meet him outside to settle their differences, but again Edmundson vetoed the plan, convinced that Sumner would simply decline and instead invite Brooks to come to his desk and talk.

Finally, the woman finished her conversation with the sergeant at arms, turned, and walked directly past Brooks and Edmundson and out the Senate chamber door. Brooks waited another minute, his eyes boring into Sumner, who seemed oblivious to everything except the speech copies he was signing.

It was time.

✳ ✳ ✳

Brooks glanced at Edmundson, nodded, rose, and began walking toward Sumner with his usual pronounced limp, the result of a bullet wound he'd sustained during a duel in 1840. In his hand, Brooks carried his cane.

He made his way up the aisle toward Sumner, later saying he did so "under the highest sense of duty."

Brooks stepped closer, now directly in front of Sumner's desk.

Sumner, sitting behind a large stack of documents, still had his head bent low, writing feverishly, his chair drawn up close and his long legs snugly under the desk.

The Massachusetts senator was completely unaware of Brooks's presence.

"Mr. Sumner . . ." Brooks began.

✳ ✳ ✳

Vanity prevented the nearsighted Sumner from wearing eyeglasses, so when he heard his name spoken, he looked up from his seat and squinted at the tall, blurred, and indistinct figure standing before his desk. Sumner had never met Brooks and would not have recognized the South Carolinian even if he had been wearing spectacles.

Brooks tightened his grip on the cane.

"Mr. Sumner," Brooks said again in a low voice. "I have read your speech twice over carefully. It is a libel on South Carolina and Mr. Butler, who is a relative of mine."

Sumner, still seated, moved as if to rise, and Brooks stopped speaking and struck him hard on the top of the head with the smaller end of the cane, a blow simply "intended to put him on his guard," as he described it. The force of the blow caused blood to erupt from Sumner's scalp and so shocked him that he lost his sight immediately. In terror, he threw up his hands to protect himself. Brooks struck him again and again on his head and face with the heavy end of the cane.

For the first five or six blows, Sumner struggled to rise but his legs were still pinned under his desk and he forgot to push back his chair, which was on rollers. After about a dozen blows to the head, his eyes blinded with gushing blood, Sumner roared and made a valiant effort to rise. His trapped legs wrenched the desk—which was bolted to the floor by an iron plate and heavy screws—from its moorings.

Sumner staggered down the aisle, arms outstretched in a vain attempt at defense, now an even larger and easier target for Brooks, who continued to beat Sumner across the head with the cane "to the full extent of [my] power." Bloodlust now consumed Brooks—he rained down vicious blows upon the Massachusetts senator. "Every lick went where I intended," Brooks recalled. "I plied him so rapidly that he did not touch me."

As he pounded Sumner, Brooks's cane snapped, but he continued to strike the dazed senator with the splintered piece. "Oh Lord," Sumner gasped, "Oh! Oh!" He stumbled and reeled convulsively around the seats in the Senate chamber, tearing another desk from its screws as he began to fall to the floor.

But Brooks showed no mercy and would not let Sumner escape that easily—he had discarded his initial plan to merely teach Sumner a lesson and now seemed intent on killing him. He grasped the helpless Sumner by the lapel and held him up with one hand while he continued to strike with the other. Brooks would later confess that he did not stop hitting Sumner until he had thrashed him with "about 30 first-rate stripes."

Witnesses later testified that they heard shouts of encouragement for Brooks, including "Go, Brooks!" and "Give that damned abolitionist hell!"

✱ ✱ ✱

New York Times reporter James W. Simonton was the first to move, running forward followed by a group of other men, seemingly determined to stop Brooks, but as they got near the action, Brooks's friend Congressman Keitt rushed in, his own cane raised menacingly over his head, yelling, "Let them alone! Goddamn, let them alone." With his hand hovering near his holstered pistol, Keitt threatened anyone who interfered.

The tactic worked. Brooks continued to beat the dazed Sumner unimpeded. "I repeated it [the beating] till I was satisfied," he would say later in his official account of the incident. "No one interposed and I desisted simply because I had punished him to my satisfaction." Near the end of the horrific beating, Sumner was "entirely insensible," Brooks admitted, though just before the Massachusetts senator finally succumbed, "he bellowed like a calf."

New York congressmen Ambrose Murray and Edwin Morgan finally entered the fracas as it wound down. Murray seized Brooks by the arm and tried to draw him back, but Brooks's arm slipped from Murray's grasp. Later, conflicting reports emerged about this singular moment—some witnesses said Brooks's brief escape from Murray allowed him to beat a helpless Sumner several times more as the senator lay motionless, lodged against a toppled desk; others, including Brooks, denied it vehemently. Whig senator John Crittenden from Kentucky ran up the aisle and warned Brooks, "Don't kill him," and finally pulled him away from Sumner.

At that moment, Brooks, apparently realizing he had gone too far, muttered, "I did not intend to kill him, but I did intend to whip him."

Robert Toombs of Georgia, standing close by, did not help subdue Brooks, and in fact hoped that the South Carolinian would renew his assault on Sumner. "I approved [of] it," Toombs said later.

Northern senator Stephen Douglas, the subject of numerous and venomous attacks from Sumner, had run from the anteroom when he heard sounds of the struggle but also chose not to interfere. He considered trying to end the attack, but then thought: "my [strained] relations with Mr. Sumner were such that if I came into the Hall, my motives would be misconstrued . . . and I sat down again."

✳ ✳ ✳

Meanwhile, Morgan caught a near-unconscious Sumner, whose torso had begun slipping from the desk toward the floor. He cradled the fallen senator, who, head and face covered with blood, "lay at the side of the center aisle, his feet in the aisle."

Morgan heard Sumner groan piteously at first, and then go silent. The Massachusetts senator was "as senseless as a corpse for several minutes, his head bleeding copiously from the frightful wounds, and the blood saturating his clothes." Morgan's shirtsleeves were soaked with Sumner's blood.

With Sumner now splayed unconscious, and several pieces of Brooks's cane splintered across a floor slippery with blood, friends led Brooks toward a side room; along the way, Crittenden gently took the nub of the broken cane that Brooks still clutched. Brooks surrendered the remainder of his weapon without resistance but asked Crittenden to find and retrieve the cane's gold head. Other Southerners picked up splintered pieces—later, those scraps would be fashioned into rings that many Southern lawmakers would wear on neck-chains as a sign of solidarity with Brooks.

In the side room, Brooks's colleagues helped him wash a small cut he had suffered above his eye, caused by the recoil of his cane during the savage beating.

Minutes after his cut was bandaged, Brooks departed from the Capitol and walked down Pennsylvania Avenue with his protector, Keitt, in tow.

✳ ✳ ✳

Within moments, Charles Sumner regained consciousness, his bleeding head resting on the knee of Edwin Morgan.

A few colleagues helped the bewildered and wobbly senator from the floor. A Senate page gave him a glass of water. Sumner asked colleagues to find his hat and take care of the papers at his desk, then leaned on Morgan and, face covered in blood, staggered to the anteroom, where senators and a few journalists gently laid him on a sofa to rest.

Lawmakers quickly summoned Dr. Cornelius Boyle, who treated Sumner, stitching his wounds, which were bleeding profusely. Boyle noted that both head gashes Sumner received had split through the scalp to the bone, "laying it bare," and that he suffered defensive wounds and bruises on his hands, arms, and shoulders.

Friends then assisted Sumner into a carriage and accompanied him to his nearby Sixth Street lodgings. Upon arrival, they helped Sumner, still in a stupor, to first undress and then get into bed. Sumner's shirt near the neck and collar were soaked with blood. His waistcoat and trousers were streaked red. Blood covered the shoulders of the broadcloth and soaked the back and sides of his coat.

As he reached his bed, Sumner, head spinning and likely suffering from a severe concussion and a skull fracture, told Henry Wilson that he wished to resume his crusade against slavery as soon as he could return to the Senate. A patient and sympathetic Wilson did not respond directly but urged Sumner to try to relax.

An injured, shocked, and bewildered Charles Sumner could barely speak, but he managed one coherent remark before falling unconscious again:

"I could not believe that a thing like this was possible."

PART THREE

A NATION SPLIT ASUNDER

CHAPTER 17

THE VACANT CHAIR

Charles Sumner's caning sent shock waves across the country—outrage in the North, jubilation in the South. Sumner's beating inspired some, angered some, and frightened others. The shocking episode evoked raw emotion and action from newspapers, politicians, abolitionists, fire-eaters, speechmakers, and ordinary citizens.

Northerners reacted with a fury that had been brewing through years of increasing Southern aggressiveness in its efforts to perpetuate slavery—the Fugitive Slave Law, the Kansas-Nebraska Act, the violence in Kansas—and Preston Brooks's attack pushed most Northern citizens to the edge. "We all or *nearly* all felt that we had been personally mal-treated and insulted," one Boston man wrote to Sumner. The South celebrated the attack on Sumner as a lesson to abolitionists, declaring that Sumner's Kansas speech had unmasked the North's true goal—to destroy slavery, the South's economic system, and its entire way of life. "The vulgar Abolitionists are getting above themselves," the *Richmond Enquirer* declared. "They have grown saucy, and dare to be impudent to gentlemen. . . . They must be lashed into submission. Sumner, in particular, ought to have nine-and-thirty every morning."

In Kansas, Sumner's caning likely helped motivate the savage murders of proslavery men by abolitionist John Brown; in Illinois, it inspired a young Republican lawyer named Abraham Lincoln to deliver a speech that held listeners spellbound, so much so that no one in attendance took notes to record the full text of his words for others to read—many in the audience for the so-called "lost speech" declared it among the finest they'd ever heard. And maybe most important, the caning had convinced thousands to join the fledgling Republican party over the summer and fall, so much so that members held out hope that, in the November 1856 election, the presidency was within reach of the Republicans' first-ever nominee, John C. Frémont.

Sumner and Brooks would both see their lives forever altered by the caning. The beating left Sumner a shell of his formerly robust self, but it also solidified his role as the North's great antislavery voice and its greatest martyr. Brooks was the subject of a full and unprecedented congressional investigation, living in fear of reprisals, including assassination, but he too was elevated. The caning cast him as a hero and potential savior for those in the South hoping to maintain slavery.

Perhaps the most important effect of Sumner's caning was to crush any hope of conciliation between North and South—as illusory as such hope may have seemed—and harden both sides. For many in the North who had previously viewed Southern human bondage with ambivalence, or as a distant issue not relevant to their lives, the caning transformed slavery from a legal, political, social, and economic matter to a titanic moral struggle, replete with religious overtones. The steady chill in North-South relations over the years instantly intensified, fostering repugnance on both sides and obliterating compromise.

As Sumner struggled to regain his health, sectional clouds, already dark, thickened and roiled. Preston Brooks's attack on the Massachusetts senator, start to finish, consumed somewhere between sixty and ninety seconds—its tremors would reverberate across the North and South for the next four years.

A line had been crossed on May 22, 1856, and there was no going back.

⁂ ⁂ ⁂

In the first few days after the assault, Charles Sumner seemed to be recovering fairly quickly. Dr. Marshall S. Perry, a Boston physician hired by a Republican manufacturer to ensure that Sumner was receiving the finest possible care, arrived in Washington and found Sumner in satisfactory condition on May 25.

Perry said that the wound on the left side of Sumner's head had nearly healed, but the wound on the right side "had not adhered." Bothered by a "pulpy feeling" on the right side of Sumner's head, and by his patient's "unnaturally excited state," Dr. Perry recommended that the senator remain quiet and get complete rest. "His nervous system [had] received such a shock that I told him he should be very careful," Dr. Perry recalled.

Perry noticed a dramatic change for the worse in Sumner's condition on the evening of May 27, observing that Sumner was feverish and that his pulse was racing to over 90—"a very different state of things from what he had before." Overnight, Sumner experienced "great pain" in the back of his head, his neck glands were swollen, and his fever increased to 104. Perry sent for Dr. Boyle, whom he still considered Sumner's attending physician, and the two found Sumner's head wounds were hot to the touch. The doctors opened the wounds—Perry noticed a "tablespoon-ful of pus discharged," which provided Sumner with some relief from the "extreme suffering he had during the night" and allowed him to get several hours of sleep.

Perry told congressional investigators one day later that Sumner's wounds should be considered extremely serious. "Any blow received upon any part of the head with sufficient force to cut through the scalp down to the bone . . . would [present] a great deal of danger to life," he said, either from brain trauma or the possibility of extreme infection.

✵ ✵ ✵

While Sumner lay bedridden in Washington, thousands upon thousands of his fellow Northerners swarmed to rallies to show support for the Massachusetts senator and disdain for his South Carolina assailant.

Throughout late May and early June, huge public gatherings and "indig-nation meetings" were held to protest the caning in New York, Philadelphia, Boston, Albany, Cleveland, Detroit, New Haven, Providence, Rochester, and virtually every city and small town East and West—including places like Berea, Ohio; Rahway, New Jersey; and Burlington, Iowa. Attendees of all political persuasions jammed into halls and churches, stomped their feet, cheered speeches, and roared their approval for Sumner—and shouted their denunciations against Brooks, the South, and slavery. In many places, Brooks was hanged in effigy.

Further, when word started reaching the North and East about the pillaging of Lawrence, Kansas, Northern Republicans and other anti-slavery factions quickly began linking "Bleeding Kansas" and "Bleeding Sumner" in the public's mind. For more than a year, Republicans had tried to grab the attention of Northerners about the outrages in Kansas, without much success. News from the middle of the country was spo-radic, fragmented, and often contradictory, even somewhat abstract to

Northerners who lived a thousand miles away. Who could say exactly what was exaggeration and what was true? Who could say which side engaged in excesses and why? Yes, there was anger toward the South for its interference in the Kansas elections, but there was also a sense among many Northerners that abolitionists had asked for trouble by flocking to Kansas to confront border ruffians.

But the caning of Sumner, the deliberate attack upon a U.S. senator who was unable to defend himself, was concrete, shocking, unprecedented, and easily understood. Even among Southerners, there was little dispute about the facts of the incident. By stressing the Brooks assault instead of Kansas, Republicans believed that Northern differences of opinion could be smoothed over, or at least minimized, and in the words of one historian, the "instincts, passions, and sense of liberty of the free states [could be] roused against the enormous pretentions and villainous acts of the South."

✳ ✳ ✳

On Monday, June 2, ten days after the caning and following a week of testimony from twenty-seven witnesses, the House investigating committee recommended the expulsion of Preston Brooks from the U.S. House of Representatives. The committee also called for the censure of Congressmen Henry Edmundson and Laurence Keitt, who knew of Brooks's intention, though not the exact time and place he would act on them.

The 3–2 committee vote broke along party and sectional lines. Two Southern Democrats dissented, insisting that the House had no jurisdiction over an attack that took place in the Senate; thus, it should "remain silent" on the matter lest the opinion of lawmakers unduly influence the judiciary in Brooks's upcoming court case, in which he faced assault charges for his attack on Sumner.

Much like the Northern press, the majority report upbraided Brooks for his premeditation ("of at least two days"), his confronting of a defenseless Sumner ("the senator was in a sitting position), his choice of weapon ("of deadly character . . . a large and heavy cane"), and the brutality of his attack ("the blows were indiscriminately dealt . . . repeated with great rapidity and extreme violence . . . at the hazard of the life of the assailed").

The report's conclusion left no doubt about the majority's position on the caning, or the narrative that would play out in the North over the coming weeks and months: "The wounds were severe and calculated to endanger the life of the Senator, who remained for several days in a critical condition."

✳ ✳ ✳

By late June, Sumner had endured weeks of pain, misery, and deep melancholia.

While thousands thronged halls, churches, and town squares to either praise or denounce him, while speakers electrified crowds by declaring him either a courageous defender of freedom or an unsalvageable reprobate, Sumner remained mainly confined to his room and his bed, lonely and debilitated.

Much of the time he was unable to think clearly, and even when he was lucid, he despaired at his inability to partake in the monumental debate that swirled around him, though he occupied its center. Slavery was still the underlying issue, but Sumner's caning had gripped imaginations and poisoned debate like nothing ever had.

"My fingers are quite unused to the pen," Sumner wrote in a shaky hand to Henry Wadsworth Longfellow on June 13, but Sumner said he could not let another day go by without thanking Longfellow for his friendship. He had longed for the companionship of friends during his suffering, whose support he welcomed with a "throbbing grateful heart."

Sumner was trying to press on, but he was weak and disoriented. Dr. Perry reported that his patient complained of "oppressive weight or pressure of the brain," which intensified when he engaged in conversation or became excited. It often came on in waves—a sullen Sumner described it as a "fifty-six pound of weight" upon his head. At the same time, he had lost strength, his appetite was irregular, and he often lay awake at night in terrible pain. "Increased sensitivity of the spinal cord" and "weakness in the small of his back" made his walk unsteady. "Every step he took seemed to produce a shock upon his brain," Dr. Perry wrote. "After slight efforts, he would lose almost entire control of his lower extremities."

To escape Washington's June heat and aid his recuperation, Sumner was able to move to his friend Francis P. Blair's home in Silver Spring, on the outskirts of Washington. For nearly four weeks, he lay "22 hours out of 24 on my back," but by June 23, though he was still "very feeble," he could "totter a mile around the garden . . . hoping daily for strength which comes slowly."

Sumner lamented that, since the caning, he had written "only *five* letters," and only two on public matters.

"When this will end, I know not," he fretted.

✳ ✳ ✳

On July 4, New York senator William Seward visited Sumner at Silver Spring, and he found the patient bedridden and lethargic, "like a man who has not altogether recovered from paralysis, or like a man whose sight is dimmed and his limbs stiffened with age." Sumner was able to converse and expressed curiosity about goings-on in the Senate, but he admitted that his "vivacity of spirit" was gone.

Seward expressed deep concern about Sumner's condition. It had been more than six weeks since Sumner's beating, and his colleague not only seemed devoid of energy but had also turned into a sickly old man virtually overnight. "He is much changed for the worse," Seward wrote on Independence Day of 1856. "It is impossible to regard him without apprehension."

There was little doubt that Charles Sumner needed more peaceful surroundings, farther from Washington, D.C. On July 7, he arranged his affairs and headed north for further rest—for now, Boston was out of the question because he needed to avoid a steady stream of visitors. Instead, in the coming weeks, he would stop in Philadelphia, then Cape May, New Jersey, and later the mountains of Cresson, Pennsylvania, desperately seeking the restoration of his full health.

One day after Sumner left Washington, Judge Thomas H. Crawford of the Circuit Court of the District of Columbia found Preston Brooks guilty of assault for the caning of Charles Sumner and sentenced Brooks to a fine of three hundred dollars. Brooks paid the fine and walked out of court—later, his supporters in the South raised the money to reimburse him. Sumner supporters were incensed, claiming the "paltry fine" clearly showed the proslavery temperament of the federal courts in the District of Columbia.

The legal proceedings against Sumner for his actions on May 22, 1856, were concluded, and the next day, Brooks would face a congressional

jury of his peers—the full House of Representatives would begin deliber-
ations on whether he should be expelled.

✳ ✳ ✳

The tension was palpable when members crowded into the steamy House
chamber on July 9 to debate Preston Brooks's future. To consider expel-
ling a member was weighty enough, but every representative knew that
the debate over the next few days was about far more than a lone man's
fate—the nation's future could hang in the balance. Congressmen were
well aware that whatever their decision, one side would be angry, perhaps irreconcilably so. Voting to expel Brooks would satisfy the North
and infuriate the South; letting Brooks retain his seat would send renewed outrage throughout the Northern states.

One after another, members of the House stood and delivered lengthy
speeches, in part to educate their colleagues and in part to ensure that
their remarks were reprinted in the more than three thousand newspapers across the country that Americans relied on to get their information.

Their positions were predictable.

Southerners generally agreed with Representative James L. Orr of
South Carolina, who argued that Brooks felt he had a "high and holy obligation resting on him to step forward and repel the insult made on the
character of his state and his relative." Orr parroted the Southern belief
that Brooks had little choice but to assault Sumner, that Sumner's in-
tentional provocation in "The Crime Against Kansas" speech demanded
nothing less, and that Sumner's injuries were not serious. Northerners
disagreed vehemently. New Jersey's Alexander Pennington set the tone
for the remarks of virtually every other Northern member, calling the
caning "a gross and unparalleled outrage committed upon the Constitution." While he ascribed "no murderous purpose" to Brooks, he believed
the "deadly weapon [was] wielded in a murderous manner." This could
not stand in a nation that cherished the right of free speech.

Debate went on for nearly six full days inside the sweltering House
chamber, with neither side offering quarter or compromise. Every Northern representative sounded themes similar to Pennington's—that the caning was an attack against the laws of the nation. Orr spoke for virtually
all Southerners—Sumner's insult against Brooks's relative and his region
warranted such an attack. The arguments spoke volumes about how far

apart North and South were on the issue, and, by extension, on the issue that lay at the root of the caning: slavery.

When the debate ended and the roll was called, the House voted 121–95 to expel Brooks, but it was a full 23 votes short of the necessary two-thirds majority to remove him. All but one of the majority votes were from the free states. Thirteen free-state Democrats voted with Southerners against the expulsion resolution, arguing that Brooks's removal was too harsh a penalty. The House also fell short of the necessary two-thirds majority to officially censure South Carolina's Laurence M. Keitt, and the vote to censure Henry Edmundson was defeated outright.

Proud and defiant as he prepared to address the House after the July 14 vote, Preston Brooks knew how the vote would turn out. He knew Republicans would lack the two-thirds majority to expel him, but he was deeply rankled and insulted that a simple majority of members would declare him unfit to serve in the House any longer. He had "long foreseen" the outcome, was "altogether prepared for it," and as such, had ten days earlier placed a letter announcing his resignation with the governor of South Carolina, "to take effect the very instant that I announce my resignation upon this floor."

Which he did at the end of his remarks: "And now, Mr. Speaker, I announce to you and to this House that I am no longer a member of the Thirty-Fourth Congress." Brooks strode from the House chamber and, after being thronged at the doorway by sympathetic Southern women who embraced and kissed him, left the Capitol building.

* * *

Brooks's absence from the House was short-lived. Two weeks later, South Carolina held a special election in his district to fill the seat he had resigned. Legally eligible to seek reelection, Brooks did so (as did Keitt, who, two days after Brooks, resigned in the wake of his own censure). He ran without opposition and won by acclaim—receiving 30 percent more votes than his 1854 election total.

On August 1, he returned to the House chamber, approached the rostrum, and took the oath of office to support, protect, and defend the Constitution of the United States.

* * *

AUGUST 1856, THE ALLEGHENY MOUNTAINS

Abolitionist and women's rights advocate Jane Swisshelm wrote of her shock upon seeing Charles Sumner three months after his beating. "When he rises from his chair, he takes hold of the table," she observed. "His gait, at first glance, appears that of a man ninety years of age."

Swisshelm wrote this description in a long letter published in the *New York Times* on August 23, 1856, an update to readers on Sumner's convalescence. She had visited Sumner at the health resort of Dr. Robert M. Jackson, a physician in the town of Cresson, Pennsylvania, in the Allegheny Mountains, where Sumner had gone to recover from his injuries. Sumner, perhaps noticing his guest's dismay, assured her that he was improving—he would return to Washington in two weeks. She feared he was deluding himself.

While resting at Cape May, New Jersey, earlier in the summer, Sumner had complained that he felt "as if [I'm] composed of gristle instead of bone," and he admitted that a simple walk wearied him.

Demoralized and infirm, Sumner exerted additional strain on himself for being absent from the Senate "at a moment when more than ever in my life I was able to wield influence and do good."

The isolation of the Allegheny retreat weighed heavily on Sumner, and acute loneliness gripped him. His debilitating headaches, lack of focus, and insomnia all contributed to his fear that he might be losing his mind. His concern was compounded when one of his doctors admitted that he was unsure whether Sumner faced the prospect of permanent brain injury, a potential condition he dreaded and viewed as unbearable. If Brooks's cane had inflicted lasting damage, then "death would have been my best friend," Sumner admitted.

✳ ✳ ✳

Far from Washington, D.C., Sumner watched with dread as Southerners congratulated Brooks for his brutal attack; Southern newspapers commended him, and the House failed to expel him. As Brooks was reelected, Southerners organized rallies on Brooks's behalf, where banners proclaimed SUMNER AND KANSAS: LET THEM BLEED. Brooks received hundreds of canes as gifts—many inscribed with the words HIT HIM AGAIN.

Then, just six days after Jane Swisshelm's letter about Sumner appeared in the *New York Times*, throngs of Columbia, South Carolina, residents jammed the street in front of the city courthouse to see and hear from their newly crowned hero.

Brooks was making his way home from Washington for the first time since the caning. In town squares along the way, Southerners gathered to cheer and thank him for teaching a lesson to "the notorious Charles Sumner for his wanton abuse and cowardly assault upon . . . Andrew Butler, and the fair name of his state."

In South Carolina's capital, the Columbia mayor presented Brooks with a silver pitcher, a beautifully crafted goblet, and one of the "finest hickory canes with a handsome gold head" to reward his beating of Sumner and his display of "honorable conduct" in the stressful days and weeks following the assault. The goblet was engraved with the inscription: "To Hon. Ps Brooks from the Citizens of Columbia, May 22, 1856."

It was no mistake that the goblet was engraved not with the date of the rally but with the date of the caning—Columbia citizens recognized its singular importance in the swirl of events that gripped the nation.

❋ ❋ ❋

As if Southern adulation for Brooks didn't cause Sumner enough despair, his supporters' reaction to the politics of the caning, coupled with Sumner's subsequent absence from the Senate, depressed him even more.

It wasn't all bad. The most important symbol bolstering the Republican cause during the summer and fall of 1856—one that swelled its membership by thousands—was Charles Sumner's vacant chair in the U.S. Senate chamber.

The simple fact was that Sumner's continued ill health and his prolonged absence from the Senate, which would exceed five months as the November elections approached, enabled Republicans to keep the caning top of mind for voters. They recognized how deeply the caning had touched Northern sensibilities; Sumner's well-chronicled, highly publicized, and as-yet-unsuccessful efforts to regain his health and resume his duties only heightened the caning's powerful impact across the North.

For this reason, Republicans were in no hurry for Sumner to return.

His vacant chair spoke volumes about the evils of slavery and the

Southern Democrats who supported it. The greatest irony during the early months of Sumner's convalescence was the senator's earnest, sometimes desperate, struggle to get well and return to work, even as his political allies viewed his *absence* as far more advantageous to the future of the Republican Party and the antislavery cause.

"Your empty chair can make a more fervent appeal than even *you*," explained his friend Wendell Phillips.

✳ ✳ ✳

Sumner continued to chafe at his inability to speak publicly and return to work. Because he could not stump for Republican candidates, party leaders were spared from having to deliver the painful message that Sumner on the campaign trail was more a liability than a benefit to aspiring Republican office-seekers.

The reason was simple. In his reclusiveness, Sumner resumed his passionate letter-writing, focusing on the dire situation in Kansas, urging Republicans to work hard for Frémont's election, and to rally on behalf of Kansas and demand its admittance to the union as a free state.

But Republicans were grateful that Sumner's writing would only reach individuals who were the recipients of his private letters. His insistence on making Kansas the center of the debate ran contrary to the Republican campaign strategy as the November 1856 election drew near. Republican political operatives wanted the focus on Sumner *himself*—his ongoing debilitating condition and the brutal attack that had left him an invalid. No reasonable Northerner could condone either Brooks's action or Southern support of it—most Northerners, regardless of their political leanings, viewed the caning as a violent trampling of free-speech rights.

In a sense, the Brooks assault on Sumner offered Northern Republicans the opportunity to thread what previously would have been an unthreadable needle—to attack the South for barbaric behavior *without* specifically attacking slavery. Such an approach was far more palatable to Northern moderates and well-to-do business owners who relied on slave labor to provide cheap raw materials for their factories. If the caning had unified the South, must not the North also unify to protect its interests and its constitutional rights?

One Northern Democrat who switched to the Republican Party after the caning did not support abolitionism and continued to believe that blacks were inferior to whites, but could no longer tolerate Southern brutality, exemplified by Brooks's assault on Sumner. "Had the slave power been less *insolently aggressive*, I would have been content to see it extend," he said, "but when it seeks to extend its sway by fire and sword . . . I am ready to say hold enough!" To a longtime Democratic associate, he added: "Reserve no place for me [in the party]. *I shall not come back*."

✳ ✳ ✳

For Northern Democrats—those men who still balked at the fanaticism of abolitionists and believed that continued agitation on the slavery question would destroy the union—the South's response to the caning would soon become a source of alarm.

Had Southerners even mildly repudiated Brooks's actions, or remained silent, Northern Republicans would have been left with a single incident that could have been attributable to one congressman who lost his temper.

But the South's overwhelming approval of Sumner's beating fundamentally altered the dynamic—Northerners of almost all political persuasions were stunned that Brooks *wasn't* expelled from the House. They decried the multitude of pro-Brooks editorials and celebrations across the South, and Brooks's overwhelming reelection. To people in the North, these events provided demonstrable and indisputable evidence that the entire South was filled with a visceral brutality that transcended its support for slavery.

Republicans portrayed Brooks as every Southerner and the North as every Southerner's victim. Each time a news account depicted Southerners rising to Brooks's defense, Republicans reinforced the image of Southerners, slave owners in particular, as lawless and violent, and Southern society as backward and barbaric. Throughout the summer and fall of 1856, Northern Democrats begged Southern congressmen not to publicly endorse Brooks's actions; yet their gift to Republicans continued.

One New York Democrat warned Stephen Douglas that Southern reaction to the caning was doing the party "vast injury" in the North. Another party loyalist believed that the assault on Sumner would cost

Democrats two hundred thousand votes in the fall election; other key operatives thought that the losses would be even greater. Former President Millard Fillmore (who was running again in 1856) vividly articulated the dilemma:

> Brooks's attack upon Sumner has done more for [Republican candidate John C.] Frémont than any 20 of his warmest friends [in the] North have been able to accomplish. If Frémont is elected, he will owe his election entirely to the troubles in Kansas, and the martyrdom of Sumner. . . . The Republicans ought to pension Brooks for life.

✳ ✳ ✳

The final indignity heaped upon Sumner was a charge repeated again and again across the South: that he was faking his injuries. Most Southerners thought Sumner's injuries were minor and that Sumner and Northerners were exaggerating and exploiting the effects of the caning to build momentum for the Republican Party. They were right about the party's motives but wrong about Sumner and his injuries.

Indeed, the evidence is weighted heavily in the opposite direction. Throughout the summer of 1856, both Sumner himself and virtually all of the medical professionals who treated him documented his feeble condition and intense suffering. As one historian observed, if there was a plan for Sumner to feign illness, others would have been part of the conspiracy, and if there was a plot, "it was one of the best kept secrets in American history."

Sumner repeatedly let friends know how much he suffered. He was perhaps most honest with Samuel Gridley Howe when he described the peaks and valleys of his health on September 11: "This is my best day. But yesterday was a disheartening day; I seemed to be going back."

Nor is there anything in Sumner's personality that suggests he would abandon his Senate duties and sacrifice his voice for the sake of the Republican Party's advancement. Speaking out against slavery was the cause of his life. He believed, mostly correctly, that nobody could frame and argue the issue as well as he could, and he longed to do so.

✳ ✳ ✳

If the cynicism of the political response to the caning depressed Sumner, he was buoyed by the sympathetic response from ordinary citizens.

Hundreds of letters of support from Northerners clogged Sumner's mail; not surprisingly, Boston and Massachusetts were well represented, but residents of many states expressed their stunned outrage. One Illinois writer, representative of Sumner's indignant correspondents, acknowledged that "the blood boils in my veins" as he recalled the caning. Portending the dreadful events to come, he added: "I feel as though no other provocation was needed to justify the North in shouldering the musket and fighting the battles of the revolution over again."

Even children were touched. "The instant papa told me," a Massachusetts girl wrote about the attack on Sumner, "it seemed exactly as if a great black cloud was spread over the sky." Little Mary Rosamond Dana, daughter of Sumner's friend and confidant Richard Henry Dana, expressed herself with a mixture of childlike innocence and a thirst for revenge: "Mr. Brooks is a very naughty man and if I had been there, I would have torn his eyes out—and so I would do now if I could."

Northern letter writers did more than express anger and sympathy; most satisfying to Sumner, they also lauded the Massachusetts senator for his courage, his steadfast and vociferous leadership, his moral virtue on antislavery issues, and indeed, the martyrdom he had attained as a spiritual representative—now, the *unrivaled* spiritual representative—of the entire Northern antislavery movement.

Sumner's caning brought him a level of affection and admiration from Northerners that he had long sought but, until now, seemed to elude him. The hundreds of Northerners who wrote to him assumed the role of Sumner's extended family, offering comfort to a man whose injuries and sufferings elicited feelings of pity, anger, and sectional pride. Noted Boston resident James Stone: "[The Brooks attack] seems to be the last feather that breaks the camel's back of their [conservative and moderate Northerners'] sympathy with slavery."

Sumner's dear friend Longfellow agreed with this general sentiment. Sumner's wounds, his bleeding, his continued pain, his difficult convalescence—all of it had "torn the mask off the faces of traitors, and *at last* the spirit of the North is aroused."

✳ ✳ ✳

Sumner was grateful for the groundswell of Northern support and the unabashed displays of warmth and affection, but he realized the irony, too.

He had desperately sought adulation for most of his life and was now being showered with it, but his physical condition rendered him unable to fully enjoy it. He had relished the role of martyr and often anointed himself when the term did not apply, but he was now unable to appreciate his newfound status when the label truly was appropriate.

On the eve of the 1856 presidential election, Charles Sumner would experience firsthand the response to his ordeal from the people of Boston. Though suffering from intense dizziness and wracked with headaches and stabbing back pain, he was ready to leave the Pennsylvania mountains to cast his ballot.

After nearly a year away, a year unlike anything he had ever experienced, after months in Washington and months more recuperating at the seashore and in the mountains, Charles Sumner was going home.

✳ CHAPTER 18 ✳

A REELECTION AND A SHOCKING DEATH

MONDAY, NOVEMBER 3, 1856, BOSTON

More than one thousand men on horseback marched in columns, accompanying a procession of nearly twenty carriages, the whole assemblage stretching for more than a half mile along downtown Boston's Washington Street.

Thousands of cheering spectators lined the street—men brandishing their hats wildly, women tossing bouquets—and hundreds of residents leaned out the windows of their homes, shouting and waving handkerchiefs madly.

Bostonians showered praise upon the haggard and pale man who sat in an open carriage drawn by six magnificent gray horses. On this overcast but unseasonably warm Monday afternoon in November, Charles Sumner's fellow citizens turned out to pay him tribute in a remarkable display of affection and solidarity.

Sumner had arrived a day earlier at his friend Longfellow's house after a tough trip from Philadelphia. Against the advice of doctors and despite the entreaties of friends, who feared for his health, Sumner was determined to return to his beloved home city to vote for John C. Frémont for president and for Anson Burlingame in his congressional reelection bid.

He had delivered brief remarks as he entered the city earlier in the day, his voice weak and lacking its usual sonorous power; only those near the carriage could hear him, and many of those who saw him close-up were overcome with emotion at his pallid condition and lack of vitality. He felt pride that he had incurred his wounds "in the performance of duty" and believed that the forces of freedom would enjoy a "final triumph."

Now, as his procession made its way toward downtown Boston,

Sumner was overwhelmed by the crowds along the route, overcome by the hundreds of flags, streamers, and banners as his carriage wound its way through the city's streets. "Massachusetts loves, honors, and will sustain and defend her noble Sumner!" announced one banner strung high across Newton Street. "Welcome Freedom's Defender!" said another on the side of a building. On another house was a sign wreathed in black that reminded all of the fateful day in the Senate chamber: "May 22, 1856."

Sumner, normally aloof and often icy even with close friends and family, was genuinely touched when his carriage approached the Boston Female Asylum for orphans on Washington Street, where young girls lined up in front of the building, waving handkerchiefs and displaying on a white banner a wreath of evergreens covered with flowers, along with a sign that read: "We weave a wreath for Charles Sumner."

This was the only point along the route at which the unsteady Sumner rose to his feet in gratitude. "The kindness of these orphaned ones so touched his feelings, that he could not help acknowledging it in this way," one newspaper account explained.

❋ ❋ ❋

As Sumner approached the statehouse, the scene left him awestruck.

Between five and seven thousand citizens, white and black, crowded Beacon and Park Streets and the long set of stairs that led to the state capitol building itself; rooftops were packed with thousands more. The crowd greeted Sumner's arrival with raucous and sustained cheers, and it roared even louder as Sumner, with help, slowly ascended the steps of a hastily erected platform. Massachusetts governor Henry J. Gardiner, who months earlier had proposed that the Commonwealth assume the costs of Sumner's medical expenses, now urged the crowd to help him welcome Sumner. The governor pledged that the state would stand by Sumner "today, tomorrow, and forever."

When Sumner finally spoke, he labored with great difficulty, speaking in a tremulous voice for barely a minute before his strength failed him, and then he handed his prepared remarks to a reporter. The crowd cheered wildly when he sat down.

His written manuscript, publicized in many places afterward, expressed his deep appreciation to Bostonians for their support throughout his ordeal. He sought only "the triumph of truth" and vowed to continue his fight against the slave power. He also made the subtle case for his own reelection to the U.S. Senate when the Massachusetts legislature considered the matter in January 1857—he expected soon "to be permitted, with unimpaired vigor, to resume all responsibilities of his position."

It was close to five o'clock in the afternoon when a weary Sumner—wracked by fatigue and a blinding headache—was taken to his family home at 20 Hancock Street on the back side of Beacon Hill. After he entered his house, throngs of people gathered out front on the narrow street and cheered repeatedly, too excited to remember Governor Gardiner's pleas to allow Sumner his privacy.

The day honoring Sumner illustrated one indisputable fact. His beating, and his painful attempt to recover, had accomplished what heretofore had proved impossible: unifying a previously divided Boston, bringing together longtime abolitionists and staid commercial merchants alike against what its citizens now saw as the common enemy of Southern barbarism.

They, and their fellow Northerners, would weigh in when they cast their ballots on November 4, 1856, Election Day in Massachusetts and across the nation.

✳ ✳ ✳

For North and South alike, the most shocking, significant, and prophetic outcome of the 1856 presidential election was not that Republican John C. Frémont was defeated in his bid for the presidency but that he came so close to winning.

The new Republican Party, which did not even exist in several Northern states only a year earlier, made a resounding statement in its first bid for the nation's highest office and, in the process, threw a scare into Southerners and Northern Democrats. The message of the election was clear: bolstered by Sumner's caning and its aftershocks, the new antislavery party had made an astounding showing across the North, and while it fell short of its ultimate goal, voting trends clearly infused Republicans with enthusiasm and momentum for 1860. One worried Southern Democratic activist noted: "The club which broke Mr. Sumner's head has . . . turned more votes than all other causes that were at work." A Republican party leader agreed: "The most effective deliverance made by any man to advance the Republican party was made by the bludgeon of Preston S. Brooks."

Almost overnight, national power had begun shifting profoundly.

Frémont won eleven Northern states, all but five in the section, and carried a remarkable 60 percent of the Northern popular vote and an astonishing one-hundred-thousand-vote plurality in New England. His vote total in the North actually exceeded that of the new president-elect, James Buchanan, who became the first man in American history to win the presidency without carrying a preponderance of free states.

What frightened the South most was that had Frémont carried Pennsylvania or the combination of New Jersey, Illinois, and Indiana—he carried all other free states except California—he would have won a clear victory *without a single Southern electoral vote*. In the realm of presidential politics, the South needed the North and the North could ignore the South. A "solid North" could win the presidency outright—the South did not have sufficient population or electoral votes to achieve the same result with one of its candidates.

Any solid North in the future would assure the election of a Republican president.

Republicans made a note of that for 1860.

✳ ✳ ✳

While Charles Sumner was jubilant at the results nationally and in Massachusetts (Republicans swept the state, thereby virtually guaranteeing his reelection in early 1857), his ill health and slow recovery dominated his thoughts and actions during the fall and winter of 1856 and early 1857.

He was unable to travel to Washington for the fall session, instead remaining at Longfellow's home, hoping to clear his head and regain his strength. Longfellow noted in his diary that "Sumner . . . looks well in the face, but is feeble and walks with an uncertain step." Sumner tried to ride horseback most mornings and take walks in the afternoon, but every movement was a struggle. It was likely he still suffered from the effects of a serious concussion, and perhaps brain trauma. He spent the weeks after the election reading and corresponding with friends, often from bed. "I am a convalescent invalid," he wrote in December, adding that his doctors believed he was months from a complete recovery.

Dejected and lonely, he took great solace in the kindness of friends. A verse from abolitionist poet John Greenleaf Whittier made the emotionally fragile Sumner's "pulse beat quick and my eyes moisten with tears."

At the same time, he confided to Whittier, he could not bear the thought that he might "survive with impaired powers, or with a perpetual disability."

As year-end approached, Sumner's inability to return to work drained him of energy and left him dispirited. Sumner found neither peace nor goodwill during the 1856 Christmas season, unburdening himself often through letters, wrestling with deep discouragement, lamenting his pain and his maladies, and expressing frustration about his inability to raise his voice against the evils of slavery.

But the new year brought a glimmer of hope.

✳ ✳ ✳

The statehouse in Boston hummed with anticipation when lawmakers gathered on January 9, 1857, to reelect Charles Sumner, a testament to how much had changed in six years.

Gone was the acrimony that marred his first election in April of 1851.

Gone was the grumbling and resentment that a radical antislavery political novice had unexpectedly eked out a single-vote legislative majority on the twenty-sixth ballot to win election to the Senate.

Gone was the glowering disapproval and uncensored cursing of the Boston business community when the self-righteous Sumner moved from abolitionist agitator to a man of influence in Washington, D.C.

Except for Sumner, everything had changed. He was still the uncompromising antislavery warrior, still the egotist who sneered at lesser intellects and ridiculed political opponents, still the immovable sentinel of freedom who was fueled by moral certitude. Now, though, his work in the Senate, his opposition to the Fugitive Slave Law and the Kansas-Nebraska Act, and especially his caning at the hands of Preston Brooks had transformed him into a symbol—one of unrepentant Southern violence and barbarism aimed at destroying free speech, and one of Northern solidarity aimed at counteracting Southern aggression and preserving the union.

This time, when Charles Sumner stood for reelection, even as he struggled to get well, Massachusetts lawmakers drew on a reservoir of deep affection for their wounded senator. They rallied around him with a near-religious fervor, inspired by his martyrdom and borne of sectional pride and a sense of mission that transcended partisan politics and petty agendas. As the state legislature gathered to vote, the *New York Times* wrote a substantive story outlining the change in sentiments among the residents of Massachusetts. Sumner, the newspaper wrote, was now "the most popular man in the state."

The conclusion was hard to refute.

✻ ✻ ✻

The Massachusetts House of Representatives made Sumner's reelection its first order of business in 1857, even before receiving the governor's inaugural message. Without debate or suspense, the clerk called the roll, and when he finished, Charles Sumner had received an astounding 333 of the 345 votes cast (the 12 other votes were divided among nine other candidates). Sumner's victory in the House was fast and overwhelming, and it was met with uproarious applause. Four days later, the Massachusetts Senate met and unanimously cast their votes for Sumner.

He was scheduled to begin his second six-year term in the U.S. Senate when the new session began on March 4.

Massachusetts residents and newspapers were quick to point out the dramatically altered political landscape that propelled Sumner to a second term. The *Boston Atlas* enumerated the stark differences from his first election:

Sumner's reelection was virtually unanimous and occurred only three days into the legislative term; this was in contrast with his razor-thin victory in 1851, a full 114 days into the term.

Six years earlier, votes were cast in a sealed envelope, while in this latest election, "every member [spoke] aloud his party vote."

In 1851, Sumner was part of a wobbly Free Soil Party that drew about 26,000 votes in the previous election; this time, Sumner was the leading voice in a Republican Party that drew more than 108,000 votes in the previous election, about two-thirds of the entire vote.

And finally, whereas only two or three others in the U.S. Senate shared his political sympathies after his first election, Sumner was returning to a Congress in which Republicans held a majority in the House and 25 percent of the Senate.

Sumner himself interpreted his resounding victory as a sign that the people of Massachusetts had forgotten their "ancient party hates" and instead had banded together "in fraternal support of a sacred cause." While he continued to suffer, he desperately wanted to take up the cause again in the new congressional session. If at all possible, Sumner said, "My hope is to reach Washington before the [current] session closes."

✳ ✳ ✳

Before he got to the nation's capital, Sumner and the nation received earthshaking news from Washington, D.C., on the morning of January 28, 1857.

Preston Brooks was dead.

Just eight months after his brutal attack on Sumner had shocked a nation, the thirty-seven-year-old congressman had died in agony in his quarters at Brown's Hotel in D.C. Several days earlier, he'd developed a sore throat, which progressed to trouble breathing, then to near strangulation in the final moments of his life as a result of what his doctor termed "acute inflammation of the throat," quite likely an esophageal infection. While a howling blizzard and frigid temperatures paralyzed the city, several of Brooks's colleagues watched helplessly at their friend's bedside as he clawed at his throat and struggled in vain to breathe.

"He died a horrid death, and suffered intensely," noted the official telegram announcing his death.

"If he had been struck by lightning," one Northern correspondent noted, "the announcement could not have been more unexpected."

Still recuperating at Longfellow's when he got the news, Sumner did not gloat, did not suggest that Brooks's rapid demise was providential payback for his brutal and senseless attack, but instead took the news with reflection and a great sense of sadness.

In Sumner's view, the violence perpetuated by Brooks was not the deranged action of one immoral man; far worse was that Brooks served as the representative creature of thousands of immoral men who presided over slavery, the most immoral institution of all.

✳ ✳ ✳

One year before his death, Preston Brooks had been a backbench legislator. The elaborateness and pageantry of his funeral services showed how far he had come in the intervening twelve months.

On January 29, 1857, two days after Brooks's untimely death, braving heavy snow and roaring wind, thousands made their way to the Capitol.

The galleries and rotunda leading to the House and Senate chambers were soon blocked by the mass of mourners who came to view Brooks's body. The House chamber and galleries were so full that the House set aside its rule barring women on the floor. Virtually all of the country's leaders were in attendance, including President Franklin Pierce, President-elect James Buchanan, members of the cabinet, and members of the Supreme Court. Speakers used glowing terms to describe Brooks's generosity, bravery, faithfulness, and work ethic.

Southern politicians mourned and eulogized Brooks with reverential obsequies and lofty hosannas more often reserved for deceased kings than for two-term congressmen. Ordinary people—most Southerners—wept when they heard the news.

To Sumner and his allies, the honors bestowed on Brooks in death were troubling, to say the least.

A powerful case can be made that the long, mournful return of Brooks's body from Washington, D.C., to Edgefield, South Carolina, solidified a unique place for Brooks in Southern antebellum history. His attack on Sumner, coupled with his sudden death at a young age, made Brooks a tragic hero to his supporters.

✹ ✹ ✹

Brooks's hometown of Edgefield organized a committee of twenty-six "intelligent and substantial men" to travel to Washington to retrieve Brooks's body. On February 10, the committee collected Brooks's remains and set out quickly, beginning their return trip just after 5:00 P.M. Their steamer took more than five hours to plow through the ice in Aquia Creek and into northern Virginia, and the committee eventually made its way to Richmond. From there, they boarded a train that carried them to the Carolinas. Stops were scheduled in the North Carolina communities of Goldsborough, Wilmington, Charlotte, and Raleigh before the train rolled into South Carolina for stops at Branchville, Charleston, Abbeville, and Hamburg.

Brooks's final journey was documented by virtually every newspaper in the South and in dozens of personal letters and diaries. It inspired poetry, paeans, editorials, eulogies, and tears, and it spawned sad gatherings of thousands of citizens in large cities and small towns across the South.

At every location along the route, mayors and townspeople paid tribute with speeches and prayers and retrospectives. Church bells pealed.
Retail commerce ceased. Planters left their fields and flocked to town
squares. Women across the South penned poems and submitted them to
local papers, stanza after stanza of grief-filled verse packed with religious
allusions and tributes to Brooks's statesmanlike valor and righteousness,
the defender of their way of life and their honor. In Charleston, the har-
bormaster requested that all vessels lower their flags to half-mast. Guns
were fired when Brooks's train arrived, and church bells tolled as the procession wound its way through the city streets.

Four large horses drew a hearse along the final leg of the journey, from
Augusta, Georgia, to nearby Edgefield, just across the state line in South
Carolina. There, Brooks's friends thronged the streets, standing patiently
in line to view his body, and then walking silently beside the guard of
honor that accompanied his hearse to the Edgefield cemetery gravesite.

The message at every funeral stop across the South was clear: Brooks
was not slain by bullet or bayonet, but he died for the South nonetheless,
defending causes greater than all others—family, sectional honor, slavery, the protection of his region's way of life.

Two weeks after Brooks was buried, a fatigued and unsteady Charles
Sumner arrived in Washington, D.C., with every intention of resuming
his duties in the U.S. Senate.

✳ ✳ ✳

Whether Sumner should have ventured into the nation's capital at all is
open to debate.

He received tremendous support in Massachusetts and New England,
but the mood differed vastly in the Southern-leaning District of Columbia. Sumner's friends and colleagues had urged him to stay away from
Washington in the days immediately following Brooks's funeral, suggesting that his presence would not only heighten tensions but likely also
precipitate violence. One letter writer urged him to absent himself from
Washington "for some weeks" to allow highly charged emotions to dissipate.

Finally, however, Boston and New England manufacturers prevailed
on Sumner to return to the Senate earlier than he planned to vote on a
tariff bill that would reduce the duty on manufactured woolens. Sumner

took his seat at 2:00 P.M. on February 26, 1857—for the first time since May 22 of the previous year. Republicans greeted him warmly. Most Democrats ignored him.

He did not last long. Too weak to remain in his seat—he nearly passed out—he returned to his lodging, leaving instructions to be called as votes came up on the tariff bill. Sumner returned to the chamber at 9:00 P.M. and cast votes on various amendments before leaving the Capitol at 2:00 A.M., completely exhausted.

Just two days later, Sumner wrote despondently to Parker: "I have sat in my seat only on one day. After a short time the torment of my system became great, and a cloud began to gather over my brain. I tottered out and took to my bed."

✳ ✳ ✳

Despondent, exhausted, and in constant pain, Sumner decided to remove himself from the stress of the Senate and Washington, D.C., and travel to Europe to restore his health. He remained in Washington only until March 4 to take the oath as senator for his second term, the same day James Buchanan was sworn in as America's fifteenth president. For one of the first times, Sumner mentioned the current state of his health and his own mortality in the same breath. "I may die," he wrote to Theodore Parker, "but if I live a word shall be spoken in the Senate, which shall tear Slavery open from its chops [cheeks or jowls] to its heel."

Three days later, in New York, the forty-six-year-old Sumner boarded the steamship *Fulton* bound for Paris. "With a farewell to my country . . . I give my last thoughts to suffering Kansas," he wrote to a lawyer friend from the *Fulton*'s pilothouse, "that she may be lifted into the enjoyment of freedom and repose."

As it had been for the previous nine months, Charles Sumner's Senate chair was vacant once again.

✷ CHAPTER 19 ✷

THE *DRED SCOTT* DECISION AND TRIAL BY FIRE

Sumner's decision to travel to Europe in March of 1857 to restore his health marked the beginning of a two-and-a-half-year cycle of pain and infirmity, with occasional good days, as he desperately sought to achieve full health.

He would take two lengthy tours of Europe during this period, sandwiched around a frustrating and unproductive return to Washington for a four-month period at the end of 1857 and the beginning of 1858. Often plagued by excruciating pain and deep depression, he sometimes expressed a wish for death to take him.

The European trips certainly brought him some relief: he took immense pleasure from visiting museums, cathedrals, and libraries and dining with the likes of William Thackeray, William Gladstone, and Alexis de Tocqueville. Yet, his "invalid" status, as he so often referred to it—hobbled by back and leg pain, difficulty focusing on daily tasks, an inability to rise from his bed for hours at a time—was with him almost always.

On his initial trip to Paris, the lasting pain from injuries to his back and head were exacerbated by influenza, which laid him low. For ten days, Sumner did not leave his room. The grippe subsided, but the symptoms from the caning persisted. "My whole system is still morbidly sensitive," an exasperated Sumner wrote from Paris on April 23, 1857. "I drag myself along with great difficulty."

Mentally, Sumner could not shake his feelings of foreboding, even during the good physical times. The days he allowed himself to hope were more than offset by despondency. "Sometimes I wish that death would come and close the whole case," he confided to Theodore Parker, after admitting that his pain had been so disabling for several days that he had hardly been able to walk.

✳ ✳ ✳

Just one day before Sumner sailed for Europe, and with no awareness on his part, the Supreme Court handed down a decision that rocked the United States. Coming a little more than nine months after the caning, the *Dred Scott* decision unleashed yet another ferocious firestorm on the slavery issue that swept the land and threatened to scorch, and ultimately lay waste to, any last bit of common ground shared by North and South.

Had he been stateside, Charles Sumner, in pain or not, likely would have railed against the landmark ruling, among the most divisive, confusing, controversial, and sweeping—"far-reaching" is perhaps more accurate—decisions in American history. Not only was it the first instance in which the Supreme Court invalidated a major piece of federal legislation, it was also the court's most noteworthy attempt to settle a seminal national issue—in this case, slavery—through judicial fiat.

But rather than dousing the smoldering slavery debate, as the court had hoped, *Dred Scott* poured gasoline on the controversy.

✳ ✳ ✳

As broad and complex as the Supreme Court's decision was, the facts of *Dred Scott v. John F. A. Sandford* are fairly simple and not in dispute.

Dred Scott was the slave of Dr. John Emerson, an army surgeon who lived in St. Louis, Missouri. In the 1830s, Emerson had taken Scott on tours of duty to Illinois and Wisconsin Territory, regions that had been made free soil by the Missouri Compromise of 1820. In 1838, Emerson returned to Missouri, where he died in 1843, leaving his property—including Scott—to his widow. When she later moved to Massachusetts, Mrs. Emerson transferred ownership of Scott to her brother, John F. A. Sanford (the Supreme Court misspelled Sanford's name in its official citation).

In 1846, Scott sued for his freedom in Missouri state court, arguing that he had become free when the late Emerson had moved him to live in free territory. The legal process at the state court level dragged on for years, with alternative trials and appeals producing judgments for and against Scott, until the Missouri Supreme Court ruled against Scott. Then, with the backing of a group of antislavery lawyers, Scott sued as a citizen of Missouri in federal circuit court. Sanford, in response, argued that because Scott was a Negro, he could not be a citizen of Missouri or the United States and thus was not entitled to sue in federal court. In March 1854, the federal circuit court in Missouri found for Sanford—and Scott's lawyers appealed the case to the U.S. Supreme Court.

✳ ✳ ✳

The high court, led by a pro-Southern majority, including Chief Justice Roger Taney, had three key issues before it: whether Scott was a citizen (only citizens could sue in federal court); whether the time Scott lived on free soil rendered him a free man; and finally, whether prohibiting slavery in parts of the Louisiana Purchase that were governed by the Missouri Compromise of 1820 was constitutional.

On March 6, 1857, around 11:00 A.M., as Charles Sumner's ship was preparing to sail to Europe, Chief Justice Taney and the eight other black-robed judges appeared before a crowded Supreme Court chamber deep within the Capitol to announce Scott's fate.

The aging Taney, who would turn eighty in eleven days, waited for the murmuring to subside, his shaking hands clutching the fifty-five-page decision.

Initially, as spectators and journalists strained to hear Taney's barely audible voice during his two-hour oration, there was confusion among the audience on exactly what the chief justice said and, thus, what the court had decided. But in the coming days, the audacious and far-reaching nature of the decision became clear.

The court ruled that no Negro, slave or free, could be classified as a citizen of the United States, and thus Dred Scott had no right to sue for freedom in a federal court—a right reserved *only* for citizens. Citizenship was derived from the federal government, and it had never belonged to Negroes, who the court said were regarded as "beings of an inferior order and altogether unfit to associate with the white race, either in social or political relations." Despite Scott's lack of legal standing, Taney and the court still ruled on the other issues before it. As to whether Scott's residence on free soil made him free, Taney ruled it did not, arguing that it was Scott's owner who brought him to Illinois and then returned him to Missouri. Therefore, Scott's status "as free or slave, depended on the laws of Missouri, and not of Illinois."

Had Taney stopped there, the Supreme Court's decision might still have elicited howls of protest in the North, but it was the third major component in the case—whether Congress could *prohibit* slavery in territories—that unleashed a firestorm and cries of judicial misconduct and malfeasance from Republicans and other Northerners.

✴ ✴ ✴

In the most stunning part of their ruling, Taney and the Court declared flatly that the Missouri Compromise restriction on slavery north of the 36° 30′ parallel was unconstitutional.

The Fifth Amendment clearly stated that no one could be "deprived of life, liberty, or property without due process of law." Since slaves were considered property, how could Congress prohibit owners from taking slaves into a federal territory? It could not—Congress had no more right to ban slavery in any federal territory than it had the right to deny a territorial population the right to free speech, the right to bear arms, or the right to a jury trial.

With that, Taney made his historic pronouncement: the Missouri Compromise of 1820 was unconstitutional and, therefore, void.

With the ruling, Taney and the Supreme Court had essentially made slavery legal across *any* territory in the United States. And the Court's language stoked Northern fears that the spread of slavery would not stop with the territories. Abraham Lincoln soon warned that a future court ruling, what he called "the next *Dred Scott* decision," could prohibit *states* from banning slavery. In that case, Lincoln said, "we shall lie down, pleasantly dreaming the people of Missouri are on the verge of making their state free; and we shall awake to the reality instead, that the . . . Supreme Court has made *Illinois* a slave state."

✴ ✴ ✴

Dred Scott legitimized and encouraged an expansion of slavery, reeked of partisanship and bitterness, damaged the Supreme Court's reputation for decades, and forever marred the legacy of preeminent Chief Justice Roger Taney.

Lincoln would one day call the court's shocking decision "an astonisher in legal history," and one prominent historian deemed it an example of judicial failure and "the most frequently overturned decision in history."

The North interpreted *Dred Scott* as yet another abuse perpetuated by an out-of-control and belligerent slave power that controlled the federal government apparatus. The South believed the decision validated not just slavery itself but the *constitutionality* of slavery—that because slavery was not prohibited explicitly in the Constitution it was therefore legal, just, and permissible anywhere in the country. Southerners also viewed *Dred Scott* as a moral and legal bulwark that protected its way of life against the increasing encroachment of the North and the radical assaults by ever-emboldened abolitionists.

In essence, Southerners believed that the Supreme Court decision sanctioned the actions Preston Brooks took with his cane against Charles Sumner on May 22, 1856.

✳ ✳ ✳

Dred Scott further polarized North and South and created an uproar that strained the frayed bonds tenuously tying the two sections together. It hobbled the Buchanan presidency from the outset. When coupled with the President's own announcement that he would serve only one term and his subsequent indecisiveness on every major issue he faced, it helped render his administration ineffective at a time when the nation most needed bold and unifying leadership.

But rather than weakening or destroying the Republican Party, as the South had hoped, *Dred Scott* actually strengthened it further in two ways: by fracturing Northern and Southern Democrats—Northerners felt the court had far overstepped its authority—and by encouraging still more citizens to join the Republicans in an effort to stave off slave-power abuses.

While in Europe, Charles Sumner did not comment specifically on *Dred Scott*. But in July he wrote to a friend from London: "The late course of our Govt—particularly its pro-slavery character, has degraded us in the eyes of Europe more even than you are aware."

✳ ✳ ✳

Longing to return to the antislavery fight, Sumner left England and returned to Washington in December 1857 against the advice of friends, who believed he was still not fully recuperated.

On December 19, he took his seat in the Senate, but his back and leg pain, along with persistent exhaustion, prevented him from participating in debates over the controversial admission of Kansas to the United States. He attended sessions in the morning, showed up for votes, but otherwise stayed away from the Capitol; protracted debates and confrontational language—once his stock-in-trade—now filled him with anxiety. "I am unhappy, and yesterday, after sitting in the Senate, I felt like a man of ninety," he wrote to Theodore Parker. "When will this end?"

Simply by being in Washington, close to the scene of his attack, and once again surrounded by the acrimony of the deepening fissure between North and South, Sumner was unable to cope. He felt overwhelmed. When he tried to engage in active work, he became exhausted in minutes.

Depressed, Sumner again left Washington in late December 1857 and was absent often over the next five months, staying with friends in New York and Philadelphia, and occasionally with Longfellow. He would return to the capital several times to vote on questions concerning Kansas and then leave as soon as the vote ended. Outside of Washington, he often felt "entirely well," but acknowledged that once he returned to work, "I am still an invalid."

Sumner continued his commute to and from Washington until April 1858, when he suffered another relapse. His "calamitous illness" left him weak and in great pain. He was wracked with severe back pain, "pressure on my brain," and total exhaustion. He could not rise from his chair or walk without pain, and after a month with no improvement, his doctors advised him to leave Washington. "I grow old, inactive, and the future is dreary," Sumner wrote to Longfellow.

Feeling totally alone, he decided to again visit Europe in another desperate quest to seek restoration. When he sailed on May 22, 1858, exactly two years after he was caned by Preston Brooks, most of his allies and enemies alike believed his Senate career was over.

Sadly, in his immediate future, more pain—this time excruciating, almost unendurable—awaited him.

�֍ ֍ ֍

JULY 1, 1858, PARIS

Alone in his steamy Paris hotel room, Charles Sumner was fearful of the man coming to visit him.

Even though he believed this man, above all others, could make him well again.

"This evening—in an hour—my doctor comes again," he wrote to Samuel Gridley Howe. Then he added: "perhaps to burn me."

Sumner's doctor, the Paris physiologist and neurologist Charles-Édouard Brown-Séquard, specialized in treating diseases of the spine and nervous system. A native of France, he had spent time in the United States on the faculty of the Medical College of Virginia until his strong antislavery positions forced him to leave. Applying an open flame to the skin on Sumner's back, in Brown-Séquard's view, was the American's only hope to get well, the result of a diagnosis the doctor had made on the first day he encountered Sumner.

Without anesthetic—the doctor told Sumner the treatments would be more effective that way—Brown-Séquard applied a flaming compress, or "moxa," made of rolled cotton wool to Sumner's bare skin, burning him up and down his back and neck, tracing the length of his spinal cord with fire.

Brown-Séquard explained that fire was necessary to offset the injury Sumner's spine had suffered from Brooks's caning. The doctor likened the sequence of events leading to Sumner's injuries and pain to trying to drive a nail into hard wood; the blow does not necessarily bend the head of the nail, but the weakest point along the shaft. When Brooks struck with his cane, Sumner's skull protected his brain, but the beating had injured two points along his spinal cord: an upper irritation affected Sumner's brain functions and produced headaches; a lower irritation "caused the pain which gave the appearance of paralysis in his legs." Fire treatments, Brown-Séquard insisted, would "break up" and reduce fluid in the brain and spinal cord, thus easing the pressure on Sumner's back. Pain from the treatments would be enormous, the esteemed surgeon warned, but without them he offered an even more dire prediction—Sumner would remain "a permanent invalid, always subject to a sudden and serious relapse."

Sumner took a liking to Brown-Séquard. His frankness, his professional competence, gave Sumner "such confidence that I put myself at once into his hands." It mattered not that Brown-Séquard had contemporaneous critics. The open-flame treatment was generally considered advanced for the time.

Tonight's visit was Brown-Séquard's sixth in two weeks. After he arrived, with a minimum of small talk, he got to work, applying the flame without hesitation or further conversation. Sweating profusely, gripping the back of a chair for support, Sumner refused to cry out, suffering in silence, until he reached the limit of his pain, gasped, and snapped the chair in half.

Brown-Séquard stopped for a moment. Sumner caught his breath and found a new spot to brace himself, and the surgeon continued his application of the open flame for the next ten minutes. "I have never seen a man bearing with such fortitude as Mr. Sumner has shown," Brown-Séquard marveled at the time.

✳ ✳ ✳

Unsurprisingly Brown-Séquard's "treatment" only led to more misery.

What came next—blisters, sores, open suppurations, wounds, inflammation—was almost as painful as the burning. Sumner spent most of June and July in bed.

"For five weeks, I have not been able to lie on my back or turn over in my bed," Sumner confided to Longfellow in mid-July. His suffering was dreadful and almost unbearable at night. He also feared that the fire had "driven the pain" into one of his legs, which he described as "sadly disabled." Sumner admitted to Samuel Gridley Howe: "I walk with pain; lie down with pain; rise with pain." One Parisian friend was heartbroken when he saw the difficulty Sumner had getting in and out of a carriage, his body bent "almost on all fours . . . struggling and hoping for health with heroic resolution."

In the midst of it all, Sumner began to feel severe chest pains and pressure, like his heart was being squeezed in a vise. The doctors called it angina pectoris, intense pressure and heaviness in the chest, and rather than attributing it to insufficient blood supply to the heart, they concluded that Sumner's discomfort was due to "sympathy between the nerves in the region of the chest and those of the spine."

The attacks continued for a few weeks, occurring four times on some days, and were so severe that Sumner said they made "the fire seem pleasant."

He wondered: "What is life on such terms?"

✳ ✳ ✳

Back home, citizens were growing increasingly impatient with the length of his convalescence; some believed Sumner should resign. Unwilling to step down and unable to return to his duties, Sumner sought to quell calls for his resignation by issuing a public statement from Brown-Séquard and other physicians on the state of his health in November 1858. The doctors agreed that Sumner was "still suffering from the injuries he received more than two-and-a-half years ago." They also considered it "unadvisable for him to return to his public duties during the present winter," but they assured the Massachusetts public that they had "great confidence *that he would surely recover.*"

Sumner's literal trial by fire made for good newspaper copy back in the United States and rekindled North-South debate about just how much the senator was suffering.

Northern, primarily Republican, papers carried detailed accounts of Dr. Brown-Séquard's treatments in an attempt to accomplish several things: stave off Northern voices that suggested Sumner resign (how could they be so heartless while he endured such pain?), put the lie once and for all to the Southern accusation that he was shamming (why would *anyone* subject themselves to such excruciating treatments under false pretenses?), and create what amounted to a second martyrdom for Sumner as a way to remind the country of the long-term and barbaric effects of the caning—and, by association, of slavery.

Southern papers did not focus so much on the "shamming" issue any longer but simply continued to question the veracity of reports about Sumner's health. The *Charleston Courier* questioned whether Brown-Séquard's fire treatments had actually occurred or were a figment of irresponsible journalists' imagination.

Sumner's well-chronicled European trips during 1857 and 1858 lent credence to Southern skepticism about his condition. He ventured to France, England, Scotland, Belgium, Holland, Germany, Austria, Czechoslovakia, Switzerland, and Italy. He attended receptions, lectures, and concerts, visited the countryside in France and Italy, sat through sessions of Parliament, strolled through parks with the archbishop of Canterbury, dined with political and literary luminaries. He rode horseback past shepherds in the snow-capped Pyrenees and walked for miles through the streets of Paris, Rome, Berlin, Marseilles, Florence, Genoa, Dresden, Prague, Pompeii, Turin, Zurich, Nuremberg, Vienna, Verona, and Venice.

With this itinerary, many Southerners scoffed, how serious could his injuries be? Sumner's behavior was indicative of the behavior of *all*

abolitionists, their argument went: cowardly, destructive, and untrust-
worthy.

* * *

The answer to the Southern skepticism requires some speculation, but it
seems clear that Sumner suffered a combination of severe physical and
mental ailments following the caning.

Physically, based on symptoms he recounted and the writings of his
doctors, Sumner almost certainly suffered from a concussion, brain
trauma, and likely brain swelling when Brooks smashed him over his
head repeatedly with his cane. Because of his difficulties walking, and at
times even moving his legs, it also seems likely that he sustained a serious
shock and at least a temporary injury to his spinal cord.

But these alone do not account for Sumner's long absence. The stress,
headaches, and mental anguish that he complained of indicate a form of
psychosomatic infirmity—an affliction close to what modern physicians
label as post-traumatic stress disorder (PTSD). Sumner suffered his worst
pain when he turned his attention to work matters, when he visited, or
got close to, Washington, D.C., or when he took his seat in the Senate
chamber where he was attacked. He relapsed more than once in Washington, and his condition always improved when he left the city. He was
able to tour Europe—hike mountains, swim lakes, walk cities—for long
periods with few if any symptoms, yet he often suffered near-paralyzing
headaches after a single day back in the Senate chamber.

Sumner's friends refused to authorize an autopsy after his death in
1874, so the extent of the physical damage to his brain and spinal cord
was never determined. But in the words of one of Sumner's previous bi-
ographers, "it is clear that the Brooks assault produced psychic wounds
that lingered long after the physical injuries had disappeared."

* * *

The pain Sumner endured convinced him once again of his martyr status, and, by extension, of the ultimate and near-providential righteousness of his antislavery cause; Sumner's suffering in Europe redoubled his
commitment to eradicate slavery in the United States.

At the same time, he took umbrage with Europeans who scoffed at the
U.S. notion that "all men are created equal." When his companions sniffed

with haughty sanctimony about America's shortcomings, he reminded them that most European countries had practiced slavery vigorously up to only a few decades earlier, and even now they were governed, contentedly in most cases, by monarchical and royalty systems that treated ordinary people as "subjects" and not "citizens." Unlike European nations, America's founding documents provided his home country with the legal framework not only to abolish slavery forever but to do something no other country had ever done—ensure equality for all citizens.

If only the political will existed to do so.

By late 1858, while still in his self-imposed exile, Sumner longed more than ever to exert his own political will on his home country. He vowed again that he *would* get better, would return to Washington and reclaim his Senate seat, and would continue his passionate antislavery fight with renewed tenacity.

He drew strength from envisioning how he would deal with slave owners when he returned to Washington. "If health ever returns, I will repay slavery and the whole crew of its supporters [for] every wound, burn . . . ache, pain, trouble, grief which I have suffered," he promised. "*That* vow is registered."

✳ ✳ ✳

By March 1859, Sumner felt better and believed his worst "gloomy hours" had passed. "I am satisfied that I have completely turned the corner," he wrote from Turin, Italy, on May 18. "I can walk and do many things which I could not do 6 weeks ago."

In June, he returned to Paris, where he wrote a letter to Theodore Parker of his plan to return. "In the autumn expect me back well," he pledged, "my long suffering ended—and ready for action."

On November 5, 1859, nearly three and a half years after the caning, Charles Sumner sailed from Liverpool bound for the United States.

"Before me," he wrote, "are [the] *fiercest* battles."

✷ CHAPTER 20 ✷

RETURN FROM EXILE

Martyr or madman? Like so much else in the United States in late 1859, the answer depended on which geographic region was answering the question.

To most Northerners, especially abolitionists, John Brown, who was hanged for treason against the state of Virginia on December 2, engaged in a noble and righteous cause when he led an unsuccessful October raid on the federal arsenal at Harpers Ferry (which would later become part of West Virginia). Brown's goal was to obtain weapons, liberate slaves, and—prosecutors would argue successfully though Brown denied it—ignite a slave uprising that would bring the South to its knees.

Across the North, but in Boston in particular, and among abolitionists most fervently, Brown was hailed as a religious and moral crusader, whose unjust death would fuel a mighty cause. Indeed, even as Brown awaited his hanging and some called for the Virginia governor to reduce his sentence in the name of mercy, many Northerners saw Brown's execution as a benefit to the abolitionist cause. "Let no man pray that Brown be spared!" declared antislavery clergyman Henry Ward Beecher in a widely circulated reprint of a sermon. "Let Virginia make him a martyr!"

On the day of Brown's execution, when thousands gathered in downtown Boston to pay tribute, William Lloyd Garrison said: "Today, Virginia murdered John Brown; tonight, we have witnessed his resurrection."

Southerners were appalled by the Northern reaction. The South cheered no symbolic rebirth, but rather, they celebrated Brown's wounding by U.S. Marines (led by Robert E. Lee), the death of half of his eighteen-man raiding party, Brown's rapid trial, his conviction on multiple counts of conspiracy and first-degree murder (the jury took only forty-five minutes to reach its verdict), and his swift execution. No other results were acceptable or even tolerable. "I want these modern fanatics who have adopted John Brown as their Jesus and their cross to see what their Christ is!" thundered Senator Andrew Johnson of Tennessee as the U.S. Senate was preparing to investigate the Harpers Ferry raid. "This old man, Brown, was nothing more than a murderer, a robber, a thief, and a traitor."

Martyr in the North, madman in the South. John Brown's raid, capture, trial, and execution had set up the most ominous sectional standoff yet. Secessionist fury, expressed first by a small number of Southern fire-eaters after California's admittance as a free state, now fully swept the South, while an ardent desire to end slavery, once and for all, infused the North.

It was into this cauldron that Charles Sumner stepped when he returned to Washington, D.C.

Much had occurred in his absence. Several times during his European trip he confided to friends that he had gone weeks or months without reading a U.S. newspaper; it was important to avoid stressful news as he attempted to "turn the corner" with his health.

Now that he was back in the United States, "as the great hours of history seem to be tolling," Sumner caught up on the events he had missed.

* * *

Sumner had been on his first post-caning trip to Europe and was just beginning his whirlwind tour of the French provinces when America learned of the death of Andrew P. Butler, distinguished senator from South Carolina. Butler died on May 25, 1857, six months shy of his sixty-first birthday, and just over a year after Sumner had made him the object of derision and insults in "The Crime Against Kansas" speech.

Butler's death was not the only event Sumner missed while abroad.

Minnesota and Oregon had been added to the union as free states, disrupting forever the balance between slave and free states. The battle for the soul of Kansas, the event that started Charles Sumner's long and painful ordeal, intensified and came to a head while he was in Europe— "the prairies are on fire," one New York paper declared as proslavery forces in Lecompton attempted to ram through a "slave state" constitution for Kansas. But the Lecompton Constitution was heartily rejected, and Kansas's admission as a free state was on the Senate docket in the spring of 1860 when Sumner finally returned.

And then there were seven epic debates in Illinois. The entire North had been riveted in the summer and fall of 1858 by the intellectual exchanges between wily and ambitious incumbent Stephen Douglas and ascending political talent Abraham Lincoln as the two squared off for one of Illinois's U.S. Senate seats. Through the parched heat of summer and into the autumn chill, on days baked by bright sun or darkened by soaking rain, thousands upon thousands of Illinois residents thronged squares, halls, and fields to hear what one Virginia newspaper called "the great battle of the next Presidential election."

Again and again, the two men staked out their ground—Douglas to argue in favor of "popular sovereignty," the right of people in new territories to decide for themselves on the question of slavery; Lincoln to argue that the Founders had placed slavery on a "course of ultimate extinction" by making no provision for its extension. Thus, new territories and states should be designated as free. Douglas also attacked Lincoln for his famous line uttered prior to the debates that "a house divided against itself cannot stand"—this, Douglas said, was tantamount to a declaration of war against slavery. Lincoln staked out the high ground on slavery when he accused Douglas of "blowing out the moral lights around us by encouraging the extension of slavery."

Ultimately, the Illinois legislature reelected Douglas to the Senate. But the voters' enthusiasm for Lincoln's oratorical brilliance and razor-sharp arguments would have made him the clear favorite if senators were elected by popular vote as they are today. The debates helped Lincoln acquire a nationwide reputation.

By the time Charles Sumner returned to the Senate in December 1859, Abraham Lincoln's name was on the lips of some Republicans as a presidential candidate in the fall 1860 election.

❋ ❋ ❋

Lincoln's emergence was only one instance of massive change that occurred in national politics while Sumner was away.

Douglas clung to his seat in Illinois, but Democrats suffered badly in the 1858 midterm elections anywhere the people voted directly for candidates. Republicans dominated across the North, as voters made their feelings known about slavery at the ballot box.

Republicans picked up twenty-six seats in the U.S. House, regained

power in Ohio and New York, increased their hold on Massachusetts
and New England, won Michigan and Wisconsin, and made substantial
gains in Illinois, Indiana, Pennsylvania, and New Jersey. Democrats also
saw threatening signs in the Senate. They held on to the majority, but Republicans gained six seats. Charles Sumner was now one of twenty-four
Republicans, compared with one of only three members of the old Free
Soil Party when he first entered the Senate.

In short, the 1858 midterm election was a political revolution, a threat
to slavery and Southern dominance, a triumph of Republicanism that
set the stage for the presidential election two years away. President Buchanan knew that he and the Southern Democrats had been trounced.
He dined with friends as election results came into the White House
and wrote afterward: "We had a merry time of it, laughing among other
things at our crushing defeat. It is so great that it is almost absurd."

All these events occurred while Sumner was out of the country, but
certainly not out of mind. Now physically recovered and mentally strong,
he was encouraged by Republican prospects and more confident than
ever that slavery, inherently evil and destructive to any civilized nation's
fortunes, must be eradicated.

After four years of silence, Charles Sumner felt compelled to deliver
this message to the nation—loud and clear and, as always, without regard
to consequences.

❆ ❆ ❆

Never in the history of the U.S. Congress had a speech been delivered
like the one Sumner envisioned—one calling for the total excoriation,
denunciation, and abolition of slavery everywhere within the country's
borders, the only position any righteous man *could* hold in the "solemn
battle between right and wrong, between good and evil."

Yet, when he began to gather material for the speech in early 1860,
virtually no one wanted to hear it—the South because their contempt for
Sumner had only become more deep-seated since his return; the North,
and especially Northern Republicans, because they had their eyes on the
White House in 1860 and were about to nominate their presidential candidate. In a familiar story, they did not want Sumner saying anything that
would alienate moderates, especially this early in the process, or provide
Democrats and their nominee, Stephen Douglas, with an opening that

might unify Northern and Southern Democrats. A divided Democratic Party was exactly what Republicans wanted.

The situation was made worse when it became clear to Sumner that, in addition to the generally poisoned atmosphere in Washington, Southern hostility toward him personally continued unabated. Some Virginians talked openly of kidnapping him. Another Southern letter writer warned him that he was "spoiling for another licking" and told Sumner not to harbor any illusion of safety by betting that Southerners would refrain from attacking him again for fear of Northern reprisals. "If giving you *another pummeling* will be the means of bringing it about, then here gos [*sic*] it," one letter writer warned.

A discouraged Sumner wrote of the nation's capital city: "This is a barbarous place. The slave-masters seem to me more than ever barbarians—in manner, conversation, speeches, conduct, principles, *life*."

He also fretted about his uncertain role in the Republican Party, especially after leaders begged him to restrain his antislavery rhetoric until after they nominated their presidential candidate. Party managers all but ignored him during the early months of 1860. Sumner again felt like an outcast in his own party, a party he had essentially built based on core antislavery beliefs that he had articulated for years. "Nobody writes to me now & I feel solitary enough here," he confided to Samuel Gridley Howe in late April. But even Howe believed Sumner's uncompromising views against slavery were "too full of fight" for the current time and recommended that he tone down his public utterances. Others urged him to refrain from taunting his Southern tormentors and further inflaming tempers. "You have floored those dirty fellows," pointed out one letter writer, "I would not stop to piss on them while they are down."

Ultimately, Sumner agreed to remain quiet, at least until Republicans nominated their presidential candidate.

But the decision gnawed at him.

✳ ✳ ✳

It was precisely *because* the Republicans had a good chance to triumph in November that Sumner wanted to speak.

Winning the election became less of a concern for him than convincing his party to remain faithful to its founding principles. Success had clouded the good judgment of many men, and Sumner sought to prevent the seductive lure of national power from obscuring the clarity of the Republicans' core vision: the abolition of slavery. He alternated between anger and despondency at admonitions to stand down or temper his rhetoric—he wanted Republicans to use "the whole arsenal of God" to renounce slavery, including "arguments, sarcasm, scorn, and denunciation."

In May, Republicans nominated Abraham Lincoln for president at their convention in Chicago. Despite Lincoln's rising popularity, Sumner and other party leaders felt that the nod would go to the more experienced Senator William H. Seward. Nonetheless, Sumner wrote, he believed Lincoln was a "good honest anti-slavery man," and while inexperienced on the inner workings of government or Washington, "those who know him speak of him as a person of positive ability, and of real goodness."

He added: "We think he will be the next President."

With Lincoln's nomination, Sumner no longer felt shackled by his promise to Republican leaders to remain silent on the slavery issue. And the speech he was contemplating would *benefit* Lincoln, not harm him.

His time finally arrived in June 1860, two weeks after Lincoln's nomination, when the Senate took up a bill seeking, at long last, to admit Kansas to the United States as a free state.

It was not lost on Sumner that the issue that had led to his beating four years earlier and his suffering since now provided him with the impetus to emerge from exile with glory.

✳ CHAPTER 21 ✳

"THE BARBARISM OF SLAVERY"

An eerie combination of déjà vu and nervous anticipation gripped the Senate chamber when Charles Sumner entered a few minutes before noon on Monday, June 4, 1860.

His gait was slower, his long dark hair speckled with more gray, and his face fleshier than most remembered; but at age forty-nine, he stood as tall as ever, and his broad forehead, piercing dark eyes, patrician nose, and proud bearing projected the aura of a serious statesman.

He was resplendent in formal dress, including white gloves—one observer would say later that he glistened with the sheen of nobility. He clutched a sheaf of galley proofs that contained the thirty-five-thousand-word text of a speech he entitled "The Barbarism of Slavery."

Washington, D.C., had been abuzz in anticipation of this moment. The Senate galleries were almost full, though not as shoulder-to-shoulder jammed as they had been four years earlier for the "Crime Against Kansas" oration. Curiosity abounded—inside the chamber and across the city, people mulled and mused about the speech to come.

Would Sumner have the physical strength to engage in one of his patented lengthy and impassioned orations? Would he mention his own beating and his struggle to recover? Would he refer to his deceased assailant, Preston Brooks, or Brooks's second cousin, the late Senator Andrew P. Butler? Would he moderate his position on slavery at all given the concerns expressed by Republican Party leaders? Would he speak for himself only, or for Abraham Lincoln and the Republicans in general?

And the most titillating question of all—how would Southerners respond?

✳ ✳ ✳

The Senate chamber, on this Monday in June 1860, was transformed into Charles Sumner's theater.

His fellow senators, while important, were not his primary audience. All of them, Sumner believed, even his allies, were, to one degree or another, mired in political quicksand and thus incapable of recognizing the transcendent debate before them—between slavery and freedom—a debate that should not, *must not*, be tempered, diluted, or abandoned, regardless of politics or policy considerations.

Nor was his primary audience the visitors to the Capitol. Most were here for the spectacle of Sumner's return, and perhaps an unspoken desire to witness a recurrence of the drama and violence of four years earlier.

As Sumner rose to speak, uppermost in his mind were the millions of Americans, especially Northerners—but many in the South and West, too—who would read his printed speech in the coming days; and the historians, also, who would dissect his words and ideas in the years to follow. He was about to deliver an unprecedented and all-out assault against American slavery, party and politics be damned. He believed that all but hardened slave owners trusted his instincts on the most compelling issue the country now faced, or had *ever* faced.

With so much at stake, he believed in his heart that the people would follow him.

✳ ✳ ✳

It is not merely that Charles Sumner refused to give an inch of ground during his four-hour address—though he certainly did not—but that he broke unplowed ground in the annals of American antislavery oration.

Reading from printed galleys because he thought memorizing the speech, as he usually did, would prove too taxing, Sumner unleashed his full rhetorical arsenal. When it came to the subject of slavery, the twin political staples of conciliation and compromise were simply foreign notions to him; he had never backed down or wavered, and he did not start now.

He answered one question on everyone's mind quickly: How much emphasis would he give the Brooks assault? The answer: aside from one fleeting reference, none.

Almost without preliminary, Sumner launched into a searing indictment of slavery and slave owners, a polemic unsparing in forcefulness and tone, virtually every sentence and paragraph clubbing into submission the South's proslavery arguments. He chastised the men who profiteered from the shackled misery of other men and berated the Southern economic system that perpetuated such an injustice.

Senate Republicans listened intently, if warily. Southern Democrats walked around, grumbled loudly, pretended to read newspapers, ridiculed him, and left the chamber in disgust.

None of it fazed Sumner.

His language, at once stinging and eloquent, roiled the chamber with a turbulence that had been missing while his chair remained vacant.

He summoned all the passion of the powerful Massachusetts abolitionist movement, of which he served, in practical terms if not by formal title, as a standard-bearer and champion on a national level. He invoked religious themes as never before, referring to slavery as a violation "*against the eternal law of God*." Between slavery and freedom, he declared, there was an "essential incompatibility—if you are for one, you can not be for the other—the embrace of Slavery is the divorce from Civilization."

In fact, a slave society was no civilization at all. Far from it, Sumner declared. Slavery was "barbarous *wherever it shows itself*, Slavery must breed Barbarians!" The insidious, evil nature of Southern slavery was contained in the devilish laws that governed the institution. Think of the contradiction by which the South governed itself, Sumner declared: a Southern Negro might be "marked like a hog, branded like a mule, yoked like an ox, maimed like a cur, and constantly beaten like a brute, *all according to law*."

How could such a system be just in the eyes of God? Or in the eyes of man?

✳ ✳ ✳

Sumner's arguments transcended the religious and moral; the practical consequences of slavery, too, were debilitating and destructive to any society.

In relentless statistical detail—a shift from his usual lyrical and emotional rhetoric—Sumner compared the populations of North and South. He concluded that slavery had "stunted" economic and educational progress in the South, and it was likely not a coincidence that he singled out South Carolina to prove his thesis, pointing out that a smaller percentage of its white population than of Massachusetts' free

Negroes attended school. And in what could only be a sign of mental deficiencies among Southern slave owners in general, they seemed not only to accept their backward situation but to flaunt it and "go to any lengths to protect it."

Sumner also dashed the Southern argument that slavery was protected by the Constitution—this long-standing Southern canard was so unfounded as to border on the delusional. The Constitution, Sumner said, contained "not one sentence, phrase, word—not a *single suggestion, hint, or equivocation, even*," to justify Southern claims. The Constitution's true purpose and principle, he insisted in an argument he had made his whole adult life, was to render "Freedom *national* and Slavery *sectional*"—to establish "the laws of impartial Freedom without distinction to color or race."

Boiled down to its essence, Sumner's argument rested on three fundamental principles:

Slavery was inherently evil, and thus forbidden under God's law.

Slavery was given no explicit life within the language of the Declaration of Independence or the Constitution, and thus had no legal basis to exist under U.S. law.

Slavery was detrimental to societal progress, and it crushed ambition, economies, the arts, and the human spirit.

Immoral to its core, illegal by any definition, poisonous to the human condition—taken together, these constituted Sumner's "barbarism of slavery."

By the time a drained and weary, albeit triumphant, Sumner concluded his speech, his Senate colleagues, North and South, had borne witness to a simple fact: during his lengthy absence, the outspoken senator from Massachusetts had lost neither his antislavery zeal nor his ability to infuriate his opponents.

✳ ✳ ✳

As Sumner returned to his seat, South Carolina senator James Chesnut rose and responded only briefly:

"After ranging over Europe . . . craving pity, and reaping a harvest of contempt, this slanderer of states and men has reappeared in the Senate." Explaining why Southern senators had listened quietly to Sumner's scathing speech (though many had not), Chesnut said he had hoped the

Massachusetts senator, "after the punishment he had received [the Brooks caning] for his insolence," would have learned propriety and manners.

Unflappable, Sumner replied that he planned to print Chesnut's remarks in an appendix to his speech, both to ensure that the record was complete and to dramatically illustrate the barbarism he had just recounted.

Charles Sumner had taken on the entire sweep of slavery, had indicted and repudiated the entire system of human servitude in the American South. He dismantled its framework and, in the process, impugned the morality of the entire slaveocracy and, by extension, the entire region.

Sumner was the first member of Congress to do so with such thoroughness, such religious fervor, such boldness, such eloquence, and such utter unconcern for any political consequences—from either friend or foe.

He would also be the last. "The Barbarism of Slavery" was the final major congressional antislavery speech in American history.

In less than a year, the slavery debate would change venues once and for all—shifting from speeches in the halls of Congress to screams and war cries on blood-soaked battlefields.

* * *

Sumner's political allies again feared for his safety.

From the moment he vacated the Senate chamber after "The Barbarism of Slavery" speech, his friends insisted that he submit to guards and escorts whenever possible. Fellow Massachusetts lawmakers Henry Wilson and Anson Burlingame, both armed, accompanied him on the one-mile walk to his lodging immediately after the speech.

In Washington, D.C., barrooms and hotel parlors, Southerners conspired to commit additional violence against Sumner for his explosive and heretical words about slavery; across the South, the speech generated fresh fury.

Four days after the speech, a drunken Virginia slave owner banged against the door and forced his way into Sumner's room. A startled Sumner was alone in his quarters, and the man, though he brandished no weapon, began shouting that he was one of four men from Virginia who would hold Sumner accountable for his insulting speech. "Leave now!" Sumner ordered, surprised when the man seemed to listen to him and retreated toward the door. "I'll be back with my friends—we will get our revenge," the Virginian shouted as he bolted from the room.

A nervous Sumner sent for Henry Wilson, who immediately came to sit with him. At nine o'clock that same night, three other men came to Sumner's door but declined to enter when they learned he was not alone. They vowed they would return in the morning for a "private interview" with Sumner, and if they could not have it, they would cut his "damned throat" before the next night. Faced with a genuine threat, Sumner's friends agreed that he should not spend the night alone, despite his ve-hement protests that he needed no additional protection. Burlingame and another congressman, John Sherman, slept in the front room that opened into Sumner's bedroom.

The Virginians who threatened to cut Sumner's throat did not return the next morning.

As word of the violent threats against Sumner made their way north, they prompted offers of assistance. On June 9, his friend Edward Pierce wrote from Boston: "We have just heard of the threat of violence made to you last evening. Be careful, *very* careful." A military veteran from Dux-bury, Massachusetts, assured Sumner: "I am ready to shoulder my musket and march to the Capitol [to protect you]." Fearing for Sumner's safety, his secretary, A. B. Johnson, arranged for protection in Sumner's quarters at night and designated a series of armed escorts to follow Sumner— revolvers in hand—as he walked to and from the Capitol. Many of these armed bodyguards were citizens of Kansas, who had visited Washing-ton for the debate on statehood. They volunteered to guard Sumner in thanks for his unwavering efforts on their behalf.

Save for the occasional angry words, no additional violence occurred. Those Southern slaveholders who might have been inclined to organize something more concrete than a drunken break-in at the senator's lodg-ing were already focused on more elaborate plans, ones that Sumner's speech would no doubt help advance:

Secession and rebellion.

✳ ✳ ✳

If Sumner's great antislavery speech elicited raw hatred from his enemies, it also drew initial criticism from his political and journalistic friends.

At best, his stirring oration received a tepid response from Republican leaders in the North, who sought to distance the party from the controversial senator.

Things had changed since 1856, when Sumner's beating provided the incentive and ammunition for the meteoric growth of the Republican Party. And while John C. Frémont's showing was impressive four years earlier, he still had not won. With Lincoln's nomination, and a real shot at the presidency, Republican strategists continued to fear that Sumner's remarks would alienate moderate voters. Most concurred with Iowa senator James W. Grimes, who concluded that Sumner's speech "sounded harsh, vindictive, and slightly brutal. His speech has done Republicans *no good*." When Sumner sent a copy of the speech to Abraham Lincoln, expressing his "earnest hope that what I said may help our great cause," Lincoln—a cagey politician—replied a week later with his best noncommittal response. He had yet to read the speech, but he "anticipate[d] both pleasure and instruction from it," he wrote to Sumner.

Sumner deeply resented the "cold shoulderism and heartlessness" with which fellow antislavery Republicans responded to his speech. With all he had been through, had he not earned their respect? He was accustomed to standing tall, to making himself a target, to absorbing slings and arrows from many quarters. By now, though, he felt he didn't deserve to endure the attacks alone. He deserved better.

During his convalescence, despite his struggles, Sumner had developed an even stronger belief in the righteousness of his cause. Far from regretting or apologizing for "The Barbarism of Slavery," he declared that "*I would make it again*."

"*That* speech," he predicted, "will yet be adopted by the Republican Party."

✳ ✳ ✳

He was correct.

The political operatives, the journalists, the party elite—all of them lagged well behind the people. Again, as in 1856, members of the general public became Sumner's earliest and strongest allies.

In general, Sumner lacked sharp political instincts, and his own self-centeredness often prevented him from understanding what truly lay in the hearts of his fellow citizens. But in this case, he had channeled thousands of Northerners. In expressing his ideas about slavery, he had expressed theirs.

Now they repaid him for their own evolution. Hundreds of letters poured into Sumner's post from ordinary men and women in the North—an astounding 450 letters in the first 30 days after the speech, more than he ever received before—virtually all supportive of him, a groundswell that buoyed his spirit and reinforced his resolve.

The people wrote with fervor and pathos and a single mind. They expressed their profound satisfaction with Sumner's speech and concluded it was his best ever; they read it aloud at the family tables or in front of hearths. They urged him to ignore Republican leaders who took pains to avoid confronting head-on the evils of slavery for the sake of political expediency and expressed their immense satisfaction that Sumner was again speaking "with full vigor and unterrified spirit" from his Senate pulpit. His view was the populist view.

Sumner grasped that he was now—eleven years after his first speech on slavery's evils—the country's strongest and most eloquent antislavery champion.

So he stayed on the offensive during the critical and profound summer and fall campaign season of 1860.

✷ CHAPTER 22 ✷

LINCOLN'S ELECTION AND SOUTHERN SECESSION

The people could not get enough of Sumner.

And so after the congressional session ended on June 28, 1860, Sumner spent his time addressing one Republican rally after another. He wrote letters condemning slavery and urging support for Republican candidates. He told voters the choice in November was between Northern civilization and Southern barbarism, between the ideas of John Quincy Adams and John C. Calhoun—between "the glorious Pilgrim ship, *Mayflower*, and the first slave ship, with its fetters, its chains, its bludgeons, and its whips . . . choose, ye, fellow-citizens between the two."

In one extraordinary demonstration for Sumner and his "Barbarism of Slavery" speech, more than three thousand cheering supporters jammed the Cooper Institute in New York City on the evening of July 11 to hear his remarks, one of the largest crowds ever to assemble at that location.

Sumner received thunderous applause when he appeared on the rostrum. He spoke for two hours, keeping the audience spellbound. In his remarks, entitled "The Origin, Necessity, and Permanence of the Republican Party," he reiterated the themes he espoused in "The Barbarism of Slavery" and added political sections on the importance of supporting the Republican ticket in the upcoming fall elections. The Republicans, he stressed, were the party of the Constitution, America's cherished founding document, which slave owners were trying to co-opt to suit their devious agenda.

The Founders would be appalled to learn that the Constitution, "from which they had carefully excluded every *word* [of slavery], would be held, in defiance of reason and common sense, to protect the *thing*" that most statesmen found offensive even seven decades earlier.

The crowd erupted.

✴ ✴ ✴

The New York appearance was Sumner's first before a live audience, outside of Congress, since his beating, and the crowd responded as though
he were a conquering hero.

They knew how long he had suffered and admired the fact that neither
his pain nor fear of retribution had compromised his principles.

Newspapers printed his New York remarks in their entirety, and the
Young Men's Republican Union distributed more than fifty thousand
copies of a pamphlet edition. The speech was circulated as far away as
California, where the Republican committee published another ten
thousand copies in pamphlet form. Mentally and physically, Sumner's
latest speeches were an elixir.

"I feel at last *completely restored*," he exclaimed to a friend.

Republican leaders began to fall in line. Those who shied away in June
now enthusiastically sought his support—in an astonishing about-face,
congressional Republicans now circulated the "Barbarism of Slavery"
speech as a campaign document.

From New York, Illinois, Ohio, New Jersey, and Maine, Sumner received
invitations to speak and stump for candidates. Despite his newfound popularity, Sumner refused to campaign outside of Massachusetts, believing he
needed to stay close to home to reassert his leadership among state Republicans.

Still, his clear and strong voice carried throughout the North. He
urged Northern voters not to be cowed by Southern threats to secede if
Republicans were successful in November. He reminded voters that the
Deep South slaveholding states had threatened secession again and again
since the nation's founding: during discussions of the Constitution,
the Missouri Compromise, the Nullification Acts in South Carolina, and
the Compromise of 1850.

The time had come for Republicans to draw their own line in the sand,
to call the Southerners' bluff and stand fast for the antislavery principles
upon which the party was founded.

Republicans' first duty, Sumner stressed, was to "stand straight" and
refuse to wilt under threats of disunion.

Sumner concluded one of his Massachusetts campaign speeches with an exhortation that once again brought an adoring crowd to its feet: "Let people cry 'Disunion.' We know what the cry means, and we answer back—The Union shall be preserved, and made more precious, by its consecration to Freedom."

✳ ✳ ✳

The ideas Sumner promulgated, the arguments he crafted, the language he employed, and the example he set formed the basis not only for the strong antislavery platform the Republicans adopted but also for Lincoln's ongoing evolution on the slavery question, and for the antislavery view that caught fire throughout the North leading up to the pivotal 1860 election and beyond.

His refusal to retreat from his principles for the sake of any short-term political gain, a rarity among elected officials, awakened and catalyzed a renewed sense of antislavery enthusiasm in the North. And the fact that he saw the Declaration of Independence and the Constitution as foundational for—not detrimental to—the antislavery cause made him more attractive to Northerners than those abolitionists who believed the founding documents were unsalvageable and needed to be scrapped for the country to move on from slavery.

Lincoln and Sumner were like-minded on this issue, and Lincoln would eventually express these sentiments in the Gettysburg Address; but they were ideas Sumner had initially formulated and expressed, and then reiterated for years.

✳ ✳ ✳

Sumner delivered his final campaign speech on November 5, 1860, the eve of the presidential election. Before several hundred citizens at Boston's Faneuil Hall, Sumner anticipated a Republican victory but declared that the magnitude of the next day's election could not be overstated. "Tomorrow we shall have not only a new President, but a new government," he predicted. "A new order of things will begin, and our history will proceed on a grander scale."

But even as he made his upbeat public comments, his newfound optimism was tempered with a sense of trepidation, perhaps even foreboding, emotions that often took up residence in Sumner's mind when things seemed to be going too well. A few days earlier he wrote a letter in which his excitement about a possible Lincoln election was mixed with his predictions of a harsher reality. "Lincoln will be chosen," he asserted. "Then, however, will commence a new class of perils and anxieties . . . I shall prepare myself in advance for many disappointments."

✻ ✻ ✻

Sumner was right about both Lincoln's election and the perils that followed.

In what historians would one day come to call the most important and pivotal presidential election in American history, Abraham Lincoln won the presidency in 1860 without earning a single Southern electoral vote. He carried no slave states, and in ten Southern states, not a single ballot was distributed for Lincoln (parties distributed ballots on behalf of candidates prior to the secret ballot that emerged in the 1880s). Indeed, more people voted against Lincoln than for him, but in the four-person race, Lincoln's 40 percent of the overall popular vote (54 percent of the Northern popular vote) and 180 electoral votes proved more than enough. On the surface, at least, it was a less-than-rousing mandate for a man who, generations later, would be acclaimed as one of America's greatest presidents.

But the larger reality was encouraging. In only their second national election, Republicans had captured the Executive Mansion and established themselves as the most powerful party in the nation. Speaking to a crowd in Concord, Massachusetts, on the evening after the election, Charles Sumner called the Republican win "a victory not of the cartridge-box, but of the *ballot* box." Reverberations of Lincoln's election would be felt and "heard around the world." In the weeks following, Sumner, of all people, urged moderation and humility among Republicans; gloating would not help Republicans accomplish their goals. Their mission now was to stand fast by their principles—"they are of living rock, and no power can prevail against them"—never surrender to a threat of disunion, and trust the instincts of Abraham Lincoln.

Sumner was convinced that Lincoln would take up the Republican antislavery cause, backed by the Constitution, and speak loudly that "the Union *shall be preserved* and made more precious by a consecration to Human Rights."

✳ ✳ ✳

But speaking would not make it so.

Following Lincoln's election, the union that Sumner loved so dearly began to unravel with lightning speed.

Hysteria over Lincoln's election gripped the Deep South. Most Southern planters saw Lincoln's victory, propelled by his antislavery views and the support of abolitionists, as an invitation for their slaves to rise up, for Northern assassins to storm Southern communities and kill slave owners, for bands of Northern abolitionists to overrun and confiscate Southern plantations. There was only one "deliverance from this great danger," Mississippi governor John J. Pettus declared, and that was the "reserved right of the states to withdraw from injury and oppression."

Southern states set up secession conventions and appointed secessionist commissioners to visit every slave state. In December, as South Carolina was awaiting its own secessionist convention, the state's two U.S. senators resigned their seats in Congress, and the legislature prepared to arm a defense force of ten thousand men. In an analogy Sumner and Bostonians recognized well, the *Charleston Mercury* proclaimed: "The tea has been thrown overboard; the revolution of 1860 has been initiated."

Sumner, who, along with many Northern Republicans, misjudged the South's burning desire to secede, quickly recognized his error in a letter to Longfellow in early December: "S.C. will go out," he predicted, "then Alab & Missip; the great question is, can Georgia be saved? Some say yes; others say no."

He added: "Then, if all these go, where will the contagion stop?"

Some Northerners, especially those in Sumner's home state, suddenly became skittish with the Republicans' intractable antislavery position. Distinguished orator Edward Everett blamed the Republicans and their abolitionist supporters for pushing the country to the brink of a "final catastrophe." More than twenty thousand Massachusetts Unionists signed a petition favoring a compromise on slavery and slavery expansion and delivered it to Congress.

Sumner dismissed it as "all wind" and ventured that it was far too late for compromise.

✳ ✳ ✳

And it was. On December 20, 1860, South Carolina—once home to Preston Brooks, Andrew Butler, and the estimable John C. Calhoun—became the first state to secede from the union.

Meeting in Charleston, secession convention delegates submitted the ordinance to dissolve the union shortly after 1:00 P.M.—by 1:30, all 169 members had voted "yes." Church bells pealed, business activity ceased in celebration, whooping and cheering took place throughout the city. Later that night, in a more somber event, South Carolina officials signed the Ordinance of Secession, declaring that the former state was now "an Independent Commonwealth." South Carolina secession convention delegates also endorsed the idea of appointing commissioners—sometimes referred to as "apostles of disunion"—to travel to other states to discuss secession strategy and the formation of a new confederacy.

Charles Sumner acknowledged that Lincoln's election had been followed by the "menaced storm," and that "it is clear that the South is more in earnest than ever before." Despite his own genuine desire to see the nation remain intact, Sumner refused to consider any compromise on the slavery question. When union-loving Kentucky senator John J. Crittenden, Henry Clay's successor, proposed a compromise to stave off further secession (including an irrevocable constitutional amendment that would guarantee slavery in *all* current or future territories below the 36° 30′ latitude), Sumner was appalled.

And when a group of Massachusetts businesses submitted petitions calling for compromise, Sumner urged state lawmakers to stay strong in opposition. "Pray," Sumner pleaded with Governor John Andrew. "Keep Massachusetts sound and firm—FIRM—FIRM—against every word or step of concession." When outgoing President Buchanan urged Sumner to persuade Massachusetts to adopt the Crittenden proposition, Sumner replied that the Commonwealth's people "would see their state sink below the sea and become a sandbank before they would adopt those propositions that acknowledge property in man." His home state was an example that other states would look to—"if Massachusetts yields anything now to the outcry of the traitors, other states will yield everything," he said.

If the choice was between concession and secession, and it appeared it was, Sumner would take his chances with the latter.

"I fear nothing now *but* compromise," he wrote.

✳ ✳ ✳

And yet, for weeks in late 1860 and early 1861, Congress tried unsuccessfully to hammer out various "peace" compromises—it was far too late. In January, five more Southern states followed South Carolina out of the union: Mississippi, Florida, Alabama, Georgia, and Louisiana. Texas voted to secede on February 1. "Madness rules the hour—among our Southern friends," Sumner wrote to Dorothea Dix. "I think the contagion will spread through all the states South of M[ason] & D[ixon] line."

On February 4, representatives of the seven seceded states gathered in Montgomery, Alabama, to form the provisional government of the Confederate States of America (CSA). In the words of one historian, while President-elect Lincoln was constructing his cabinet, "the country was falling to pieces."

Some moderate congressional Republicans, desperate to keep the union together, debated admitting New Mexico as a slave state to appease the South, a move Sumner deemed "a fatal, dismal mistake." Such a move would split the party just as it had ascended to power on an unshakable antislavery platform. "Nothing is gained by it," he said. "But everything is lost—our principles—the cause for which we have contended."

Attempting to placate the South at this late hour, especially by surrendering principles, was tantamount to succumbing to extortion. It meant that every future presidential election would be conducted with the defeated party threatening secession.

✳ ✳ ✳

Sumner stood resolute against all attempts at compromise on the slavery issue.

Blessed as he believed the union was, he could not justify or countenance any political agreement that extended or perpetuated the evils of slavery, or widened its sphere in even a temporary way. Sumner did not deceive himself; he was aware of the potential consequences if there were no compromise. He detested violence almost as much as he detested slavery. "Much as I desire the extinction of slavery, I do not wish to see it go down in blood," he said.

But he was astute enough to know that prolonged civil war was all but inevitable. "The existing hallucination of the slave-masters is such that I doubt if this calamity can be avoided," he wrote. "They seem to rush to their destiny." His view differed from some unrealistic Republicans who predicted that even if war did occur, it would last only two or three months—he knew that the South would fight long and hard to preserve slavery.

So be it. If a climactic, existential clash was required to end slavery and preserve the soul of the country, then the North must fight, the Republicans must fight, and *he* must fight.

In his view, the time for compromise was long past. "*No, No, No,* let the North cry out to every compromiser and to every retreat," Sumner underscored.

"*The question is to be settled now.*"

✳ CHAPTER 23 ✳

"AT LAST THE WAR HAS COME"

As Inauguration Day approached, President-elect Abraham Lincoln slipped into Washington aboard a secret overnight train, acting on the advice of bodyguard Allan Pinkerton, who feared for Lincoln's life.

On Saturday, February 23, 1861, the day after Lincoln's arrival, news spread through the nation's capital that Lincoln had arrived almost ten hours earlier than expected, and in disguise, to foil an assassination plot hatched against him in Baltimore, Maryland, by proslavery and pro-Confederacy agitators.

The Southern press responded by calling Lincoln a coward, and even Northern papers, while generally kinder, labeled his decision to sneak into Washington as less than dignified. But one of the more sympathetic responses to Lincoln's decision came from abolitionist and former slave Frederick Douglass, who wrote a column comparing Lincoln's midnight train ride to the plight of runaway slaves trying to flee bondage. Did Lincoln's evasive tactics to avoid assassination appear cowardly on the surface? Perhaps, Douglass said. But ultimately, his efforts to avoid "slave-holding assassins" showed "the merit of wisdom, forethought, and discretion."

Lincoln would need all of those qualities as he entered the maelstrom that engulfed Washington and the nation.

✳ ✳ ✳

Sumner, too, did not envy Lincoln for what lay ahead, and he was curious at how the Midwesterner would respond to the secession crisis. On the day after Lincoln reached the capital, Sumner called on him in his room at Willard's Hotel. It was the first meeting between the two men, and despite their similar views on the slavery question, their differences were immediately apparent. Sumner was stiff and formal, and Lincoln's Midwest folksiness and homespun expressions threw him off balance.

Lincoln's humor also baffled Sumner. At one point in their meeting, Lincoln, impressed by Sumner's height, suggested the two "measure backs" to decide who was the taller. A perplexed and unamused Sumner replied with his characteristic stiffness that now was "the time for uniting our *fronts* against the enemy and not our backs." Sumner later told a friend that he "could not get rid of his misgivings as to how this seemingly untutored child of nature would master the tremendous task before him." He came away with mixed feelings, at once "greatly amazed" to find Lincoln lacking in the social poise and sophistication associated with being president but also impressed that he demonstrated "extraordinary flashes of thought and bursts of illuminating expression."

Sumner was not alone in his assessment of the new President-elect. Even as many would underestimate him in the coming days and weeks, almost all saw something that set Lincoln apart as a leader. Republican congressman Charles Francis Adams, Sr., of Massachusetts, who called on Lincoln on the same day as Sumner, went away feeling that this "tall, illformed man, with little in the way of grace of manner or polish of appearance," nonetheless possessed a "plain, goodnatured, frank expression which rather attracts one to him."

For his part, Lincoln sized up Sumner's formal and perhaps pretentious demeanor at their first meeting in remarks he supposedly made to a newspaper reporter: "I have never had much to do with bishops where I live, but, do you know, Sumner is my idea of a bishop."

✳ ✳ ✳

On March 4, 1861, a raw and windy day, Charles Sumner was in high spirits as he witnessed the swearing-in of the nation's first Republican president.

During his inaugural address, Abraham Lincoln tried to reassure the South that "their property, their peace, and their personal security" would not be jeopardized by a Republican administration. But he also issued a warning that: "No State, upon its own mere motion, can lawfully get out of the Union . . . and that acts of violence . . . against the authority of the United States are insurrectionary or revolutionary, according to circumstances."

Lincoln was hopeful that the country could settle its differences without violence. He emphasized that the North and South were "friends, not enemies . . . though passion may have strained, it must not break our bonds of affection." In his memorable inaugural close, Lincoln predicted that the "mystic chords of memory . . . will yet swell to the chorus of the Union, when again touched . . . by the better angels of our nature."

But Lincoln was wrong.

The better angels no longer exerted influence in the North or the South—nor would they for years to come.

✳ ✳ ✳

Sumner was ecstatic that Lincoln's inauguration was not interrupted by Southern agitators, and even more jubilant that the new President proposed no compromises to the South. Encountering a friend on his walk home from the Capitol, he offered that Lincoln's inaugural address "seems to be best described by Napoleon's simile of 'a hand of iron in a velvet glove.'"

Four days after Lincoln's inauguration, Sumner was selected by his colleagues as chairman of the influential Senate Committee on Foreign Relations, a position he would soon make more powerful than ambassadors or even most secretaries of state.

Yet, over the next week, Sumner's upbeat mood was tempered by the push and pull of patronage and politics that affect all new administrations; people came to him regularly in search of government jobs. "I am tired, sick & unhappy," he wrote to Longfellow late on a mid-March night. "My rooms are full from early morning till midnight, with debaters about 'office'—and the larger part go away discontented & . . . hostile." He also expressed frustration with Lincoln's efforts to deal with patronage-hungry constituents, claiming that the new President's effort to make everyone happy "fritters away his valuable time."

Sumner was convinced that a breakup of the union was imminent—"things were never worse than now"—and he believed that the inexperience of Lincoln and his cabinet prevented them from recognizing the seriousness of the situation. "[New York senator] Seward is infatuated," he exclaimed to John Jay. "He says in 60 days all will be well!"

Fifteen days after Sumner penned those words, it became clear to Seward—as well as the North, the South, and the world—that all was definitely not well.

✳ ✳ ✳

On April 12, 1861, at 4:30 A.M., the sky over Fort Sumter in Charleston Harbor exploded with bursts of cannon fire, signaling the dreadful and by now inevitable moment when America split asunder.

The Civil War had begun.

Tensions had been building for a month between the seceded and now independent Commonwealth of South Carolina and the United States, and they finally led to the attack on the federal garrison stationed at Sumter. Major Robert Anderson, a Kentuckian and former slave owner, commanded the federal troops, and his men were in desperate need of food and supplies. They faced starvation if they were not reprovisioned.

Just after his inauguration, President Lincoln learned about the fort's supply shortage, and he faced a dilemma. He could send armed ships steaming into Charleston Harbor, ready to fight their way to Fort Sumter, which would surely provoke an attack by South Carolina. Such overt aggression, however, would serve to unite the South—including critical upper South states like Virginia, which had not yet seceded—and divide the North, which contained many leaders who still hoped to avoid war.

Lincoln might have chosen to simply withdraw Anderson's garrison and surrender the fort, but that risked emboldening the South and discrediting the federal government. It would be akin to surrendering the Union.

The new President chose a third option. He sent word to the South Carolina governor that he planned to send only unarmed supply ships—carrying mainly food—to Fort Sumter. "If such attempts be not resisted," Lincoln said, "no effort to throw in men, arms or ammunition, will be made, without further notice, [except] in case of an attack on the Fort."

✳ ✳ ✳

Now the South and Confederate President Jefferson Davis faced their own dilemma.

If the South attacked unarmed ships carrying food for hungry men, such an act of aggression would be seen as dishonorable; in the reverse of the Northern conundrum, it could unify the North and divide the South, whose people held deep reverence for military service and soldiers. The South would be blamed for firing the first and unprovoked shots of war.

Lincoln's plan had backed the South into a corner. Davis was under pressure to take some kind of action. "If something is not done pretty soon," said one Alabama newspaper, "the whole country will become so disgusted with the sham of southern independence, that the first chance people get at a popular election, they will turn the whole movement topsy-turvy."

When it became clear that Lincoln was not going to order the evacuation of Sumter, Charleston military commander P. G. T. Beauregard sent word to Anderson requesting that he surrender. Anderson thanked Beauregard for the "fair, manly, and courteous terms proposed," but he refused the offer on the grounds that a surrender would be tantamount to shirking his duty. While he and his men possessed ever more meager supplies, they would defend the fort. But, he informed Beauregard, "If you do not batter us to pieces, we will be starved out in a few days."

Anderson promised to evacuate the fort on April 15 once his provisions were exhausted, which would allow him and his men to leave the fort with their honor intact. He would take this action only if the Confederates committed no hostile act against the fort or the U.S. flag that waved above it, and providing he received no additional provisions from his government. If he received more food, his men would stay on and defend the fort.

The chess game continued.

Who would make the next move?

✳ ✳ ✳

Jefferson Davis, his military leaders, and the South acted next.

Davis believed that the North was the aggressor, *regardless* of whether Lincoln's supply ships were armed or not. "The order for the sailing of the fleet was a *declaration of war*," he wrote. "A deadly weapon has been aimed at our heart—only a fool would wait until the shot has been fired."

At an April 9 meeting, Davis and his lieutenants decided that they were left with only one choice to blunt Lincoln's deceitful and underhanded act of aggression, preserve their honor, and mollify Southerners who demanded action to establish the credentials of the new Confederacy. The South needed to attack and capture Fort Sumter *before* the supply ships arrived, which they were scheduled to do between April 13 and April 15.

An hour before the first long arcing shell was lobbed at the fort from the Confederate battery, the South's Colonel James Chesnut delivered a message to Anderson warning that the attack would begin. Over the next thirty-six hours, between forty and forty-five Confederate guns fired between three and four thousand shells and hot shots (heated cannonballs) at the federal fort in Charleston Harbor. Charlestonians gathered on balconies, wharves, and rooftops along the Battery to watch.

The hot shot rained down upon Anderson and his men. They sustained no casualties, but the shot ignited their personal effects and living quarters, and the shells themselves tore out chunks of the fort's walls. Anderson did not return fire. His ammunition, along with his food, was nearly gone.

Finally, at just after 1:00 P.M. on Saturday, April 13, Anderson ordered the American flag taken down. After negotiations with Confederate emissaries that evening, arrangements were made to evacuate the fort on Sunday morning, April 14. Anderson asked for terms that included his troops being allowed to salute the flag one last time and fire fifty two-gun salutes as they marched from the fort onto waiting Confederate transport ships.

When the surrender was complete, the Confederate and South Carolina palmetto flags were raised above Fort Sumter to wild cheers from spectators onshore and the roar of guns fired in salute from Confederate ships in the harbor. From the balcony of the Charleston Hotel, South Carolina governor Andrew Pickens delivered a rousing speech: "We have met them and conquered them. We have humbled the flag of the United States before the Palmetto and Confederate flag . . . today it has been humbled before the glorious little state of South Carolina!"

An awful war had begun, one that would plunge the nation into a nightmare and require it to pay a terrible price for its reunification and preservation.

✳ ✳ ✳

The news from Fort Sumter infuriated and unified the North.

In New York City, more than a quarter million people turned out for a pro-Union rally in a place that once harbored strong pro-Southern sentiments because of its trading partnerships and economic interests. In Chicago, Democrat Stephen Douglas, who had spent years offering olive branches to the Southern slaveocracy, got swept up in the pro-Union fervor when he told a huge crowd: "There can be no neutrals in this war, *only patriots—or traitors.*"

On April 15, Lincoln issued a proclamation calling on the Northern states to commit seventy-five thousand militiamen to suppress the Southern rebellion. Four days later, Lincoln ordered a blockade of Southern ports to prevent cotton and other raw materials from reaching domestic and European markets, and to prevent war matériel from reaching the Confederacy (by July, the Union Navy had established blockades of all major Southern ports).

Lincoln's decrees led to two critical moves—the mustering of troops all across the North to fight for the Union cause, producing a different battle cry from the militias that normally defended individual states; next, Virginia, the most important upper South state, made the decision to secede (North Carolina, Tennessee, and Arkansas would follow, bringing the total number of CSA states to eleven). Otherwise, under the terms of Lincoln's order, Virginians would be asked to take up arms against South Carolinians. In May, Virginia officially seceded— bringing to the Confederacy a brilliant military commander named Robert E. Lee—while ardent pro-Union forces in the western region of Virginia split off from the state and in June formed the Union state of West Virginia.

"At last the war has come," Charles Sumner wrote. "The day of insincerity and duplicity is now passed, and *all* the cabinet is united in energetic action. It will be needed, for the Slave States will be united."

Sumner's home state took his words to heart. If South Carolina had fired the opening salvo to destroy the Union, it made sense that its alter ego in every way, Massachusetts, would be the first state to respond to Lincoln's call to begin the country's restoration.

Massachusetts governor John Andrew quickly ordered out the first wave of troops: the Third, Fourth, Sixth, and Eighth Massachusetts Regiments. On April 17, the Sixth Massachusetts left Boston by train en route to Washington to defend an unprotected capital—huge crowds cheered as the train left; Bostonians rushed to support the war from all quarters.

Even Massachusetts abolitionists, who normally deplored bloodshed, saw the war as a chance to abolish slavery forever. If war put an end to the slave system, said William Lloyd Garrison, this war would be "more glorious in history" than the American Revolution.

✻ ✻ ✻

On his way home from Washington, Charles Sumner stopped in Baltimore on the evening of April 18 to rest overnight. He registered at Barnum's City Hotel and walked to a friend's house for tea.

As he walked back to his hotel at around 9:00 P.M., Sumner spotted a large, violent crowd gathered in the square in front of Barnum's, shouting and shaking their fists. Looking to avoid the scene, Sumner slipped into a side door of the hotel, where he was met by a worker who delivered a shocking message:

"That mob in the square is for *you*," he said. "Their leaders demanded *you*."

The worker had informed the crowd that Sumner was out, that nobody knew where he was, and that perhaps he had left town. The pro-Southern mob was not convinced and continued to scream for Sumner, the man they held most responsible for the current Northern aggression against the South.

Undeterred, Sumner walked down the long corridor of the hotel's main floor, turned into the office, and asked for his room key. The establishment's owner and his assistant approached Sumner and requested that he leave the hotel. They feared that the mob would storm the lobby, damage the hotel, and injure or kill Sumner. "We cannot guarantee your safety," the owner said. "To remain is perilous."

Regretful for the scene his presence had caused, a shaken Sumner replied that he had nowhere else to go. He refused to return to his friend's house, fearful that the mob would exert its wrath on an innocent person. Because he had paid for lodgings, Sumner believed the hotel had an obligation to provide him with a room. Surely, in such a large structure, a safe place could be found where he could sleep for one night. The Barnum's owner finally relented, and led Sumner to the third floor of the hotel, down another long corridor to a small chamber, and assured him that no one else would know where he was. Not even the staff would be informed of his new location—the hotel could risk no leaks. There they left him alone.

From the window of his new room, Sumner looked below and could "see the swaying multitude and hear their voices," bloodthirsty at this point.

Screaming for him.

Early the next morning, after the mob had tired and dissipated, Sumner slipped from Barnum's City Hotel and boarded a train for Philadelphia. On the way north, the southbound train carrying the Massachusetts Sixth passed him, and he was "struck by the gayety of soldier life which overflowed" as the train went by.

* * *

But gayety for the Massachusetts Sixth was short-lived.

On the morning of April 19, the regiment was set upon by a mob in Baltimore and four of its members were killed—the first battle casualties of the Civil War. The state's support for the war grew only more strident and unified when it received word of the attack. Across Massachusetts, outraged residents, newspaper editors, clergymen, and politicians focused on the historic date of the attack, drawing parallels between the actions of the Sixth and the "shot heard 'round the world" in Lexington, Massachusetts, that opened the American Revolution in the early morning hours of April 19, 1775.

Any vestige of sympathy for the South and any hope that war could be avoided were obliterated with the news from Baltimore. Massachusetts militiamen and merchants alike, stunned by the civilian mob's attack on American soldiers, demanded revenge and full support for the war effort. Across the state, young men rushed to enlist, the wealthy contributed to the war effort, and women signed up to aid the wounded. The Massachusetts Fifth mustered on Boston Common, anxious to head southward to avenge their colleagues. Those feelings reached a fever pitch when word arrived from Richmond that thousands of Virginians had participated in a torchlight celebration to *honor* the acts of the "gallant Baltimoreans" who had attacked the Massachusetts Sixth.

* * *

Upon his arrival in Philadelphia as he headed north, Charles Sumner learned by telegraph of the attack upon the Massachusetts soldiers in Baltimore just hours after he had left the city. Still rattled by his own near miss and the mob violence against the Sixth, Sumner felt a need to speak to other troops. On April 21, traveling toward Boston, he met the Third Battalion of Massachusetts Rifles, commanded by Major Charles

Devens, at the New York armory. Devens ordered his battalion into line, and Sumner addressed them.

Amid their applause and cheers, he thanked them for their service and for the mission they were undertaking. He felt he had done his part for the antislavery cause—now the cause was in their hands. "Elsewhere it has been my part to speak," he told the troops. "It is your part now to act."

He told the Massachusetts battalion that his "soul was touched" when he heard that members of the Sixth had fallen in Baltimore. The heroes of the Sixth "have died well, for they died at the post of duty, and so dying, they have become an example and a name in history!" He swelled with pride when he learned that Massachusetts, as in 1775, had spilled first blood in a conflict for a new kind of independence—freeing the nation of the bonds of slavery. Other times were said "to try men's souls," but as he witnessed how willing patriotic citizens volunteered to save their country, and to die if necessary, "I look in vain for signs that souls are tried."

The Rifle Battalion cheered wildly.

Sumner did not minimize the dangers and hardships the troops would face but urged them to be brave in the duty for which they had been called. "And if you need any watchword, let it be, Massachusetts, the Constitution, and FREEDOM!"

Again, the troops roared their approval and surrounded Sumner, shaking his hand, clapping his back, and thanking him for his words and role in the Union cause. They showered him with genuine affection, an uncommon feeling for him, and as these Massachusetts troops headed off to war, they let him know of their devotion and admiration.

CHAPTER 24

"ELEVATE THE CONDITION OF MEN"

As much as Charles Sumner despised war, the onset of the Civil War imbued him with a sense of hope and even a dare-not-be-spoken feeling of elation. "Nothing could be more painful than this conflict," he wrote, "except that I feel that it was inevitable, & that its result will be the extinction of slavery."

But at first, Sumner's attempts to portray the conflict as an antislavery crusade were at odds with the goals of President Lincoln, Union troops, and the majority of Northern citizens.

From the outset, Sumner believed that the idea of declaring full emancipation was permitted under President Lincoln's war powers. After the attack on Fort Sumter, Sumner rushed to the White House to pledge his support to the President "heart and soul," and told Lincoln that under his "war power[s] the right had come to him to emancipate the slaves." Sumner, as chairman of the Senate Foreign Relations Committee, had briefed Lincoln several times on overseas affairs—Lincoln had almost no foreign policy expertise—and in the process had grown closer to the President. "The President speaks simply and plainly of the state of the country, and I think he understands it," he wrote on April 16. "As I see more of him I like him better." Still, Sumner wished Lincoln would move more boldly on the issue of emancipation.

But in the spring of 1861, Lincoln had practical reasons for declining such a move.

The President was desperate to hold the slaveholding border states of Delaware, Maryland, Kentucky, and Missouri as part of the Union. These states gave the North a huge numerical advantage in the number of troops required to fight a war, and in the farmland and factories needed to feed and supply them. The white population of the four border states alone was about half the total population of the eleven states of the Confederacy. Maryland bordered and provided a buffer to the nation's capital. Kentucky was rich in minerals and was a major producer of grain and livestock; plus, because it was bordered by the Ohio River to the north and the Mississippi River to the west, it held important strategic advantages both for Union troop movements and in the defense of Indiana, Illinois, and Ohio. Framing the conflict as one to abolish slavery threatened any attempt to retain these states and, Lincoln believed, would actually encourage them to secede.

The President couldn't risk it. "I hope to have God on my side," Lincoln purportedly quipped early in the war, "but I *must* have Kentucky."

Later he went even further on the importance of the Bluegrass State: "I think to lose Kentucky is nearly the same as losing the whole game," he said. "[With] Kentucky gone, we can not hold Missouri, nor I think, Maryland. . . . We would as well consent to separation at once, including the surrender of this capital."

✳ ✳ ✳

Fear of antagonizing the border states was only one reason for Lincoln to avoid the potential abolition of slavery as a war aim.

He needed the full support of Republicans in the Midwest and West, who had far less sympathy for the antislavery movement than their Eastern counterparts, and he required backing from those non-Republicans in the Northern states who were lukewarm toward abolition and skeptical of the national government's authority to bring it about. Both groups saw the preservation of the Union as the reason for the North to undertake the conflict and would balk at any effort to transform the war into a fight against slavery.

Northern soldiers also desired to "fight for Union" and, at least at the outset of the conflict, had little interest in interfering with slavery. To reinforce this ethos, Union Army leaders issued formal orders that slave uprisings should be suppressed, if possible, and some officers even offered to return fugitive slaves to their masters. Blacks were forbidden to leave Washington, D.C., unless they showed sentries proof that they were free. Government officials reacted accordingly. The Justice Department, in a letter of instruction, recognized the *duty* of U.S. marshals to return fugitive slaves. The secretary of the interior denied the right of the national government to interfere with slavery in any state. President Lincoln revoked orders from generals emancipating slaves within their commands in Kentucky and Missouri.

America's overseas diplomatic correspondence contained similar provisions, much to the detriment of the North. The lack of a strong and explicit imperative against slavery weakened support for the Union among foreign leaders. One English lord noted in a London speech that the absence of a forceful antislavery message as a reason for civil war not only threatened British support for Lincoln and the North but actually provided many in England with an excuse to support the underdog South, whose cheap cotton supplied British textile factories. If the United States could not bring itself to take a strong antislavery stance, why should the English support the Union cause?

For his part, Sumner bided his time, but he remained hopeful of the North's ultimate success and convinced of the war's long-term result—"the extinction of slavery."

✷ ✷ ✷

No one should have been surprised by the United States' official early wartime stance on the slavery issue—for three months, even before the attack on Fort Sumter, noninterference with slavery was the foundation of the new administration's stated policy. "I believe I have no lawful right to do so, and I have no inclination to do so," Lincoln said publicly.

Privately, however, influenced by ideas that Sumner had promulgated for years, President Lincoln's thinking seemed to shift by the spring of 1861. In early May, Sumner and the President were enjoying an evening carriage ride, during which Sumner again pushed Lincoln to make emancipation a war priority. The President balked, suggesting that such a drastic move was premature and, at that point, counterproductive. A disappointed Sumner agreed that the timing was delicate, but took heart when Lincoln did not refute his urging to be "ready to strike when the moment came."

On May 7, one of the President's secretaries, John Hay, met with Lincoln to let him know that his daily correspondence was "thickly interspersed" with suggestions that he should declare the "entire abolition of slavery" as the primary reason for the war. Lincoln's response so impressed Hay that the secretary copied it into his diary and, years later, printed it verbatim in his biography of Lincoln.

Lincoln began his response conventionally enough.

> I consider the central idea pervading this struggle is the necessity that is
> upon us of proving that popular government is not an absurdity. We must
> settle this question now, whether, in a free government, the minority have
> the right to break up the government whenever they choose. If we fail, it
> will go far to prove the incapability of the people to govern themselves.

Hay agreed with these sentiments, and Lincoln's language did not surprise him, but what the President said next *did*—however obliquely and
guardedly Lincoln spoke.

> There may be one consideration used in stay of such final judgement, but
> that is not for us to use in advance. There exists in our case, an instance of
> a vast and far-reaching disturbing element, which the history of no other
> free nation will probably ever present. That however, is not for us to say
> at present.

Hay was startled by the import of what he had heard. Lincoln had not
used the word "slavery" or "emancipation" in their conversation, but
his reference to *one consideration in stay of such final judgement* and *a
vast and far-reaching disturbing element* could only mean that the President had acknowledged, for the first time, the possibility that a decree of
emancipation, though *not for us to use in advance*, might become necessary during the course of the war.

The loyal Hay, of course, breathed not a word of this publicly.

That however, is not for us to say at present, the President had warned.

✳ ✳ ✳

Hay noted something else in his diary on May 7: President Lincoln was
already working on a major message to Congress for delivery on July
4, 1861, America's Independence Day and the first day of a special congressional session he had called to lay out his war goals. The President
labored on his report day and night for weeks, and on June 19, Lincoln
took the extraordinary step of announcing publicly that he would receive
no visitors until after his message was delivered.

Lincoln shared his final draft with Sumner and a handful of others.

His words would be his first broad expression of the Union's goals for the war, and they signaled a public change in his own thinking. Lincoln's message contained elements of Sumner's point of view that the war opened a window for the North to trumpet a higher moral calling—crushing slavery once and for all as a means of saving the Union. During Sumner's several conversations with the President, he had sensed a willingness on Lincoln's part, latent and reluctant though it was, to consider such a move.

Lincoln called for the congressional session to open on July 4, 1861. It seemed appropriate to lay out his plan for saving the nation on the occasion of its birthday. In keeping with tradition, his private secretary John Nicolay would hand-deliver Lincoln's message to the Capitol, where it would be read aloud by the clerks of the House and Senate chambers. It was not lost on anyone in Washington, or anywhere else, that, depending on the course of the war, this could be the nation's last Independence Day celebration.

As if to confirm the aura of solemnity and grandness that marked the moment, a celestial occurrence graced the city and the country, too. Washingtonians were still talking about a massive and brilliant comet that traversed the night sky starting on July 1—after the rainstorm cleared—and continued on the nights of July 2, 3, and 4, its head the size of a three-quarter moon and its sweeping tail dazzling and splendorous as it streaked across the dark summer sky. The *New York Herald* labeled the majestic event the "War Comet of 1861."

Now, on the fourth—with the city on a razor's edge, with wary congressmen uncertain about what lay ahead, with armed Union troops drilling across Washington, D.C., with the sound of hammers clanging from the unfinished Capitol building, with the citizenry frightened about the nation's very future—President Lincoln shared his own brilliance, in its way as fiery as the great comet, and, it would turn out, complete with a tail that would burn bright for decades.

✳ ✳ ✳

The first half of Lincoln's Independence Day address described the events leading to secession and war and requested that Congress appropriate money and additional troops to the Union effort. He also offered a compilation of reasons why controversial measures such as the suspension of habeas corpus and a blistering attack on the Confederacy as an "illegal organization" engaged in an illegal act were necessary.

None of these points particularly impressed or surprised lawmakers. But what came next did.

Lincoln alluded to the slavery question and offered a glimpse of the emancipation issue when he described the war as a "people's contest." For the Union,

> it is a struggle for maintaining ... that form and substance of government, whose leading object is to elevate the condition of men. To lift artificial weights from all shoulders—to clear the paths of laudable pursuit for all—to afford all an unfettered start, and a fair chance in the race for life— *this is the leading object* of the government for whose existence we contend.

It was extraordinary language—*elevate the condition of men ... lift artificial weights ... an unfettered start ... a fair chance in the race for life.* Lincoln had gone well beyond even what he privately shared with Hay in March. Charles Sumner had expressed such thoughts for years, but he was often a lone voice among elected officials; it was astonishing for a U.S. President to present such profound ideas in order to describe the reasons to engage in the struggle ahead, indeed, to save the Union.

Many abolitionists would criticize Lincoln for resorting to ambiguous language about slavery. They missed the President's subtle meaning, or perhaps refused to see it. Surprisingly, the editors of the proslavery *Baltimore Sun* were far more perceptive when they inferred the meaning of Lincoln's veiled words. The President's use of "unfettered" and "elevate the condition of men" in his message could only mean one thing, the paper surmised: "the abolition of slavery, and the social, civil, and political equality of the Ethiopian, Mongolian, Caucasian, and all other races."

✳ ✳ ✳

Lincoln's Independence Day message marked public milestones for him—in the evolution of his own thought process on slavery, and on his reputation in Washington and across the country. President Abraham Lincoln, the backwoodsman who hailed most recently from Illinois, and Kentucky before that, had expressed powerful arguments about freedom with more eloquence and intellect than any Eastern university scholar. Both North and South took notice.

For the next fifteen months or so, he faced *political* choices on when and how vigorously to label the war as a conflict to overturn slavery, and on the nature and timing of a potential decree of emancipation. But his July 4, 1861, message to Congress foretold the intellectual and deep moral convictions he would hold for the rest of the war (which would cover the rest of his life), convictions that mirrored and were deeply influenced by Charles Sumner's.

Lincoln's language in the dark and anxious summer of 1861 presaged words and ideas that would ring across the world and reverberate down through history in his Emancipation Proclamation, the Gettysburg Address, and his masterful Second Inaugural speech.

"Henceforth he might be—would be—reviled," one historian noted, "but he would never be underestimated."

✳ ✳ ✳

Lincoln's 1861 Fourth of July message also sparked modest but perceptible movement in a Congress now sitting without seceded Southern members.

On July 8, four days after the President's message was read, Illinois congressman and radical abolitionist Owen Lovejoy offered a two-part resolution in the House: that Union soldiers assume no responsibility to capture and return fugitive slaves—some moderate members had suggested they do so to keep the focus of war only on preserving the Union—and that the Judiciary Committee consider a bill to repeal the Fugitive Slave Law.

The resolution passed the next day by a convincing vote of 93–55.

A jubilant Charles Sumner congratulated Lovejoy on the progress. Lovejoy, who had been dedicated to eradicating slavery ever since the murder of his brother by an anti-abolitionist mob in Illinois, was thrilled that the resolution passed. In his July 11 reply to Sumner, he noted that the timing of the motion, following Lincoln's message, forced previously reticent members of the Senate to finally take a stand. They had not necessarily become braver overnight, but the President's bold and unexpected words had left them with little recourse other than to stiffen their backbones before the public.

"Our conservative people were timid and vexed," Lovejoy said, "but they had to vote *right* at last."

✹ ✹ ✹

If Lincoln's Fourth of July message marked the beginning of a change in the Union's war aims, an event that took place seventeen days later— July 21, 1861—created the irreversible momentum that would soon make emancipation the North's priority for the rest of the war.

On the surface, the event was a jarring disaster for the Union—the stunning and humiliating defeat of their forces in the conflict's first major battle, just thirty miles from the nation's capital. The Confederates referred to their victory as the Battle of First Manassas, named after the closest Virginia town to the fighting; the Union called it the First Battle of Bull Run, for the long creek that wound its way through the battlefield.

It was the first fighting experienced by most men on both sides. Around 3:00 P.M., Union troops, though thirsty, hungry, tired, and choked with dust, appeared to have the upper hand. But Confederate reinforcements overwhelmed and routed them, forcing them into a panicked, chaotic retreat toward Washington, D.C., to seek refuge. Frightened Union troops nearly collided with a crowd of civilians and congressmen who had come out to view the expected Northern victory. So total was the Confederate victory that rebel military officers were later criticized for not pressing their shocking advantage and pursuing Union troops across the Potomac into Washington, and capturing the national capital.

The defeat was a blow to Lincoln, and a surprise, because he'd received favorable news from the battlefield earlier in the day. Believing the Union would achieve victory, he went for an afternoon carriage ride. On his return to the White House, he received the demoralizing update that the Union Army was in full retreat. "The day is lost," the telegram read. "Save Washington and the remnants of this army."

Defeat was one thing; a humiliating rout was something worse. The panic that Union troops had demonstrated was shameful. Thoughts of a swift and mostly bloodless war evaporated. Lincoln was dismayed, the North discouraged.

Were Northern troops cowards?

Would they even fight for the Union?

These were the words on Northerners' lips and the feelings in their hearts.

But shortly, the cloud of despair that dampened Union spirits after a catastrophic first defeat began to dissipate and, for Charles Sumner and other emancipation advocates, a bright light shone on the great issue of the day.

* * *

The Union learned a great deal from its dispiriting defeat at Bull Run and—with Sumner and Lincoln together nurturing the response—that knowledge brought forth the issue of emancipation as a critical goal of the war.

First, military leaders and soldiers alike saw vivid evidence that emancipation could hurt the South's on-the-ground war effort. Northern soldiers reported that slaves by the thousands labored for the Confederacy. Many Union troops had watched as slaves, coerced by their Southern officers, manned gun emplacements during Bull Run. Other slaves took care of necessary battlefield chores—cooking, washing uniforms, setting up encampments, hauling supplies—thus freeing up Southern troops to fight unencumbered. One cavalryman also pointed out correctly that slavery in general enlarged the Confederate Army by permitting a large proportion of white Southern men to join the ranks "while their negroes are at home raising crops to support their families." His solution: "free the slaves and the white men will be obliged to come home to look after the welfare of their families and go to work themselves or starve."

He was right. Slaves constituted about half the Southern labor force, and slave labor was so important to the Southern war effort that the Confederate government impressed slaves into service before it began drafting white men as soldiers. "The *very stomach of this rebellion* is the negro in the form of a slave," an astute Frederick Douglass observed. "Arrest that hoe in the hands of the negro, and you smite the rebellion in the very seat of its life."

In fact, freeing the slaves would not only hurt the Confederacy, it could actively *help* the Union with its own wartime strategy; at Bull Run and long afterward, Union officers were aided by reports from runaway slaves who identified Southern positions, offered intelligence on Confederate troop movements and strategy, or arrived at Union lines after sabotaging Southern artillery or stealing rifles—all at enormous personal risk. And this was well before any strategic effort to enlist border-state slaves to fight on the side of the Union. Merely from a tactical perspective, emancipation would severely hinder the South's ability to wage and win the war.

But the Union's defeat at Manassas/Bull Run had a far more profound impact on its view of emancipation. For Republicans especially, but not exclusively, something deeper and more visceral had changed after Bull Run, something that touched the core of the North's character and defined the very essence of what the "Union" stood for in the first place.

✳ CHAPTER 25 ✳

"THE REBELLION IS SLAVERY ITSELF!"

The South's ferocity at Manassas was eye-opening.

It illustrated with starkness to the North how rabidly the rebels would fight to preserve their way of life—and at the heart of this "Southern way" was the embedded and pervasive system of slavery, a hallowed cause to which they were bound by duty, honor, and righteousness.

After Manassas, the North recognized that sidestepping the slavery issue as a reason for war—by focusing only on "preservation of the Union"—actually *hindered* its own moral position. For what did "preserving the Union" refer to if not the protection and expansion of freedom and liberty? If the South fought so hard to save slavery, how could the North achieve victory without eradicating it?

Union troops on the ground recognized this point and expressed these thoughts early. Men from Massachusetts, New York, Rhode Island, Pennsylvania, and elsewhere had heard often about Southern fanaticism to maintain a slave-based society, but now they witnessed it firsthand. Northern troops saw up close how slaves risked their lives to flee to Union lines, revealing a desperate longing for freedom. Uprooting slavery might help not only to somewhat justify the slaughter of war but also to ultimately improve—and redeem—the Union into something worthy of preservation.

One soldier explained that the Union must be saved to certify the success of "the experiment of our popular government." A Missouri private observed to his wife that "it was slavery that caused the war," and it would take "the eternal overthrow of slavery" to win it.

✳ ✳ ✳

Sumner accurately viewed Bull Run as a turning point, a profound moment in which the entire North seemed to shift in its war priorities to align with his own. The day after the disastrous battle, the Senate passed legislation declaring that the Union had a right to confiscate any slaves employed by the rebels for military purposes. Lincoln signed the Confiscation Act into law on August 6. While language in the law did not clarify explicitly whether these slaves were free, it did strip their owners of any claim to them. It was a "military emancipation" of sorts, and the law was vague on the overall fate of the slaves, but Sumner believed it was long-overdue progress and a harbinger of a general emancipation policy later in the war.

The Union defeat at Bull Run/Manassas made it possible. "In the providence of God, there are no accidents," Sumner wrote on the passage of the Confiscation Act, "and this seeming reverse helped to the greatest victory which can be won."

Sumner told Lincoln that the defeat at Bull Run "was the worst event and the best event in our history . . . the worst, as it was the greatest present calamity and shame—the best, as it made the extinction of Slavery inevitable."

✳ ✳ ✳

Throughout the summer and fall of 1861, in speech after speech, Sumner pounded away at the theme of emancipation, even expressing his willingness to compensate slave owners regardless of cost. "Never should any question of money be allowed to interfere with human freedom," he said. "Better an empty treasury than a single slave."

He spoke in Worcester, Massachusetts, then in Boston, Providence, Albany, Philadelphia, and Boston again before finishing the circuit at the Cooper Institute in New York on November 27 before a wild and enthusiastic crowd. In every city, audiences greeted him with loud applause, often forcing him to pause and wait for the cheering to subside; in New York, the crowd erupted in thunderous cheering as he raged against the institution of slavery, claimed it was the *sole* cause of the rebellion, and insisted that emancipation offered the only means to both military and moral victory.

In some of his most soaring rhetoric ever, Sumner inspired the New York crowd:

"All must see, and nobody will deny, that slavery is the ruling idea of this rebellion. . . .

"It is slavery that stamps its character alike upon officers and men.

"It is slavery that inspires all, from general to trumpeter.

"It is slavery that speaks in the word of command, and sounds in the morning drum-beat."

He built toward a crescendo, and the crowd kept roaring its acclamation:

"It is slavery that digs trenches and builds hostile forts . . .

"It is slavery that sharpens the bayonet and runs the bullet; that points the cannon and scatters the shell—blazing, bursting unto death."

With the crowd delirious and roaring its approval, Sumner's voice swelled as he reached the climax of his remarks:

"Whenever this rebellion shows itself, whatever form it takes, whatever thing it does, whatever it meditates, it is moved by slavery—nay, *the rebellion is slavery itself*—incarnate, living, acting, raging, robbing, murdering, according to the essential law of its being!"

In the summer and fall of 1861, as the Union hung in the balance, Charles Sumner seized the moment. He forced a bleary-eyed nation to look in the mirror, reacquaint itself with its ideals, and find its moral courage and true purpose for existing. It was his "prophet-like voice and determination which prepared the way for Lincoln's proclamations, and made them the events they became," one contemporaneous writer said.

Sumner held firm and stood tall even while heartbroken over the tragic death of one dear friend and the inconsolable grief of another.

✳ ✳ ✳

Through all of Charles Sumner's personal turmoil and difficulty maintaining relationships, there was one constant: his deep and cherished friendship with Henry Wadsworth and Fanny Longfellow.

The Longfellows accepted and looked past Sumner's social awkwardness and appreciated the gentle and thoughtful, if insecure, soul within. It helped that Sumner felt relaxed in the presence of Henry, Fanny, and their children. He and Henry had a long kinship based on mutual respect and deep affection, and Sumner was also proud that he had an independent relationship with Fanny, who nurtured him in a way no one else did.

Sumner appreciated Fanny's razor-sharp wit and intellect. Henry described Fanny as a genius, and Sumner agreed. She was a voracious reader in several languages and a talented artist, and she had accumulated a rich body of writing and sketches. She and Sumner regularly discussed literature, art, history, religion, travel, domestic politics, and international affairs. She delighted him, for certain, but even more important to Sumner, he appeared to delight *her*—something he could say about almost no one else in his life.

More than once, Sumner told Henry that he envisioned Fanny as a friend for life.

✳ ✳ ✳

The Longfellows' resplendent Georgian mansion in Cambridge, Massachusetts, was stifling in the steamy early afternoon of July 9, 1861. Normally, Henry and Fanny and the children would be enjoying the refreshing sea breezes at their Nahant home on the North Shore of Massachusetts, but Fanny had just spent the morning visiting with her dying father in Boston.

When she returned to Cambridge, she set up in the drawing room and decided to preserve several locks of her seven-year-old daughter Edith's beautiful curly hair. While she was sealing a snippet in an envelope, wax from a lighted candle spilled onto Fanny's hooped muslin dress, setting her ablaze in an instant. Engulfed in flames, Fanny screamed and leapt from her chair, and, hoping to protect Edith, stumbled and whirled away from her daughter—but as she did so, Fanny's convulsive movements fed the blaze and it consumed her.

Henry, working in his nearby office, heard his wife's anguished wails, rushed to Fanny's aid and—his eyes and brain registering the horror in a split second—grabbed a small rug and tried in vain to snuff out the flaming pyre that Fanny had become, and finally, in desperation, hugged his beloved close to his body to extinguish the flames, severely burning his hands and face in the process.

Fanny survived the night, her horrible pain lessened only somewhat by ether, but her burns were far too widespread and severe—there was no hope. She died the next morning, "perfectly calm, patient and gentle, all the lovely sweetness and elevation of her character showing itself in her looks and words."

✳ ✳ ✳

Sumner received the terrible news in Washington on July 11 when his friend Richard Henry Dana wrote of the "fearful disaster and loss at Cambridge."

Late in the day of July 21—the same day Union troops were routed at Manassas—Sumner wrote a long letter to an anguished Longfellow, who was suffering from the loss of Fanny and from his own third-degree burns that left his hands and face disfigured (Longfellow grew his iconic beard after Fanny's death to hide his scarred face). The poet's injuries were so severe that he had been unable to attend Fanny's funeral on July 13. A typical Sumner epistle, his letter combined sympathy for Longfellow with despair over his own suffering, as if the two were equivalent. "Daily, hourly, constantly I think of you and my thoughts end with myself," Sumner admitted, "for I cannot forget my own great and irreparable loss." Sumner could not conceive of life without Fanny and "counted upon her friendship to the last."

He urged his friend to cherish the "great happiness" and "precious memories" he and Fanny had shared, and hoped Longfellow's children could provide the poet with some consolation. He promised to accompany Henry on a visit to Mount Auburn Cemetery in Cambridge—Fanny's burial spot—when he returned to Boston. Sumner's first stop when he arrived in his home city in August 1861 was Longfellow's house, where he attempted to console a devastated Henry. The two spent several days together over the course of Sumner's recess.

But soon a far more pressing public reality intruded on the two friends' privacy.

✳ ✳ ✳

Sumner was forced to leave Longfellow and return to Washington in late November. The United States, already taxed to the utmost in its own brutal civil war, was on the brink of a foreign war with the greatest naval power in the world. Great Britain was angry and emitting a roar that was heard across the Atlantic and around the world.

The President and the nation called upon Charles Sumner to find a solution.

If he could not, America was doomed.

CHAPTER 26

BRITISH TREACHERY

OCTOBER 12, 1861, 1:00 A.M., CHARLESTON HARBOR

The small Confederate steamer *Theodora* departed from Charleston Harbor sight unseen, slipped the Union blockade, and hit open water amid sheets of windswept rain.

On board were two Confederate emissaries; former Virginia senator James Mason and Louisiana's John Slidell, a prominent New Orleans lawyer who once served as President Polk's special envoy to Mexico. Their mission: reach Europe and enlist assistance for the Confederate States of America.

Mason and Slidell carried letters of introduction from Confederate President Jefferson Davis. Mason's recognized him as "envoy extraordinary and minister plenipotentiary" of the Confederate States to the United Kingdom of Great Britain and Ireland. Slidell was "special commissioner" of the Confederate States to the Republic of France.

Up to now, Great Britain and France had maintained diplomatic relations with the United States, and they had recognized the CSA as a belligerent power but not a sovereign nation. Davis wanted full diplomatic recognition for the Confederates, which would lend instant credibility to the South's cause and allow full trading between the CSA and the European giants.

Davis believed from the beginning that European dependence on Southern cotton for its textile industry would lead to the full recognition that the CSA sought, and perhaps convince England and France to intervene in the war, offering mediation if not outright military assistance. Combined, the South's cotton and its recent battlefield victories might persuade the Europeans to help the CSA achieve "a place [among nations] as a free and independent people."

It was this heady stuff that Mason and Slidell pondered as the *Theodora* steamed on through the darkness. In many ways, they knew, the fate of the CSA depended on them.

What they had no way of knowing was that *their* fates would soon be in the hands of the despised Charles Sumner.

✳ ✳ ✳

The *Theodora* was scheduled to dock in the Bahamas first and then make its way to St. Thomas—then a part of the Danish West Indies—where Mason and Slidell would book passage to Southampton, England. Plans changed slightly when the *Theodora* laid up on the outskirts of Nassau harbor and the captain received word that no ships were available to take the Confederate emissaries to St. Thomas. Instead, the ship sailed on to Cuba, where it docked on October 16.

Unfortunately, the once-a-month steamer to St. Thomas had departed earlier on the day the *Theodora* arrived. Mason and Slidell were forced to spend three more weeks in Cuba before leaving Havana for St. Thomas on November 7 aboard the British mail steamer, the RMS *Trent*. When they departed Cuba, the envoys were aboard a neutral mail steamer sailing under the British flag on a scheduled voyage between neutral ports.

Unbeknownst to Mason and Slidell, Union captain Charles Wilkes, commanding the USS *San Jacinto*, had arrived in the area, redeployed from the African coast to assist in a planned Union assault on Port Royal, South Carolina. However, when Wilkes read in a Cienfuegos, Cuba, newspaper that the Southern envoys were scheduled to leave Havana on November 7—neither their presence nor their mission was a secret on the island—he ignored his orders and decided to lay off the coast of Cuba and capture Mason and Slidell.

When the *Trent* appeared around noon on November 8, the *San Jacinto* fired a warning shot across her bow. The *Trent* hove to, and Wilkes sent his lieutenant and a boarding party to remove Slidell and Mason and their secretaries, all of whom Wilkes decided were "the embodiment of dispatches" and thus "contraband of war."

The actual dispatches from Jefferson Davis to the leaders of England and France remained hidden aboard the *Trent*.

✳ ✳ ✳

Normally, international law required that when contraband was discovered on a ship, the ship should be taken to the nearest "prize court" for adjudication, something Wilkes was planning to do. But his lieutenant who boarded the *Trent* argued that transferring crew members from the *San Jacinto* to the *Trent* to bring the ship into port would leave the *San Jacinto* dangerously undermanned. It would also inconvenience other passengers aboard the *Trent* and delay the *Trent*'s mail deliveries to British outposts in the Caribbean.

Wilkes agreed and allowed the *Trent* to proceed to St. Thomas without the Confederate envoys, who were removed at the point of bayonets. Wilkes had, essentially, made the two men prisoners of the United States and allowed the dispatches—the real contraband—and the ship to go free. In mid-November, after a stop at Hampton Roads, Virginia, Wilkes took his captives to Boston, where they joined other Confederate prisoners at Fort Warren.

Wilkes, acting as an officer of the United States, did all of this without an official legal proceeding or permission from Washington, although he said later that he "carefully examined all the authorities on international law to which I had access." Nonetheless, two ranking Confederates were in Union custody, and at first, most of the North vigorously celebrated what would soon become known as "The *Trent* Affair."

But the jubilation was short-lived. Soon afterward, all hell broke loose.

✳ ✳ ✳

In the autumn of 1861, the North desperately needed a win, and at first glance seemed to get one with the capture and detention of two Confederate traitors aiming to seek aid and comfort from a foreign government.

The war had gone poorly for the United States. After the embarrassing defeat at Manassas, Union forces had met with disaster in Ball's Bluff in Maryland and lost ground in Missouri, Mississippi, and Kentucky. The Union Army in Virginia, under the command of General George McClellan, was still lollygagging, maintaining only defensive positions around Washington while mustering and drilling for a possible advance at some undetermined time in the spring. The Confederates were confident and full of hope.

Then, finally, from out of nowhere, after seven months of Union failure, a victory of sorts—the capture of Mason and Slidell. Most Northerners learned of the *Trent* incident on November 16 when the news broke in the afternoon newspapers, and elation swept across the Northern states.

Most newspapers and prominent lawyers called Captain Wilkes's actions legal and fully justified under international law. Richard Henry Dana, considered a maritime law expert, literally beamed and clapped his hands in satisfaction when he heard the news and said he would risk his professional reputation on the legality of Wilkes's actions. Slidell and Mason, he argued, were engaged "solely in a mission hostile to the United States," making them guilty of treason. On November 26, two days after Wilkes had arrived in Boston with his prisoners, the city's most prominent citizens hosted a banquet in his honor, and one speaker after another lauded Wilkes and called him a hero.

In Washington, too, officials could not move fast enough to heap hosannas upon Wilkes. Secretary of the Navy Gideon Welles wrote the captain a congratulatory letter, stamping the "emphatic approval of this department" on his actions. Meeting in early December without now-seceded Southern members, the U.S. House of Representatives passed a unanimous resolution thanking Wilkes for his bravery and "patriotic conduct." President Lincoln and his cabinet initially responded to the capture of the confederate envoys with effusive praise.

Across the North, nearly everyone's first reaction was joy and justification for Wilkes's detainment of the *Trent* and the capture and imprisonment of Mason and Slidell.

Nearly everyone's.

✳ ✳ ✳

Charles Sumner was getting off the train from Providence, where he had delivered a speech, when a friend rushed up to him, provided the details of the *Trent* seizure, and asked for Sumner's reaction to Wilkes's capture of Mason and Slidell. The friend quoted Sumner as saying: "We will have to give them up."

There are other indications that—initially at least—Sumner agreed with the general view that Wilkes had "won a great triumph," but after additional reading, reflection, and research, he saw the U.S. position as untenable. To remove Confederate diplomats from a neutral vessel was a clear violation of international law, and it contradicted America's long-established opposition to search and seizure on the high seas. Wasn't this forced capture—"impressment," the United States called it—one of the factors that had led to the War of 1812?

Now, fifty years after a conflict that led to the burning of Washington, D.C., by British forces, tensions with England were boiling again—over the Northern blockade of Southern ports, over the potential recognition of the Confederacy by the Crown and Parliament, even over rumors that Secretary of State William Seward had considered an invasion of British Canada as a means to reunite the United States against a common enemy.

The *Trent* Affair would make matters far worse.

Sumner, who had traveled extensively in England and had numerous high-level contacts there, realized that it was best not to speak on the *Trent* Affair until he got to Washington on the last day of November. He needed more intelligence from across the Atlantic.

Meanwhile, the British finally got word of the *Trent* Affair on November 27.

In response, England began preparing for war with the United States.

✳ ✳ ✳

The British were apoplectic.

Because Slidell and Mason were traveling on a neutral vessel, much of the government and the general public viewed their capture not as an act of self-defense by the United States but as a deliberate provocation to involve Britain in a war with the Northern states. So be it—one American visitor to London wrote to Seward and declared: "The people are frantic with rage, and were the country polled, I fear 999 men out of 1,000 would declare for immediate war."

Charles Sumner's British friend Richard Cobden, with whom the senator corresponded often, wrote that a large swath of British leadership would use the *Trent* Affair to push for intervention on the South's behalf. His ominous prediction: "Three-fourths of the House of Commons will be glad to find an excuse for voting for the dismemberment of the great [American] republic."

Nor was this mere saber-rattling. The British government was infuriated, and it moved fast. Prime Minister Lord John Palmerston called emergency cabinet meetings on November 29 and 30 and reportedly began the first session by throwing his hat on the table and declaring, "I don't know whether you are going to stand [for] this, but I'll be damned if I do." Apocryphal or not, the statement accurately reflected the atmosphere in London. Palmerston urged that planned reductions in the military budget be put on hold; the British government demanded the immediate release of Mason and Slidell and a formal apology from the United States. Her Majesty's government demanded "reparations for the international wrong" the United States had committed.

It also ordered its U.S. minister to leave Washington, D.C., and to communicate the *Trent* outrage to all vessels of the British Navy in American waters and to the governors of all British possessions in the Americas.

As the calendar flipped to December, Charles Sumner and President Abraham Lincoln held their first of what would become daily meetings on the crisis.

✵ ✵ ✵

Three days later, in the midst of what felt like a torrent of warlike preparations, came the greatest of all: the British cabinet authorized the dispatch of a large force of troops to Canada and made preparations to send an even larger one.

British military planners decided to send a contingent of eleven thousand additional troops to reinforce soldiers already stationed in Canada. Not only could these troops defend British Canada if the United States decided to attack, but they could also easily conduct an offensive into the United States if war broke out. In such an event, British military leaders would attempt to coax Maine to leave the Union and join England, thereby offering the Crown's troops easy access to other Northeast states. Between December 12, 1861, and January 4, 1862, these eleven thousand officers and men, along with arms, ammunition, clothing, and supplies, departed for Canada.

Civil War had weakened the United States, and its failure to release Mason and Slidell provided England with an opportunity to justifiably strike if America failed to release the envoys. The British position was that the Americans had acted illegally in detaining the *Trent* and capturing the Confederates, and such brazenness could not go unavenged. The queen wrote to her uncle that war would result in "utter destruction to the North Americans."

As the British prepared for war, their ultimatum that could avert it—demanding the release of the prisoners and a formal U.S. apology—reached Washington on December 18, 1861.

✷ ✷ ✷

Preoccupied with reversing the Union's war failures, and possessing little foreign policy experience and almost no international relationships, President Abraham Lincoln first underestimated the danger of the *Trent* Affair.

Charles Sumner changed that.

Since his arrival in Washington, Sumner had warned the President that letters from his English friends, particularly liberal leaders John Bright and Richard Cobden, emphasized the danger of war with England if Mason and Slidell were not released. The Duchess of Argyll was blunter, calling the seizure of the *Trent* and the two Confederate commissioners "the maddest act that ever was done, and, unless the [U.S.] government intends to force us to war, *utterly inconceivable*." Sumner's contacts also wrote of the British fear that Seward was interested in provoking a war with England and urged Sumner's intervention to prevent one.

A troubled Sumner shared the correspondence with Lincoln, who was astonished that the situation had grown so dire in England. "There will be no war unless England is bent on having one," the President assured Sumner. Lincoln wondered if it would be appropriate to ignore diplomatic protocol and speak face-to-face with Lord Lyons, the British minister to the United States—"I could show him in five minutes that I am heartily for peace." Sumner warned of the impropriety of such a move, suggesting that it could make the situation worse. In this delicate moment, following proper channels was essential.

On December 23, Lyons presented to Seward the formal British demand for the release of Mason and Slidell and an apology from the U.S. government. The British minister also informed Seward that unless a satisfactory answer was received within seven days, he had instructions to close the British embassy and leave Washington, D.C.

The clock was ticking.

Lincoln called an emergency cabinet meeting for Christmas Day and invited Sumner, whom he now trusted more than anyone on foreign affairs, to take the lead.

✳ ✳ ✳

The 1861 Christmas meeting was a somber four-hour affair. Each cabinet member realized that the decision they made on this historic occasion would determine, in the words of Attorney General Edward Bates, "probably the existance [sic] of the nation."

Sumner read letters from Bright and Cobden urging the release of the two Confederate diplomats, and he also laid out points he had made in a letter to Lincoln the previous day on the likely disastrous outcome of war with England—the immediate recognition of the Confederacy by London, followed soon by recognition from France, and de facto Southern independence; the breaking of the Union blockade against the Confederates and the capture of the Union fleet; a retaliatory British blockade of the U.S. Eastern Seaboard from "Chesapeake to Eastport," which would mean the destruction of the U.S. economy; and England's opening of trade with the Confederate states, whereby the British would then feed products into the Northern states according to its own economic needs, "making the whole North American continent a manufacturing dependency of England."

War with England would be cataclysmic for the United States in its fight against the Confederates, and Lincoln, Sumner, and everyone else agreed that it was essential to avoid it. Lincoln also fretted about the potential disaster of having "two wars on his hands at a time."

Persuaded by Sumner's summary to Lincoln, Seward finally awakened to the gravity of the situation and read a paper he was preparing to deliver to the British. It acknowledged that Captain Wilkes had violated international law, and that Mason and Slidell must thus be released. Cabinet members agreed with the sentiment but assigned Seward the task of meeting the demands of the British without seeming to yield to the *pressure* of the ultimatum.

✳ ✳ ✳

Seward's job was tricky. In his new draft, he downplayed the importance of the continued detention of Mason and Slidell. He stated that Wilkes had acted correctly in stopping the *Trent* for a proper search for contraband, but he had erred by not seizing the ship as a "prize" under international law. Mason and Slidell, therefore, would be released, but the United States would issue no formal apology. Lincoln's cabinet endorsed Seward's reply to Lord Lyons with no dissent, though several members regretted that the United States was supplicating itself to Great Britain.

Later, on December 26, Seward informed Lyons that Mason and Slidell would be released. Even without the formal apology, the British accepted the language of the American reply.

War fever had cooled in England for several reasons. On December 14, 1861, public attention was diverted away from Mason and Slidell to the death and mourning of Prince Albert. Three days later, Seward's dispatch arrived to the American minister stating that Wilkes had acted on his own, without orders from Washington, and that the United States was working on a resolution. Finally, the British were worried about Napoleon III; neither the queen nor Lord Palmerston trusted the French leader to control his own aggressive impulses if Britain became distracted by a war with the United States.

All of this meant that the U.S. response, though not entirely satisfactory to the British, would have to do. The threat that the American Civil War would expand into a U.S. war with England had ended, and Charles Sumner was most responsible for the de-escalation.

"The case of the *Trent* is *settled*," Sumner wrote with deep satisfaction to Bright later that night.

✷ ✷ ✷

The *Trent* Affair was the first time Charles Sumner used his considerable diplomatic skills during the Civil War to avert a catastrophic war with England, but it would not be the last.

Less than two years later, British treachery caused an outraged Sumner to demand that the powerful island nation stand down, which would result in an international crisis that remained unresolved for nearly a decade. The Confederate warship *Alabama* disrupted Union merchant shipping during 1863 and 1864, conducting an unstoppable sinking spree that would earn her an almost mythic stature while striking fear into the hearts of Northern captains and coastal dwellers alike. Eventually, over nearly two years at sea (before she was finally sunk off the coast of France in 1864), the *Alabama* terrorized U.S. merchant vessels and warships in the Atlantic, off Newfoundland and the New England coast, and off the coasts of Brazil, South Africa, the West Indies, Europe, and all the way to Singapore.

Worse, from the Union point of view, was the fact that the *Alabama*, the pride of the Confederate Navy, had been constructed and launched in England after Confederate envoys convinced the British to assist them— albeit secretly—in building a navy. The *Alabama* was at the center of a brewing storm in British-American relations since its construction began in 1861 (it was launched in May 1862), even as the *Trent* Affair festered. Additional Confederate ships had been built in England, too, and more were under construction as the *Alabama* crisis reached full boil.

Once again, the two countries were on the brink of war. Once again, Charles Sumner was determined to prevent it.

Sumner believed the English position was untenable and nearly unforgivable. Unlike *Trent*, when the British arguments were legally correct and the United States was technically in violation of law and custom on the high seas, the British were now actively engaged in assisting a traitorous belligerent in its war against the United States. If additional Confederate ships were built in English ports and allowed to sail and prey on Union shipping, war would be unavoidable.

"All who talk peace will be powerless," Sumner predicted. And later, a plea to the British: "Stop the ships."

❋ ❋ ❋

For Sumner, the British position was even more infuriating because, like the *Trent* Affair, at its root, it signaled England's support for American slavery.

British elites, diplomats, royalty, politicians, and media people all vociferously claimed to despise slavery, yet most sympathized with the Confederacy because cheap Southern cotton powered a robust English economy that benefitted this group most of all—allowing many of them to accrue personal fortunes. But since the outbreak of the war and the Union blockade, those British textile factories were largely silent, which threatened British upper-class prosperity. In addition, many members of the British aristocracy, who often resented the rebellious spirit of their own working class, were kindred spirits with—and perhaps secret admirers of—the monarchical slaveocracy that imposed ironfisted order and rigidity across the American South.

These attitudes meant that American animosity toward England had grown more pronounced since the Civil War had transformed into a titanic battle about the future of slavery. Sumner spoke for many when he asked whether England really desired to align itself with a "disgusting slave empire" on the borders of the United States. Such a position was sheer madness, Sumner charged, and it seemed inconceivable to him that the British would pursue such a course.

Eventually, with Sumner's influence, and tide-turning Union victories in 1863 at Gettysburg and Vicksburg, the British relented. On September 8, 1863, Lord Russell notified the American minister that the British would release no more Confederate ships from English shipyards.

And with those words, the crisis was over.

For the second time in less than two years, Charles Sumner's influence and diplomacy had averted war with England.

✳ ✳ ✳

In 1869, four years after the war ended, Sumner would demand reparations from England in a scathing anti-British speech in the Senate that landed like a thunderclap on both sides of the Atlantic.

Sumner demanded that Britain provide monetary recompense for damage done by Confederate cruisers financed by Britain and built in English shipyards, and for prolonging the war by as much as two years. Eventually, these cases were lumped under a single moniker named for the historic Confederate ship that struck the deepest fear into Union hearts during the Civil War—the two sides would refer to these collectively and forevermore as the "*Alabama* claims." In his speech, Sumner offered his shocking sum as a remedy for British treachery.

Sumner would estimate at a colossal $100 million the cost of goods and tonnage that the *Alabama* and other CSA ships had sunk and now lay on the bottom of the ocean, the increased insurance costs on all American vessels, and the overall damage to U.S. commerce. But that figure was simply "one item in our bill," Sumner said. Since the total cost of the war was approximately $4 billion, and British assistance to the Confederacy prolonged the war for two years, it was only appropriate that the British be held responsible for half the cost—or $2 billion dollars. It was an unimaginable sum.

He justified it simply: England had inflicted upon the United States "an injury most difficult to measure." Worse, it occurred at "a great epoch in history . . . when civilization was fighting a last battle with slavery."

✳ ✳ ✳

A Joint High Commission of American and British officials was formed to adjudicate the *Alabama* claims, and it would hammer out what become known as the Treaty of Washington, which was finally finished and signed on May 8, 1871. Sumner took no part in the official negotiations, but he reviewed draft copies and worked behind the scenes with British commissioners. Had Sumner drafted the agreement himself, it would be hard to imagine that he could have come up with a document that tracked more fully to the demands he made in his 1869 "*Alabama* claims" speech.

The new Treaty of Washington expressed "the regret by Her Majesty's Government for the escape . . . of the *Alabama* and other vessels from British ports and for the depredations committed by those vessels." Most important from Sumner's point of view, the High Commission had gone along with his desire that the *Alabama* claims for monetary repayments would be submitted to a five-member international tribunal that would meet in Geneva, Switzerland, in December 1871.

Sumner and forty-nine other Republicans voted in favor of the plan, while twelve Democrats were opposed. Sumner took great pleasure that "every point I made . . . is met in the treaty [of Washington]. Of course, the amount of damages . . . will be considered at Geneva."

After two preliminary meetings, the examination of hundreds of pages of written cases by U.S. and British officials, and several days of substantive hearings as they approached a final decision, the international tribunal rendered its verdict on September 14, 1872, in Geneva. By a vote of 4–1 (British arbitrator Sir Alexander Cockburn dissented), the tribunal awarded the United States $15.5 million in damages for Britain's role in the destruction of Union property caused by Confederate ships during the Civil War (Sumner's suggested amount was considered outlandish)— Britain would pay the damages by surrendering U.S. bonds that it held equal to the value of the award.

In Geneva, an artillery salute celebrated the tribunal's decision, church bells clanged, and Swiss gunners held aloft the flags of Geneva, Switzerland, the United States, and Britain. Amid the general good cheer, Cockburn snatched up his hat in disgust and stormed from the hotel.

The *Alabama* treaty and arbitration were landmarks in the settlement of international disputes—one of the very few instances in history when the world's preeminent and most powerful nation, England in this case, agreed to submit a national issue to an international tribunal for resolution. The treaty also ended many years of ugly British-American tension and controversies, which had reared their head since the War of 1812 and, perhaps more accurately, since the American Revolution.

For all practical purposes, the *Alabama* claims decision in Geneva in 1872 cleared the way for the United States and England to become allies, and they remain so to the present day.

Never again were the two nations enemies.

✳ ✳ ✳

Charles Sumner's reputation was burnished by the *Trent* Affair and the *Alabama* crisis, both as a trusted advisor to presidents and as the nation's foremost expert in foreign policy.

It is no exaggeration to say that Sumner's efforts literally saved the country; without his expertise and diplomacy, the North certainly would have blundered into a devastating war with England that—waged simultaneously with its battle with the Confederacy—likely would have destroyed the United States of America.

War with England had been averted.

But two other battles—against the rebels and the slavery system they cherished—had a long way to go.

PART FOUR

DEATH OF SLAVERY, DEATH OF A REBELLION, DEATH OF A PRESIDENT

✳ CHAPTER 27 ✳

EMANCIPATION IN THE NATION'S CAPITAL

FEBRUARY 20, 1862

Willie Lincoln was dead.

The President's eleven-year-old son, the light of his father's life and the joy of his mother's, lost his month-long fight with typhoid fever at 5:00 P.M. as he lay bedridden in an elegant White House guest room. Willie's eight-year-old brother Tad, suffering from the same disease, which he had contracted two weeks after Willie had, lay gravely ill in the same room (Tad would recover from the fever, but he would die at age eighteen from tuberculosis and pneumonia).

Willie was an ineffable delight to his parents, and both were devastated by grief. An exhausted President Lincoln, who had spent night after night sitting bedside vigil with his ill sons, walked down the hall to John Nicolay's office and, in a voice choked with emotion, said to his secretary: "Well, Nicolay, my boy is gone—he is actually gone!" and then burst into tears. In the years after Willie's death, Abraham Lincoln enjoyed occasional uplifting moments, but never again did he experience true joy in his life.

Willie's death crushed his mother. Inconsolable that she had lost her "favorite child . . . the idolized child of the household," Mary Todd Lincoln could not bear to attend Willie's funeral and withdrew from public life, taking to bed for three weeks. For nearly a year, all social activities at the White House were suspended. Mary never fully recovered from Willie's death.

✳ ✳ ✳

Charles Sumner, whose relationship with the Lincolns had grown more intimate in the past months, handled Willie's death with a sense of decorum and sensitivity that did not come naturally to him.

Always a good friend to Mary Lincoln, Sumner drew closer to the First Lady after she lost Willie. Four days after Willie died, President Lincoln, unable to console his wife and thankful for the senator's friendship with her, scribbled a plaintive note to Sumner: "Mrs. L. needs your help. Can you come?"

When Mrs. Lincoln emerged from mourning, she welcomed regular visits and conversations with Sumner; he, too, had known pain and loneliness, and their shared suffering helped establish a lifelong bond. Later in Mary's life, when she was a widow and financially destitute, it was Sumner who convinced Congress to approve a bill awarding her a pension.

Politically, Willie's death snuffed out any of President Lincoln's buoyancy about the successful outcome of the *Trent* Affair and a few small Union victories in early 1862. Plus, much to the grieving Lincoln's frustration, a recalcitrant General George McClellan, commander of the Union Army of the Potomac, seemed determined to do everything in his power to *avoid* a direct attack on the Confederates in northern and eastern Virginia, despite the President's repeated entreaties to seize the offensive.

Sumner, though eager to push forward with his antislavery agenda—he and Lincoln had continued to meet almost daily on a potential plan for compensated emancipation in the border states—knew enough to give the President plenty of space during Willie's illness. "One day in January, he [Lincoln] said sadly that he had been up all night with his sick child," Sumner recounted. "I was very much touched, and I resolved that I would say nothing to the President about this [potential emancipation] or any other business if I could help it until that child was well or dead. And I did not."

Sumner's patience and forbearance were rewarded when, even before the senator was dressed in the early morning of March 6, 1862, Lincoln's secretaries, Hay and Nicolay, arrived at his door with an urgent summons to the White House.

President Lincoln had something he wanted to share immediately.

A first in American history.

✳ ✳ ✳

For the past three months, Lincoln had discussed with Sumner the idea of developing a "compensated emancipation plan" that might convince slave owners in Union border states and Washington, D.C., to free their slaves. The President was now prepared to present the plan to Congress, and he was eager to hear Sumner's opinion. "I want to know how you like it," Lincoln said. "I am going to send it in [to Congress] today."

Lincoln recommended a joint congressional resolution that would offer "pecuniary aid" to any of the border states that would initiate a gradual emancipation plan. The President went out of his way to assure the border states that the decision on whether to support his plan, "the absolute control of the subject [of emancipation]," rested solely with the state and its people.

Lincoln had spent hours on his plan. He pored over the federal budget and the slave population totals in the border states and D.C. . . . . *more than 87,000 slaves in Maryland, 225,000 in Kentucky, 115,000 in Missouri*, and so forth. In all, the combined number of slaves in the four Union border states and Washington, D.C., exceeded 432,000. Lincoln proposed a remuneration to owners of $400 per slave, a total cost to the federal government of about $173 million—or about the cost to wage war for 87 days—which seemed a small price to pay for beginning a process of emancipation that could shorten the war.

So long as slavery continued unchecked, Lincoln expected that the bitter war would continue. Lincoln, Sumner, and others believed that if the Confederacy saw progress on emancipation, the rebels' will would diminish; freedom's foothold in the border states would signal an ever-shrinking haven for slavery on the American continent, and perhaps rebel states would consider a compensation plan as a condition of returning to the Union. The alternative was a bloody, protracted war with the potential to destroy large swaths of the South and, if the North prevailed, end slavery *without* compensation to slave owners.

The valid counterargument, of course, was that Lincoln's border-state emancipation proposal would bolster the spirit of the rebellion and strengthen Confederate tenacity, defiance, and willingness to fight to the bitter end.

Sumner and Lincoln discussed all of this at their March 6 meeting, and overall, Sumner agreed with Lincoln's plan. He seemed unable to part with the document, which he began to read one final time, until Lincoln finally said: "There, now, you've read through it enough, run away. I must send it in today."

Then he gave it to Hay and Nicolay to produce several handwritten copies.

* * *

Sumner had high hopes for Lincoln's border-state compensation plan, in part as a distraction from his own stumble that occurred in February when he presented a series of resolutions on how Confederate states might be handled if they returned to the Union.

It was, for all intents and purposes, the first foray into what would one day be called "Reconstruction."

Sumner's proposals were based on what he labeled "state suicide"—a theory that the rebel states had forfeited all rights to their statehood status in the Union when they seceded and trained their guns on the United States. They were now equivalent to territories, and as such, these former states and their "pretend governments" fell "under the exclusive jurisdiction of Congress." Within this national territory, all "peculiar local institutions" automatically ceased to exist unless they were sanctioned by an act of Congress. Slavery, which could not exist without an affirming law, was therefore abolished throughout the seceded states—or the new "territory." In addition, Sumner insisted that Congress ordain black suffrage in the former rebel states before they could rejoin the Union.

Unfortunately for Sumner, his resolutions were greeted with widespread and instant disapproval and tabled by the Senate. Senator Waitman T. Willey of western Virginia, speaking on behalf of the border states, was furious that Sumner was attempting "by one fell swoop of his pen to blot ten or twelve States out of the Union *forever,* to remit them back to a territorial condition." Most lawmakers felt congressional oversight of such a vast territory would be impractical and unwieldy, and would stiffen the backbone of the rebels. Republican senator James Doolittle of Wisconsin offered grudging admiration that Sumner had convinced more than twenty Republican senators to support his proposal. In a relatively short time, Doolittle said, these men have "*Sumner-ized* the Senate."

Against such resistance, Sumner did what he usually did—began preparing an elaborate speech defending his position. But he did not deliver it. The widespread hostile reactions to his resolutions, and his approaching reelection contest, may have convinced him not to make any additional political enemies at this crucial time. Lincoln, about to submit his compensated emancipation border-state proposal, may also have appealed to Sumner to stand down.

Though incremental in comparison with Sumner's sweeping state-suicide resolutions, the President's plan would have to do—Sumner could live with baby-step progress.

If the border states supported Lincoln's proposal, slavery would be one small step closer to eradication.

✳ ✳ ✳

But they rejected it overwhelmingly.

Despite days of meetings between Lincoln and border-state members of Congress, twenty of the twenty-eight representatives politely declined to act on the President's compensated emancipation plan. In a long letter to Lincoln, they cited a variety of reasons: the burden on the national treasury to pay slave owners to free their slaves, which would amount to a tax on slave owners that would offset the compensation they received; the unconstitutionality of allowing the federal government to even make such a proposal in the first place, since it was a clear infringement on states' rights; fears that emancipation in the border states would further unite the South and increase its desperation; and perhaps most important, that such a proposed "radical change of our social system" had been hurried through Congress without reasonable time for debate, and with "not time at all for consultation with our constituents."

Lincoln was bitterly disappointed. He thought he knew and understood the border states, and he believed they knew and understood him. Their refusal to accept what he considered a fair, reasonable, and gradual emancipation plan stung him deeply.

Yet, there was a silver lining, or in Sumner's eyes, *several* silver linings. While Lincoln's plan failed, in the succeeding weeks and months it

stimulated Republicans in Congress to push through several practical antislavery measures—forbidding the army and navy to aid in the return
of fugitive slaves; diplomatically recognizing the mostly black nations of
Liberia and Haiti, something heretofore opposed by Southern lawmakers
who feared the countries would send black diplomats to mingle in Washington society; and completing a treaty with Great Britain to finally stamp
out the Atlantic slave trade. The latter measure, approved unanimously in
the Senate, moved Sumner to tears—for him, it ended several centuries
of an evil practice and illustrated the groundswell of antislavery fervor in
the North.

The failure of Lincoln's proposals to resonate with the individual border states also compelled Congress to look much closer to home, to a
jurisdiction over which the federal government *did* have control, one
in which the very existence of slavery despoiled the nation's founding
promise, and now, in the midst of a rebellion, seemed to mock the very
reason the Union was fighting in the first place.

It was finally time for Congress—after years of debate, of fits and starts,
of rationalization and hesitation—to abolish slavery in Washington, D.C.

✳ ✳ ✳

Since December 1861, the Senate had been reviewing what had come to
be known as the "Compensated Emancipation Act of 1862." It was sub-
titled "For the release of certain persons held to service or labor in the
District of Columbia," and the Senate finally took up the bill for debate
on March 12.

Inspired and driven by Charles Sumner, supported by Senate Republicans, and dislodged from committee purgatory by Lincoln's bold border-
state compensation proposal, the bill called for freeing more than three
thousand slaves in the nation's capital.

It also provided for a three-person commission to appraise claims by
slave owners for any slaves set free—limiting their allowance in the ag-
gregate to $300 per slave. Congress appropriated $1 million to pay slave
owners and added another $100,000 to pay them an additional $100 per
slave for those who chose to immigrate to Liberia or Haiti.

Charles Sumner hailed the bill, and the prospect of its speedy adoption, with "unspeakable delight." It was only a "small installment" of the

debt the United States owed to the enslaved people within its borders, Sumner pointed out, yet it would be "recognized in history as a victory of humanity."

✳ ✳ ✳

Jubilant and defiant at the same time, Sumner titled his March 31 speech in support of the bill "Ransom of Slaves at the National Capital." He was willing, albeit reluctantly, to vote money for emancipation, but he would not recognize the title of "master" implied in compensation. Because of his long-held view that there could be "no property in man," he considered the grant of money as a "ransom" for the slave rather than compensation for the illegitimate "master."

Still, while the bill was far from perfect, Sumner's exuberance was palpable during his remarks, which captured the full import of the moment. The act before the Senate was the first solid, tangible stride for emancipation *anywhere* in the United States, and it would bring the country closer to his goal of emancipation *everywhere*.

He used his time to trace the history of slavery in the District, and also to justify Congress's right to abolish it—"if Congress cannot abolish slavery *here*, then there is no power *anywhere* to abolish it." Indeed, for too long, Congress had abrogated its responsibility by allowing slavery in a district under its jurisdiction without support of any kind in the Constitution. "There is no power in the Constitution to make a king, or, thank God, to make a slave," he said. And absent such power, all laws and statutes sustaining slavery in the national capital must be unconstitutional and void. Approve the Compensated Emancipation Act of 1862 and watch "the whole widespread tyranny begin to tumble," he predicted to his colleagues.

As was customary after he delivered a speech, Sumner received praise from newspapers and constituents. No words better captured the feelings of those who had supported Sumner since his emergence on the national scene than that of Frederick Douglass:

"The events taking place seem like a dream," the former slave wrote to Sumner. "If slavery is really dead in the District of Columbia . . . *to you more than to any other American statesman belongs the honor of this great triumph of justice, liberty, and sound policy. . . .* You have lived to strike down in Washington the [slave] power that lifted the bludgeon against your own free voice."

✳ ✳ ✳

On April 3, the Senate passed the Washington, D.C., Emancipation Act by a decisive vote of 29–14. Opponents were an unlikely mix of border-state senators who felt the bill was too sweeping (and feared Congress looking to emancipate their slaves next), radicals who felt D.C. slave owners deserved no compensation, and some Western senators who believed Congress was overstepping its authority, especially since the Southern-sympathizing D.C. city government was opposed to the measure.

On April 11, the House approved the act resoundingly, 94–44.

President Lincoln reviewed the bill for a few days—hesitating because he had questions. Had Washington, D.C., slave owners been given enough time to review it and have their voices heard? Was the compensation plan fair and reasonable? Language in the bill provided that claims for compensation must be submitted within ninety days, but not thereafter—that seemed unnecessarily onerous, and Lincoln suggested that the deadline should be extended with an amendment or through a supplemental bill (a supplemental bill was passed in July).

Suspense loomed across Washington as Lincoln considered the legislation. After two days, Sumner visited the President and expressed astonishment that Lincoln could postpone his approval for even one more night. Slaves across D.C. were "in concealment, waiting for the day of Freedom to come out from their hiding places." Sumner resorted to chiding the President: "Do you know who at this moment is the largest slave-*holder* in this country? It is Abraham Lincoln, for he holds all three thousand slaves of the District, which is more than any other person in the country holds!"

As irritating as it was to Lincoln, Sumner's sarcasm worked.

On April 16, 1862, the President signed the Compensated Emancipation Act. For the first time in American history, Congress had passed, and the President had signed into law, a bill calling for the emancipation of slaves within the borders of the United States.

The law would also stand unique in the country's history as the only instance in which the U.S. government provided compensation to slave owners. Over the next nine months, the Board of Commissioners approved 930 petitions, fully or in part, from former owners as recompense for the freedom of nearly 3,000 former slaves.

* * *

News of President Lincoln's action raced across Washington, D.C.—the joy throughout the District's black community was dramatic and profound. "This indeed has been a happy day to me," wrote one black resident to his friend in Baltimore. He described a chambermaid leaving the room and sobbing for joy when she heard the news. Another enslaved woman, now free, exclaimed, "Let me go and tell my husband that Jesus has done all things well." The *Anglo-African*, a black newspaper published in New York, deemed Lincoln's signing fitting since it happened nearly a year to the day of the Confederate attack on Fort Sumter.

The date Lincoln signed the bill remained etched for decades in the memories of former Washington, D.C., slaves. On the fourth anniversary of the law going into effect, April 16, 1866, a year after the war had ended and four months after the final ratification of the Thirteenth Amendment had abolished slavery throughout the United States, leading African American figures in the nation's capital organized a huge parade to celebrate and demonstrate their pride, solidarity, and political strength. More than five thousand people marched and another ten thousand turned out to cheer them on.

The parade would become an annual celebration until the start of the twentieth century.

* * *

For Charles Sumner, emancipation in the nation's capital, compensated or not, did to Washington what Joshua's trumpets did to Jericho—in the name of justice, the walls of despair around D.C. that the slaveocracy had erected and fortified for decades came tumbling down.

It had been nearly thirty years since he first visited and saw slaves; fourteen since the nation's largest slave uprising, the *Pearl* incident, had occurred within the nation's capital; and a decade since Sumner had helped free Sayres and Drayton from an unjust prison term for their unsuccessful effort to help those slaves escape. Hard as it was to imagine that these events, and others like them, took place in Washington, D.C., they would soon be mere memories along the Potomac.

Emancipation in the capital city was a joyful event in its own right, a powerful message to the country and the world that the federal government of the United States had finally rejected and thrown off the yoke of slavery within its most visible and noteworthy area of jurisdiction.

Just as important, though, was what emancipation in Washington, D.C., portended and influenced elsewhere.

Slowly, surely, the dominoes were beginning to fall. In the second half of 1862, Charles Sumner kept pushing . . . pushing.

CHAPTER 28

"AT LAST, THE PROCLAMATION HAS COME"

As 1862 wore on, Sumner's jubilance about progress in the battle against slavery was dampened by anxiety and sorrow over debilitating illnesses that befell family members.

His seventy-seven-year-old mother, who had been ill since December of 1861, was now almost completely bedridden with exhaustion and insomnia, and often too weak to talk. This began a downward spiral that left Relief Sumner more enfeebled and enervated with each passing month, until her death in June 1866.

Sumner was also concerned about the deteriorating condition of his lone remaining brother. George—incessant talker, clever debater, pretentious traveler, prolific writer of letters and pro-Union newspaper columns—had been laid low by a debilitating freak injury. While assisting Governor John Andrew by supervising the mobilization of Massachusetts troops, George was accidentally slammed in the knee by an errant railroad car. Soon, George's entire right leg was paralyzed, and by the summer of 1862, George could barely move—a manservant cared for all of his needs.

As early as April 1862, writing from Washington, Charles asked Samuel Gridley Howe about George's deteriorating health and offered to cover all of his brother's medical costs. When Charles returned to Boston in late July, he was deeply saddened by his brother's condition. George's boundless energy and glib chatter had always enlivened the Sumner house. Now he lay silent and still.

With both his brother and mother bedridden and his only surviving sister, Julia Hastings, now married and living in California, Charles was struck by the deathly quiet of the Sumner house.

The weight of worry and the pang of loneliness gripped him.

✳ ✳ ✳

A tumultuous and grueling, though productive, spring and early summer in Washington was now giving way to an almost irrepressible anxiety and anticipation Sumner felt for the fall.

Time and again, before leaving Washington, Sumner had urged President Lincoln to issue a general proclamation of emancipation as a means to shorten the war. The two met on the Fourth of July, and Sumner argued that Independence Day was the perfect time to issue such a decree—it would make July 4 "more sacred and historic than ever."

In one fell swoop, Sumner said, Lincoln could change the course of the rebellion by freeing the slaves and allowing them to serve in the Union Army, which would swell the ranks of Union troops and create grateful and passionate new allies. He was disappointed when Lincoln failed to act, more so when Lincoln said: "I would do it if I were not afraid that half the officers would fling down their arms and three more States would rise." A frustrated Sumner disagreed with Lincoln's assessment, pointing out that Lincoln's last call for three hundred thousand troops had been greeted with enthusiasm in the North because it signaled that he was "pushing the war vigorously."

A general proclamation of emancipation would show the same resolve. But, Sumner lamented in one letter, on this topic Lincoln "is hard to move."

Would the President be ready to move by fall?

✳ ✳ ✳

Sumner was convinced that every positive development over the previous few months—full emancipation in Washington, D.C., the recognition of Haiti and Liberia, the treaty with England outlawing the slave trade, even Lincoln's failed border-state compensation initiative—signaled that a major announcement from the President was imminent.

Then, on July 17, 1862, Lincoln signed the Senate-and-Sumner-led "second confiscation act," which authorized presidential seizure of rebel property, including slaves, and provided that those slaves coming within Union lines "shall be deemed captives of war and shall be forever free." They would not be subject to return under the Fugitive Slave Law.

The legislation indicated that congressional Republicans—led by

Sumner—were growing impatient with Lincoln and were willing to exert additional pressure to persuade him to act more boldly on the emancipation issue. While some in Congress believed lawmakers were interfering with the President's war powers, Sumner dismissed this notion, declaring that confiscation was a "step to Emancipation," not a challenge to presidential authority. Besides, war powers were not limited to the President—Congress also had extensive war authority under the Constitution.

Regardless of the tension between Sumner and Lincoln, the President signed the Senate-sponsored confiscation bill. But he did so with the knowledge that he would make minimal effort to enforce it. Instead, he was preparing to exercise his presidential power in another way. For weeks, even as Sumner accused him of moving too slowly, the President had shifted closer to the senator's way of thinking. For weeks, Lincoln had thought about and labored over a "paper stronger than an army."

A first draft of his proclamation for emancipation was in one of the drawers of his writing desk, "but no other living soul was aware of it."

✳ ✳ ✳

As Lincoln mulled the timing of revealing the secret document, *New York Tribune* editor Horace Greeley excoriated him for fighting the war without acting against the evil that caused it.

In his August 22, 1862, response to Greeley, Lincoln explained his position and offered a hint of what lay ahead. As always, his paramount goal was to save the Union. "If I could save the Union without freeing any slave, I would do it, and if I could do it by freeing *all* the slaves I would do it," Lincoln wrote, "and if I could save it by freeing some and leaving others alone I would also do that." Within this context, however, it was important for Greeley to understand that he stood by his "oft-expressed *personal* wish that all men everywhere could be free." He conceded that slavery was at the root of the rebellion and viewed the Emancipation Proclamation as a wartime measure; the timing of its issuance was dependent on the advantages it might offer to suppress the rebellion.

On September 17—coincidentally the same day the congressional Confiscation Act was due to take effect—the Union's slender victory at the horrific Battle of Antietam provided Lincoln with the moment he sought. From the smoke and the screams and the dreadful carnage at Antietam Creek, on the Burnside Bridge, and in the cornfield, a sharp bolt of clarity emerged for Lincoln on the single bloodiest day in American history.

When he met with his cabinet afterward, the President concluded: "I think the time has come now."

✲ ✲ ✲

SEPTEMBER 23, 1862

It was the moment Sumner had so long prayed for, had so often cajoled, wheedled, and tussled with Lincoln over, a moment he despaired of ever happening. It evidently caught him by surprise—just days earlier he had complained to Congressman John Fox Potter of "fatal irresolution" in the Lincoln administration. Unsure of whether Lincoln would act, Sumner was pinning his hopes on the Confiscation Act, which promised to free slaves of those still in rebellion by September 17, at least a measure of emancipation regardless of what Lincoln did.

On his decision to finally move ahead with the proclamation, the President said: "I felt that we had . . . about played our last card and must change our tactics, or lose the game." As Salmon Chase recalled later, Lincoln vowed to himself that "if God gave us victory in the approaching battle he would consider it an indication of Divine will." After Antietam, the President said: "God had decided the question in favor of the slaves."

Lincoln's words to his assembled cabinet so impressed Chase that he recorded them in his journal:

> When the rebel army was at Frederick, I determined, as soon as it should be driven out of Maryland, to issue a Proclamation of Emancipation such as I thought most likely to be useful. I said nothing to anyone; but I made the promise to myself and (hesitating a little)—to my Maker. The rebel army is now driven out, and I am going to fulfil [sic] that promise.

Antietam's outcome was enormous for another reason. As historic as the Emancipation Proclamation was in the fall of 1862 and would be when it formally took effect on January 1, 1863, the document was toothless unless and until the Union won the war. Despite enormous losses in the battle on both sides—more than twenty-three thousand had been killed or wounded—Antietam proved finally that the Union *could* win an important battle, and perhaps the war.

After the proclamation was issued and published in newspapers across the North, Lincoln told a group of well-wishers who had serenaded him at the White House, "What I did, I did under a very heavy and solemn sense of responsibility."

Then he added: "I can only trust in God I have made no mistake."

✳ ✳ ✳

If Charles Sumner was disappointed that Lincoln's proclamation delayed for one hundred days the freeing of slaves in the rebel states, or that it didn't go far enough because it ignored border-state slaves entirely, he was too politically astute to show it.

Sumner recognized the deftness of the Emancipation Proclamation. In fewer than five hundred words, Lincoln had figured a way for the nation to take the most meaningful leap toward freedom since the Declaration of Independence while also avoiding two major obstacles. First, by limiting the proclamation to states defying federal authority, he would not disturb the property of slave owners in the border states so critical to the Union cause, since they were not "in rebellion" against the United States. Second, by declaring the proclamation a military necessity, he sidestepped any constitutional issues raised by congressional action against slavery, such as the Confiscation Act.

The issuance of the Emancipation Proclamation now placed Lincoln and Sumner in harmony heading into the fall election season, and Sumner saw value in reinforcing this message to his Massachusetts constituents. He spoke often about the power and necessity of the proclamation as a war measure, including at a major October speech at Faneuil Hall, where he received a thunderous ovation as he stepped to the platform. When the applause subsided, a black man in the audience rose and cried out in a trembling voice: "God Bless Charles Sumner!" and the cheering resumed. "Thank God that I live to enjoy this day!"

Sumner labeled the fight against slavery one of the grandest events of history, "one of those epochs from which humanity will date"—emancipation would forever be remembered as beginning with Lincoln's proclamation. It signaled the beginning of the end of slavery not only in the United States but in other places in the world—Brazil, Cuba, Puerto Rico—where it continued to exist and stain the honor of foreign nations.

"Nowhere can [slavery] survive extinction here," he said. "We conquer for liberty everywhere."

It was a profound mission that Union troops were embarked upon, Sumner reminded the crowd. Dying bravely for one's country was honorable enough—"but all who die for country now die also for humanity . . . as heroes through whom the Republic was saved and civilization established forever."

✳ ✳ ✳

Sumner's full-throated support of Lincoln and the Emancipation Proclamation paid off politically for him and Republicans in Massachusetts. On November 4, 1862, 59 percent of Massachusetts voters again chose John Andrew as governor and selected an overwhelmingly Republican legislature that pledged to give Sumner a third term in the Senate. On election night, more than one thousand Republicans gathered outside Sumner's house on Hancock Street, serenading him on his victory and upcoming reelection by the legislature.

In early January 1863, the new legislature sent Sumner back to Washington by a more than five-to-one margin.

The cause of emancipation was victorious, Massachusetts supported it irrevocably, and Sumner, now at his political pinnacle, had consolidated his power base at home and in Washington as he prepared to begin his third term in the U.S. Senate.

✳ ✳ ✳

JANUARY 1, 1863, BOSTON

Charles Sumner was in Washington on New Year's Day, but he found out later that many of his Boston constituents were on tenterhooks for the entire day. The suspense was maddening.

As the 11:00 P.M. hour struck at the city's Tremont Temple, tension built among the thousands assembled there. Only sixty minutes from midnight, and still no official word that President Lincoln had issued his promised Emancipation Proclamation. Boston had been celebrating for the entire day; church bells rang throughout the city, and singing and dancing could be heard on most street corners as blacks and whites joined together to mark what they hoped was a new era in the country's history.

In a speech to the Tremont Temple crowd, Frederick Douglass thanked God that he was alive to see the beginning of the end of slavery. He knew that Lincoln's proclamation would not have the immediate effect of liberating the slaves, but Douglass had no doubt of its ultimate weight and historical significance—it finally put the full power of the U.S. government on the right side of the struggle between "beautiful right and ugly wrong."

But precisely when, on this first day of 1863, would that time arrive?

Anxious citizens wondered aloud whether Lincoln would keep his promise; there had been rumors of the President hesitating, perhaps even equivocating. While Douglass led the meeting at the Tremont Temple, Boston's literary and social elite packed the nearby Music Hall. Emerson, Longfellow, Whittier, Harriet Beecher Stowe—all awaited the long-sought news from the nation's capital. Messengers had been stationed at Boston's telegraph office since early evening, charged with bringing word to the Tremont Temple and Music Hall rallies that Lincoln had signed the proclamation.

"We . . . waited on each speaker, keeping our eye on the door, and no proclamation," Douglass would say later. "And I said, 'We won't go home til morning.'"

✳ ✳ ✳

What the Bostonians could not know was that Lincoln had signed the document nine hours earlier, on a clear and brilliant New Year's Day in Washington, D.C.

After a morning meeting with General Ambrose Burnside to discuss the Union's bloody and devastating defeat at Fredericksburg less than a month earlier, Lincoln spent a few minutes polishing the proclamation. He was still writing at 11:00 A.M. when guests began to arrive for the annual New Year's reception held at the White House. Lincoln dressed in formal clothes and went downstairs to greet guests—government officials, dignitaries, members of the diplomatic corps.

For three long hours, he shook hands and made small talk, unconcerned that his social duty was delaying the official issuance of the country's most important document since its founding. "Vast as its consequences, the [proclamation] itself was only the simplest and briefest formality," wrote Nicolay and Hay. Lincoln's "mental conflict and the moral victory" occurred back in July, when he prepared his draft, and then in September, when he announced to all that the proclamation was coming.

After Lincoln greeted the last of a few thousand well-wishers, he went back upstairs to his office. His right hand was so cramped, stiff, and numb from three hours of shaking hands that he could hardly hold his pen. While he assured his aides that "I, never in my life, felt more certain that I was doing right, than I do in signing this paper," he worried that his signature would be "closely examined" for all of history. "If they find my hand trembled, they will say, 'he had some compunctions'" about signing, he predicted. "But, any way, it is going to be done."

Then, President Lincoln steadied his hand, grasped the pen firmly, dipped it, and signed the document—not the usual *A. Lincoln* but the full *Abraham Lincoln*. The signature was bold and clear.

The Emancipation Proclamation was official.

✳ ✳ ✳

But right up until the final moment, it was not *inevitable*. Charles Sumner, exerting his influence on Lincoln, helped make it so.

In the ninety-nine days since Lincoln had announced his intentions, speculation was rampant on whether he would issue the proclamation or withdraw it. Lincoln received pressure from both sides, but those opposed to the document were often more vocal. The President's good friend Orville Browning, senator from Illinois, claiming to reflect the views in the President's home state, said the document would "unite and exasperate" the South and "divide and distract us in the North." These kinds of sentiments, plus Lincoln's reluctance to mention the proclamation as the days ticked off in October, November, and December, alarmed abolitionists.

Was Lincoln losing his nerve?

They turned to Sumner for help.

Sumner, who often spoke publicly during the fall in support of the proclamation, visited the President on December 27 to ensure Lincoln was on track for the January 1 signing. The President was hard at work on the draft, writing it out in longhand. Sumner interrupted to present Lincoln with a number of pleas from proclamation supporters: a letter from Boston clergymen urging him to stand by his commitment; an insert from a Boston paper advertising a musical celebration on January 1 in honor of the proclamation; a list of electoral college members from Massachusetts who supported the proclamation, "*which he proceeded to read aloud,*" Sumner exclaimed.

Sumner then put aside his props and spoke from his heart—of the importance and grandeur of the act. He urged Lincoln to make the document a military decree, cosigned by Secretary of War Stanton, since it would show the measure as an act of "military necessity and just self-defense" as well as "an act of justice and humanity." (Eventually Secretary of State William Seward, not Stanton, would cosign the proclamation.) Such action would serve to dissuade opposition to the document, Sumner said.

Lincoln listened intently and then said, as a way to explain the great care he was taking before finalizing the proclamation: "I know very well that the name connected with this document will never be forgotten." But there was no doubt, he assured Sumner: he would sign and issue it on schedule.

Sumner wrote with confidence to a friend the next day: "The President says he could not stop the Proclamation if he would, and would not if he could."

For Sumner, his visit to the Executive Mansion on December 27—mere days before the Emancipation Proclamation was scheduled to take effect—could not have gone much better.

"Let the music sound and the day be celebrated," he wrote.

✳ ✳ ✳

Back in Boston, shortly after 11:00 P.M. on January 1, 1863, Judge Thomas Russell, who had gone to the telegraph office himself for news from the capital, burst through the Tremont Temple's front doors, shouting to the crowd and clutching the Emancipation Proclamation text in his hands, along with the notification that Lincoln had signed it.

"Hats, muffs, cushions, overcoats, and even umbrellas were thrown heavenward, and dancing and stamping became general all over the hall," one reporter recounted. Crowd members unknowingly echoed celebrants in Washington earlier in the day when they shouted, "God Bless Abraham Lincoln," "Glory to God," and "Bully for Old Abe," as the cheering reached a crescendo. Frederick Douglass recounted later: "I never saw Joy before! Men, women, young and old were up; hats and bonnets were in the air."

Abolitionist Charles W. Slack ascended the rostrum, raised his hands, and called for order. The crowd quickly complied, and Slack read a portion of the historic text:

"That on the 1st day of January, in the year of our Lord, 1863, all persons held as slave, within any State or designated part of a state, the people whereof shall then be in rebellion against the United States, shall be then, thenceforth, and forever free . . ."

Slack was interrupted with thunderous applause, waited for the noise to subside, and continued:

"And the executive government of the United States, including the military and naval authority thereof, will recognize and maintain the freedom of such persons . . ."

More sustained applause.

"And will do no act or acts to repress such persons on any of them in any effort they may make for their actual freedom."

With the crowd in a near frenzy, Slack reached the Emancipation Proclamation's soaring conclusion, a passage suggested by Charles Sumner:

"And upon this act, sincerely believed to be an act of justice, warranted by the Constitution, upon military necessity, I invoke the considerate judgment of mankind, and the gracious favor of Almighty God."

Again, the Boston audience erupted with cheers. Frederick Douglass led the singing of the psalm "This is the Day of Jubilee" as the meeting concluded and the ecstatic crowd spilled onto the street for further celebration.

Douglass summed up the crowd's delirium at that moment: "We got up such a state of enthusiasm that almost anything [anyone said or shouted] seemed witty—and entirely appropriate to the glorious occasion."

✳ ✳ ✳

For the crowds who celebrated into the wee hours of January 2 in Boston, for slaves already liberated in Washington, D.C., for thousands of abolitionists across Northern cities and small towns, for nearly four million slaves in the Confederacy, and for Charles Sumner—the Emancipation Proclamation was so much more than a presidential order.

It was a sacred document, one awaited, considered, and accepted with near-biblical reverence, one unimagined as recently as a decade earlier, when abolitionists were considered fringe radicals and Northern acquiescence to the Southern slaveocracy was seen as essential and necessary for the nation's commerce to survive.

No longer. Like Sumner, most Northerners fully recognized the power and potential of the Emancipation Proclamation's content, and most concurred with the *Boston Daily Advertiser*'s editorial position on January 2: "No instrument of more momentous impact has ever been published since the Declaration of Independence challenged the attention of the world, and this proclamation affects the welfare of as large a number of human beings as did that."

The paper's editorialists were not so starry-eyed as to suggest that a "mere dash" of Lincoln's pen "secures freedom to the full . . . [or] that it straightaway crushes the rebellion and ends the war." Still, the proclamation provided the North with numerous advantages. It cleared the way for colored troops to fight in the federal army and deprived the South of a vital manpower source during a time of war. It all but removed frivolous political spats and disputes that detracted from the war effort. It silenced those voices who questioned Lincoln's opposition to slavery. The proclamation's greatest value was more symbolic in nature, the *Advertiser* argued. After nearly two years of war, Lincoln's words meant that the North, at long last, would enjoy "the immense support which springs from the cordial sympathy of the moral sense of the whole world."

And that moral sense, the publication believed, would endure.

✳ ✳ ✳

Charles Sumner believed all these things, too.

The drawn-out process of issuing the proclamation had simultaneously brought him a greater appreciation of Lincoln's more deliberate approach to emancipation and drew the President nearer to his position on the subject. Never one to compromise, Sumner was initially displeased that the Emancipation Proclamation's "gradualism" did not include freeing slaves in border states. But he eventually recognized what Lincoln had argued all along—those states were vital to a potential Union victory, and *without* victory, the proclamation's words would remain merely hollow rhetoric, the document itself relegated to an obscure historical footnote.

For Lincoln's part, the months spent working through the proclamation's ideas, language, and tone had solidified for him what Sumner had been saying all along—at its core, from the Union's perspective, the war was about nothing less than the elimination of slavery from the United States, a premise Lincoln had first disputed, then reconsidered, then circled with caution, then gravitated toward, and now, finally, gripped like a vise with his large and strong hands.

Sumner and a handful of others—but Sumner above all—relentlessly and unabashedly put forth the arguments and applied the pressure that led to the evolution in Lincoln's thinking.

Long grueling months, epic battles, savage fighting, unimaginable pain, and incomprehensible carnage lay ahead before the war would end and any final verdict would be rendered on slavery.

But a Rubicon had been crossed.

The Union and the Confederacy both knew it.

"It is done," Charles Sumner wrote with satisfaction upon Lincoln's signing of the Emancipation Proclamation. "And the act will be firm throughout time."

CHAPTER 29

"THE RESULT IS CERTAIN—SOONER OR LATER"

THURSDAY AFTERNOON, OCTOBER 8, 1863

In a secluded spot in Mount Auburn Cemetery in Cambridge, Massachusetts, far from the main entrance, the casket of George Sumner was lowered into the ground. Charles, his mother, and a few close friends, Howe and Longfellow among them, attended the otherwise private burial.

Paralyzed for nearly two years, the forty-six-year-old George had died on October 6 at the Massachusetts General Hospital. Since his Cooper Union Institute speech in the fall of 1861, Charles had declined numerous speaking requests and other social engagements to be with George as his brother's condition deteriorated. Charles was at George's bedside when he passed. "My poor brother is at last released from his trials," he wrote to Howe the next day. "The funeral will be *private*, but his friends can never be otherwise than welcome."

It is hard to neatly pigeonhole Sumner's relationship with George. The two brothers could not be described as close—at one point, they hadn't laid eyes on each other for fifteen years, and George disagreed with Charles on many major issues. But they exchanged letters often, and since George's return from Europe, they had been friendly and spoke often; their relationship, cool but never in abject disrepair, had noticeably strengthened.

As for Relief Sumner, also in failing health, she had now suffered the pain of burying seven children—only Charles and Julia remained—astonishingly, all of whom had died as adults.

Sumner struggled with all of this. George's death and what it signified about the family "afflicts me more than I had anticipated," Charles wrote. "It reminds me again of my loneliness in the world."

✳ ✳ ✳

CHRISTMAS DAY, 1863, WASHINGTON, D.C.

With his mother and sister miles away, and other Washington acquaintances otherwise occupied, Charles Sumner spent Christmas in the nation's capital in a contemplative and selfless way, unusual for him during the heat of political battle but perhaps expected as he struggled with the recent death of his brother and his own deep loneliness.

He visited the wounded in nearby army hospitals.

Sumner did not identify precisely which of the more than fifty hastily constructed hospitals in Washington he visited, but from his descriptions, it appears he toured the Lincoln General Hospital on the corner of East Capitol and 15th Street, and the more well-known Armory Square Hospital on the National Mall in the shadow of the U.S. Capitol building, whose new dome, capped by the Statue of Freedom, had been completed only weeks earlier.

Wounded, sick, and suffering Union soldiers made up the overwhelming majority of patients, but Sumner also visited a rebel ward that housed about eighty bedridden soldiers. While the Confederates were treated "precisely like our own soldiers," Sumner conceded that he had "never before noticed so great a contrast in . . . human beings." Union soldiers, even in their suffering, appeared reasonably content to Sumner, or at least quietly resigned to their fates, but "the rebels seemed in a different scale of existence . . . mostly rough, ignorant, brutal, scowling." Sumner talked with several Confederates, inquired about their health, offered his best wishes that they enjoy their holiday meal, and in many cases "softened them into a smile." Still, Sumner admitted, "when they knew who I was they seemed uncertain whether to scowl *extra* or be civil."

Convalescing Confederates may have been agitated when they learned of Sumner's identity, but as the congressional session got underway in late 1863 and moved into 1864, Sumner felt a sense of calm about the state of the nation, perhaps another reason he decided to visit army hospitals on Christmas. Recent Union victories and shifting political attitudes convinced Sumner that it was simply a matter of time before the United States prevailed and slavery was abolished forever.

"The result is certain—sooner or later," he said.

* * *

In fact, President Lincoln, in his short but soaring commemoration of the military cemetery at Gettysburg just a month earlier, had expressed sentiments that drew him and the North even closer to Sumner's lifelong positions.

In less than three minutes, in one grand swoop, the President had linked the current great struggle between North and South—at its root a war to end slavery—to the nation's founding documents and the principles of human freedom and equality. In the speech's brevity lay its genius; in fewer than three hundred words, Lincoln's Gettysburg Address had rendered indissoluble the sacrifices of those who had given their lives in the great battle to the principles espoused in both the Declaration of Independence ("all men are created equal") and the Constitution ("a government of the people, by the people, for the people"). Without mentioning the battle itself, the words "North" or "South" or "slavery," Lincoln's address made clear that the cause for which the soldiers at Gettysburg had given "the last full measure of devotion" represented a "new birth of freedom" for America—one no longer stained by the sin of slavery.

In his own economical but poetic way, Lincoln had reaffirmed what Sumner had long believed and espoused—the Declaration and the Constitution provided clear direction to end slavery and guide the nation's rebirth. It was not the founding documents that were flawed, Lincoln and Sumner agreed, but the misguided, though sometimes well-intentioned, decisions of men—first in the eighteenth century and now in the nineteenth—who had interpreted them too narrowly, who had sacrificed sacred principles for profits or politics or prejudices, to retain the unequal status quo.

Inherent in both the Declaration and the Constitution, plain for all to see, was the *promise* of the United States—equality and self-governance in a nation *conceived* in liberty and *dedicated to the proposition that* all men were created equal—and the sacrifices at Gettysburg had gone a long way toward fulfilling that unfulfilled promise.

Sumner had been expressing similar sentiments his entire public life, and especially since the first shells exploded over Fort Sumter. Civil war, as dreadful and bloody as it was, had given America a second chance to fulfill its rightful destiny. Heading into 1864, even as fighting raged and casualties mounted, the country had turned a corner. For the first time in decades, the road ahead—still long and still dangerous—was at least no longer littered with detritus and debris strewn by the slaveocracy to sabotage America's journey to freedom for all.

"The way seems at last open," he said. "Nobody doubts the result."

✳ ✳ ✳

FEBRUARY 9, 1864, SENATE CHAMBER, WASHINGTON, D.C.

Senators remained silent and unmoving as two tall black men carried the massive roll of petitions across the chamber and laid it upon Charles Sumner's desk.

Lawmakers held differing views on how best to tackle or abolish slavery, but none of them failed to grasp the symbolism and solemnity of what was now happening before them—exactly the effect Sumner had desired when he orchestrated the dramatic and unorthodox moment. "I offer the petition now on the desk before me," Sumner said when the two men departed. "It is too bulky for me to take up. I need not add that it is too bulky for any of our pages to carry."

Sumner proudly presented "The Prayer of One Hundred Thousand," petitions from across the country containing a total of 100,000 signatures of residents above the age of eighteen, "earnestly pray[ing]" that Congress pass "an act emancipating all persons of African descent held to involuntary service or labor in the United States."

The single giant roll was made up of six thousand forms glued end to end, with each state's petition rolled separately in yellow paper, tied with red tape, and marked on the outside with the number of men and women who had signed it.

The petitions were delivered to Sumner by abolitionists and women's suffragettes Elizabeth Cady Stanton and Susan B. Anthony, who, early in 1863, had organized the Women's National Loyal League (WNLL), which hoped to secure a million signatures to petitions demanding the complete abolition of slavery through a constitutional amendment. The one hundred thousand men and women who signed this first batch of petitions,

Sumner explained, "ask for nothing less than Universal Emancipation, and they ask directly at the hands of Congress."

During the summer of 1863, the project garnered support from anti-slavery men, including William Lloyd Garrison, who begged Sumner, as the leading antislavery senator, to fight for a congressional edict abolishing slavery throughout the country. The American Anti-Slavery Society had endorsed the signature-gathering drive at its convention the previous December, urging Sumner to present the petitions to Congress.

Anticipating a flood of petitions, Sumner in January 1864 asked the Senate to create a special commission to "take into consideration all propositions and papers concerning slavery and the treatment of freedom."

Sumner was appointed chairman of the Select Committee on Slavery and Freedom, whose formation he characterized as "an epoch of history." Only a short time ago, Sumner said, the Senate would have refused to authorize such a committee, and even proposing it "would have created a storm of violence."

✳ ✳ ✳

Though the first batch of 100,000 signatures—65,601 from women and 34,399 from men—fell far short of the WNLL's goal of one million (Stanton and Anthony promised another 300,000 signatures soon), the impressive number and widespread geographical scope of the signatures demonstrated clearly that the "slavery monster, wherever it shows its head, is a *national enemy*," Sumner said, "to be pursued and destroyed as such." Nearly 18,000 New Yorkers signed the petition, along with 15,000 Illinois residents and more than 11,000 people from Massachusetts. Large numbers of residents of Ohio, Michigan, Iowa, Maine, and Wisconsin also affixed their names to the historic petition. Sumner assured his Senate colleagues that the petitioners were "a mighty army, one-hundred-thousand strong . . . the advance-guard of a yet larger army."

The arrival of the gigantic WNLL petition in the Senate chamber was high theater, a symbolic event that illustrated the change in attitude that had permeated the Senate and the country on the issue of slavery. As a matter of procedure, it required no technical action by the Senate. But its spirit, combined with Union war advancements and Sumner's pertinacity, infused the Senate with a sense of urgency to bring about an end to slavery.

✳ ✳ ✳

Some dominoes began to fall quickly; others shook, wobbled, and tee-
tered before finally toppling.

In the spring of 1864, Sumner introduced successful legislation allowing
"colored witnesses" to testify in federal courts across the country, something he had helped achieve two years earlier in D.C. alone. He demanded
equal pay for colored troops, who currently made ten dollars per month
compared to thirteen dollars for their white counterparts (the bill passed in
June, and the attorney general implemented it in July 1864); and he pushed
hard for the desegregation of all streetcar lines in Washington, D.C., which
he deemed a public and highly discordant symbol of inequality while Union
troops were purportedly fighting and dying for freedom (his resolution
cleared the Senate quickly and became law in March 1865).

Sumner was unsuccessful in his May 1864 efforts to amend the city
charter in Washington, D.C., over which Congress had jurisdiction, to
allow black suffrage in the District; the bill was ultimately defeated in
June. Such discrimination in the nation's capital was "the tail of slavery,"
Sumner said when he saw his proposal going down to defeat. "Slavery dies hard. It dies hard on the battlefield. It dies hard in the Senate
chamber."

But then, in rapid-fire fashion and with widespread reverberation,
two major legislative initiatives rode upon a wave of political and social
momentum to passage. Two initiatives whose audacious arrival in the
spring of 1864 served notice that—as hard as slavery dies—slavery, indeed, was doomed.

✳ CHAPTER 30 ✳

THE THIRTEENTH AMENDMENT AND THE END OF THE FUGITIVE SLAVE LAW

Since President Lincoln issued the Emancipation Proclamation, Charles Sumner had oscillated on whether a constitutional amendment to abolish slavery was even necessary.

Amending the constitution was by design a lengthy and laborious process, and therefore rare, with many opportunities for derailment along the way. Since the Bill of Rights was adopted in 1791, the Constitution had been amended only twice, and the most recent was ratified a full sixty years earlier. Sumner had long believed and contended with vociferous conviction that both the Constitution and the Declaration of Independence—by their very language guaranteeing freedom and a republican form of government for all—already cleared the way for Congress to eradicate slavery. "By a single, brief statute, Congress may sweep slavery out of existence," he declared, a sentiment he repeated often.

Passing a simple law that abolished slavery would be more immediate and would eliminate the long waiting period necessary for the ratification of a new amendment. He feared that a months- or even years-long process would provide ample opportunity for lawmakers to engage in political mischief, excuse-making, or backpedaling, any of which could relegate a proposed antislavery amendment to political purgatory or a permanent graveyard.

On the other hand, Sumner recognized the lasting power and declarative finality of an amendment. Future lawmakers would be less tempted and less able to reverse course. More to the point, an amendment would give "completeness and permanence to emancipation, and bring the

Constitution into avowed harmony with the Declaration of Independence."

＊ ＊ ＊

On his way to Washington in early December 1863, Sumner broached the subject of a constitutional amendment with well-known abolitionist Henry C. Wright.

The two were aboard the steamboat *Empire State*, traveling on Long Island Sound from Fall River, Massachusetts, to New York—Sumner en route to Washington and Wright to Philadelphia. Sumner sketched out language for the amendment in the form of a petition to Congress and convinced Wright to put it to a vote at the American Anti-Slavery Society at its anniversary meeting on December 4. Sumner's simple language declared that "slavery shall forever be prohibited within the limits of the United States." The society adopted the petition without a single dissenting vote.

The society's congressional petition, prompted by Sumner's shipboard suggestion and language, and recounted by Wright several years later, appears to be the first public movement for the Thirteenth Amendment to the U.S. Constitution.

＊ ＊ ＊

When the congressional session began, two House members offered versions of an antislavery amendment, and on January 11, so did Senator John B. Henderson of Missouri. Henderson's language read: "Slavery or involuntary servitude, except as a punishment for crime, shall not exist in the United States." His proposal was referred to the Judiciary Committee, chaired by the estimable and dominant lawyer-lawmaker Lyman Trumbull of Illinois, the appropriate starting place for any proposition to change the Constitution.

Sumner, one day before he presented "The Prayer of One Hundred Thousand" on the floor of the Senate, offered his own "amendment to the amendment" and reflected his belief that liberty *and* equality were one and inseparable. First, he rejected as outdated and barbaric the notion that slavery as punishment for crime was tolerable in the United States; thus, he found unacceptable Henderson's proposed exception to a slavery ban. Instead, Sumner's language provided that "all persons are equal before the law, so that no person can hold another as a slave."

There it was again—"equal before the law"—a phrase, a concept, precise words that conveyed the full idea of human rights enunciated in the Declaration of Independence. Sumner had introduced the phrase in the United States back in 1849 when he argued the Boston school case on behalf of little Sarah Roberts. Fifteen years, a divided country, and a violent bloody war later, Sumner hoped to enshrine in the U.S. Constitution the small phrase that carried enormous consequences.

He also suggested that the entire question of a Thirteenth Amendment be moved from Trumbull's Judiciary Committee and referred to his own Committee on Slavery and Freedmen, whose mandate was "broad enough to cover every proposition relating to slavery."

Sumner was concerned that his "equal before the law" language would receive insufficient consideration from Trumbull's committee, that without his presence in the room to press the argument in favor of incorporating the phrase into the proposed amendment, Judiciary members would find its inclusion too far ahead of its time.

✳ ✳ ✳

Sumner lost on his motion to bypass the Judiciary Committee and was correct that his amended language would be dismissed by committee members.

On the first, senators seemed perfectly content to allow Sumner his theatrics when presenting "The Prayer of One Hundred Thousand" petition, but they were reluctant to jettison years of Senate tradition, risk retaliation from the powerful Trumbull, and satisfy Sumner's desire for credit by placing the future of the Thirteenth Amendment in his committee's hands.

On the second point, much to Sumner's frustration, Trumbull and others confirmed his fears—an amendment to abolish slavery was a momentous enough change to the Constitution; inserting language that stipulated equality between whites and blacks was beyond the pale for many senators and could jeopardize everything if such an idea reached the full Senate.

The irony, then, was that Charles Sumner—more than any other

individual most responsible for bringing the country to this historic junc-
ture, and the unquestioned and unimpeachable conscience of the Senate,
and the entire North, on the issue of slavery—had little to do with the actual writing of the amendment that ended slavery in the United States.

* * *

Even as the amendment was being crafted in the Judiciary Committee,
Sumner continued to push for a congressional vote banning slavery, an
insurance policy of sorts should the amendment process bog down. He
wanted slavery "in a condition from which it could not recover."

Sumner warned his colleagues not to operate "under the illusion that
we settle this question by an attempt—for it will be *an attempt only*—at
a constitutional amendment." He urged them to focus on the more practical approach as well, by approving simple congressional legislation to
end slavery and its spiderweb of attendant laws and statutes once and for
all. His colleagues heard him out, some even agreed, but on the specific
issue of the abolition of slavery, the die was cast.

Senate Republicans were all in on the Thirteenth Amendment.

* * *

When the proposed amendment emerged from Trumbull's committee on
March 28, Sumner was disappointed but unsurprised that it contained
no language on equal rights. Instead, the Judiciary Committee agreed
on language that would become the historic and profound Thirteenth
Amendment to the Constitution of the United States:

Section 1.

Neither slavery nor involuntary servitude, except as a punishment for
crime whereof the party shall have been duly convicted, shall exist within
the United States, or any place subject to their jurisdiction.

Section 2.

Congress shall have power to enforce this article by appropriate legislation.

Trumbull, proud of his committee's work, argued that the simplicity
and clarity of the amendment were its strengths. He urged swift approval
by the Senate, noting that it would likely receive, within a year, ratifica-

tion from enough states remaining in the Union to become part of the Constitution. Trumbull's remarks were followed over the next several days by long speeches, passionate debates, substitute language proposals, and numerous "amendment to the amendment" offerings.

All were defeated.

Finally, on April 8, the last day of Senate debate, Charles Sumner, who still found the amendment lacking, once again put forth his "equal before the law" language. But Trumbull and others, impatient for a final vote, convinced him to withdraw the proposal. Sumner read the mood of the room—senators were weary, impatient, and "wished to vote and get their dinner," he explained. He would later say he regretted not pushing harder for equal rights language, and fighting against the clause that could still allow slavery as "a punishment for a crime."

But he would offer no more amendments.

However, before the final vote on April 8, 1864, he would speak one last time on the most important and divisive issue that the country had grappled with in its history.

* * *

Because passage of the Thirteenth Amendment in the Senate was not in doubt, Sumner's speech was not designed to persuade but to deliver a brief history lesson and allow him to take a victory lap to commemorate his years of fighting against slavery.

His remarks, which he entitled "No Property in Man," borrowing from and paraphrasing James Madison, was wide-ranging and covered his favorite slavery touchstones—its blatant illegality under the Constitution, the impropriety and injustice of compensating slaveholders, the "judicial perversions" of the Constitution in cases such as *Dred Scott*, and, again and again, his fervent belief in equality under the law.

He made it clear that he would support the amendment, but he believed it would become part of the Constitution "too tardily . . . it postpones till tomorrow what ought to be done *today*." He would continue to be as vigilant and irrepressible as ever as the Thirteenth Amendment wound its way through the ratification process. "So long as a *single slave* continues anywhere beneath the flag of the Republic," he promised, "I am unwilling to rest."

When Sumner sat down, the Senate voted 38–6 to approve the

Thirteenth Amendment—with Sumner casting his "yes" vote with the majority—well beyond the two-thirds margin necessary to move the measure forward.

Sumner's fears that the gears of political discourse would grind slowly on the Thirteenth Amendment's progress were confirmed, at least temporarily, when the House of Representatives failed to achieve a two-thirds majority to approve the measure. In a presidential election year, enough Northern Democrats voted against the amendment so as not to risk disenchanting their base voters.

The session of Congress closed without further action.

✳ ✳ ✳

Even after the Senate had passed the Thirteenth Amendment and sent it to the House, Charles Sumner refused to rest.

More than anything or anyone else over the previous two decades, his voice and his work had brought the Senate—and by extension, the country—to this point. Now, on the intertwined issues of slavery and equality, he wished more.

Since he had delivered his first major speech in the Senate twelve years earlier, a blistering attack on the Fugitive Slave Law, Sumner had envisioned a day when this most odious component of the Compromise of 1850 was forever stricken from U.S. law, along with its less harsh 1793 counterpart. Now, with the Thirteenth Amendment fresh in the minds and hearts of his colleagues, Sumner, during a stirring April 19, 1864, speech, said that it was time "to remove this shame from our statute-book."

If the Thirteenth Amendment ultimately secured passage in the House and ratification in the Senate, the repeal of the Fugitive Slave Laws would largely be academic and symbolic—if slavery was abolished, there could hardly be any fugitives from slavery.

But congressional repeal of the fugitive laws was one of his insurance policies, the practical legislative manifestation of his philosophical pledge to strike against slavery any chance he could.

✳ ✳ ✳

He met resistance from some senators who were content to repeal the 1850 law but balked at eliminating the 1793 act because it was crafted by the "men who framed the Constitution" and declared valid and constitutional by every tribunal since. The eighteenth-century law was seldom enforced and thus hardly onerous; by repealing the 1850 law and retaining the 1793 act, could not the Senate accomplish its goals while showing appropriate reverence for the Framers?

No, Sumner replied in his speech—"the argument against one is the same against all." He answered objectors by challenging them to look at the sacrifices made by colored Union troops at Fort Wagner and at the grisly massacre of black officers and soldiers at Fort Pillow. How could they possibly draw distinctions between the severity of the two laws?

As April dragged into May and then June, Sumner continued to meet opposition and battle through it. Inspired by his arguments, the House of Representatives passed its own resolution calling for the repeal of both Fugitive Slave laws and sent it over to the Senate. The Senate delayed it for another week, and when Sumner brought it up again on June 22, exasperated border-state senator Willard Saulsbury of Delaware demanded the Senate adjourn without a vote. "Let us have *one day* without the nigger," he begged, a sentiment shared by many slaveholding border-state lawmakers who continued to fear that abolitionists would turn against them next, regardless of their importance to the war effort.

Saulsbury's motion failed, and the Senate haggled late into the night. Sumner pressed for a vote—but as close as he was to success, tempers were frayed and members exhausted. Sumner received some aid from Ohio Republican John Sherman, who decried parliamentary delays and declared that he was "perfectly willing now to go into a contest of physical endurance" to pass the bill.

But deep into the night, the Senate adjourned one more time.

✳ ✳ ✳

Finally, on June 23, after beating back additional efforts by border-state senators to omit the Founder-drafted 1793 bill from the legislation, the Senate voted, finally, to repeal all Fugitive Slave Acts.

President Lincoln would sign the bill into law on June 28, 1864.

Sumner could not wait to let Longfellow know of the Senate's action. Noting in his letter that he was writing from the Senate chamber at "10 minutes before 4 o'clk P.M." on the twenty-third, Sumner dashed off a short message: "My dear Longfellow—All fugitive slave acts were to-day expunged from the statute-book. This makes me happy."

He signed it, "Ever Thine, Charles Sumner."

And then Sumner added a postscript: "Thus closes one chapter of my life. I was chosen to the Senate in order to do this work."

✳ ✳ ✳

The congressional session ended on July 4, 1864, and Sumner thought Independence Day appropriate to recount to his British friend the Duchess of Argyll the satisfying success of Congress over the previous six months:

Congress will disperse today, having done several good things:

(1) All fugitive-slave acts have been repealed;
(2) All acts sustaining traffic in slaves on the coast from one domestic port to another have been repealed . . .
(3) The railroads here in Washington have been required to admit colored persons into their carriages.
(4) Greatest of all in practical importance, the rule of evidence excluding colored testimony in the United States courts has been abolished.

All these measures are now *the law of the land*.

Sumner could not resist taking credit, but in this case, it was fully appropriate: "They were all introduced by myself. I feel happy in this result."

✳ ✳ ✳

Among his accomplishments, Sumner might have added his demand for the creation of a new federal agency to assist former slaves in finding a place in the ever-deteriorating society across the South and to protect them from the possibility of once again falling under their former masters' domination.

While war raged, his hope was to create an agency that would provide food and shelter for thousands of displaced and often starving slaves who roamed the South. He also foresaw the peacetime continuation of the "Bureau of Freedmen" to help former slaves find land and employment. The agency was necessary, Sumner argued, to "safeguard against serfdom" and ensure that "there must be no slavery under an *alias*."

After debate on whether the special bureau would sit within the Treasury Department or the War Department, and whether it was appropriate for its charter to continue beyond the end of the war, the Senate passed the bill on June 28 by a vote of 21–9. Again, Sumner was frustrated by foot-dragging and long debates in the House, whose Democrats prevented the bill's final passage until the following session.

Sumner made his views known throughout the long debate—emancipation must "not be nullified," he argued, and former slaves must be "protected in the rights now assured to them." For him and many other Republican abolitionists, the issue was a moral *and* legal one—blacks deserved equality with whites, and assisting freedmen after the war was essential to protecting their rights and moving the country forward.

Finally, on March 3, 1865, lawmakers agreed to create the Freedmen's Bureau within the War Department; President Lincoln signed the bill into law on the same day.

CHAPTER 31

"ARE YOU FOR YOUR COUNTRY, OR ARE YOU FOR THE REBELLION?"

The war stretched on, the fighting became more savage, and horrific casualties mounted on the Union side. Sumner lamented that "the blood and treasure lavished to subdue belligerent slavery are beyond precedent."

Despite his strong personal relationship with Lincoln, Sumner had misgivings about the President's ability to see the war through to a successful conclusion, which he and other Republicans defined as a total Union victory and the reunification of the United States—North and South—into a nation without slavery.

War weariness spread across the North, and morale ebbed as the bloody fighting continued and victory still seemed distant. Democratic newspapers relentlessly opined about the President's inability to achieve victory and peace. "The people are tired of the war," one Illinois paper commented, "tired of the vain sacrifices of so many thousands of lives . . . and they are sternly determined on a change in Administration."

Unlike many party leaders who held secret meetings to plot ways to undermine Lincoln's reelection and select a stronger candidate who would prosecute the war more aggressively, Sumner never took part in these sessions, saying that a different candidate should be nominated *only* if Lincoln withdrew. He was displeased when, in May 1864, a convention of Republican dissidents nominated John C. Frémont for president on a more radical antislavery and equal rights platform. It was a candidacy Sumner normally would have supported philosophically, but other considerations took precedent. First, he was loyal to Lincoln and generally satisfied with the job the President was doing. Plus, he believed a divided Republican ticket would potentially elect a Democrat in November, which threatened everything he had worked and fought for over the past decade. Thus, he would support the nomination of an alternate candidate only with *"the good will of the Presdt."*

If Lincoln desired to remain as the Republican candidate for President, Sumner said, he should do so without opposition.

✳ ✳ ✳

A realist and pragmatist always, and a defeatist on occasion, Lincoln himself had doubts about his ability to win in November.

He knew that his chances of reelection hinged on military success in a war now in its fourth terrible year, with little hope for a speedy conclusion. General Ulysses S. Grant had warned of a prolonged and grueling battle near Petersburg, Virginia—the fall of Richmond seemed like a long way off—and William Tecumseh Sherman was making only incremental progress toward Atlanta. Worse, the Confederates had made their way to the outskirts of Washington in July.

Things looked so bleak for Lincoln that in mid-August, Republican insider Thurlow Weed told the President that his reelection was an impossibility. Later in the month, Republican party chairman Henry Raymond also brought the President grim news: if the election were held then, Lincoln would surely lose the critical states of New York, Pennsylvania, and Illinois, and perhaps every state. "We are not to have peace . . . under this Administration until [the] slavery [issue] is *abandoned*," he warned.

Raymond urged Lincoln to send a delegation to meet with CSA President Jefferson Davis to offer peace terms "on the sole condition of acknowledging the supremacy of the Constitution"—leaving the issue of slavery to be resolved at a later date. Raymond's prediction: Davis would turn it down and insist on Confederate independence, and the country and the world would see that Davis, not Lincoln, was the true implacable obstructionist.

For a brief moment, Lincoln went along with Raymond's idea, drafting a memo authorizing a commission to meet with Davis and propose an immediate cease-fire based only on the restoration of the Union. But then, within twenty-four hours, the President, after intense self-reflection and wrestling with perhaps the biggest decision of his presidency, changed his mind. Sending a commission hat in hand to Richmond was tantamount to "surrendering in advance," and he would not do it. Weighing the options between abandoning his own moral stand on emancipation and his reelection chances in November, Abraham Lincoln chose to risk the latter.

✳ ✳ ✳

The day after his meeting with Raymond, on August 23, 1864, Lincoln penned one of the most extraordinary memoranda in American history. It read:

> This morning, as for some days past, it seems exceedingly probable that this Administration will not be re-elected. Then it will be my duty to so cooperate with the President-elect, as to save the Union between the election and inauguration; as he will have secured his election on such ground that he can not possibly save it afterwards.—*A. Lincoln*

Lincoln folded the note, pasted it closed so that the text could not be read, and took it to a cabinet meeting. He instructed his cabinet members to sign the outside of the memo, sight unseen, which they did. Historians would one day call the document the "Blind Memo" or "Blind Memorandum," since cabinet members did not read it before signing it.

His cabinet did not know it, but Lincoln did: by signing the memo, he and his administration had pledged that they would accept the will of the people in November and help a new incoming President save the Union if Lincoln lost.

✳ ✳ ✳

It came as no surprise to anyone that Democrats nominated former general George B. McClellan for the presidency on August 31, 1864, at their Chicago convention. He was popular among party members, had broad name recognition, and still harbored just enough resentment toward Lincoln for his firing that he had the incentive to campaign hard against the incumbent.

The surprise came when party leaders who crafted the platform boxed in McClellan before he decided whether to accept his nomination—a colossal and ill-timed self-inflicted wound that irretrievably threw away any chance Democrats had for the presidency.

The Democrat peace platform declared that the war had been "four years of failure" and demanded that "immediate efforts be made for a cessation of hostilities" and a convention of states assembled that would work to restore peace. The Democrats "peace plan" rejected the notion that Union *and* emancipation should be conditions for peace, and only called for "Union" as a condition to end hostilities. What was worse, in the eyes of Charles Sumner and Lincoln, the platform insisted on the restoration of "the rights of States unimpaired," which all but guaranteed the preservation of slavery. Finally, delegates chose as McClellan's running mate Ohio congressman George Pendleton, a slavery sympathizer and vociferous opponent of the war who had voted against supplies for the army.

What would McClellan do?

Lincoln believed the Democrats had gone too far and left McClellan in a poor spot; a former general—his leadership ineffectiveness notwithstanding—running alongside an anti-war congressman on a platform that had declared the suffering and sacrifice of Union soldiers a failure and a waste. McClellan faced a conundrum, and Lincoln observed during the days of waiting that the general "doesn't know yet whether he will accept or decline." And then in a disdainful reference to the indecisiveness that had cost McClellan his battlefield command, Lincoln added: "And he will *never* know. Somebody must do it for him. For of all the men I have had to do with in my life, *indecision* is most strongly marked by General McClellan—*if that can be said to be strong which is the essence of weakness.*"

Finally, a week and a half after the Chicago convention, McClellan issued a letter formally accepting the nomination while disavowing the peace plank of the platform. However, he indicated that he had no objection to a compromise settlement leaving slavery intact within a restored Union.

"The *Union* is the one condition for peace," McClellan said. "We ask no more."

✳ ✳ ✳

But after three and a half years of shattered limbs, crushed spirits, ghastly suffering, and devastated families, most Union voters desired *much* more.

After what Sumner referred to as the "Chicago treason," a rejuvenated Lincoln predicted that "the danger [of his possible defeat] has passed . . . after the expenditure of blood and treasure that has been poured out . . . the American people were not prepared to vote the war a failure." It was not the nomination of McClellan but the Democrats' platform itself that lifted Lincoln's flagging spirits—indeed, he predicted that if the Democrats had nominated McClellan on a platform pledging the party to "a vigorous prosecution of the war," Little Mac likely would have won the presidency.

As it was, the extreme position of Democrats handed Lincoln new political life. The party platform, along with the defiant nomination of the anti-war Pendleton, pushed thousands of moderates and conservatives who once considered abandoning Lincoln firmly back into his corner. Morale soared within the campaign and across the North. Republicans who had all but buried Lincoln flocked to support him; bitter party opponents now heartily expressed their support.

Sumner viewed the possibility of McClellan's election as "damnation." The Chicago platform was simply too abominable to contemplate voting for anyone *but* Lincoln. To a Boston audience, Sumner declared that those who voted for McClellan ". . . will give the very vote which Jefferson Davis would give were he allowed to vote in Massachusetts."

✳ ✳ ✳

If the tide turned in Lincoln's favor after the Democratic Convention adjourned on August 31, support for the President became a tidal wave when news broke from Atlanta a mere two days later.

After a brutal four-month campaign, General William T. Sherman's federal force had finally taken Atlanta, second only to the capital city of Richmond in importance to the Confederacy. Atlanta's network of roads and railroad lines made it vital to Confederate troop and supply movements; its location deep in the heart of the slaveholding South made it a coveted symbolic prize for the Union, not to mention the federal army's first major military victory of 1864.

Sherman's troops had shelled the city and choked off supplies from the north, west, and east, forcing Confederate general John B. Hood to evacuate his army or risk being trapped in the city and starving. Hood ordered the retreat on September 1, and by midnight, the last of his infantry units were marching out of Atlanta, destroying left-behind munitions as they went. The next day, Mayor James Calhoun formally surrendered Atlanta to Sherman, and late that afternoon, the Stars and Stripes flew over the city for the first time in more than three years.

The victory had come at enormous cost to both sides. The Union suffered thirty-seven thousand battle casualties during the campaign, and the Confederate killed, wounded, or missing tally exceeded thirty-two thousand troops. Some 70 percent of soldiers fell sick at one time or another. Telegraphing Washington, D.C., after taking the city, Sherman wrote: "Atlanta is ours and fairly won."

The fall of Atlanta electrified the North in early September 1864, and celebratory one-hundred-cannon salutes boomed from Washington to Boston. It was a crushing blow to the morale of white Southerners, who had staked everything on the Confederacy. Beyond the effect on the Southern psyche, the destruction of Atlanta effectively ended the Confederates' ability to supply their army in the West.

"The capture of Atlanta is surely a great point in the war," Sumner observed.

For both North and South, the ignominious fall and subsequent burning of Atlanta illuminated one indisputable fact: the outcome of the war was no longer in doubt.

Nor was the outcome of the presidential election.

✳ ✳ ✳

The Democrats' "Chicago treason" and Sherman's overwhelming victory in Atlanta propelled President Abraham Lincoln to a solid reelection victory on November 8.

He won 55 percent of the popular vote, and he carried the electoral vote of all participating states with the exception of New Jersey and the border states of Kentucky and Delaware. While McClellan had a surprisingly strong showing in the North, it wasn't enough.

As 1864 drew to an end, Charles Sumner viewed the events of the fall as watershed moments in the life of the United States. His long-sought goals of freedom and equality appeared closer than ever as the nation headed into 1865, and he looked to the new year with hope and promise.

And yet, he acknowledged often, especially in 1864, that the war had caused great pain. The Union's Overland Campaign in Virginia— the Battles of Wilderness, Spotsylvania, Cold Harbor, and the siege of Petersburg—had come at a cost that was both terrible and indescribable in polite Washington society.

Men on both sides who enlisted early, who were once infused with a sense of noble purpose, dashing romanticism, sectional glory, unabashed patriotism, an almost religious zeal—men who fought with the valor and earnestness inspired by exalted causes—now buried their faces in mud to protect themselves from merciless shelling, wiped their blood-slippery blades on tattered uniforms after murderous hand-to-hand combat, screamed with pain caused by their own gaping wounds or the unforget- table images of their broken comrades, prayed for their return from the killing fields with limbs and minds intact, and wept for their innocence forever lost.

By sheer weight of numbers and strength of conviction, federal troops had turned the tide against a courageous and stubborn rebel force whose battlefield commanders were, in the main, more competent and whose will, even amid its last gasps, appeared unbreakable. Fully mindful of the shock- ing bloodshed suffered by his own army, General Ulysses S. Grant was un- deterred in his almost divine quest to capture Richmond and, once and for all, force the Confederacy to its knees and end the war.

Neither the horror nor the pain of war was lost on Sumner, a pacifist by nature.

When Colonel Charles R. Lowell of Massachusetts was killed in the Battle of Cedar Creek in Virginia, Sumner poured his heart out in a condo- lence letter to Lowell's in-laws. "When at last our triumph is won, his name must be inscribed on that martyr list, without which slavery would have been supreme on this continent." He saw in Colonel Lowell's death what he saw in his own tribulations over the years—a painful martyrdom in a righteous crusade against slavery, a sacrifice made in the country's pursuit to realize its founding promise of equal justice for all.

Now, the result of the November election, whose outcome had ap- peared uncertain as late as August, seemed to confirm that a corner had been turned in the nation's fight to become a more perfect union. Slavery was headed for extinction.

"Here I close this chapter of my life," Sumner wrote to President Lincoln.

✳ ✳ ✳

But on the issue of slavery, there was one final chapter left.

At the opening of the next congressional session on December 6, 1864, President Lincoln, in his annual message, reminded the House of the pending Thirteenth Amendment that would abolish slavery forever. He put the full force of his office behind the amendment, urged its reconsideration and passage, and suggested that his own recent reelection proved that the will of the people was "most clearly declared in favor" of the amendment.

The Senate had done its job months before—it was time for the House to follow suit. "May we not agree the sooner the better?" Lincoln asked. "In a great national crisis like ours, unanimity of action among those seeking a common end is very desirable—almost indispensable."

House members took the President's message to heart. The House began its debate on January 6, 1865, and on January 31, before a packed gallery filled with anticipation, the Speaker called the roll. By a vote of 119–56—achieving the two-thirds majority required—the House passed the language approved by the Senate nine months earlier.

The Speaker's dramatic announcement of the final vote was met with an outburst of enthusiasm and applause. Republican representatives sprang to their feet, shouting and clapping their hands. Spectators danced and cheered in the crowded galleries. Ebon Ingersoll, representative from Illinois, recognized the historic moment immediately and said: "In honor of this immortal and sublime event, I move that the House do now adjourn!"

With nothing before it that could even approach the magnitude of its previous vote, the House did so.

More than ten months later—a full twenty months after the Senate vote—on December 6, 1865, the provisional Union-controlled government of Georgia became the twenty-seventh of thirty-six states to ratify the Thirteenth Amendment. The three-fourths threshold for adoption had been reached.

On December 18, as the historic year 1865 drew to a close, Secretary of State William Seward announced to the world that—eighty-nine years after it had declared its independence, seventy-eight years after the ratification of its Constitution, and four years and hundreds of thousands of deaths after war had cleaved the country in two—the United States had constitutionally abolished slavery.

⁕ CHAPTER 32 ⁕

WITH MALICE TOWARD NONE?

MARCH 5, 1865

On the day after he was inaugurated for his second term, President Abraham Lincoln sent the following dispatch by courier to Charles Sumner:

Executive Mansion, Washington, March 5, 1865

Hon. C. Sumner,

My dear sir—I should be pleased for you to accompany us tomorrow evening at ten o'clock, on a visit of half an hour to the Inaugural Ball. I enclose a ticket. Our carriage will call for you at half-past nine.

Yours truly,

A. Lincoln

The next evening, a Monday, the President's carriage arrived at Sumner's lodging at the designated time. As Lincoln's party entered the ballroom, the President, who was accompanied by Speaker of the House Schuyler Colfax, was announced first, followed by Sumner escorting his friend First Lady Mary Todd Lincoln.

Sumner's personal invitation from the President reflected a deepening closeness in their relationship. Lincoln's heavy reliance on the senator's expertise on virtually every important foreign policy issue the administration faced, their now indistinguishable positions on the need for the country to abolish slavery as part of a Union victory, and Sumner's close relationship with the First Lady—all contributed to the deepening friendship.

When Lincoln's private carriage arrived at Sumner's lodging, it also signified something else: the President was extending an olive branch to the senator who had, over the past two months, opposed him with vehemence on how and when seceded states should be allowed to return to the Union.

Sumner insisted that Lincoln alter his position, and Lincoln needed Sumner's cooperation for any meaningful plan to move forward at all.

* * *

The challenge was unprecedented—prior to 1860, no state had ever seceded from the Union—and the issues were mainly twofold: Did the President or Congress have primary jurisdiction over states rejoining the Union? And what requirements must states fulfill before they were allowed to return?

Sumner and Lincoln agreed on many things regarding reconstruction: both agreed that there could be no peace or readmittance without the end of slavery; both agreed that former slaves—freedmen—and white Southern Unionists needed guarantees of safety before a state could seek readmission; and both agreed that before a state returned to the Union, it must provide its citizens with the constitutional guarantee of a "republican form of government" through free elections and protection from domestic violence.

But their differences were real and sharp.

Lincoln believed that the President, acting under his war powers, had full authority to take the initiative in reconstruction, and he did so by installing provisional military governors in states under Union control. He agreed that Congress had *final* authority over readmitting states to the Union, but believed that the will of the President carried significant weight in the process—similar to an executive request for a declaration of war or the nomination of a justice to the Supreme Court. In both cases, Congress possessed an enumerated constitutional role, but in both cases, deference to the President was appropriate and consistent with political precedent.

Sumner disagreed—he was firmly committed to almost total congressional jurisdiction over the reorganization of the South. As even Lincoln acknowledged, if Congress alone could admit new states to the Union, then it stood to reason that only Congress had authority to *readmit* them. For such authority to have any real teeth, Congress must take the preeminent role in establishing the ground rules for readmission. Sumner conceded that, for the sake of checks and balances and overall national harmony, it would be beneficial for the country if congressional action on readmitting states met with "the approval of the President," but, based on the thrust of his arguments throughout, Sumner's meaning of the word "approval" was intended as informal concurrence rather than a legal presidential sign-off.

Sumner and Lincoln also differed in their definitions of what constituted a republican form of government. Sumner insisted that "a government founded on military power, or having its origins in military orders, cannot be 'republican in form' according to the requirements of the Constitution." Lincoln, aware of the weakness of the provisional regimes set up in the South, especially in their earliest stages, felt the military needed to protect and nurture the "embryo" governments, arguing that "we shall sooner have the fowl by hatching the egg than by smashing it." Sumner retorted: "The eggs of crocodiles can produce only crocodiles; and it is not easy to see how eggs laid by military power can be hatched into an American state."

Finally, Lincoln and Sumner differed on the other major component of a republican form of government—universal suffrage.

In early 1865, President Lincoln's stance on voting rights for former slaves was not entirely clear. He favored a slow approach, and privately conceded that voting rights perhaps should be extended to "the very intelligent [freedmen], and especially those who have fought gallantly in our ranks." Sumner insisted on a sweeping guarantee of complete black male enfranchisement before any state could return to the Union. Without the votes of freedmen, "we cannot establish stable govts in the rebel states," he said. "Their votes are as necessary as their musquets [*sic*] . . . without them, the old enemy will reappear, and put us all in peril again."

Without universal suffrage, Congress would be, de facto, sanctioning a return to power of the previous white slaveholding class.

Between Lincoln and Sumner, strong political allies who had become close personal friends, the battle was joined. It would play out in Louisiana.

✳ ✳ ✳

Lincoln had placed General Nathaniel P. Banks in control of reconstruction in Louisiana and supported the general's plan to reconstitute the government of the state under its antebellum constitution, with only the proslavery clauses omitted. Some twelve thousand Louisianans swore an oath of future allegiance to the Union, establishing a constitution providing for separate but equal public schools for whites and blacks and empowering the legislature to confer voting rights on African Americans *when it deemed appropriate*. Legislators had also pledged to ratify the Thirteenth Amendment to abolish slavery if the state was readmitted to the Union in time for the vote. Banks spent the end of 1864 and beginning of 1865 in Washington urging Congress to seat representatives and senators from Louisiana, even though—without mandated black suffrage—political power would still continue to rest with the planter class.

Lincoln believed it was a solid start. "These twelve thousand persons are thus fully committed to the Union, and to perpetual freedom in the state," he said. "If we reject and spurn them, we do our utmost to discourage and disperse them." As for the former slave population, rejection of Louisiana would leave them in an undefined limbo, Lincoln maintained, delaying full citizenship and liberty until "some vague and undefined when, where, and how."

From a pure political perspective, Lincoln argued, failure to admit Louisiana would also mean a loss of one state that had agreed to ratify the Thirteenth Amendment. Even without full explicit universal suffrage in the moment, wasn't it more likely that blacks would attain voting rights—and all other rights—sooner by *sustaining* rather than *discarding* the proposed new state government?

Nonsense, said Charles Sumner.

✳ ✳ ✳

To Sumner and other Radical Republicans, the Louisiana reconstruction plan, and anything resembling it that might come along, negated the hard-fought gains the Union had made during the war.

How could it be in any way considered just—in the wake of hundreds of thousands of Union deaths and the Confederates' desire to destroy the United States—to allow these same traitorous slaveholders, who had conspired with England to ensure the Union's demise, to return to power in their state and in Washington merely by repudiating their decision to secede? Sumner was convinced that slaveholders would "never again be loyal to the Union" but would remain "a disaffected element, always ready to intrigue with a foreign enemy." He was unwilling ever to trust them again. "The only Unionists of the South are black," he declared, making it essential "to extend the suffrage to the Negroes." Sumner threatened to kill Lincoln's plan in February 1865 when it came before the Senate by filibustering during the debate.

Infuriated Democrats and even many Republicans questioned Sumner's defiance. Strengthened by reelection results, Lincoln was at the apex of his popularity. The war was on the verge of ending with the Union triumphant, the House had approved the Thirteenth Amendment abolishing slavery, Sumner and the radicals had won major gains the previous session on equality issues.

Was this the time to challenge Lincoln on universal suffrage in Louisiana?

Republican leaders attempted a compromise: admit Louisiana as the President proposed, but then adopt for all other Southern states a Reconstruction act "giving the electoral franchise to all citizens without distinction of color." Even Sumner felt like he could support this measure. It was clear to him that equal suffrage needed to be established one way or another during Reconstruction, or—he feared—it never would be. If it meant that other states could drag Louisiana into the fold, rather than vice versa, he could live with the compromise.

But the agreement soon unraveled. Conservative Republicans believed imposing universal suffrage on all other states was constitutionally questionable and an unacceptable capitulation to the radicals. Radicals believed that Lincoln still wielded too much say on Louisiana's return. Moderates saw huge problems with inconsistencies on black suffrage from state to state—if universal suffrage was essential to a republican form of government in South Carolina, for example, then why was it not obligatory in Illinois or New York, or a dozen other Northern states, which still either disenfranchised or discriminated against blacks at the ballot box?

Thorny questions—with no easy answers. The attempted compromise died.

✳ ✳ ✳

Though the majority of Republican senators were ready to readmit Louisiana, Sumner vowed to prevent the vote by stalling all other legislation if his party insisted on moving ahead with Lincoln's Louisiana plan.

He also launched into a full-scale attack upon the "pretended state government of Louisiana" with his customary candor. "It is a mere seven-months' abortion, begotten by the bayonet in criminal conjunction with the spirit of caste, and born before its time," he said of the bill that omitted universal suffrage, "rickety, unformed, unfinished—whose continued existence will be a burden, a reproach, and a wrong."

Sumner's efforts almost single-handedly sank the Louisiana plan. After three days of debate, on February 27, 1865, a week before Inauguration Day, the Senate dealt President Lincoln a defeat by voting to postpone until the next congressional session further consideration of Louisiana statehood. Democrat Lazarus Powell of Kentucky denounced Sumner in an angry tirade: "You and a handful of fanatics are engaged in destroying the country," he shouted, just before barely missing Sumner's shoe with a wad of tobacco he spat on the carpet.

Sumner believed that blocking Louisiana bought time to persuade citizens and lawmakers to embrace the idea of universal suffrage.

"I think that during the summer and autumn, before the next Congress, the country can be rallied," he said.

✳ ✳ ✳

Lincoln—whose political temperament generally leaned toward the philosophical, the evenhanded, the wry—was furious.

He had set his heart on Louisiana becoming the first readmitted state, viewing it as a harbinger that the country's wounds could be healed and the nation restored. To his secretaries Hay and Nicolay, he complained that Sumner was attempting to "change this government from its original form to a strong centralized power." Press and pundits alike speculated that the intimate personal relationship between Lincoln and Sumner would suffer an irreparable break after Sumner—in the colorful words of the *New York Herald*—had "kicked the pet scheme of the President down the marble steps of the Senate Chamber."

But there was no break.

Despite Lincoln's disappointment, and even his frustration with what he considered Sumner's childlike idealism, he respected Sumner's position and his rights as a senator and grudgingly admired his backbone. "I can do nothing with Mr. Sumner in these matters," he reportedly said to his secretaries, referring to the universal suffrage issue. "While Mr.

Sumner is very cordial with me, he is making history in an issue with me on this very point."

Lincoln was fully aware that the battle-tested Sumner had carried the day in what was one of the senator's toughest parliamentary fights. It was Sumner's spirit alone that had defeated the President's plan for Louisiana; in so doing, he had, virtually single-handedly, insisted on both unfettered congressional oversight of reconstruction and full citizenship for African Americans.

It was because of Sumner's statesmanship that universal suffrage—regardless of color or race—became first a part of the Republican core ethos and, eventually, a fixture in the minds of the American people.

Perhaps, then, Lincoln saw something fully developed in Sumner that stirred in nascent form within his own heart. Sumner admitted that Lincoln took the defeat of his Louisiana plan "very kindly" and interpreted the President's mature response as a hopeful sign for the country's reconstruction efforts.

"I think that his mind is undergoing change," Sumner predicted.

✳ ✳ ✳

In the aftermath of the Louisiana debate, Lincoln's invitation to Sumner to attend the inaugural ball, and Sumner's acceptance, had practical advantages for both men.

For Lincoln, remaining close to the Massachusetts senator was crucial as the war neared its end and the task of rebuilding the country moved to the forefront. Sumner represented the millions of people who, over the past four years of hideous bloodshed, had shifted their views on slavery and equal rights toward his. A headstrong fringe radical at the time of Lincoln's first election, Sumner now represented and reflected the opinions of the mainstream Republican Party. Without Sumner's support, as the Louisiana matter showed, the President would be relegated almost to lame-duck status before his second term gained traction. With Sumner as an ally, Lincoln was protected from sniping Northern "ultra-abolitionists" who constantly prodded him to move faster and further on equal rights.

For Sumner, despite his differences with Lincoln, there was no better time to be perceived as a confidant of the President. The Thirteenth

Amendment was off to the states for ratification, Grant's forces were finally closing in on Richmond, and Lincoln had been resoundingly reelected—all helped to propel the President to the highest popularity of his career. The many opportunities Sumner had to stand next to the President in early 1865 only enhanced the senator's reputation and influence.

Some people thought Lincoln's influence had softened Sumner's bitterness and ego; others believed Sumner had bolstered Lincoln's courage and conviction.

Each observation contained elements of truth.

In either case, Sumner benefitted.

✳ ✳ ✳

Within the halls of Congress and in D.C. smoking rooms, the feeling was widespread that Lincoln would soon reorganize his cabinet—Sumner's deep alignment with the President made him the odds-on favorite to replace Seward as secretary of state.

Excited by the prospect of joining the cabinet, Sumner envisioned repairing U.S. relations with England and introducing a stronger, united, slave-free America to the European powers. Some cynical Washington veterans whispered that Lincoln dangled the secretary of state position before Sumner to persuade him to support the Louisiana plan, but there is no documentation to suggest this; in any case, Lincoln knew full well of Sumner's aversion to political favors and patronage.

Sumner believed that Lincoln possessed similar integrity. The President could separate strong and honest political disagreement from his assessment of whether a man was competent and capable of carrying out leadership responsibilities.

Lincoln's second term seemed to promise all manner of progress—social advancement, equal rights, human prosperity, and world recognition for the United States—and Sumner relished the opportunity to sit on a potentially historic cabinet for the next four years. He had come to recognize the populist appeal of the President—befitting Lincoln's modest Midwest background, Sumner felt that Lincoln was touched by greatness in a most understated way.

"It is plain that Mr. Lincoln has a hold on the public heart, such as few men have had in history," he would say later.

✴ ✴ ✴

Lincoln's appeal was on full display on Inauguration Day, Saturday, March 4, 1865—two days before the ball Sumner attended with the Lincolns. It had rained heavily for several days, and inauguration morning once again broke with sweeping rain and gale-force winds. Pennsylvania Avenue and most of Washington's streets were sodden with several inches of thick mud.

Despite the horrendous weather, crowds began gathering at the east front of the Capitol before ten o'clock; by noon they were drenched. But the rain stopped before the ceremonies began, and the gray overcast sky held at least the promise of clearing.

The makeup of the crowd, and eventually the inaugural procession, augured for an even more promising future. For the first time in the nation's history, African Americans, thousands of them, participated in a presidential inauguration. Many in the crowd, perhaps most, were former slaves who had toiled in the District of Columbia and whom Charles Sumner had fought tirelessly to free. A battalion of colored troops formed part of the military escort that accompanied President Lincoln along Pennsylvania Avenue, and members of a black Odd Fellows lodge were also part of the procession. One observer rejoiced that the great bronze Statue of Freedom now crowned the dome of the Capitol building, "her guardianship justified by the fact that the Thirteenth Amendment virtually blotted slavery from the Constitution."

Tens of thousands of visitors had streamed into town to attend the historic inaugural, filling "every available room, bed, nook, and corner." Northern reporters on the scene contrasted the hopefulness of this day with the despair of Lincoln's first inauguration, when the President-elect, in disguise, had literally slipped into the federal city in the dead of night to avoid potential assassination.

Lincoln, worn down by the stress of his first four years, appeared weary. The poet Walt Whitman attended the inaugural and watched as Lincoln passed by, close enough for Whitman to observe that the President looked "very much worn and tired; the lines, indeed, of vast responsibilities, intricate questions, and demands of life and death, cut deeper than ever upon his dark brown face." But beneath the surface, Whitman saw "all the old goodness, tenderness, sadness, and canny shrewdness."

Lincoln seemed to know that a feeling of peace and safety enveloped the city and his inauguration.

One journalist concluded: "The solemnity of 1861 had given place to the joyousness of 1865."

✳ ✳ ✳

The first order of business was the swearing in of the Vice President–elect, which took place in the Senate chamber. Andrew Johnson had arrived in Washington on March 1 and was exhausted from his long trip and a recent bout with typhoid fever. Not one to need an excuse to imbibe, Johnson drank several glasses of whiskey to calm his nerves, and when he was escorted out for his swearing in, it was apparent to all that he was hopelessly intoxicated.

Slurring his words, Johnson proceeded to deliver a rambling, self-centered diatribe, talking about his "plebeian" roots that he "gloried in" and stumbling over names and phrases. When he took the oath, he held up the Bible and said, "I kiss this Book in the name of my nation the United States." Ashamed and embarrassed, President Lincoln, Republican senators, and onlookers squirmed and cringed. During Johnson's screed, Lincoln "closed his eyes and seemed to retire into himself as though beset by melancholy reflections." When Johnson finally finished and took the oath, Lincoln leaned over to the parade marshal and whispered: "Do not let Johnson speak outside."

Sumner thought the Vice President's sordid behavior was "the most unfortunate thing that had ever occurred in our history." He gathered the Republican caucus and demanded that Johnson be forced to resign the office he had besmirched. His colleagues voted down his motion, with a few noting that, as ribald as Johnson's behavior was, his intoxication would not have drawn so much attention "if Sumner hadn't been so exquisite about it."

Sumner never forgot or forgave Johnson's reprehensible demonstration in the Senate chamber, but for now he shrugged it off as the President-elect, newly sworn-in senators, lawmakers, and everyone else moved outside to the east front of the Capitol, where Lincoln would take his oath and deliver his inaugural address.

✳ ✳ ✳

When Lincoln moved forward to speak, the multitudes assembled before him erupted in thunderous cheers, and thousands waved American flags. Some estimates put the crowd at thirty thousand, others at forty thousand; the throng filled every square foot of space in front of the Capitol, and they continued to roar—rolling waves of cheers—as Lincoln stood patiently. "The grandeur of the spectacle before me was indescribable," one witness marveled. "Thousands of colored folk, *heretofore excluded* from such re- unions, were mingled for the first time with white spectators."

Finally, the Senate sergeant at arms called for quiet. The President stepped forward holding a sheet of foolscap on which his inauguration speech was printed, and scores of witnesses swore the finger of God im- printed itself upon the historic scene when the sun burst through the clouds just as Lincoln began to speak. Chief Justice Salmon Chase de- scribed the moment as "an auspicious omen of the dispersion of the clouds of war, and the restoration of the clear sunlight of prosperous peace." (Lincoln himself would ask journalist Noah Brooks the next day: "Did you notice that sunburst? It made my heart jump.")

At a mere 700 words, Lincoln's inaugural speech was one of the shortest in American history. For the next 160 years, scholars and historians would refer to this masterpiece reverentially as Lincoln's "Second Inaugural Ad- dress" or simply the "Second Inaugural"—its name always capitalized, its content and language and eloquence scrutinized, analyzed, poeticized, *immortalized* for enriching the political literature of the Union. Among Lincoln's many oratorical gems, only the Gettysburg Address surpassed it for soaring idealism and enduring iconic value.

The 1865 inaugural address expressed Lincoln's fervent hope—his prayer—that now, with war's end near, forgiveness and magnanimity were the best ways to achieve lasting peace. For him, all that mattered was how to manage the peace once the combatants laid down their arms. There was only one way, he believed, and with the vast, expectant crowd seeming "to hang on his words as though they were meat and drink," Lincoln delivered his answer with soaring eloquence in a concluding paragraph that would become one of the most oft-quoted in American history:

> With malice toward none; with charity for all; with firmness in the right,
> as God gives us to see the right, let us strive on to finish the work we
> are in; to bind up the nation's wounds; to care for him who shall have

borne the battle, and for his widow, and his orphan—to do all which may achieve and cherish a just and lasting peace among ourselves, and with all nations.

✳ ✳ ✳

Lincoln's final paragraph "fell like a benediction from heaven," noted one mounted member of Lincoln's bodyguard team. Lincoln himself wrote that he expected the speech "to wear as well as—perhaps better than—anything I have produced."

Two audience members were far less impressed with Lincoln's inaugural address.

One was Charles Sumner. He found Lincoln's final paragraph far too conciliatory to the South, especially on the heels of the President's Louisiana doctrine. The speech seemed to confirm that Lincoln was again considering the readmission of states without universal suffrage and without blacks having a strong role in the formation of new governments.

The other man, a Southern sympathizer, objected to Lincoln's biblical allusions, his blasphemous contention that God had brought forth war as a necessary punishment for the sin of slavery. Outrageous! What a pathetic attempt by Lincoln to absolve himself of guilt! Was it God who had defiled Atlanta, or was it the Devil in the form of Sherman? Was it the Almighty who had slaughtered so many outnumbered Confederate boys amid the thick underbrush of the Virginia Wilderness—or was it the merciless and cold-blooded Grant?

Contemptuous of the President and his war crimes, disdainful of Lincoln's cheering, fawning acolytes in the crowd, the man seethed as he stood next to his fiancée, Lucy Lambert Hale. Lucy was the daughter of New Hampshire senator John Parker Hale, and through her father she had obtained two coveted tickets to the inauguration platform. She and her husband-to-be had a perfect up-front view of the President and could hear his remarks clearly.

They were *so* close, recalled Lucy's fiancé later, that he had an excellent opportunity to shoot the President if he had wished to do so. But for now, the man, an actor by trade—tall, dashing, and wildly popular—was content simply to bide his time.

John Wilkes Booth had other plans.

✳ CHAPTER 33 ✳

RICHMOND HAS FALLEN

Charles Sumner watched in awe as Lincoln shook hands with virtually every wounded and sick Union soldier, nearly five thousand in all, who were bedridden in tent hospitals near the Army of the Potomac's headquarters at City Point.

Lincoln's physical stamina was impressive enough—the President shook his head when Sumner asked him if his shoulder or hand was tired—but even more noteworthy was the way Lincoln so easily connected with these men, most of whom had suffered grievous wounds or were dying from debilitating diseases. A handshake and a brief conversation here, a chuckle and a mirthful smile there; a "Where are you from, boy?" at one bed stop, a "How do you do?" at another; a "Thank you for your sacrifice" to an emaciated soldier whose head was swathed in bloody bandages, and even a magnanimous "I hope a Confederate colonel will not refuse me his hand" when Lincoln reached the bedside of a captured rebel officer, who gratefully clasped the President's hand in both of his.

It seemed to come naturally to Lincoln, Sumner observed—knowing what to say, how to say it, how long to visit, when to move on to the next bed, when to inject gentle humor even as he expressed grave concern. Sumner possessed little in the way of these instincts, and as he watched the President in action, he marveled that Lincoln's mannerisms were neither contrived nor disingenuous. The President comforted all of the men but patronized none. He asked questions and listened with patience for the answers.

The men picked up on his kind and unaffected manner in an instant. A Vermont sharpshooter threw off his blankets just as Lincoln arrived at his bedside so the President could see that his right leg was gone, amputated just above the knee. "What, a leg gone?" Lincoln inquired. When the man replied "Yes," Lincoln looked at the placard at the head of the patient's bed and said, "and a Vermonter?" The patient answered that he prided himself on being a Green Mountain boy, at which point Lincoln gently took the man's hand in both of his. The wounded man looked up at Lincoln and asked:

"Well, Father Abraham, have we done our work well?"

The President replied: "Very well, indeed, and I thank you."

The sharpshooter recollected: "I never shall forget the pressure he gave my hand, nor can I forget that sad, careworn face . . . I often see that sad and worn face in my memory, and I can hardly keep back the tears."

✳ ✳ ✳

It was a long day at the hospitals, but Sumner thought the President looked and sounded energized. Lincoln had been away from Washington since March 23—the longest absence from the capital of his presidency—meeting with Grant and Union officers at their City Point, Virginia, headquarters, then visiting Richmond two days after the Confederate government fled the city on April 2 before returning to City Point for final strategy sessions. Lincoln's hiatus from D.C. had done him enormous good physically and emotionally, and the extraordinary reception he received upon his arrival in Richmond on April 4 brought his rejuvenated spirits to a whole different level.

Sumner understood why. On April 6, after rendezvousing with the President in City Point, Sumner and Mrs. Lincoln, along with a small entourage, also visited Richmond, as far South as Sumner had ever ventured. He too was flush with a sense of jubilance when he entered the Confederate-abandoned capital city.

For certain, both Lincoln and Sumner felt a sense of relief and joy that the Confederate government, including President Jefferson Davis, had finally surrendered Richmond and fled in fear into the night.

What was even more uplifting was *who* greeted Lincoln and Sumner when each arrived, two days apart, in the once proud Confederate capital.

✳ ✳ ✳

Lincoln's April 4, 1865, arrival in Richmond became the stuff of legend, and it was perhaps the most gratifying day of the President's life.

Despite pleas from cabinet members who feared for the President's safety, there was never any doubt in Lincoln's mind that he would go to Richmond. As soon as the navy removed the Confederate booby traps from the James River, Lincoln and a small party set out aboard two ships, the *River Queen* and the *Malvern,* accompanied by a draft barge pulled by a tugboat, which would be used to transport the President in the shallower water near Richmond.

Arriving without fanfare, the President and his party stepped ashore surrounded by marines carrying carbines. The President questioned the need for protection, but Admiral David Porter said the guards were a precaution against any animosity the white population of Richmond might have toward Lincoln. The President was first recognized by dozens of black workmen, who pushed to the edge of the dock and repeatedly called out: "God Bless our liberator." One man of about sixty dropped his shovel and rushed forward: "Bless the Lord," he said, "there is the great Messiah! Glory, Hallelujah!" He and others fell to their knees, taking the President's hand and kissing it. "That is not right," Lincoln said, embarrassed. "Don't kneel to me. You must kneel to God only, and thank him for the liberty you will hereafter enjoy."

Word of Lincoln's arrival spread quickly as he walked toward the center of town; it was a warm day, and he removed his overcoat but continued to wear his telltale stovepipe hat. Soon he was surrounded by hundreds of black people—most former slaves—who shouted, "Bless the Lord, Father Abraham's come!" The crowd pressed against Lincoln, "so fearfully that I thought we all stood a chance of being crushed to death," noted Admiral Porter, who ordered his men to fix bayonets.

But Lincoln calmed the situation. "My poor friends," he said. "You are free—free as air. You can cast off the name of slave and trample upon it; it will come to you no more. Liberty is your birthright!"

The crowd roared its approval and continued to accompany the President as he made his way to the center city.

✸ ✸ ✸

The President visited the Confederate White House, where he sat in Jefferson Davis's study, and also stopped at the Virginia statehouse, where the Confederate Congress had done its work.

Before and after these stops, he was accompanied by a "colored population that was wild with enthusiasm," in the words of one black Northern correspondent, T. Morris Chester, who was filing dispatches for the *Philadelphia Press*. Fully recognizing the historic nature of the moment, Chester dutifully recorded the unprecedented scene of throngs of former slaves surrounding Lincoln: "It must be confessed that those who participated in this informal reception of the President were mainly *negroes*. There were many whites in the crowd, but they were lost in the great concourse of American citizens of African descent."

Men clung to the tops of telegraph poles and high tree limbs, craning to get a view of Lincoln, itching to get closer. His jaw set and his gait strong, Lincoln seemed to relish the moment, continuing into the business section of the city, which was devastated by fires the Confederates had set to the area as they evacuated. Here he stopped at the notorious Libby Prison, where so many Northern troops had been held—and mistreated—during the war; it now held captured rebels. Lincoln asked for a glass of water after trudging through dust-blown streets for more than thirty minutes in the broiling sun.

Then Union troops raised the American flag over the prison, fastening the staff to a beam that left it leaning to one side. "Boys, I'm glad to see you have the flag up," Lincoln said, "but straighten that staff." Again, the President's remarks were greeted with whoops and cheers.

That night, Lincoln slept aboard the *Malvern,* and the captain insisted on posting a guard outside his door after Union troops brought a report from a captured Confederate soldier that the President was in danger and should take greater care if he went ashore again.

Exhausted but ebullient over events in Richmond, Lincoln dismissed the threat, saying: "I cannot bring myself to believe that any human being lives who would do me any harm."

✳ ✳ ✳

Sumner and Mary Lincoln's visit to Richmond two days after the President's was not heralded nearly as much, but black residents, especially, greeted both with warmth and cordiality. Sumner was joyful. "Even our stately, dignified Mr. Sumner acknowledged himself transformed into a lad of sixteen," observed the First Lady.

It was the presence of hundreds of former slaves, exuberant with joy, that reinforced Sumner's unshakable belief in universal suffrage. "*The only people who showed themselves were negroes,*" he exclaimed to Salmon

Chase. "All others had fled or were retired in their houses. Never was I more convinced of the utter impossibility of any [re]organization which is not founded on the votes of the negroes."

His long-held contention that universal suffrage was the key to the nation's future, to this point based on hope and conjecture, was amply illustrated and indelibly confirmed in all its glory on the streets of a now vanquished Richmond.

✳ ✳ ✳

Back at City Point, Lincoln, Sumner, and their group received word that Secretary of State Seward had been seriously injured in a carriage accident; while not life-threatening, his afflictions included a jaw broken in two places and a badly dislocated shoulder. The pain had been so severe that Seward had been in delirium for three of the four days since the fall.

Late on the evening of April 8, the day Lincoln had shaken the hands of wounded troops, the party boarded the *River Queen* to return to Washington. Sumner enjoyed the intimacy of the small group—"breakfasting, lunching & dining in one small family party"—and the access he had to Lincoln.

Lincoln deftly managed both the conversation and Sumner. He steered away from specific reconstruction plans, knowing Sumner preferred a more unforgiving and radical Congress-led approach. In fact, when Mrs. Lincoln mentioned that Jefferson Davis deserved the most "extreme penalty," Lincoln replied: "Judge not that ye be not judged," repeating the same phrase he used when pressed by others.

Avoiding a deeper conversation with Sumner about reconstruction, Lincoln began to reminisce about the past four years, read aloud to the group from Shakespeare and Longfellow, and even attempted to mollify Sumner with hints of a cabinet appointment. Lincoln was puzzled as to why people believed Seward had been the primary influence in his administration. "I have counselled with you twice as much as I ever did with him," Lincoln said to Sumner.

The President's entire tone suggested that Sumner might soon "be called to decide the question, whether to quit the Senate" and join Lincoln's cabinet.

✳ CHAPTER 34 ✳

"WE ARE NEAR THE END AT LAST"

After he disembarked from the *River Queen* around 6:00 P.M., President Lincoln rushed to visit the injured Seward, whose swollen and discolored face was wrapped in bandages, his damaged jaw clamped in an iron frame.

"You are back from Richmond?" Seward struggled to speak in a hoarse whisper through barely parted lips. "Yes," Lincoln replied, "and I think we are near the end at last." After about thirty minutes, he left quietly, and his carriage took him back to the White House.

Later that night, as the tired President prepared for bed, a War Department messenger brought Lincoln an urgent telegram from General Grant, sent to the secretary of war from a place called Appomattox Court House in central Virginia:

April 9, 1865—4:30 p.m.

Hon. E. M. Stanton,

Secretary of War:

General Lee surrendered the Army of Northern Virginia this afternoon upon terms proposed by myself. The accompanying additional correspondence will show the conditions fully.

U. S. Grant,

Lieutenant General

✳ ✳ ✳

Grant's surrender terms were generous.

Confederate troops could return home "not to be disturbed by U.S. authority so long as they observe their paroles and the laws in force where they may reside." In essence, this significant clause guaranteed the rebels immunity from prosecution for treason. Grant also conceded to Lee's request that Confederate soldiers be allowed to keep their horses to travel to their homes and "put in a crop to carry themselves and their families through the next winter." Lee expressed his gratitude: "This will . . . do much toward conciliating our people."

Reflecting the wishes of his commander in chief, Grant's magnanimity did not stop there. He also ordered three days' worth of rations sent across the line for twenty-five thousand starving Confederate troops and mandated that joyful Union cannon celebrations cease as news of the surrender spread throughout the camps. "The war is over," Grant said, "the rebels are our countrymen again, and the best sign of rejoicing after victory will be to abstain from all demonstrations." Finally, at the formal surrender ceremony at Appomattox, as the Confederates marched up the dusty road to stack their arms and surrender their battle flags in silence, Grant ordered Union troops to "carry arms," a salute of honor that signified respect for the bravery of the defeated Southerners.

Thus, enemies who had engaged in unprecedented savagery, who suffered crippling wounds, debilitating disease, maddening starvation, and acute despair—these men were allowed to end a horrific war, not with one side crowing in victory and the other cowering in shame but with a soldier's "mutual salutation and farewell."

✳ ✳ ✳

In a North that had barely finished celebrating the fall of Richmond, news of Lee's surrender produced another wave of joyousness and carousing: in city after city, bands played, cannon boomed by the hundreds, men and women jammed the streets and danced and laughed and hugged and kissed, singing "The Star-Spangled Banner" at the top of their lungs.

Against this tableau, the Lincoln-Sumner dance continued. On April 10, the White House sent flowers to Sumner to celebrate Lee's surrender at Appomattox. On the eleventh, with Washington fully illuminated and what seemed like the whole city thronging the streets, Mrs. Lincoln sent a note to Sumner inviting him to the White House to witness the spectacle and mentioning that "a little speech" from the President was expected.

But Sumner did not go. He anticipated, correctly it turned out, that Lincoln would bring up the subject of a lenient reconstruction process and especially highlight the benefits of his Louisiana plan as a model for readmitting seceded states. Sumner did not want to leave a public impression that he supported any of it. To some extent, he felt he had been used by Lincoln at the inaugural ball, and he had no intention of repeating his mistake. As Sumner put it: "I was unwilling to put myself in the position of opposing him on his own balcony or assenting by silence."

Much of the content of Lincoln's April 11 remarks—what is now termed his "Last Public Address"—was precisely what Sumner feared. In a section that fell flat with an audience intent on hearing victory huzzahs and patriotic platitudes, Lincoln offered a vigorous defense of his Louisiana plan for readmittance *without* universal suffrage and with only twelve thousand residents who swore allegiance to the Union.

However, for the first time, he publicly reiterated what he had said to his closest confidants—that he could support suffrage for blacks who were "very intelligent, and [for] those who serve our cause as soldiers." With those words, he became the first American President to publicly announce his willingness to confer voting rights, albeit selectively, upon black men.

While Lincoln's speech fell short in Charles Sumner's eyes, it went unacceptably too far for twenty-six-year-old John Wilkes Booth, who was again in the audience. When Booth heard Lincoln's willingness to support even gradual African American suffrage, he was incensed. "This means nigger citizenship," he muttered as Lincoln spoke.

"This is the last speech he will ever make."

✳ ✳ ✳

"I am very unhappy," Sumner wrote to Salmon Chase in a private note dated April 12, 1865. "For I see in the future strife and uncertainty for my country."

Lincoln's speech, coupled with his repeated entreaties to all Union supporters to demonstrate mercy and kindness to the South, left Sumner feeling anxious that the Union was in danger of losing the fruits of its victory. Stanton wondered "if it was not *Grant* who surrendered to *Lee*, instead of Lee to Grant!" an outraged Sumner complained to Chase. "He is sure that Richmond is beginning to govern Washington."

Still despondent on the evening of April 14, 1865—Good Friday— Sumner stopped by the lodgings of California senator John Conness to have a glass of wine with Conness and William M. Stewart, senator from the newly admitted state of Nevada.

They chatted for several minutes before Conness's servant burst in, shouting:

"Mr. Lincoln is assassinated at the theater! Mr. Seward is murdered in his bed!"

The servant was only half right, though the three senators did not know it at the time.

Frantic and frightened, they rushed out into the night.

✳ ✳ ✳

The three senators ran first to the White House, and learning nothing there, went to the theater, and then across the street to Lincoln's bedside about a half hour after the fatal shot had been fired. Sumner remained with the President until Lincoln drew his last breath the following morning.

During his all-night vigil at Lincoln's bedside, Sumner would piece together the events of the President's murder.

He learned of the intricate conspiracy by Southerners to kill Lincoln—a man who, "to the last . . . had been gentle and forgiving"—and other cabinet members. He learned of actor John Wilkes Booth's entry into the presidential box at Ford's Theatre after he displayed his calling card to an unsuspecting White House footman; of Booth's noiseless steps toward Lincoln until he was only two feet away, where he fired a bullet from his derringer into the back left side of the President's head; of Booth's leap from the balcony onto the stage below, where he landed heavily on one foot and broke a bone just above his ankle, even as he shouted to the stunned theater crowd, "Sic semper tyrannis"—"thus always to tyrants," the Virginia state motto. And then he learned of Booth, the assassin, shouting, "the South is avenged," before limping away and making his escape through the rear of the theater.

But in the moments after the President succumbed to his head wound on the morning of April 15, 1865, Sumner's thoughts were on the secretary of state, who had reportedly also been attacked by a would-be assassin the previous night as he lay bedridden from his carriage accident. Sumner had heard nothing of Seward's condition, or that of his son, Frederick, the assistant secretary of state, who had also been assaulted.

"Now for Mr. Seward!" Charles Sumner exclaimed moments after leaving the deceased Abraham Lincoln's bedroom.

Sumner opened the front door "in the gray of a drizzling morning" and saw General Henry Halleck just getting into his carriage. Sumner requested a ride to the Seward house. Halleck agreed, but said he must first stop at Andrew Johnson's quarters—when they arrived, Halleck went in to inform the President-to-be of Lincoln's death and warn him that he "must not go out without a guard."

✳ ✳ ✳

When Sumner arrived at Seward's house, he raced inside and found Mrs. Frances Seward seated, dazed, on the stairs leading to the third floor. "Charles Sumner," she cried, gripping his hand, "they have murdered my husband, they have murdered my boy. Fred is dying. He will never speak to me again." Sumner sat beside her, consoled her for a few moments, but suddenly she rose and shouted, "I must fly!" and disappeared further into the house. Sumner would never see her again—although both the secretary of state and his son ultimately recovered from their attacks, Frances Seward did not. Distraught and disoriented after the violent intrusion into her home, she died within a few weeks.

The attack against the already incapacitated William Seward and members of his family was savage and dastardly.

Around the time President Lincoln was assassinated, one of Booth's accomplices in the conspiracy—later identified as former Confederate soldier Lewis Powell—talked his way into Seward's house by claiming he had a message from the secretary's doctor about follow-up treatment for Seward's carriage injuries. Powell made his way to Seward's bedroom, where he encountered Frederick; Powell quickly brandished a revolver, which misfired when he pulled the trigger. In the dimly lit hall the two men struggled, and Powell soon gained the upper hand and pounded the pistol against Frederick's head again and again, breaking the gun and fracturing Frederick's skull in at least two places.

After Frederick collapsed, his attacker rushed to the elder Seward's bedside and slashed the helpless secretary of state repeatedly with a bowie knife. Seward, already encumbered with a rigid iron frame to hold immovable the broken jaw he suffered in the carriage accident, could do little to defend himself. As Powell slashed away, the white bandages on Seward's head and face reddened instantly with streams of blood. Seward's nurse, Robinson, burst into the room and attempted to drag

Powell away but received serious stab wounds himself. Coming upon the scene to investigate the ruckus, Seward's daughter Fanny screamed in distress, and, hearing the commotion, Seward's other son Augustus rushed in and wrenched the would-be murderer away from his father— but not before Augustus's head was cut "twice to the bone" and his hand slashed.

Finally, Powell tore himself free, fled down the stairs and out into the street, mounted his horse, and galloped away.

✳ ✳ ✳

Powell had cut Secretary of State William Seward's throat on both sides and nearly severed Seward's right cheek from his face. Seward and Frederick were both unconscious and bloody; Augustus and Robinson, though injured and covered in blood, remained conscious. Frederick was essentially comatose for more than forty-eight hours, and surgeons removed eight "pieces of bone from his brain," which was visible and exposed through his cracked skull. After two weeks, almost miraculously, Frederick was conscious and lucid.

William Seward took weeks to recover from his knife wounds. In late May, when thousands of members of the Army of the Potomac marched in review down the avenue in front of Seward's house, Seward was propped up in the window to watch the spectacle. General William T. Sherman, leading his troops, looked to Seward's window, moved his horse toward the house, removed his hat, and saluted the injured secretary of state. "He recognized the salute, returned it, and then we rode on steadily past the President, saluting with our swords," Sherman wrote with admiration in his memoirs.

When the anxiety-ridden Frances Seward died on June 21 at the age of sixty, Sumner remarked that "the poor Seward has been called to bear yet another blow." On the positive side, the fact that the secretary of state was even alive after such a brutal attack was incomprehensible.

"His escape is a marvel," Sumner wrote.

✳ ✳ ✳

After leaving Seward's house, a shaken and exhausted Charles Sumner reached his own quarters at the corner of F and 13th Streets at 8:00 A.M. When he arrived, Sumner saw that Stanton had posted guards outside.

He thought such precautions were unnecessary, but the secretary of war insisted that the outspoken and Southern-despised senator might be a target for assassination by Booth's conspirators. Stanton had also received information that *he* was a potential target.

Sumner went inside his house and sat unmoving for several minutes. His secretary, A. B. Johnson, described the senator as "sitting stern and haggard over his untasted breakfast as he contemplated the rebellion defeated and degraded to assassination."

In the succeeding days and weeks, Sumner called on Mary Lincoln several times to express his sympathies. In gratitude, she sent Sumner two souvenirs of her late husband. One was a likeness of British politician John Bright, a friend of both Lincoln's and Sumner's "and a noble and so good friend of our cause." The other—and Mrs. Lincoln saw no irony given the 1856 assault on Sumner—was President Lincoln's cane.

The cane was accompanied with the following note from Mrs. Lincoln:

My dear Mr. Sumner—Your unwavering kindness to my idolized husband, and the great regard he entertained for you, prompts me to offer your acceptance of this simple relic, which being connected with his blessed memory, I'm sure you will prize. I am endeavoring to regain my strength sufficiently to be able to leave here in a few days.

I go hence broken-hearted, with every hope almost in life crushed. Notwithstanding my utter desolation through life, the memory of the cherished friend of my husband and myself will always be most gratefully remembered.

Sumner struggled mightily with the shock of Abraham Lincoln's murder, the third president to die in office and the first by assassination. The two men had developed a friendship "of unbroken intimacy," and he was bewildered that Southern conspirators could destroy a man "so essentially humane and gentle that he could not make up his mind to any severity, even to Jefferson Davis."

Sumner took some solace in the smooth transition of power to Andrew Johnson upon Lincoln's death. Hours after Lincoln died, Johnson took the oath of office, and that very evening, Sumner met with Johnson to discuss business in the common room of the hotel in which the new President was staying.

✳ ✳ ✳

Two days after Lincoln's death, Sumner organized a meeting of the small number of senators and representatives still in Washington and chaired the committee that planned the funeral arrangements.

Lincoln's April 19 funeral was massive; six hundred invited guests attended services at the White House (a distraught Mary Todd Lincoln was not among them), and afterward they talked with somber reverence of General Ulysses S. Grant, sitting alone at the head of the catafalque in full uniform, "the hero on a pedestal, his face glistening with tears." The mile-long funeral procession then headed to the Capitol, where Lincoln's body would lie in state. The next day, more than forty thousand mourners filed by the casket in the rotunda during fourteen hours of viewing.

Dignitaries were on hand the following day at the train depot for a final farewell, and Lincoln's remains were then transported through cities across the country en route to the President's final resting place in Springfield, Illinois. The funeral train largely traced, in reverse order, the route Lincoln had taken on his way to Washington for his first inauguration. Along the way, more than one million people viewed Lincoln in death, and more than seven million kept vigil along the route of the passing train. The twenty-day odyssey transformed Lincoln from man to myth.

President Andrew Johnson designated June 1 as the day for the entire nation to commemorate Lincoln, and Boston leaders invited Charles Sumner to deliver the city's eulogy. Sumner accepted and convinced municipal authorities to choose Reverend Leonard Grimes, "the colored preacher" of the Twelfth Baptist Church—an abolitionist and a conductor on the Underground Railroad—to deliver the benediction at the funeral.

"It was for his race that President Lincoln died," Sumner wrote. "If Boston adopted him as chaplain on the day when we mourn, it would be a truer homage to our departed President than music or speech."

✳ ✳ ✳

Sumner delivered a heartfelt eulogy, but Lincoln's death had clearly disoriented him. Attendees remarked that some of his oratorical fire was missing. He seemed sluggish as he read from a manuscript, looked down at the paper far more than usual, and paused many times to adjust his glasses, which kept falling.

And yet, his two-hour tribute to Lincoln contained stirring language. He emphasized Lincoln's compassion, humor, and forgiving spirit, asserting that the late President's most ringing achievement was that he "pronounced the great word by which slaves were set free." The Emancipation Proclamation, Sumner declared, placed Lincoln "so far above human approach that human envy cannot reach him."

Sumner also spent an uncomfortable length of time imploring the funeral audience to support African American suffrage, a plea that many attendees, black and white, found inappropriate. But Sumner's heavy-handed appeal was a way to preserve the ideas Lincoln espoused in the Gettysburg Address and Second Inaugural. "*All* turns on the colored suffrage," he said. "This is the centre and pivot of national safety."

The Thirteenth Amendment to abolish slavery was a necessary first step, but without the right to vote, former slaves would enjoy no political standing or influence, would always fear a retrenchment and rebuilding of the slaveocracy, and the horrific war that had just ended, as well as Abraham Lincoln's death, would have been in vain.

The country owed it to Lincoln to adopt black suffrage. Former slaves—"freedmen"—were far from free without the vote.

"Liberty has been won," Sumner proclaimed to his audience at the Boston Music Hall. "The battle for Equality is still pending."

PART FIVE

"FOR ALL EVERYWHERE WHO SUFFER FROM TYRANNY AND WRONG"

☀ CHAPTER 35 ☀

ANDREW JOHNSON'S BETRAYAL

Even as Charles Sumner mourned the loss of his friend Abraham Lincoln, he knew he could waste little time influencing Lincoln's successor on the crucial issue of reconstruction.

At first, Sumner was convinced that he and President Andrew Johnson were *simpatico* on the reconstruction issue, and his euphoria knew no bounds. The President had assured him: "There is no difference between us." On May 1, 1865, after Sumner and Johnson had discussed the fate of the South's reconstruction several times, Sumner described the outlook for the country's future as "never so grand and fair and beautiful."

Johnson would prefer such a movement "appear to come from the people," an unstoppable groundswell of popular support, rather than via a presidential decree. Sumner agreed and sent word to like-minded allies in Massachusetts to organize visible events in support of suffrage for all.

Sumner was convinced that, with Johnson's full blessing, the postwar future would produce a new and better United States, a "regenerated land" whose commitment to equal rights would finally rest firmly on the principles articulated in the Declaration of Independence. "I feel more confident that this will all be fulfilled," he exclaimed in May. "*In the question of colored suffrage the President is with us*," Sumner declared triumphantly to John Bright.

But only days after he penned the letter, Sumner was dismayed to learn that he was badly mistaken.

President Johnson—acting without reason and without warning, according to Sumner, and perhaps suffering from some "strange hallucination"—betrayed him.

☀ ☀ ☀

It all began to unspool on May 9, one month after the surrender of the Army of Northern Virginia, when President Johnson recognized Francis Harrison Pierpont as the rightful governor of the restored state of Virginia. Pierpont had helped establish West Virginia as a separate state and had served as de facto governor of Virginia since 1863.

But the Pierpont government did not give blacks the franchise, which seemed to contradict everything Sumner and Johnson had agreed upon.

On May 11, a bewildered Sumner met with Johnson for an hour before heading back to Massachusetts. He told the President that his decision on Virginia was a "miscarriage," that "the Pierpont government is nothing but a sham." He met with Johnson hoping to "save the rest" of the readmitted states from a similar fate.

It was to no avail.

Sumner had not been home ten days when all of his hopes for a "just and speedy reconstruction on the basis of equal rights were dashed." On May 29, President Johnson appointed William W. Holden provisional governor of North Carolina and asked him to organize a convention to form a government in preparation for the state's reentry into the Union. Johnson's proclamation stipulated that voter qualifications would be the same as before secession—that is, *no black suffrage and no black participation in the convention.* Only those whites who had taken an oath of allegiance to the United States and received amnesty could vote for delegates to the state's constitutional convention. Johnson issued similar proclamations and chose provisional governors for Alabama, Georgia, Mississippi, South Carolina, Texas, and Florida, and affirmed the validity of similar reconstruction efforts begun under Lincoln in Tennessee, Louisiana, and Arkansas.

Sumner opposed "reconstruction by Executive action," but Johnson refused to call Congress into special session; by mid-September, the President had granted 13,500 pardons to rebel leaders and functionaries. It appeared that Johnson was determined to complete reconstruction unilaterally and present Congress with a fait accompli when it finally convened in December. Rabid abolitionist congressman Thaddeus Stevens—Sumner's counterpart in the House—asked Sumner whether there was a way "to arrest the insane course of the President." He worried that without intervention, Johnson would "be crowned king" before Congress met.

Sumner was at once baffled and outraged. The President had at first agreed with the core principle that before any state could be readmitted to the Union it *must* enshrine into its constitution universal suffrage without regard to color.

Something had so altered Johnson's course on reconstruction that he seemed intent on careening without restraint down a dangerous road.

But what?

* * *

Theories abounded about why Johnson changed his mind—or *if* he even did.

Was it his ego, plied by the flattering of Southern leaders who urged him to escape Lincoln's shadow and make his own mark by upstaging Congress? Was it payback fueled by his smoldering anger toward Sumner and other radicals for calling out his besotted condition on Inauguration Day? Was he drinking again, which left him unable to reason clearly? Or was the simplest answer the most likely—was Johnson reverting to his political roots as a former Tennessee slaveholder and Democrat?

One other possibility presented itself: Did Sumner simply *misread* Johnson from the beginning, allowing his own hopes for universal voting rights to deceive him as to Johnson's intentions? "It was Johnson's habit to listen without replying to those who disagreed with him," one historian noted, "and Sumner had too often taken silence for consent."

The easiest and least sinister explanation for Johnson's change of heart is that, while Congress was out of session during the summer of 1865, he sought to assert his presidential authority and heal the nation, and readmitting states was the easiest way to do so. The President understood that most of the North was exhausted by war, by death, by the destruction and chaos that had ravaged the country. The abstract notions of equal rights and universal suffrage did not resonate with Northerners in the same way as preserving the Union or abolishing slavery had served as rallying cries. In addition, Northerners were anxious for reopening Southern markets, which had remained closed to merchants for four long and unproductive years.

For the majority of the country, the faster reunification occurred the better, and it appeared Johnson was moving swiftly to accomplish this goal.

* * *

In the summer of 1865, Johnson emphasized to several provisional governors that the governments of the South should be controlled by "the white population alone." In September, he articulated a more politically cynical approach, suggesting to Southern state governors that if the vote was also granted to "all persons of color who can read the Constitution of the United States, and write their names, and to all persons who own real estate" valued at more than $250 and pay taxes, "you would completely disarm the adversary [Radical Republicans like Sumner] and set an example the other States will follow." Johnson knew that almost no former slaves could fulfill these requirements, so in essence, suggesting such a sham plan for universal suffrage would mean no freedmen suffrage at all.

If Johnson's policy was not "arrested," Sumner said, then "nothing can save the country from destruction."

Sumner outlined his own Reconstruction goals in a late-August letter to his friend, Francis Lieber:

> (1) Refer the whole question of Reconstruction to Congress; (2) Lead public opinion in the right direction; (3) Obey the existing laws of Congress which expressly exclude from public service any person who has sustained the rebellion; (4) Obey the Constitution which refuses to make any distinction of color; (5) Redeem the promises of the Declaration of Independence instead of openly setting them at defiance.

He reiterated these steps publicly at the Massachusetts state Republican convention in September and even called for a constitutional amendment guaranteeing black suffrage.

But many Republicans were reluctant to challenge Johnson so forcefully, and they certainly had no political incentive to break with him. Republicans controlled several large Northern states by only a few thousand votes, and many citizens believed Johnson had taken on an unprecedented, unenviable, and monumental task with a measure of good faith and "honesty of purpose," in the words of Massachusetts governor John Andrew, who urged cooperation with the President. Sumner's old friend and legal adversary in the Sarah Roberts case, Peleg W. Chandler, warned of a "feverish dread . . . of *any* breach with the President. It would be a terrible misfortune at this crisis to have a divided North."

Sumner assured his allies that he had no plans to break with Johnson "unless it becomes absolutely necessary," but as the congressional session began in December 1865, he remained resolute in his calls for universal suffrage. He now expected the fight with Johnson to be a grueling one, and this on the heels of the grinding battles he had waged with Southern slave owners for a decade and a half. He usually relished his time in the arena, but he admitted to Salmon Chase that it was difficult to maintain a positive outlook during such struggles. "I was born too early," he wrote wistfully. "I wish that I had come into the world 30 years later—how beautiful this world will be 30 years from now."

Even so, he was convinced that Congress would intervene and right the wrongs of Johnson's Reconstruction policies. "This Republic cannot be lost," he wrote. "Therefore the policy of the President *must* fail."

✻ ✻ ✻

SATURDAY, DECEMBER 2, 1865

Sumner requested an audience with Johnson on the very evening of his arrival in D.C. The issue was too urgent to delay for a moment—he had to convince the President to alter his disastrous course on reconstruction.

Johnson began the White House meeting "warmly and antagonistically," a description Sumner employed to indicate the wariness with which both men approached the sensitive topic after a summer of jousting. But their intensity, coupled with the stakes of the issue, skimmed away the veneer of politeness in minutes, and the tone of the meeting deteriorated from bad to worse.

Sumner viewed Johnson as "hide-bound in prejudice, and painfully insensible to the real condition of things" among freedmen in the South. On the entire subject of reconstruction and protecting former slaves, Johnson was "impenetrable," Sumner declared, and most of what Johnson said during their discussion was "pig-headed and painful, from its prejudice, ignorance, and perversity." Not surprisingly, Johnson found Sumner's manner arrogant and dictatorial, and inferred from Sumner's language that "the radicals in Congress would open war" upon the President's policies.

As the two men argued, a furious Sumner told the President that he "had thrown away the fruits of the victories of the Union army" with his inane policies that would leave former Southern slaves without the vote and without protection from their former owners. When Johnson asked for more specifics, a tired and agitated Sumner could only muster a response that was woefully inadequate. "The poor *freedmen* in Georgia and Alabama were frequently *insulted* by rebels," Sumner said.

Johnson could hardly believe his ears. After a war that had split the nation in two, killed hundreds of thousands of Americans, wounded thousands more, brought the country to the brink of war with England, destroyed the Southern economy, and demolished the slavery system, the leading Senate champion for freedom and equal rights was threatening to crush a workable reunification plan—demanding that the administration *change its entire reconstruction policy*—based on mere insults?

Unmoved, Johnson asked with sarcasm: "Mr. Sumner, do murders ever occur in Massachusetts?"

"Unhappily, yes, Mr. President."

"Do people ever knock each other down in Boston?" Johnson continued.

"Unhappily, yes, Mr. President, sometimes."

"Would you consent," Johnson asked, "that Massachusetts should be excluded from the Union on this account?"

"No, Mr. President," Sumner conceded with exasperation, "surely not."

It was clear that the differences between the President and the senator were irreconcilable. "He was without any sympathy for the freedmen," Sumner recalled.

The best illustration of how badly the Johnson-Sumner relationship had degenerated came toward the end of the meeting. When he entered Johnson's office, Sumner had removed his fine silk hat and laid it upside down on the floor next to his chair. President Johnson, becoming animated during one heated exchange, paused for a moment, and—either "unconsciously," as Sumner described, or perhaps deliberately to make a point—expectorated violently, using Sumner's hat as a spittoon.

Unintentional or not, the President's vulgar gesture encapsulated, in Sumner's view, the entire depressing summer and fall of 1865—after a promising start to the Johnson administration—and the outright disdain he and Johnson now felt for each other.

✳ ✳ ✳

On Christmas Day, 1865, while most Americans celebrated with family and friends, Charles Sumner pored over lengthy and disturbing reports that convinced him—insomuch as the self-assured Sumner *ever* needed independent convincing—that his position was right and just.

He was engrossed and sickened by the stories he read about conditions in the war-ravaged American South:

In Bladon Springs, Alabama, a freedman was run down, captured, chained to a pine tree, and set afire by a marauding group of former slave owners.

Near Goldsboro, North Carolina, Chanie, an "aged woman of color," was whipped more than one hundred times by former plantation owner William Barnes, his wife, and his son. The three then tied Chanie between two trees ("feet to one tree and hands to another"), cut off her hair, and watched as three of their snarling dogs tore her clothing and bit her repeatedly. Barnes then gave her two hundred lashes with a paddle and declared that "no damned nigger should be free under him."

In Clinton, Mississippi, a planter boldly declared to a U.S. government official: "These niggers will all be slaves again in twelve months. You have nothing but Lincoln proclamations to make them free."

On July 4, 1865, in Mobile, Alabama, a procession of freedmen, "6,000 well-dressed and orderly colored people," paraded the streets in celebration. Town officials screamed obscenities at them from street corners, and young black women in the group were forced to have sex with town police officers under threat of incarceration in the guardhouse. One black church was burned, and threats were made against others.

And on and on . . .

Sumner digested this gruesome collection of reports from freedmen bureaus in Southern states as well as the voluminous and equally depressing *Report on the Condition of the South* by Major General Carl Schurz, a German-born Union general and friend of Sumner's, who had been asked by President Johnson to make a tour of the South for the purposes of reporting on racial conditions, a trip Sumner supported.

Schurz visited South Carolina, Georgia, Alabama, and Louisiana, spending time in cities and across the countryside. He spoke with and interviewed civilians, military officials, civil authorities, and citizens "from the highest to the lowest [classes] of society" in city taverns, on roadsides, on steamboats, and on farms.

Schurz found what Sumner feared he would find, and perhaps in some ways *hoped* he would find as the senator sought to derail President

Johnson's Reconstruction plan: an "utter absence of the national spirit" from Southern whites toward the United States (*only* freedmen celebrated the Fourth of July in the South); former Confederates who were profuse in their praise for Johnson's Reconstruction policies, anxious for the withdrawal of federal troops, and desirous of swift readmission to the Union with little change in rights for freedmen; and a large contingent of "incorrigibles" who still indulged in the "swagger" of the South before the war and hoped for a time when the "southern Confederacy" would achieve its independence.

And, of course, the almost universal, systematic oppression and brutal physical violence toward former slaves.

"I heard [one message] hundreds of times," Schurz said, "I heard it everywhere I went, heard it in nearly the same words from so many different persons—'you cannot make the negro work, without physical compulsion.' This is the prevailing sentiment among the Southern people."

Schurz provided example after example of freedmen who were whipped, shot, drowned, lynched, or clubbed into submission. Ironically enough, because the slaves were now free, former slaveholders no longer felt the financial need to protect their once valuable property against outright violence, grievous injury, or death. As Sumner noted: "In most places the freedmen are worse off than when [they were] slaves—exposed to the brutality and vindictiveness of their old masters, *without* the old check of self-interest."

Halfway through his Christmas reading of Schurz's report, Sumner paused a moment to write the general a letter. Two facts were clear, he told Schurz: first, that the report proved without a doubt that Congress must assert its jurisdiction over the Reconstruction process to ensure the physical safety of the freedmen, and, second, Schurz's detailed stories of the mistreatment of freedmen provided ample evidence that no former rebel states should be readmitted to the Union without agreeing to universal suffrage.

✳ ✳ ✳

Three weeks earlier, on the first day of the congressional session, Sumner had introduced a series of resolutions on the Senate floor asking Congress to guarantee that every reentering state maintain a "republican form of government" and that no government could be considered republican without allowing universal suffrage.

He urged Congress to seize control of the Reconstruction process, sweep away what he viewed as the corrupt regimes Johnson had set up in the Southern states, and insist that "all persons shall be equal before the law" throughout the former Confederacy "whether in the court-room or at the ballot-box." He proposed that each state hold a constitutional convention—soldiers or officers of the Confederacy would be forbidden to serve as delegates—and vote to disavow secession, prohibit slavery, and permanently prohibit all high-ranking Confederates from holding office. Only when this process was approved by eligible voters—under Sumner's plan that would include blacks but exclude most ex-Confederates—could a state be readmitted to representation in Congress.

Two weeks later, he also called on Congress to block the so-called "Black Codes" of southern legislatures, which were focused on controlling the movement and labor of freedmen who wished to take part in the South's post-slavery free labor system. The defining feature of the codes was an oppressive vagrancy law, which allowed local authorities to arrest former slaves for minor infractions and commit them to involuntary labor.

"In the name of God, let us protect them," Sumner said, referring to the freedmen.

But despite his pleadings, it would soon become clear that, as had been the case since the 1840s, Sumner's ideas on achieving racial equality were far ahead of most of his congressional colleagues.

✷ ✷ ✷

Fellow senators were simply unwilling and unprepared to endorse his proposals.

Instead, still concerned about the balance of power in the North and the 1866 midterm elections, Sumner's colleagues hoped to achieve a compromise with President Johnson.

Republican leaders agreed to establish a Joint Committee of Fifteen on Reconstruction to develop a more moderate program. It was chaired by Senator William Fessenden of Maine, one of Sumner's bitterest enemies in the party. The committee included few radicals and deliberately omitted Sumner as an inducement for the President's cooperation—

Fessenden was fearful that the "yelping of the dogs" of radicalism might drive Johnson into the Democratic camp.

Committee members did agree that further legislation and a constitutional amendment were necessary to assure the loyalty of readmitted states and protect freedmen. By mid-February they took the initial step of extending the life of the Freedmen's Bureau and passing a civil rights bill that provided legal guarantees on the streets and in court for freedmen. But despite the Senate's hopes of building a bridge with Johnson, the President vetoed both bills and on February 22, 1866, delivered an invective-filled speech to a crowd at the White House, comparing Republican leaders who opposed him, including Sumner, to Jefferson Davis.

"These are trying days for us," Sumner wrote in response. "I am more anxious now than during the war." He had high hopes that the constitutional amendment Fessenden's committee was considering—a proposed Fourteenth Amendment to the U.S. Constitution—would settle the issue of black suffrage once and for all, with clean, unequivocal, and final language. The freedmen required such protection for their own safety and advancement.

What emerged instead was messy and cloudy, once again leaving Sumner's desire for universal voting very much up in the air.

CHAPTER 36

THE FOURTEENTH AMENDMENT: "FREEDOM WITHOUT SUFFRAGE IS STILL SLAVERY"

The push for a Fourteenth Amendment by Radical Republicans had one critical question at its core: How far should the Constitution go to protect the rights of freedmen, and African Americans in general?

For several months during the winter and spring of 1866, it was clear that the answer would depend on a combination of the practical (what language would satisfy two-thirds of members?), the poetic (Sumner's long-heralded ideals of equality, universal suffrage, and equal justice under the law), the puerile (Radicals and their ongoing feud with President Johnson), and, as always, the political (what did Republicans dare pass that would not hurt them in the North in the November congressional midterms?).

When the dust cleared, a muddled piece of legislation emerged. Sumner promptly dismissed it as "another compromise with human rights."

And yet, despite Sumner's initial resistance and even his early opposition to the Fourteenth Amendment, the measure validated a large chunk of his lifetime work by enshrining into the U.S. Constitution, for the first time, the principles of black citizenship, due process for all, and equal protection under the law.

These were Sumner's priorities, Sumner's battles, and Sumner's ideals. On each day of debate, though he played only a small role in the actual *crafting* of the new amendment, Sumner's voice played over and over in the heads of representatives and senators who eventually brought the amendment to the floor.

But it would take him some time to recognize the Fourteenth Amendment for the victory it was. At first, he tried to alter it, and failing that, to kill it altogether.

✳ ✳ ✳

"It is not I who speak," Sumner told a packed Senate chamber on February 5, 1866. "I am nothing. It is the cause, whose voice I am, that addresses you."

What he witnessed that day, what had *never* happened before, was that more than one-quarter of the Senate gentlemen's gallery was made up of Union troops from colored regiments—black soldiers, resplendent in full uniform, anxiously awaiting Sumner's words about their future. They had fought bravely for the Union and now anticipated Sumner's fight for them. As much as the residents of Massachusetts, these men—and thousands more like them, along with black women and children—had been Sumner's constituency for most of his public life. One newspaper correspondent described the unprecedented spectacle in the Senate chamber as "worthy of a thousand miles' journey" to witness.

Sumner began speaking at about one o'clock, though the chamber was packed with spectators well before noon. He would speak for two hours on the fifth and another two hours on the sixth. A Maine reporter called it "not only the great speech of Charles Sumner's life, but . . . the great speech of the age."

Sumner spoke of the Constitution's guarantee of providing a "republican form of government" to its citizens, and as he had maintained for years, such a promise was impossible without the right to vote. For him, it was—it always had been—about the ballot, about universal suffrage, about enfranchising freedmen and blacks in general to ensure their full rights were protected now and forevermore.

The proposed Fourteenth Amendment did not provide for such ballot access, so he was opposed to it, even suspicious of the motives of those who *had* proposed it as employing yet another in a countless array of delaying tactics and half measures.

Universal suffrage, he maintained, was a universal right. Freedom without suffrage was another form of slavery. Ballot access was everything—it was the "*peacemaker*," which if denied, would make the freedman "the victim of perpetual warfare" and domestic strife; it was the "*reconciler*," which helped estranged people live and work together in harmony; it was the "*schoolmaster*," which went beyond basic education in reading and writing to teach "manhood," especially important to a race whose manhood had been denied; it was the "*protector*," to prevent a slave's old master from "bind[ing] his victim in new chains."

To those who argued that freedmen had little knowledge of the workings of government and that rewarding them with the vote thus presented unimaginable risks, Sumner reserved his most evocative language. "Let not the tyranny of the past be apology for further exclusion," he said. "Prisoners long immured in a dungeon are sometimes blinded as they come forth into the day, but this is no reason for continued imprisonment—to every Freedman, *the ballot is the light of day*."

He asked his colleagues to remember that the colored soldiers in the gallery, and thousands of others, had fought bravely for the Union. "If he was willing to die for the Republic, he is surely good enough to vote," he said. Liberty and equality went together, and equality required—*demanded*—universal suffrage. Liberty alone was insufficient, indeed perhaps a mirage, without equality. Together, the two elevated the American republic, he said, and offered it deliverance from the terrible crime of slavery.

"If that 'more perfect union' proclaimed in the National Constitution as a primary object [is to be] obtained at last," Sumner said, then universal suffrage must be included in the proposed Fourteenth Amendment.

Without it, he warned, "the work is only *half done*."

✳ ✳ ✳

As a matter of oratory and argument, Charles Sumner's remarkable address (entitled "The Equal Rights of All") over two days in February 1866 contained among the most eloquent and convincing arguments for equal rights in history—not just *American* history but all of history.

But as a practical *political* matter, Sumner's speech fell flat. Many Northern and former border states either did not allow black suffrage or discriminated against blacks who could vote, and they balked at including the unfettered right in the Constitution as the 1866 midterm elections approached. Republican margins in many Northern states were narrow, and the party was hoping to expand its majorities in Congress to allow for overrides of President Andrew Johnson's expected vetoes of key legislation moving forward.

As a compromise of sorts, the House of Representatives had included language in the proposed Fourteenth Amendment declaring that states that did not allow black suffrage would have their proportional representations in the House reduced by the number of black male residents. Northern lawmakers accepted this compromise because black populations in the North were much smaller than in Southern states, and thus any Northern loss of representatives in Congress would be minimal. Southern states, on the other hand, would suffer.

Sumner was having none of the compromise. He denounced it as a "delusion and a snare" and said that "even the bribe offered cannot tempt" the former slave master to confer suffrage without distinction of color. He predicted (accurately, it would turn out) that the South would find ways to evade the requirement and still retain its political influence. He antagonized moderates, who believed the compromise language was a good-faith effort given the political realities, when he said that their proposed compromise, "borrowing an example from Pontius Pilate, turns over a whole race to sacrifice."

To include or not include universal suffrage in the Fourteenth Amendment: passionate debate lasted for well over a month and covered an uneven range of deep and principled moral questions laced with a political pastiche of issues that had bedeviled lawmakers throughout the war and during the first year of Reconstruction.

✳ ✳ ✳

Strained feelings between Sumner and moderates continued through the spring, especially after his opposition led to an initial rejection of the Fourteenth Amendment. Maine senator Fessenden claimed that Sumner's impractical notions, his vanity, and his hatred of the President were "doing infinite harm." Republican representative Thaddeus Stevens pleaded with Sumner that, if the amendment was "to be slain, it will not be by our friends."

Sumner's good friend Salmon Chase urged him to support the amendment, believing it was the best Republicans could do in the current session of Congress and pointing out that it contained language enshrining into the Constitution many of Sumner's cherished and long-held views— black citizenship, due process, and equal protection. Suffrage for freedmen would come *eventually*, Chase predicted, but insisting on it now could upend everything Republicans had worked toward.

Such warnings were effective. When the amendment came up for debate again at the end of May, Sumner offered only token opposition to it. Part of his acquiescence was to help Republicans blunt Johnson's opposition, but more important was his fear that blame would fall squarely on his shoulders if the amendment collapsed entirely.

✻ ✻ ✻

The long debate over the Fourteenth Amendment, unending pressure from other Republicans, and frustrating squabbles with Johnson had placed Sumner under enormous physical and emotional strain. He was in his Senate chair every day, and after adjournment he would spend hours researching and reading in preparation for his speeches (which, for this single session of Congress, filled 556 pages of his published *Works*). He often worked past midnight, with only an hour break for dinner, and returned to the Senate early the next morning.

He became seriously ill with a painful recurrence of the angina pectoris that had affected him before. His physician suggested a vacation, but Sumner was unwilling to leave the Senate at such a crucial time. He compromised by agreeing to make no further lengthy speeches.

Adding to Sumner's stress was his aging mother's deteriorating health. Relief Sumner's physician reported in mid-May that the eighty-one-year-old woman was growing weaker "both in body and mind."

Too ill and drained to further oppose what he considered an inadequate amendment, Charles Sumner voted "yes" when, on June 8, 1866, the Senate adopted the Fourteenth Amendment.

The amendment had now passed both houses with unanimous Republican votes in each. It would take a full two years—until July 9, 1868—for a sufficient number of states to ratify it into the Constitution.

Two days after the historic vote, a worn-out Charles Sumner left Washington for a return trip to Boston.

Doctors had sent word—his mother had only days to live.

✻ ✻ ✻

Relief Jacob Sumner, who was born two years before the adoption of the United States Constitution, died on Saturday, June 15, 1866. After his hurried departure from Washington, Charles was able to spend four days at his mother's bedside before she passed.

As large as the family had been, he was the only relative at the funeral service, which was held the day after Mrs. Sumner's death at the Sumner home at 20 Hancock Street. Sumner's only living sibling, his sister Julia Hastings, lived in San Francisco and, suffering from chronic ill health herself, had not been east since 1862. Julia's three daughters were Relief Sumner's only surviving grandchildren. Only a few old friends joined Charles at the sparse funeral; Sumner did not announce his mother's death, "except to intimates . . . wishing to avoid the crowd."

His mother's death left Charles with mixed feelings. In the early years, their relationship had been cool, though she often "softened the hard places" created by his father; yet in the twenty-seven years of her widowhood, Charles often sought and found solace and peaceful refuge in his mother's company. He had been a dutiful if not devoted son, writing to her with some regularity, inquiring about her comfort, providing her with the best possible care when he was away from home, managing her finances, and spending pleasant time with her when he was in Boston. "She was an excellent and remarkable person, whose death leaves me more than ever alone," he stated with his characteristic reserve when describing family relationships.

Charles, along with Henry Longfellow and two other family friends, accompanied Relief Sumner's body to Mount Auburn Cemetery for burial. That evening, Charles had dinner with his friend Julia Ward Howe. Returning to the empty family house afterward, a grieving Sumner bowed his head and said aloud: "I have now no home."

Days later, he wrote to his dear old friend Longfellow: "I have come to an epoch in my life. My mother is dead. I have a moderate competency. What next?"

What came next would shock his friends, his enemies, official Washington, and virtually everyone else who knew Charles Sumner.

To Longfellow, he hinted: "When we meet again, I may have something to tell you."

CHAPTER 37

"I BEGIN TO LIVE!"

Before Sumner returned to Washington after his mother's funeral, his friend E. L. Pierce invited him on a long carriage ride to the suburb of Milton and a drive around the beautiful Blue Hills.

The pair had made the trip during each congressional recess.

But this one was a little different.

Sumner, suddenly and unexpectedly, turned the conversation to "the conditions which inclined people to marriage." He told Pierce that he now had the means to support a family (particularly with his inheritance), and, with his mother's passing and his caretaking duties concluded, he felt at liberty to marry if he were to meet someone who "inspired" him.

Just as quickly, Sumner ended the conversation, forbade a puzzled Pierce to speak of it again, and commanded his friend never to reveal that Sumner had expressed such thoughts.

In fact, Sumner's musing was not based on a hypothetical situation at all.

✹ ✹ ✹

Pierce did not know during the carriage ride that Sumner had already met, wooed, and planned to marry the "someone" who inspired him—the news he wished to tell Longfellow.

She was twenty-eight-year-old Alice Mason Hooper, the widowed daughter-in-law of Sumner's friend Massachusetts representative Samuel Hooper. After her husband's death in 1863, Alice and her seven-year-old daughter, Isabella, or "Bell," spent the 1865–66 social season in Washington, living with her in-laws at Samuel Hooper's insistence. Alice was familiar with the nation's capital; in the summer after her husband's death, she worked in the city as a volunteer nurse, and even when she was not on duty, she rarely let more than a day or two go by without visiting the wounded in military hospitals around Washington.

While the Senate was in session, Sumner was a frequent visitor to the Hooper house, and he quickly grew smitten with the strikingly beautiful, graceful, and intelligent Alice, whom he had known only in passing until about a year earlier. (Sumner neither mentioned, nor apparently observed, any of Alice's purported personality shortcomings enumerated by one contemporary writer, who cautioned that Alice "had an extremely variable disposition which she could show in teasing or temper . . . with the disposition to rule the circle in which she moved.")

Alice had other suitors, including Senator Fessenden and Speaker of the House Schuyler Colfax, but she seemed to take to Sumner. She was grateful that Sumner had helped secure an appointment and promotion for her brother, an army officer, and treasured public documents and photos Sumner occasionally sent to her. She also agreed with and encouraged Sumner's approach on Reconstruction. When Sumner was in town, he doted on Alice each time she visited the Senate chamber.

In one of Alice's three surviving letters to Sumner, written the previous December, she wished him a happy Christmas in Boston and playfully hoped she would not find Sumner in "gloomy" spirits the next time she saw him in Washington.

✳ ✳ ✳

Until now, even *contemplating* a romantic relationship was unusual for Sumner.

He was by temperament and lifestyle a loner and a bachelor, and before his mother's death, he relied mostly on his Senate income, which made it difficult to support a family. Also working against this particular relationship was the fact that the fifty-five-year-old Sumner was nearly twice Alice's age, and physically the difference seemed even greater. Alice looked like "a young lady of 16," while Sumner's visage appeared old and haggard from overwork and ill health; he had put on weight, and his hair had turned almost entirely gray.

But their age difference seemed to fade somewhat when Sumner became ill in the spring and Alice, an experienced nurse, cared for him in his Washington, D.C., quarters. The two chatted and laughed and got to know each other on a more genuine and less formal basis.

No explicit documentation explains Alice's apparent openness to Sumner's advances. Later, Washington, D.C., gossip speculated that she believed Sumner would make her "First Lady of the land." Another cynical rumor suggested she was well aware that a relationship with one of the most powerful members of the Senate—one of the most influential men in the country—would boost her own social and economic status. But it seems just as likely that Alice genuinely enjoyed Sumner's rich conversation and gentle deportment, found him a strong figure capable of supporting her and her child, and yet also felt a certain attraction to his vulnerability while he was ill as she reprised her role as tender caretaker.

Or maybe, as it has for centuries, love's ageless mystery simply defied explanation.

In any case, shortly after Sumner's return to Washington following his mother's funeral, he and Alice were engaged.

* * *

Sumner brimmed with a mixture of exuberance and bewilderment as he began to share his engagement news in letters and notes to friends at the end of the summer.

"Do not be too surprised," he told one correspondent, "but you cannot be more so than I am!" He wrote similar letters to friends and colleagues and received congratulations from a wide circle—Howe, Longfellow, Whittier, John Bright, Lieber, Chase, former senator (and soon-to-be secretary of state) Hamilton Fish, Mary Todd Lincoln, the Argylls, diplomat George Bancroft, and scores of others. All expressed their unbridled joy but for the regret that Sumner had delayed this step for so long.

Like any longtime single person about to embark on a relationship with another, Sumner also had his doubts, which he was not afraid to voice more than once—even to Alice. "Unless we are both satisfied that this union is to be a happy one, we had better separate now," he wrote to her. Alice felt no such anxieties and went ahead with wedding plans, even though her relatives, put off by Sumner's age, took "no pains to conceal how distasteful the whole affair was to them."

On a glorious fall day, October 17, 1866, at 3:00 P.M., Charles Sumner and Alice Hooper were married by the Episcopal bishop of Boston, Manton Eastburn, at the home of Alice's sister, Isabella Mason Appleton. Only a handful of relatives and close friends attended.

By 4:30 P.M., the newlyweds, along with eight-year-old Bell and her dog, Ty, were on their way to Newport for a three-week honeymoon.

Afterward, in Washington, Sumner himself was ebullient. His little family had rented a house at 322 I Street, where he hoped to be "very happy."

To one friend he wrote: "Thus I begin to live . . . *Tardily*, I begin."

✳ ✳ ✳

Personally and politically, December 1866 and the early weeks of 1867 were among the most pleasant of Sumner's entire life. Energized both by his marriage and the election results, Sumner wasted little time taking advantage of the prevailing climate and advancing his agenda.

Republicans had enjoyed an overwhelming victory at the polls in November and would have a three-to-one advantage once the new Congress was seated. Their one-sided victory signaled a rejection of President Johnson's Reconstruction policies and an acceptance of the Congress-led approach Sumner advocated. The *Nation* concluded that the Republican victory was "the most decisive and emphatic . . . ever seen in American politics."

On December 3 (the first day of the "holdover session" of the Thirty-Ninth Congress), Sumner proposed a bill conferring full voting rights on blacks in the District of Columbia. By mid-December, fully recognizing popular sentiment, both houses agreed (the Senate passed Sumner's bill 32–13), and Congress overrode Johnson's veto in early January 1867.

After a years-long fight, universal suffrage was, finally, law in the nation's capital. Sumner stated with satisfaction: "Here at least my ideas have prevailed!"

But it was not just in relation to Washington, D.C., that Sumner's ideas triumphed.

Throughout the war, and especially after Lincoln issued the Emancipation Proclamation, Sumner had urged that freedom and universal suffrage extend beyond those states that had taken part in the rebellion; if entrenched attitudes and political considerations made such a dream impractical in the North and the border states, surely it could apply to territories and new states looking to enter the Union.

Sumner finally got his wish when Congress voted on admitting Nebraska as a state.

＊ ＊ ＊

In the previous session, a bill had failed proposing Nebraska's admission with a constitution limiting suffrage to white citizens. Now, motivated partially by a long overdue sense of justice, and partially by a desire to increase their majority by two more senators, Republicans had come full circle—they moved to admit Nebraska *only* if the state permitted universal suffrage.

Some senators argued that the proposal was meant for show only, since merely a handful of blacks lived in Nebraska. Sumner urged support for the bill and called on senators not to create another "white man's government," regardless of the number of black citizens who resided in the state. To admit Nebraska without a universal suffrage requirement would be an egregious denial of human rights, especially after honoring those rights the previous day by establishing voting for all men in Washington, D.C., irrespective of color.

The Nebraska admission bill passed both houses of Congress after the House added an amendment requiring the assent of the Nebraska state legislature on the issue of universal suffrage, which Sumner and other Radical Republicans agreed they could live with. Again, in a sign of continued abrasiveness with the executive branch, both houses of Congress overrode President Johnson's unsurprising veto.

On March 1, 1867, Nebraska entered the Union as the thirty-seventh state, with full voting rights for its black citizens, a victory for Sumner above all.

He was happy, philosophical, and reflective:

"And thus ends a long contest, where at first I was alone."

＊ ＊ ＊

There were still more victories for Sumner and the Republicans in early 1867.

More determined than ever to hamstring Johnson, Congress on March 2 passed the Tenure of Office Act, a piece of legislation perched on a rickety legal foundation stating that any federal official whose appointment required Senate confirmation could not be removed without the Senate's consent. The act allowed the President to suspend an official if the Senate were not in session, but if the Senate, upon reconvening, did not concur with the removal, the official must be reinstated. Johnson, promptly recognizing the politics behind the act, and arguing—correctly it would turn out—against its constitutionality, vetoed the legislation, and again Congress overrode it with ease.

Republicans had cagily set a snare for Johnson with the legislation. Rumors swirled about his dissatisfaction with Secretary of War Edwin Stanton, a Lincoln appointee, who was far more politically aligned with Radical Republicans than with Johnson on the issue of Reconstruction. At the same time, several congressional Republicans, Sumner among them, had already begun a campaign urging the impeachment of President Johnson (an unsuccessful resolution for impeachment was offered in the House in January). Republicans were furious about Johnson's approach to Reconstruction, yet they recognized that a mere Legislative-Executive disagreement on policy did not meet the "high crimes and misdemeanors" constitutional threshold for impeachment.

Frustrated congressional Republicans needed more.

The Tenure of Office Act provided the means. It was a legal trapdoor for Johnson to drop through should he move ahead with the removal of Stanton—or anyone else whom the Senate had confirmed—without Senate concurrence. It was a naked power play by Congress, and Sumner knew it. But it was justified, he said, because Johnson was "the enemy of the country" and the "successor to Jefferson Davis" in his manner of governing. Sumner would support any measure that would constrain the "presidential usurper menacing the Republic."

This pledge led to the greatest Republican achievement of all in early 1867: the move by the Republican Congress to wrest control of Reconstruction from the President and their total endorsement and adoption of Sumner's plan on how to handle the former Confederate states.

✳ ✳ ✳

The South gave Sumner and other congressional Republicans all the ammunition they needed.

Violence against freedmen continued across the region—more of the beatings, lynchings, clubbings, and murders that Schurz had detailed in his report—and it was clear that Johnson's provisional governments had neither the inclination nor the wherewithal to stop it. Egged on by President Johnson, who, in a series of invective-filled speeches, openly called for its rejection, every rebel state except Tennessee voted against the Fourteenth Amendment.

Republicans had seen enough; moderates and radicals alike were at last ready to agree with Sumner on the need for more forceful and disruptive action on the former Confederacy.

The Joint Congressional Committee on Reconstruction swiftly approved a bill to impose military rule on the South and a second measure that required black suffrage and ratification of the Fourteenth Amendment as conditions for readmission to the Union. One congressman described it as a turning back of the political clock to "the point where Grant left off the work, at Appomattox Court House." Sumner believed Congress had finally wound the clock *forward*, concluding that each bill was "excellent . . . one is the beginning of a true reconstruction—the other is the beginning of a true protection."

After weeks of wrangling about details, Congress meshed the bills together and approved the Reconstruction Act of 1867. In its final form, the law divided the eleven Confederate states, except Tennessee, into five military districts under commanders "empowered to employ the army to protect life and property." And though it did not immediately replace Johnson's provisional governments, the law enumerated steps by which new state governments could be created and recognized by Congress: basically, by conferring black voting rights, approving the Fourteenth Amendment, and forbidding all interference with the Reconstruction Act by "the pretended State governments" organized by the President.

✳ ✳ ✳

The sweeping bill, which was hammered out initially by a small group of Republican caucus members, became law on March 2, when Congress again overrode what had become an almost automatic veto by an increasingly vindictive President Johnson.

The bill did not contain everything Sumner wanted—it omitted his wish for free education and land ownership for freedmen—but he did manage to step back and rejoice that Congress had finally adopted his views of black suffrage for the former Confederacy. He agreed entirely with one contemporaneous author who duly noted the importance of the momentous occasion: "An entire race, recently in slavery, was thus at one stroke admitted to the suffrage in the reconstructed states."

Within a few years of emancipation, the U.S. Congress, led by Charles Sumner, had granted the right to vote upon former slaves in the rebel states.

However, Sumner's goal of universal voting rights across the *entire* country, the North included, remained unfinished business.

✳ ✳ ✳

As he slayed one slaveocracy dragon after another in late 1866 and early 1867, Sumner found tranquility and contentment in his new role as husband and stepfather.

Sumner spent the first few weeks of his marriage busy with what he called "the trials of a young house-keeper." Domestic life was unfamiliar to him, and he worked hard to get it right. The Sumners ordered household items like soap and crystal and china and linens; they hired a nursemaid and a French teacher for Bell, rented a pew in the Church of the Epiphany for the devoutly Episcopal Alice, acquired a team of horses, and engaged the services of a coachman for their carriage excursions around Washington. Sumner wrote of his "little kingdom," where he hoped his "subjects" would be "content and happy."

Reciprocating the social obligations Sumner had amassed during his bachelor years, the Sumners invited guests over nearly every evening (Longfellow and Francis Lieber among them), though only a few at a time. "We live very quietly," Sumner reported on his first weeks in Washington, "seeing one or two persons at dinner and such as call in the evening." Visitors to the Sumner home, and those who saw the couple at the few parties they did attend, were struck by Sumner's robust and happy disposition, a transformation from his widely known and oft-criticized brooding and dourness.

For Sumner, his first several weeks of marriage were a dream come true.

But soon he learned that dreams were fragile things—and shattered dreams could cause immense pain and suffering.

CHAPTER 38

"MY HOME WAS HELL . . ."

With the force of a violent Washington, D.C., thunderstorm, conditions in Charles Sumner's household turned angry and dark with a sudden, raw ferocity he never saw coming, upending his life and leaving him exposed, unprotected, and profoundly damaged.

The deterioration of the Sumners' marriage appears to have started in late January 1867, as Charles Sumner's Senate work became more laborious and Alice's boredom and restlessness became more acute. By the end of the month, tired from Senate sessions that would run into the evening, Sumner cut down on the number of small gatherings the couple hosted at home.

Alice, however, "with half her husband's years and twice his energy," continued to accept the many invitations the Sumners received for Washington parties.

By mid-February, the gossip on the party circuit held that Alice enjoyed staying late at parties "and refuses to go home when he [Charles] wants to." At one dance that continued past midnight, Sumner politely asked, "[I]s it not time to go home?" and Alice replied sharply: "You may go when you like—I shall stay." On several occasions, she showed up at parties without Charles, unsympathetic about his claims of exhaustion. "I am always left alone," she lamented. "Mr. Sumner is always reading, writing, and snoring."

✳ ✳ ✳

Sumner also witnessed several examples of Alice's quick temper during this period. She cursed at him in public several times, and the couple became embroiled in a heated argument over Sumner's tendency to invite Samuel Hooper, the father of Alice's first husband, to dinner almost every week. She made it clear that she could not bear Hooper's presence, that "he was stupid and a nuisance."

Alice's displays of temper and anger soon became more frequent. Ill-equipped to respond, Sumner either made clumsy comments or requests—including entreaties for her to remain calm—which seemed to infuriate her more, or held his tongue and turned inward, which left her angry and frustrated.

On top of it all, as a way to befit their social standing, the Sumners felt that their rented furnished quarters were insufficient and decided to build a house on the corner of H Street and Vermont Avenue, facing Lafayette Square. Again, Charles fretted about expenses—the estimated cost was $30,000, about ten times his annual salary. While Alice drew a modest income from her first husband's estate, most of the burden of buying and furnishing the new house fell on Sumner.

He was taking on this enormous risk and expense at the very moment he wondered about his future with Alice, a prospect that soon became immeasurably bleaker.

✳ ✳ ✳

Sometime in mid-February 1867, as Sumner was absorbed in the work of the Senate and the future of Reconstruction, Alice was seen more and more in the company of Baron Friedrich von Holstein, an attaché of the Prussian embassy in Washington. Young and handsome, the German nobleman had come to America in 1865 to view the workings of representative government, and while there he had called on Sumner as chairman of the Senate Foreign Relations Committee and visited the Sumner home many times for dinner or conversation.

Soon Holstein was accompanying Alice around Washington, and the two were seen flirting in public places. Convinced she had nothing to hide, Alice made no attempt to keep her meetings with Holstein secret, or even show discretion. Once Sumner returned home unexpectedly and saw Alice about to enter a carriage with Holstein and another couple from the diplomatic corps.

"Where are you going, Alice?" Sumner asked her.

"I am going to enjoy myself," she retorted.

"But where are you *going*?" he asked.

"That does not concern you," she snapped at Sumner, and the carriage drove away.

Sumner's pleas for her to be more discreet seemed to inflame her temper more. "God damn you, 'tis none of your business," she shouted when he asked another time where she was going. "I will go where I please, with whom I please." One day, Holstein and Alice visited a cemetery outside the Washington city limits and stayed so long that servants had to unlock the door when they returned after midnight. "All the time, day and late in the night," Sumner wrote, "she was off with her paramour."

Soon, Washington was abuzz with rumors of crisis in the Sumner household, gossip that intensified when Holstein allegedly bought Alice an expensive amber necklace. When Sumner learned of this, he insisted that he pay for the jewelry himself, a weak gesture that only increased Alice's contempt for him.

For his part, Sumner now dreaded time he and Alice spent together; Alice was unpredictable and often enraged. He cringed at her hellacious temper and continued to find himself stupefied about what course of action to take. When they traveled together to social gatherings, she often berated him as a husband.

Later he confessed: "I never entered the carriage with her to drive to dinner that she did not treat me so that I was obliged to find relief in tears."

✳ ✳ ✳

Things came to a head in April.

Sumner told Alice he could no longer bear the public humiliation and said they could not continue to live together without "a change on her part." He was ready to take drastic action, both personally and professionally. "One of us must leave this house," he recalled saying a few months later. "I have already written half of a letter to my constituents resigning my place [in the Senate] and will go and bury myself in some obscure Swiss valley where [there] is peace at least. I am unfit for work."

"No," Alice replied. "If one is to go, I will go, but how do you send me from you—a degraded wife?"

"No," Sumner recalled the exchange. "You shall bear my name and I will go with you on board the steamer, engage your rooms, and you shall have my countenance until that hour."

Doing his best to remain civil and even chivalrous, Sumner believed he could offer Alice little else. "Life is utter misery to me," he wrote to a friend.

The uneasy truce—the couple would split, and Sumner would provide for Alice's passage to virtually anywhere she wanted to go—collapsed on April 16, when Holstein received orders from Berlin to return to Prussia as soon as possible. Alice was furious, believing Sumner used his senatorial influence to orchestrate the transfer; this, despite Sumner's protestations that he had not raised a finger to get Holstein recalled.

No evidence exists to suggest that Holstein's transfer was outside the normal course of events—though it is reasonable to speculate that the German embassy in Washington had gotten wind of the Holstein–Alice Sumner affair and recalled its indiscreet diplomat to avoid angering the powerful chairman of the Senate Foreign Relations Committee.

Alice never believed Holstein's recall was coincidental, and she smoldered throughout May 1866. When the Senate adjourned in June, the unhappy couple took the train to Boston, and Sumner—again, incapable of talking to his wife about their marital problems—asked her instead to read a French novel about a woman who had betrayed her husband, perhaps hoping she'd see the error of her ways and repent.

Instead, when the Sumners arrived at the Hancock Street house, a furious Alice tossed the book at him, shouted "God damn you," rushed to the bedroom, slammed the door, and insisted on separate sleeping quarters from then on.

In mid-June, Alice left and took Bell to Lenox for most of the summer, and later she traveled briefly to Europe.

Sumner never spoke or wrote to his wife again.

But if Sumner thought Alice's departure would end his misery, he was mistaken.

＊ ＊ ＊

As his marriage was breaking apart during the spring of 1867—"my home was hell, and became an *inferno*," Sumner recalled later—and throughout a long, lonely summer in Boston, Sumner breathed not a word about his domestic situation. His silence was borne of his own humiliation and despair, a hope for a change in Alice's demeanor, and a desire to protect Alice and Bell from gossip and scandal. He sat alone and brooded in his empty house in Boston, which he was in the process of selling to pay for the unfinished mansion in Washington,

Selling the family home was an ordeal, too. In early October, as he was leaving the house for the last time, he confessed to Longfellow that his "eyes moistened as I shook hands with the good domestic. [Then] I went away alone and homeless." The solitude he felt from keeping his marriage problems secret, coupled with the emotions of departing from Beacon Hill, produced an almost unbearable pressure on Sumner as he departed. "My eyes often filled with tears as I thought of the unhappy waif that I am and must be."

In mid-October, shortly after Alice returned from her trip to Europe, news of their marital problems began to seep out. The *New York Express*, a paper edited by Democratic congressman James Brooks, published a scurrilous article on the "Senator Sumner, Baron Holstein Affair," accusing Sumner of writing to German foreign minister Otto von Bismarck to recall Holstein.

The *Express* hinted at something beyond mere jealousy on Sumner's part or simple incompatibility, adding ominously that there was "some scandal afloat beyond all this, relating both to the Senator and the Lady."

❈ ❈ ❈

The *Express* account spread quickly, and Sumner's political opponents pounced with delight at his now very public marital problems. The gossip became more salacious.

In late October, Charles Francis Adams wrote in his diary of persistent rumors that Alice Sumner was planning to sue her husband "for a divorce on the ground[s] of impotence." Soon, the rumors were accepted as unquestioned fact—to Sumner's enemies, it explained why Sumner waited so long to get married, provided a reason for the separation, and offered the more spurious insight into what they felt was his "selfishness and over-bearing disposition."

The floodgates opened. Some college classmates recalled—though no one had ever suggested before—that Sumner was always known to be impotent, and at Harvard they had nicknamed him "The Stag." Another correspondent wrote to Moorfield Storey, who was about to become Sumner's secretary: "Please ask Charly confidentially if his wife left him because he could not *perform the functions of a husband . . .* this is what

Madame Rumor says." Southerners, in the moment and for years after the scandal, referred to Sumner as "The Great Impotent."

Now it was Sumner who was enraged, swearing that the charge was "shamelessly untruthful," and accusing Alice—without hard evidence, merely due to the circumstantial timing—of spreading the rumor upon her return from Europe. It was a complete betrayal on her part, especially considering he never "gave a hint with regard to *her* conduct . . . I bore it all in silence."

He saw no need for such decorum now. For the next several months, well into 1868, Sumner broke his silence, defended himself, and impugned Alice's reputation to all who would listen. As much as he desired to shield Alice "for her own sake—her daughter's sake—and for her family," the scandalous reports of his impotence had unshackled him from further restraint.

"I was willing that all should be left to smoulder [*sic*] in darkness," he wrote, "but she and her friends have willed it otherwise."

✳ ✳ ✳

Any hopes of reconciliation were over.

Sumner considered the relationship irreparable. He was determined that Alice would be out of his life forever. How could he have ever loved her? She was a "bad woman, to be remembered only with hissing and scorn—unworthy of her sex, on which she has brought shame," he wrote to Anna Cabot Lodge.

So angry and distraught was Sumner that he even contemplated giving up the new house he was building in Washington if there were any chance Alice would return to it; he talked of renting lodgings where there would be no room for her. Only when her former father-in-law, Hooper, assured Sumner on Thanksgiving Day, 1867, that Alice would "brave anything rather than continue to live with you" did Sumner move into his still unfinished home, where he hoped to find privacy and sanctuary.

"After the terrible experience of [the] last year," he wrote to Samuel Gridley Howe in mid-December, "my solitude is happiness."

✳ ✳ ✳

In May 1873, by mutual agreement, Alice, without protest, allowed Sumner to officially divorce her on grounds of desertion, and she did not remarry (nor did Charles Sumner). Neither Alice's relationship with Holstein nor Sumner's alleged impotence were part of the decree, as lawyers for both sides intended "to keep out of sight the real cause or causes of the separation."

Alice and Bell spent most of their time in Europe, with occasional visits to the United States. Calling herself "Mrs. Mason," she became a friend of Henry James, who remarked on her "great beauty . . . honesty, frankness and naturalness" but also observed that she was "limited by a kind of characteristic American want of culture." Sharp-tempered and opinionated throughout her life, she quarreled with painter John Singer Sargent, whose portrait of her, she sneered, "made her look like a murderess."

Alice died in 1913.

Sumner never forgave her and never spoke her name again.

✳ ✳ ✳

As Sumner left Boston for Washington in November 1867, despondency enveloped him and made it impossible for him to embrace his recent political achievements.

Sumner's instrumental roles in the successful congressional takeover of Reconstruction and the neutering of President Andrew Johnson with the Tenure of Office Act did little to salve the wounds inflicted by the public scandal his marriage and breakup had become, nor did they dispel the sadness he felt when he bid a final adieu to the family home at 20 Hancock Street, where he had lived since his father purchased it in 1830.

"I have buried from this house my father, my mother, a brother and sister," he reminded Longfellow, "and now I am leaving it the deadest of them all."

By the time he arrived in Washington, his new house was ready, but he was in a quandary. Should he move in or not? The $30,000 home—conveniently located as it was looking out on Lafayette Park and within easy walking distance of the Capitol, the White House, departmental offices, and foreign consulates—was large for one person. He "took this house for another," and thus "have no heart about it or anything else. I am afflicted and unhappy. What can I do?" Longfellow advised Sumner to remain in his rented lodgings: "Why go into an empty haunted house? You would only feel your loneliness the more." But Sumner, yielding to repeated pressure from Hooper to occupy the house and start his life afresh without the strain of a disastrous relationship, finally moved in just before Christmas 1867.

He seemed to relax while performing domestic tasks involved in setting up a household ("I am to examine carpets today!" he wrote in late December) and personalizing his living space with his souvenirs, bronzes, engravings, oil paintings, artwork, manuscripts, books, and, from Europe, his clocks, vases, and porcelain—"household companions" he called them.

The house provided him with ample space and a chance to host small dinners that allayed his loneliness; he seldom dined alone. Seward, Fish, Hooper, Carl Schurz, and many others were among his guests. One of Sumner's favorite evenings was a dinner with Stanton and British novelist Charles Dickens, who was in the United States promoting *A Christmas Carol*. To all who visited, Sumner seemed less combative, less anxious, calm, and conversational in the intimate social setting, a side of him that Washington, D.C., luminaries had seldom witnessed. Still crushed by what he viewed as Alice's betrayal, Sumner worked hard to be agreeable and to settle into his new home and lifestyle.

But dinner parties and a house full of bric-a-brac could not replace the love he had lost or combat the desolation he struggled with each day. Author Mary Abigail Dodge shrewdly concluded after a tour of Sumner's lodgings:

"It is full of books and pictures, and many rare old engravings, but it looks like the home of a lonely man."

✳ CHAPTER 39 ✳

"GUILTY OF ALL AND INFINITELY MORE!"

Although more gracious and agreeable at his dinner table, Sumner was as combative as ever in the Senate in early 1868 as Congress prepared to do what he wished it had done two years earlier—impeach and remove President Andrew Johnson.

Johnson stepped willfully into the trap Congress had baited with the Tenure of Office Act. In August of 1867, while Congress was out of session, Johnson suspended Stanton as secretary of war and directed him to turn over the office to General Ulysses S. Grant, who was appointed secretary *ad interim*. Stanton yielded, but said for the record that he submitted "under protest, to superior force."

When Congress reconvened, both houses voted by wide margins not to concur with the suspension and reinstated Stanton—the House on December 7, 1867, and the Senate on January 13, 1868 (the latter by a vote of 35–6). Immediately after the Senate vote, Grant vacated the secretary of war position, despite pleas from President Johnson to defy the Tenure of Office Act and remain at his post until the constitutionality of the law could be tested in court.

Mindful of his stellar reputation and his likely upcoming presidential candidacy in November, Grant steadfastly refused—he would not compromise himself by breaking the law. He wrote to President Johnson that "my functions as Secretary of War, *ad interim*, ceased from the moment of the receipt of the within notice [of the Senate's vote]."

With the backing of congressional Republicans, a smug Stanton returned to the War Department executive office one hour after Grant left.

✳ ✳ ✳

But Johnson wasn't finished.

On February 21, 1868, in a brazen and unapologetic affront to Congress and the Tenure of Office Act, the President sent Brigadier General Lorenzo Thomas, no friend of Stanton's, to the War Department to inform Stanton that he was removing him—yet again—and that Thomas would replace him. Stanton refused to leave. "I want some little time for reflection," Stanton said. "I don't know whether I'll obey your orders or not." Many senators wrote letters of encouragement to Stanton, including Sumner, who sent a note, written in pencil, with a single word: "*Stick.*"

The very next day, a frenzied House of Representatives began impeachment proceedings against President Johnson for "high crimes and misdemeanors." An initial motion to adopt articles of impeachment without debate failed. The outcome was no mystery in the House—the huge Republican majority favored it and the Democrats opposed it, both overwhelmingly—but members on each side wanted their say for posterity. On the first day of contentious debate, more speakers addressed the House than ever before on a single day; the content filled more than two hundred columns of the *Congressional Globe*.

On February 24, after only three days of debate but with the volatile tempers of members slaked to their satisfaction, the House voted 126–47, along strict party lines, to impeach President Andrew Johnson, the first time in U.S. history such a momentous action had occurred. On March 4, House managers delivered eleven articles of impeachment to the Senate, most notably Johnson's violation of the Tenure of Office Act and the appointment of Lorenzo Thomas as secretary of war even though there was no vacancy in the office. President Johnson's violent and "scandalous" language in attacking Congress, mostly on the issue of Reconstruction, was also contained in a distinct article of impeachment.

At exactly 1:00 P.M. on March 5, 1868, the Senate convened a court of impeachment, with eminent Chief Justice Salmon P. Chase presiding. Oaths were administered and procedures adopted. The President, through his attorneys, entered his formal response on March 13. For the next two months, without interruption (and with one final session ten days beyond that), the trial of Andrew Johnson proceeded.

Sumner hoped for what he saw as the best and most probable outcome, Johnson's conviction by the Senate and removal from office. "One of the great blunders of our history was that the President was *not* impeached two years ago," he wrote.

✳ ✳ ✳

For Sumner, impeachment was "a political proceeding before a political body with political purposes," aimed at "*expulsion from office,*" not a criminal trial whose prosecutorial goal was conviction and imprisonment.

Sumner never pretended that the trial was anything *but* a referendum on Johnson's poor leadership, including his sympathy for Southern slave owners and his failings on Reconstruction. (Nor had he ever forgiven Johnson for his drunken appearance at Lincoln's inauguration.) Senators were forbidden to speak once the trial got underway, but in Sumner's letters and in a long treatise published after the proceedings, he called the impeachment trial "one of the last great battles with slavery." Johnson, he said, was "the impersonation of the tyrannical slave power. In him it lives again."

It was shameful, Sumner said, that slavery had been "driven from these legislative chambers, driven from the field of war, [yet] this monstruous power has found a refuge in the Executive Mansion." Political offenses were indeed impeachable, and Johnson's high crime—his "*transcendent crime*"—was his continued support of slavery, itself a defiance of law, both man's and God's. By his repeated obstructionism of Congress, Johnson had turned his veto power into "an engine of tyranny."

Sumner labeled as a superfluous distraction the arguments of Johnson's defense team, who asserted that the veto was merely a constitutional tool at the President's disposal (on its face, an accurate statement) and that an impeachment conviction could be pursued only for criminal offenses indictable in civil trials (much more debatable). Such arguments were "petty and miserable," Sumner scoffed, foisted on the timid by "the legal mind"—they were "utterly unworthy of this historic occasion."

It was his duty to vote "guilty" on all the articles, and if given the opportunity, he would vote "guilty of all and *infinitely more!*"

If Johnson was not guilty, then never was a political offender guilty before, and "never can a political offender be found guilty again." He added: "To my vision, the path is clear as day."

Not all his colleagues agreed.

✳ ✳ ✳

On Saturday, May 16, 1868, a beautiful spring morning in Washington and the day the Senate would vote on Andrew Johnson's fate, the Capitol building was bursting at the seams.

More so than any other day throughout the highly attended trial, the Senate chamber and its spacious galleries were filled to capacity with spectators; members of the public who did not have tickets to be present for this once-in-a-lifetime event filled available space outside the chamber. Virtually the entire House membership were provided seats on the Senate floor. The diplomatic gallery was filled with representatives of foreign countries curious to see how the United States would deal with a President accused of malfeasance in office. The press area was jammed with correspondents eager to transmit news of the day to readers around the country.

Chief Justice Chase sat "erect, broad-shouldered, deep-chested" and directed the clerk to call the roll of fifty-four senators in alphabetical order for the prosecution's first and strongest article of impeachment, the President's alleged violation of the Tenure of Office Act. The result of this vote would provide a strong indication of how the Senate would vote on other articles. "How say you?" the clerk asked with high drama. "Is the respondent, Andrew Johnson, President of the United States, guilty or not guilty of a high misdemeanor, as charged in this article?"

As one senator after another rose to announce his vote, the crowd and journalists kept track. All twelve Democrats voted "not guilty." Thirty-five Republicans, including Charles Sumner, voted "guilty." But seven Republicans, including Fessenden of Maine, voted with the Democrats for acquittal. The final vote was 35–19 to convict President Andrew Johnson, a single vote shy of the necessary two-thirds needed to remove him from office.

Johnson had survived.

In utter disbelief, Sumner labeled as a painful "calamity" the votes by the seven dissenting Republicans and, without evidence, accused at least two of being bribed. Black citizens in the South, newly freed, "should have had a Moses as President," but in Johnson, "they have found a Pharaoh."

As for Johnson and his allies, Sumner declared, their triumph "is marked with blood."

✻ ✻ ✻

In the end, for all of Andrew Johnson's shortcomings, for all of his petty and spiteful behavior, for all of his efforts to thwart advancement of the freedmen—removing him from office was a bridge too far for the seven Republicans who helped him cling to survival. Timing and politics played crucial roles in Johnson's acquittal.

As dramatic as the impeachment trial was, America was weary of drama and tired in general. North and South had been torn apart by slavery and secession, enduring four years of brutal civil war and barely avoiding a war with Great Britain. Americans read about or lived in an utterly unrecognizable South, now on the brink of economic collapse; grieved (or rejoiced) over a presidential assassination; and witnessed or participated in a painful and often violent period of Reconstruction. The removal of a sitting President from office, for anything less than blatant "high crimes," might be one shock too many for the nation's people and the system to absorb.

At this point, Johnson was but a figurehead, a lame duck, and thus his forcible removal, especially due to what appeared to many as flimsy charges, was seen by some moderates as doing more harm than good. Congress had repeatedly demonstrated both its capability and inclination to override his vetoes, rendering him almost powerless to halt the will of Republicans. Why antagonize potential Republican voters by piling on a president who was already viewed as hapless?

That Johnson came within a single vote of being convicted, even with all these considerations, illustrated how loathed he was by Republicans; that he escaped removal in the face of all of his transgressions proved Sumner's contention that an impeachment trial was, above all else, a *political* activity and a political reality.

And the most salient political fact was this: the President could foment mischief from the Executive Mansion, but he could not materially disrupt the Republican agenda.

✻ ✻ ✻

Andrew Johnson's impeachment trial consumed energy, and its spectacle captured the interest and imagination of the American public, but in the long run, it was not even the most important development in the spring and summer of 1868. Indeed, after Grant's election to the presidency in the fall, Johnson's trial dropped out of sight and mind. Republicans seldom counted impeachment among their achievements, and few voices were raised wishing the verdict had been different.

Another action by Congress had more profound long-term effects on the nation's future: passage of the Fourth Reconstruction Act, which finally paved the way for the readmission of Southern states to the Union.

The Third Reconstruction Act had required that a majority of *registered voters* approve ratification of the Fourteenth Amendment. Southern whites responded by registering in large numbers and then refusing to vote, making it nearly impossible to ratify. Frustrated with such obstructionism, Congress closed the loophole and passed the Fourth Reconstruction Act, which became law automatically on March 11, 1868, after President Johnson refused to sign it. It stipulated that a majority of voters *casting ballots*, rather than a majority of registered voters, would determine the outcome of the ratification process in the Southern states.

The new law produced the results Sumner and the Republican Congress were seeking.

After seven years of being separated from the United States, several former Confederate states rejoined the Union in the summer of 1868—Alabama, Arkansas, Florida, Georgia, Louisiana, North Carolina, and South Carolina (in September, Georgia expelled three black senators and twenty-four black representatives from its state legislature, prompting Congress to reimpose federal military rule in the state and bar Georgia's representatives from holding seats—Georgia was finally readmitted to the Union in the summer of 1870). All these states were admitted with the fundamental conditions that they would not deprive any citizen of the right to vote and must ratify the Fourteenth Amendment (Virginia, Mississippi, and Texas were readmitted to the Union in 1870 with the same conditions).

At long last, with a mixture of reluctance, wariness, and perhaps promise, the Southern states had agreed to universal suffrage.

With a sense of hope tinged with unease, the Union had reconstituted itself.

Still, in the summer of 1868, it was shocking to Sumner and others that only eight *Northern* states guaranteed African Americans the right to vote.

✳ ✳ ✳

Sumner lingered in Washington until mid-August, mainly to serve as pallbearer at the funeral of House antislavery champion Thaddeus Stevens. Just before leaving the capital, Sumner wrote to E. L. Pierce: "I am hot and weary and many things trouble me."

He was still bitter about Johnson's acquittal and fuming about Alice's treachery and the public breakup of his marriage, and he dreaded his return to a "homeless" Boston. He was also hearing rumors that Massachusetts powerbrokers were floating other names for his Senate seat. He was up for reelection in the Massachusetts legislature in early 1869, and his fate would be decided by the state elections in November. Sumner was philosophical about his future:

"If the people from Mass turn from me, I shall not complain," he assured Longfellow. "I have done my duty."

He also suffered from strained vocal cords and a sore throat, which sidelined him for most of the late summer campaign season and kept him from advocating with the legislature and the public for his own seat.

But he had little to worry about. On September 9, Republicans, meeting in Worcester, Massachusetts, unanimously nominated him for a fourth term as a U.S. senator. In a letter to Longfellow, Sumner acknowledged his enthusiasm about the resounding acclamation and concluded:

"So at last I have conquered," he said, "after a life of struggle."

✳ ✳ ✳

And with the legacy of his struggle in mind, Sumner focused on a project he had contemplated for some time—collecting his speeches and writings into a comprehensive revised edition of his work, which he had first published more than a decade earlier. "They will illustrate the progress of the great battle with Slavery, and what I have done in it," he wrote.

For the rest of his life, his spare hours were occupied with this effort. His prized collection of speeches grew to more than fifteen volumes as he added newspaper articles that provided commentary on his orations, wrote his own annotations and footnotes, altered the original texts at times to offer "clarification" (and paint himself in a more favorable light) years after the fact, and included extracts of his correspondence that dealt with speech topics. "The booksellers propose to call them *Works*," he told Longfellow. "I do not like the term, but what else is there?"

Anytime Sumner conversed with friends and associates, the topic of his collection was never far from the surface. "I think he loves the author of it!" quipped one Boston publisher. If others thought him obsessed, Sumner was undeterred. His goal was to publish a completed edition of his work before he died.

"If this were done," he told Howe, "I should be ready to go."

✳ ✳ ✳

In January 1869, the Massachusetts legislature rewarded Sumner with overwhelming reelection to his fourth term, making him the longest continuously serving member of the Senate since he entered in 1851—and certainly the most conspicuous and powerful.

Tributes poured in from across the country, from private correspondents, elected officials, and journalists. Even those who generally disagreed with Sumner treated him with esteem, as though he were already a historical figure whose philosophical and policy imprints were forever stamped on the country's character. There was a sense that this election was the fifty-eight-year-old Sumner's final hurrah, and it seemed that anyone inclined to put quill to paper felt the need to comment on the senator's intellectual capacity, work ethic, sound judgment, incorruptibleness, and dignity that he brought to his office.

One of the most sterling tributes came from longtime fervent abolitionist William Lloyd Garrison, who at one time envied the fact that Sumner had dethroned him as the preeminent antislavery voice in the nation but now recognized that the Massachusetts senator was without peer in the lengthy struggle. "Your senatorial career covers the most important portion of American history," Garrison wrote with prescience in his lengthy missive. "For a long period, you were in an almost hopeless minority, misunderstood, grossly caricatured . . . in constant peril of your life while discharging the official duties of your position . . . but from that darkness, *what light has sprung!*"

The work Sumner had "so astonishingly advanced" was not yet complete, Garrison wrote, but he was convinced that Sumner would continue to fight with the same "unquenchable zeal . . . [and] heroic devotion . . . that have characterized your public labors from the beginning."

Garrison's reference to Sumner's uncompleted work was related to congressional debate on a proposed Fifteenth Amendment to the Constitution, sponsored by Republicans, that would prohibit the denial or abridgment of voting rights for men based on race.

It was a cause that cried out for his leadership to lift and lock into place—on behalf of Congress and a largely reunited nation—a crowning capstone atop the country's reconstructed edifice that would signify a triumphant victory for equality and human rights.

Instead, as debate began on the amendment, Sumner was filled with "a sense of sadness so heavy as oppresses me at this moment."

CHAPTER 40

"THERE CAN BE NO BACKWARD STEP"

The most appropriate way to characterize Charles Sumner's role in the Fifteenth Amendment debate is to place his response somewhere between the just-vague-enough "strange" and the subject-to-interpretation "peculiar"—hardly enthusiastic descriptions for a man about to culminate a lifetime of work and struggle.

As always, Sumner distrusted the amendment process itself—its length, its uncertainty, its fragility—and argued, as he had for years, that an act of Congress guaranteeing voting rights and other civil rights to black men would be faster, more all-encompassing, and less likely to meet derailment. For him, the state ratification process left too much room for unpredictable and disastrous outcomes; for example, if the amendment failed to gain ratification of three-quarters of the states and died, would Southern states who had *already* granted black suffrage as a condition for reinstatement to the Union reverse their course?

Breaking with many Republican lawmakers, Sumner asserted that an amendment on the seminal issue of voting rights was both unnecessary and risky. Congress held the power to guarantee voting rights under the Declaration of Independence and the Constitution, and it ought not eschew its duty and abrogate its responsibility by surrendering such precious rights to the risky uncertainties of the amendment process. Moreover, since the Fourteenth Amendment recognized blacks as citizens, they were now eligible to vote de facto. There simply was no need for a Fifteenth Amendment that specifically dealt with color—a physical "quality" and "not a qualification" to vote.

The universal right to vote could be codified into law quickly with an act of Congress.

✳ ✳ ✳

Sumner was also disappointed by the proposed—and to his mind, limited—language drafted by the House for this particular amendment:

Section 1.

The right of citizens of the United States to vote shall not be denied or abridged by the United States or by any State on account of race, color, or previous condition of servitude.

Section 2.

The Congress shall have the power to enforce this article by appropriate legislation.

If an amendment were to be adopted, he believed it should include *all* civil and political rights. He offered "amendments to the amendment" calling for the enshrinement into the Constitution of the right to hold office, regardless of color or race, in all national, state, territorial, and municipal elections.

He demanded that the amendment contain language mandating fines against anyone hindering any citizen from voting—by imposing poll taxes, for example—and granting citizens of all races the right to sue for damages if their rights were threatened or deprived in any way.

He and other Radical Republicans wanted the amendment to make voting requirements "uniform throughout the land," forbidding literacy, property, or education tests that, while nonracial, might effectively exclude the majority of blacks from the polls.

Noted one skeptical observer with whom Sumner concurred: "The Fifteenth Amendment was more remarkable for what it does *not* than for what it does contain."

✳ ✳ ✳

But Sumner's sweeping proposals portended potential disaster for the amendment.

The unspoken secret among congressmen was that most Northern states *wanted* to retain their voting qualifications as restrictive measures for granting the franchise. For example, Pennsylvania required payment of state taxes to vote; Massachusetts and Connecticut demanded literacy; Rhode Island required foreign-born citizens to own at least $134 worth of real estate. In the West, ethnically Chinese citizens could not vote, and Republicans wanted to use "voting requirements" to keep it that way—if not, warned California's Republican senator Cornelius Cole, it would "kill our party as dead as a stone." Other Northern leaders feared that, without the ability for states to impose their own restrictive voting qualifications, those rebels who had *not* pledged loyalty to the country would also be entitled to the franchise.

"Whatever the reason," said a preeminent Reconstruction historian, "the Northern states during Reconstruction actually abridged the right to vote more than the Southern."

Because of these clashing interests, an insufficient number of Sumner's colleagues supported either his substitute motion for a broader amendment or his preference for an act of Congress as an effective substitute remedy to end racial discrimination when it came to voting. Sumner's motion for a substitute and, in his view, stronger Fifteenth Amendment garnered thirty-one "yes" votes and twenty-seven "nays"—a majority, but well short of the two-thirds needed for Senate passage.

After the defeat, Sumner made a major decision.

His was the conviction that had kept the issue alive and top of mind in Congress and across the American landscape.

But now, standing at the precipice of achieving one of his long-cherished goals, he would play almost no role in the adoption of the constitutional amendment that guaranteed nationwide voting rights for African American men.

✳ ✳ ✳

Distressed with what he saw as shortcomings in the proposed Fifteenth Amendment, Sumner had little to say during the debates and avoided a series of votes leading up to final approval.

His reticence notwithstanding, Congress plowed ahead. On February 25, 1869, the House approved the Fifteenth Amendment, as written, by a vote of 144–44. The very next day, the Senate approved it by a vote of 39–13, with fourteen senators—including Sumner—not voting. Both tallies exceeded the necessary two-thirds majority to send the amendment to the states for ratification.

Despite his lack of enthusiasm, Sumner did encourage ratification by the states of the historic amendment granting black men the right to vote. On March 1, Nevada became the first state to ratify, and eleven more states ratified in March; by July 1, seventeen states had adopted the amendment. These included most of New England, West Virginia, and the four Southern states of Louisiana, North Carolina, Arkansas, and South Carolina. However, the issue of granting suffrage to ethnically Chinese citizens led California to reject the amendment, and, for the same reason, the Oregon legislature did not even consider it. (The two states finally ratified it nearly a century later, in 1962 and 1959 respectively—also, Delaware didn't ratify until 1901, Kentucky didn't until 1976, and Maryland's legislature never approved it, but the state's governor did in 1973.) A few other states ratified during 1869, and in January 1870, six more states voted in favor, including Ohio, which had previously rejected the amendment.

By February 3, 1870, the requisite three-quarters of the states had ratified the amendment, and on March 30, Secretary of State Hamilton Fish certified that the Fifteenth Amendment, duly approved, was henceforth part of the U.S. Constitution.

"At Last! The Fifteenth Amendment. The Law of the Land" proclaimed the front page of the March 31, 1870, edition of the *Philadelphia Evening Telegram*.

✳ ✳ ✳

One day later, hundreds of Washington, D.C., citizens, black and white, marched to Sumner's house to serenade him and cheer his efforts in bringing about the historic moment. Neither his misgivings about the amendment's scope nor his decision to withhold his vote dampened their enthusiasm. They all knew that without Sumner's leadership, this day would never have arrived.

They called on Sumner to speak, and he first congratulated them on the "great result that has been accomplished" before adding: "For years my hope and object have been to see the great promise of the Declaration of Independence changed into performance—to see that the Declaration became a reality." He was interrupted by loud cheers, and after they subsided, he added: "This at last is *nearly* consummated. I do not say *entirely* consummated, for it is not."

He still wanted equality in schools, the word "white" expunged from the statute books, and equal rights to prevail in all public conveyances and railroads in the United States, "so that *no one* shall be excluded by reason of color." Subdued though he was because of the narrow language contained in the Fifteenth Amendment, Sumner assured them he was pleased and urged them to celebrate, but also to remember the hard work that lay ahead.

"It is my nature, fellow-citizens, to think more of what remains to be done than of what has been done—to think more of our duties than of our triumphs."

✳ ✳ ✳

Sumner was not the only one who believed the country had missed an opportunity to broaden equality's reach with a stronger and less restrictive Fifteenth Amendment.

Many members of the women's suffrage movement felt the same way, perhaps worse—they were angry and frustrated. For years, some of the leaders of this group—Susan B. Anthony, Elizabeth Cady Stanton, Matilda Joslyn Gage, Paulina Wright Davis, Julia Ward Howe, Harriet Beecher Stowe, Isabella Beecher Hooker (Stowe's half sister), and many others—had fought shoulder to shoulder alongside Republican abolitionists in the struggle to abolish slavery. Yet, Republicans, Sumner included, had never seriously countenanced including women's voting rights in the Fifteenth Amendment.

For Anthony and Stanton, especially, this omission, this *abandonment,* was another in a long list of "humiliations" that Republicans had inflicted on their cause, and as such, both women vigorously opposed the Fifteenth Amendment's ratification, a stance that dealt a final blow to the long-standing abolitionist–women's suffrage alliance.

Women's suffrage leaders mocked a request for "patience and moderation" from Wendell Phillips and other abolitionists who, for twenty years, insisted on no compromise on the issue of slavery yet were now suggesting that women should accept the "half a loaf" offered by the Fifteenth Amendment, with a vague promise that it would lead to women's suffrage at some point down the road.

Women suffragists were right to object to calls for patience. In fact, it would take another half century—until August of 1920—for the Nineteenth Amendment, which prohibited the denial or abridgment of voting rights "on account of sex," to be added to the U.S. Constitution.

✳ ✳ ✳

While the Fifteenth Amendment's shortcomings were chronicled and decried by Sumner and a wide swath of influential women's suffragists, most Republicans, abolitionists, and reformers hailed its adoption as a triumph to savor, an accomplishment that just a few years earlier would have been inconceivable.

"Nothing in all history [equaled] this wonderful, quiet, sudden transformation of four millions [sic] of human beings from . . . the auction block to the ballot box," declared a jubilant William Lloyd Garrison.

In March 1870, the American Anti-Slavery Society disbanded—members agreed their work was now complete.

Increasingly, Republicans and other once-fervent abolitionists argued that, with the newly granted right to vote, black men now had the opportunity to truly advance on their own accord, and that the vexing and oft-referenced "Negro question"—so described by many contemporaneous publications and politicians—that had dominated debate in the country for three decades could finally be removed from the arena of national politics.

Sumner insisted that the United States had a long way to go to rectify the accumulated wrongs of discrimination, but Republicans and the nation, it seemed, were ready to move on to other issues. Influential Republican congressman (and future President) James A. Garfield of Ohio captured much of the popular sentiment when he declared that the Fifteenth Amendment "confers upon the African race the care of its own destiny—it places their fortunes in their own hands."

As though to prove Garfield right, Mississippi Republican Hiram Revels strode into the Senate chamber on February 25, 1870—as the packed Senate galleries burst into applause—to take his oath of office.

Five years after the end of a bloody civil war, and much to the joy of Charles Sumner, Revels was about to become the first African American ever to serve in the U.S. Congress.

✳ ✳ ✳

The figurative journey of Hiram Revels from Mississippi to Washington, D.C., was historic, and the three days of debates leading up to his swearing in are among the most significant yet little known in United States history.

To the surprise of no one, Charles Sumner was right in the thick of it.

Born to free parents in North Carolina, Revels worked as a pastor and schoolmaster and later served as an army chaplain for Union colored regiments in campaigns at Vicksburg and near Jackson, Mississippi. After the war, Revels left the army, relocated to Mississippi, and served as a local alderman and then as a member of the reconstructed Mississippi state senate.

In January 1870, as Mississippi awaited readmission to the Union, one of the first orders of business for the state legislature was to fill the vacancies in the U.S. Senate, which had remained empty since 1861 when Albert Brown and future Confederate President Jefferson Davis withdrew from their seats. Blacks represented about 25 percent of the Mississippi legislature and insisted that one of the vacant U.S. Senate seats be filled by a black member of the Republican Party. Impressed with Revels's work ethic and eloquence, legislators agreed that the shorter of the two terms, set to expire in March 1871, would go to him.

As for his literal journey to the U.S. Senate, Revels left Mississippi for Washington, D.C., and—state senator or not—was forced by railroad conductors and steamboat captains to sit in separate, colored compartments along the way (the quintessential example to illustrate Charles Sumner's desire to abolish discrimination in all public conveyances). Revels arrived safely in the nation's capital, received an enthusiastic reception from the local black community, and waited patiently until Mississippi gained readmission on February 23, 1870.

Moments after that vote occurred, Massachusetts senator Henry Wilson, a strong civil rights advocate, escorted Mississippi senator-elect Revels into the U.S. Senate chamber with a flourish.

The symbolism was not lost on anyone. In what one newspaper called an act of "poetic retribution," a black Republican was about to occupy Jefferson Davis's old seat and become the first African American to sit in Congress.

It was the stuff of legend as much as a dramatic representation of the nation's postwar political transformation.

But as it turned out, Revels would have to wait.

✳ ✳ ✳

Democrats immediately challenged Revels's right to sit in the Senate, which set off a full-fledged and fascinating debate on many of the issues the nation had grappled with in the past two decades: slavery, the *Dred Scott* decision, secession, the Civil War, Reconstruction, constitutional law, and the legal and citizenship status of African Americans.

For more than two days, the debate riveted spectators who crammed into the Senate chamber. Vice President Schuyler Colfax had to call for order several times after outbursts and shouting from senators and members of the public.

Democrats who opposed Revels did so on racist grounds, to be sure— these were not even well camouflaged during debates—but they also articulated sound constitutional arguments. Their thesis was simple: the Constitution (Article 1, Section 3) required that to become a senator, a man had to have been a "citizen" of the United States for at least nine years. Under the terms of the Fourteenth Amendment, Revels was made a citizen, but because it had not been ratified until 1868, he could claim citizenship for only *two* years.

Prior to 1868, Democrats protested with vigor, Revels was a *noncitizen* based on the *Dred Scott* decision, in which the Supreme Court held that blacks were ineligible for U.S. citizenship. Thus, because Revels had only been a U.S. citizen for two years, Democrats argued that he was constitutionally ineligible to serve as a senator.

It was a desperate ploy made more insidious because it carried with it a modicum of legal logic. Democrat George Vickers of Maryland acknowledged that *Dred Scott* was widely denounced and anathema in 1870, but it was the law of the land until 1868 and could not be ignored simply because Republicans objected to it. *Dred Scott* had made it clear that Revels could never even be a citizen, let alone serve as a senator. To suggest otherwise, Vickers said, was a betrayal of the Constitution.

Charles Sumner and the Republican majority argued the exact opposite.

✳ ✳ ✳

Republicans endorsed and believed in the Fourteenth Amendment, but the thrust of their argument went much further. They used the bulk of their debate time to make the case that the vast changes that had occurred in the nation's heart and soul in the past decade had disqualified the *Dred Scott* decision as the legal foundation upon which to consider the Revels question.

Put another way, *Dred Scott* had aged terribly in the wake of war and Reconstruction, and, therefore, it *must* be invalidated.

It was a dramatic and extraordinary argument. It did not contend merely that the Fourteenth Amendment had rendered *Dred Scott* null and void; such a limited legal position would make it difficult to refute the Democrats' insistence that Revels be rejected by the Senate because he had only been a citizen for two years. Instead, most Republican senators elevated the argument to a higher moral level—if the nation wished to heal and redeem itself after a decade of unparalleled and horrific struggle, then it was essential that *Dred Scott* be banished to the darkest corner of the national memory.

Senator James Nye of Nevada spoke for many Republicans when he said that the 1857 Supreme Court decision effectively had been "repealed by the mightiest uprising the world has ever witnessed," an uprising that wiped clean the country's stain of slavery and its unfair treatment of blacks. The country had changed. The world had changed. Torn asunder a few short years earlier, the United States had reunited, but its history and mood had been altered. The entire Republican line of debate focused on the need to leave behind prewar prejudices that now seemed remnants of a bygone past, the equivalent of a civic paleolithic era that was blurred by time and events and largely irrelevant.

In Charles Sumner's words, it was time to dispose of "ancient pretensions" and seat Hiram Revels in the U.S. Senate.

✷ ✷ ✷

When debate concluded on Friday, February 25, 1870, the Senate took its historic vote.

Forty-eight senators, all of them Republicans and including Charles Sumner, voted in favor of administering the oath of office to Hiram Revels. Eight senators, all Democrats, voted against. Twelve more senators, mostly Republicans, were recorded as absent.

Colfax called Revels forward to take the oath—the black Republican became a U.S. senator by swearing to "support and defend the Constitution of the United States against all enemies, foreign and domestic."

Charles Sumner could barely contain himself. "Today we make the Declaration a reality," he said. This day in 1870 was a day the Founders and Framers had predicted in 1776 and 1787 and, indeed, had *longed* for.

"Liberty and equality were two express promises of our fathers," he said. "Both are now assured. *From this time there can be no backward step.*"

Two days earlier—and for twenty years before that—Hiram Revels was a cause.

Now he was a colleague.

✴ CHAPTER 41 ✴

"GOOD-BYE AND GOD BLESS YOU!"

OCTOBER 15, 1870, BOSTON

A raucous Faneuil Hall was jammed to capacity when Charles Sumner stepped to the rostrum and was greeted with "almost indescribable enthusiasm," according to one Boston journalist.

Massachusetts Republicans had thronged the historic hall to ratify their nominees for state offices, and Sumner was serving as president of the meeting. For several minutes, the delirious crowd roared and would not permit Sumner to speak.

When the crowd finally quieted, Sumner did not disappoint. He emphasized that Republicans must be "constant, incessant, persevering" in their fight for the principles of freedom and equality. He urged them to avoid the complacency that often accompanies popularity and success, but he also elicited a groundswell of renewed applause when he implored the crowd to spread the word about how Republicans had moved the country forward. He reminded the delegates of the astonishing and "heroic" achievements of their party: "It has put down a terrible rebellion waged by Slavery; it has secured equal rights at the ballot-box and in the courts without distinction of color; and it has reconstructed the Rebel States on the solid foundation of the Declaration of Independence!"

His vision of a slave-free nation had been realized, and—an occurrence that would have been considered unimaginable in the 1850s—both citizenship and voting rights were now secure for men who were once enslaved.

✴ ✴ ✴

The seating of Hiram Revels in the Senate and the warm reception experienced by Sumner in Massachusetts served to salve a politically wounded Sumner, who struggled and clashed with the Grant administration throughout 1870 and into 1871.

His problems with Grant began with a snub—the new President selected Hamilton Fish rather than Sumner as secretary of state. Next came Grant's irritation over Sumner's bombastic *Alabama* claims speech, which left the President and Fish with little room to maneuver with the British, or even dispose of the issue in a less antagonistic manner.

But worst of all, from Grant's perspective, was Sumner's decision to oppose and ultimately sink the President's scheme to annex Santo Domingo (the present-day Dominican Republic) as a refuge for Southern freedmen—essentially, to establish an African American state on the island. Concerned about the loss of an independent black state, Sumner also worried that the annexation of Santo Domingo would serve as an invitation for Southern Democrats to forcibly remove blacks from their region to the island, and that it would also encourage Grant to make additional expensive acquisitions in places such as Haiti. Sumner also had grave concerns about the financing of the Santo Domingo plan, and he fretted that American troops might be needed to secure annexation.

With so many variables—and with the protection of freedmen his top priority—Sumner convinced the Senate Foreign Relations Committee to reject the treaty, and on June 30, 1870, the full Senate killed it with a 28–28 deadlock (the Constitution requires a two-thirds majority vote in the Senate to ratify a treaty). Grant was livid, accusing Sumner of reneging on an earlier promise to support the plan, which Sumner disputed. Sumner responded by denouncing the President repeatedly, and the two exchanged recriminations for months afterward.

Reconciliation was impossible.

✳ ✳ ✳

When it came time for Congress to reorganize in early 1871, a furious Grant exacted his revenge. Working behind the scenes with Fish and Republican leaders, he engineered Sumner's removal as chairman of the Senate Foreign Relations Committee after ten years in the position. Republicans justified the move on the grounds that Sumner was not on speaking terms with either the President or the secretary of state. Sumner declined to accept a rank-and-file position on the committee and retired from the Republican caucus.

He said next to nothing publicly about the insult, but his removal produced a greater outpouring of support—from lawmakers and citizens—even than after his beating by Preston Brooks in 1856. Republican Speaker of the House James Blaine labeled as shortsighted and unforgivable the decision by his party in the Senate. Sumner had been struck down in the Senate chamber in 1856 for adhering to his principles, and now he was "even more cruelly struck down . . . [by] the party he had done so much to establish."

To add injury to insult, the strain of Sumner's confrontations with Grant over Santo Domingo and the fight over his removal as Foreign Relations Committee chairman left him fatigued. In February 1871, a short time before the formal vote replacing him as chairman, he suffered from a return bout of angina pectoris. Two weeks later, he was seized by a violent attack, a spasm accompanied by intense pain that radiated across the left side of his chest and down his left arm. The illness forced him to miss a week of Senate business and confined him to bed. He received many notes from well-wishers who beseeched him to rest and abstain from the stress and excitement of Senate debates.

As he recovered, Sumner kept up with some correspondence, including with a constituent who asked whether he would consider becoming a presidential candidate in 1872.

Sumner emphasized that he would not.

"I have had enough of combat and am very weary," Sumner replied. "And yet combat is before me."

✳ ✳ ✳

SPRING 1873, WASHINGTON, D.C.

Unable to sleep due to pain in his spinal column and repeated midnight pain that "invaded" his left arm, Sumner felt constant fatigue and listlessness. His longtime physician, Dr. Brown-Séquard, was in Washington at the time and administered strychnine to Sumner as a remedy for his recurring and painful spinal cord spasms. After December 19, 1872, Sumner absented himself altogether from the Senate for the remainder of the session.

Nothing had been easy for him over the past months.

Sumner's disgust with President Grant had prompted him to take the almost unforgivable step of opposing the President in his 1872 reelection campaign. Sumner's support of liberal Republican Horace Greeley— which even his dear friends Longfellow and Frederick Douglass warned him against—so angered fellow mainstream Republicans that Sumner was banished from the Republican Party and became an independent.

Then in late 1872, Sumner was censured by the Massachusetts legislature when he introduced a Senate resolution to remove the names of Civil War battles from the Army Register and from regimental colors. Sumner claimed his proposed bill was designed to put the Civil War behind the country and "promote national unity and good-will among fellow citizens," regardless of where they resided. But many Republicans saw his "battle flags resolution" as yet another slap at President Grant, the country's soldier-president. The resolution caused a national uproar—it was assailed and quickly rejected in the Senate. The Massachusetts censure claimed Sumner's bill was "an insult to the loyal soldiery of the nation."

Ever perplexed by other people's reactions to his words and actions, Sumner wrote of the outcry: "I cannot comprehend this tempest." Sumner felt he "deserved better of Mass." after all he had done to advance the state's ideals.

Poet John Greenleaf Whittier led a petition drive to overturn the censure, but the Massachusetts legislature did not rescind its action until February 1874, just weeks before Sumner's death.

✵ ✵ ✵

Sumner's poor health was also exacerbated by his ongoing uphill struggle to convince the Senate to approve a sweeping civil rights bill. Sumner's proposed bill would have prevented any form of discrimination based on color anywhere in the country by theaters, inns, "common carriers" of passengers, managers of schools, or any church, cemetery, or state or federal court—including restrictions on juror service.

Again and again, his proposal was thwarted, altered, watered down, banished to committee, or simply ignored by the Senate. Sumner refused to relent. But though his spirit was willing, his influence had weakened because of his opposition to the Grant administration. In May 1872, while a tired Sumner was absent from the Senate during an all-night session,

Senator Matthew Carpenter of Wisconsin offered an amendment to Sumner's bill at 5:45 A.M. that *excluded* schools, churches, cemeteries, and jury service from its protection. The emasculated bill passed the Senate on May 21, 1872, but still the House failed to take it up. Undaunted by either Carpenter's underhanded maneuver or the House's failure to act, Sumner continued to press the Senate to lead the way on the civil rights bill.

Due to his health, Sumner occasionally took short walks that exhausted him and received callers to his home "only in arm-chair and dressing-gown"; it was during this time in April 1873 that Sumner's former Senate colleague and now Vice President Henry Wilson visited his home. As the two men chatted in the study, Sumner uttered a confession that startled his friend: "If my *Works* [collection of speeches] were completed, and my civil rights bill passed, no visitor could enter that door that would be more welcome than Death."

✻ ✻ ✻

Throughout his illness, Sumner received dozens of letters expressing sympathy and imploring him to rest. Many of his old friends wrote—Longfellow, Whittier, Oliver Wendell Holmes, Wendell Phillips, Lydia Maria Child, Henry Ward Beecher, Richard Henry Dana. Beecher's letter from Brooklyn captured the sentiments of almost all the writers: "Thousands look into the newspapers to learn whether your health is better or worse," he said. Sumner's character and dedication to equal rights for all "have made your name national, and your life a part of the *best history of the noblest period of American affairs.*"

Sumner finally acknowledged some physical relief and "a certain sense of returning health" when, on May 10, after only a fifteen-minute court hearing, his uncontested divorce from Alice was granted. "I rejoice that you are free at last," E. L. Pierce wrote on the same day. He continued to rally a bit over the summer of 1873 and returned to Boston in August with "a sense of health and a certain elasticity."

One late afternoon in November 1873, after dining with Longfellow, Sumner traveled to Boston's South End to attend church services. As he approached his destination, a young boy jumped from a carriage, ran to him, and asked: "Mr. Sumner, will you please write your name in my album?" The two walked beneath a streetlamp for better visibility in the fading light of day, and a deeply moved Sumner obliged the young man's

request. To Whittier, he wrote later: "The heart of Massachusetts is returning."

Sumner still could not help but think of his own mortality as death
struck his circle of friends. Chief Justice Salmon Chase had died in May
1873, and his scientist friend Louis Agassiz, famous for his work on glacial formations and the Ice Age, had also recently passed. A stroke had
paralyzed his boyhood friend George S. Hillard.

"Our little circle is growing smaller," Sumner wrote to Longfellow,
"and I am on the way to solitude."

✳ ✳ ✳

Just a few days before Sumner left for Washington and the next Senate
session, he dined with the wheelchair-bound Hillard. The two longtime
friends spoke until nearly midnight, and an unidentified eyewitness to
the meeting—likely one of Hillard's attendants—described their parting.
"It was almost in silence, with a long clasp of hands, as if each felt it was
for the last time," the observer wrote.

Before Sumner left the house, Hillard's cook, a former slave, asked
if she could meet the man "who was the deliverer of her race." Sumner
stood awkwardly in the doorway of the dining room while the cook and
another African American servant stepped up and kissed his hand. "We
looked on with wet eyes," the eyewitness reported, "but he [Sumner] was
rather embarrassed, and glad to escape upstairs."

On November 24, 1873, a Monday, Sumner boarded a train for
Springfield, where he was scheduled to stop for a couple of hours before
resuming his journey to Washington. His friend and future biographer
E. L. Pierce was aboard the same train. The men spent two hours together in the drawing-room car.

"Do you not see how the heart of Massachusetts is with you?" Pierce
asked his friend at one point. After a moment's thought, Sumner answered softly: "Yes. I expected it, but not so soon."

Later in the evening, as Sumner was set to board a second train to
New York, he and Pierce clasped hands on the platform. Sumner, eyes
wet with tears, said: "Good-bye and God bless you!" and the two friends
parted for the last time. An emotional Pierce watched the man he admired most in the world step onto the departing train, and recalled later:

"In a few moments he left forever the State he had loved and served."

EPILOGUE
"Great Champion of Liberty"

In the late afternoon of March 16, 1874, Vice President of the United States Henry Wilson stood beside an open grave in the dusky shadow of a large oak tree in Mount Auburn Cemetery in Cambridge, Massachusetts. Next to him, heads bowed in prayer, stood Boston luminaries Henry Wadsworth Longfellow, Oliver Wendell Holmes, Ralph Waldo Emerson, and John Greenleaf Whittier, all longtime friends of the deceased. Scores of mourners surrounded the grave.

Charles Sumner was dead, and Boston and all of America were grieving the loss of the country's greatest antislavery champion and proponent of equal rights.

Mourners had accompanied the casket from the start of the extraordinary funeral procession: from the Massachusetts State House, where the body had lain for thousands of mourners to view; to the brief prayer service at King's Chapel; and then for the trip down Cambridge Street to Beacon Street to Charles Street, across the Charles River Bridge into Cambridge; past Sumner's beloved alma mater, Harvard College; and finally to Mount Auburn, where the cortege arrived just as the late-winter sun was setting.

Pallbearers reverently placed the casket by the side of the grave, while outside the cemetery's wrought-iron gates, thousands of additional people clustered to glimpse the burial and honor the late statesman.

"No man in this generation has done more to advance the cause of equal liberty for mankind," one publication declared. "No death in the country, since that of Mr. Lincoln, has caused a deeper feeling of sorrow."

* * *

The heart attack that claimed Sumner's life occurred during the early morning hours of March 11, 1874, while the senator was at his Washington, D.C., home.

When word spread across the city that the sixty-three-year-old Sumner had been stricken, small groups of well-wishers, black and white alike, congregated quietly outside his house. With his close friends gathered at his bedside, Sumner's last phrases were, "Tell Emerson I love and revere him," and "Don't let the civil rights bill fail." Among his deathbed visitors in Washington was his friend and former slave Frederick Douglass, but the senator did not recognize Douglass in the moments before his death.

Around 2:00 P.M., in terrible pain, Sumner begged his doctors for more morphine, but before they could administer another injection, he became quiet, less agitated, and then still.

At 2:50 P.M., as his old friend, abolitionist George T. Downing held his hand, Sumner was seized by a "convulsive moment," gasped for air, and gripped Downing's hand so powerfully that he almost crushed it.

Charles Sumner died seconds later.

✳ ✳ ✳

Congress voted to set aside Friday, March 13, for funeral services in Washington. Douglass led a "great assemblage of colored men" who followed Sumner's hearse to the Capitol, where more than five thousand mourners were waiting. Sumner's coffin was placed in the center of the great rotunda on the black catafalque where Lincoln's body had rested nine years earlier.

It was the first time in American history that a senator's memory had been so honored.

For the next three hours, grief-stricken mourners filed by the open coffin to glimpse Sumner's face, visible beneath and protected by transparent glass. Meanwhile, President Ulysses S. Grant—who had parried Sumner's political thrusts since he took office—joined senators and representatives, members of the Supreme Court, and a contingent of army officers led by William T. Sherman in the Senate chamber for services, while wives, friends, and other dignitaries packed the gallery.

Every chair in the chamber was filled, save for Sumner's, which remained vacant, as it had for three years after his caning at the hands of Preston Brooks—this time it was draped in black.

At just before 12:30 P.M., the entire assemblage watched in silence as congressional pallbearers brought the coffin into the Senate chamber, carried it to the front, and placed it before the main desk.

Services lasted for about a half hour. Then, Senator Matt Carpenter of Wisconsin, who less than a year earlier had stripped Sumner's civil rights bill of most of its key provisions, entrusted Sumner's remains to the sergeant at arms, "to convey them to his home, there to commit them, earth to earth, ashes to ashes, dust to dust, in the soil of Massachusetts."

✷ ✷ ✷

In a scene similar to Lincoln's funeral nine years earlier, Sumner's body had been transported north by special train that left Washington around 3:00 P.M. on March 13.

But unlike Lincoln's train returning to Springfield, Illinois, which stopped numerous times along the way, the train carrying Sumner's body traveled nonstop to New York—much to the deep disappointment of enormous crowds that had gathered in Wilmington, Delaware, and Philadelphia—where it halted at midnight. The next morning it continued through Connecticut, where, in New Haven and other cities, what seemed like the entire population gathered to pay their last tribute to Sumner.

And then the train crossed into Massachusetts. Beginning in Springfield, throngs gathered at every station to watch it rumble eastward, while church bells tolled along the entire route.

Meanwhile, in Boston, several thousand mourners had filled Faneuil Hall for a public prayer meeting, and later poured onto the tracks to greet the train when it arrived in the early evening of March 14. Then a long procession followed the coffin, which was escorted by a mounted guard of honor from the Massachusetts First Battalion, up Beacon Hill to the Massachusetts State House, where Sumner's body was placed in Doric Hall and, appropriately for a man who had devoted his life to equality, guarded by African American troops.

✷ ✷ ✷

The next day, Sunday, March 15, 1874, with thousands of grieving citizens waiting outside—several women fainted in the tightly packed lines—the doors to the statehouse were opened at 10:00 A.M. for mourners to pay their respects.

The resulting turnout stunned even Sumner's greatest supporters.

Somberly, silently, two or three abreast, between forty and fifty thousand people passed by Sumner's casket during Sunday and the early hours of Monday, a stupendous number of men, women, and children who waited in line to bid the senator good-bye. "Under that roof," noted the *Boston Advertiser*, "was uttered the summons of the State to him to go forth in her name to withstand the great wrong."

The thousands who filed by Sumner's coffin knew well what the country had endured to right the great wrong that Charles Sumner had fought against most of his adult life. They had witnessed firsthand Sumner's resolute voice during the divisive antislavery fights of the 1850s, a destructive civil war, a presidential assassination, and a contentious and violent Reconstruction era. They knew of his enormous contributions to America on the world stage, including his pivotal role in helping the country avoid potentially catastrophic wars with England. They knew of the physical pain and mental anguish he had endured after his 1856 caning, a shocking event that occurred directly because of the fearless expression of his beliefs.

The people of Massachusetts—many of whom had once disagreed with Sumner's uncompromising antislavery and equal rights views—collectively recognized the profoundness of his contributions as they filed through the statehouse hall.

✳ ✳ ✳

On Monday, around 2:30 P.M., church bells tolled once again, and because virtually all of Boston's businesses suspended operations, the downtown streets were jammed with spectators and mourners.

Black-trimmed drapery hung from buildings, inscriptions honoring Sumner were displayed on stores and homes, and ships moored in Boston Harbor lowered their flags to half-mast. Trains had brought thousands into the core city from the suburbs, and police were forced to clear the roadway to allow the funeral procession to travel the short distance from the statehouse to King's Chapel for the Episcopal service, chosen because it had once been the place of worship for Sumner's mother (the senator belonged to no church).

From there, the procession—headed by Vice President Wilson, members of the Massachusetts congressional delegation, the governor, and the mayor of Boston—wound its way toward Cambridge and Mount Auburn Cemetery, closely followed by other dignitaries, friends, and, perhaps more notably according to one reporter, "the representatives of the dusky race, for whom Charles Sumner battled and suffered, and in whose cause he laid down his life."

All along the five-mile route, crowds ten deep lined the streets. The procession produced a massive traffic snarl, and for forty-five minutes, the hearse was stalled in front of a house with tightly drawn blinds.

Years later, one of E. L. Pierce's correspondents told him that behind one set of blinds stood the former Alice Sumner, the dead senator's ex-wife now back in Boston, who reportedly looked out at the coffin and said:

"That is just like Charles—he never did show tact."

✳ ✳ ✳

Charles Sumner is buried in a secluded spot in Mount Auburn Cemetery, far from the main entrance, on the southwest slope of a hill along what is today called Arethusa Path. His grave is marked by a coffin-shaped granite monument inscribed only with his name and the dates of his birth and death (January 6, 1811–March 11, 1874). Beside it are the graves of his family members, including those of his siblings, with whom Charles maintained little relationship during his life, marked with small white-gray rectangular stones. Sumner's marker is sturdy and significant but relatively unpretentious compared with other large stones and obelisk-shaped monuments nearby.

In 1874, his death was observed around the world. In Europe, where Sumner had spent so much time, glowing tributes and portraits appeared in Great Britain, France, Italy, and Sweden. In the United States, publications such as *Harper's Weekly* and the *New York Tribune* ran full-length tributes. Longfellow and Whittier commemorated him in poems and letters. Whittier lauded Sumner's "tireless devotion to duty, his courage . . . his unbending integrity, stainless honor, and tender regard for the rights of all." Newspapers across the country recognized his loss as a national tragedy and were united in the generous praise they offered him. "The noblest head in America has fallen," declared the *Springfield Republican*, "and the most accomplished and illustrious of our statesmen is no more." Within a year, four books containing collected eulogies and tributes to Sumner were published.

One eulogy delivered at Kalamazoo College in Michigan lauded Sumner for being among the first to urge emancipation after civil war broke out and celebrated his "moral greatness" and integrity. In more recent years, it required little moral courage to support equal rights, the eulogist noted, "but think what it was like in the dark days when Charles Sumner put on his armor and went forth like David against Goliath, to battle against the colossal power of slavery."

The ideas that Charles Sumner had promulgated for so long were now more than part of mainstream opinion—they had been codified into law and written into the U.S. Constitution. A deeply flawed man, Sumner's courage and leadership on the antislavery issue were indisputable and unrivaled, and, in death, virtually universally acknowledged.

One particular tribute offered a profound and startling testament to how far the country's attitudes had changed in the decade following the terrible Civil War. Eighteen years after he was caned on the floor of the Senate by South Carolina congressman Preston Brooks, Sumner was honored by the reconstructed government of South Carolina, which lowered the state flag in Columbia to half-staff upon his death.

✳ ✳ ✳

Congress set aside April 27 as a day of eulogies for Sumner.

Nine senators and eleven House members, Republicans and Democrats, offered long and, in most cases, brilliantly written remarks on Sumner's personal qualities, his character as a public official, his accomplishments, and his place in history. The 112 pages of tributes were bound by the Government Printing Office, and throughout, lawmakers accorded him the foremost place in the country's history as the "undoubted leader of the political opposition to slavery" and hailed his courage in his "ceaseless war" against the evil institution. "[His] constituency *was* the Republic," asserted Senator Henry Anthony of Rhode Island.

Amid the torrent of praise, two eulogies on that day stood out, both offered by House members. South Carolina's Joseph Rainey, the first African American member of the House, who was sworn in on December 12, 1870, spoke of Sumner's graciousness in welcoming him to Congress when he first arrived. Rainey revealed that after the Brooks assault, slaves in the South secretly prayed for Sumner, small, hidden, and risky demonstrations of support "only known to those whose situations at the time made them confidants." The slaves recited the prayers "for their constant friend and untiring advocate and defender before the high court of the nation."

Rainey's remembrances and revelations were powerful, but for pure drama, they did not approach the eulogistic tribute delivered by a second House member.

✳ ✳ ✳

When Mississippi congressman Lucius Quintus Cincinnatus Lamar rose and asked to be heard, Congress held its breath. No one was quite sure what he was going to say, because no one in Congress had been as diametrically opposed to Charles Sumner.

Lamar was an old fire-eater, a secessionist Democrat, once a fierce supporter of John C. Calhoun and Jefferson Davis—the "odor of rebellion" hung about him, in the words of one biographer. When Charles Sumner returned to the Senate in 1860 to deliver his "Barbarism of Slavery" speech, Lamar was preparing to walk out of Congress; in 1861, while Sumner was urging Lincoln to issue the Emancipation Proclamation, Lamar was drafting the Mississippi Ordinance of Secession. During the war, Lamar saw action in Virginia as a colonel in the Nineteenth Mississippi Regiment, and when poor health forced him to retire, Jefferson Davis appointed him as a special CSA commissioner to Russia. Even as the war ended, Lamar was a member of the Mississippi State Constitutional Convention, which Sumner described as "little more than a rebel conspiracy to obtain political power."

Lamar's secessionist history was compounded by the fact that now, in April 1874, he was about to follow Congressman George F. Hoar of Massachusetts, who had peppered his eulogy with criticism of the Southern slaveocracy, and especially Preston Brooks's caning of Sumner in 1856.

Would Lamar dare breach the decorum of the moment and do the unthinkable—defend the brutal beating of the man whose memory Congress was honoring? When Lamar stood, the chamber, packed with lawmakers, and the galleries, jammed with onlookers, murmured in anticipation and then grew quieter . . . and then silent.

As Lamar began to speak in a strong, clear voice, it became evident to all that something unexpected and inspiring, perhaps even epochal, was happening.

✳ ✳ ✳

What Lamar said ricocheted across the country, stunned his colleagues, and touched the hearts of every listener. The former slaveholder from the Deep South offered a stirring eulogy to Charles Sumner and, in Sumner's memory, made a simple plea for lasting peace and justice between North and South.

It was not an easy speech for Lamar to make. Both of his brothers and two of his law partners were killed in Civil War battles, a war that Southerners believed was fought due to the radical antislavery policies favored by Sumner and those like him. If it were 1864 rather than ten years later, Lamar and other Southerners would have celebrated Charles Sumner's death.

But not today. Lamar believed there had been too much strife and hatred and distrust between regions—it was time for North and South to heal. Americans from every region needed to view themselves as a single people, Lamar said, "bound to each other by a common constitution, destined to live together under a common government." Sumner's death offered an opportunity for a new understanding between the sections.

Lamar made it clear that he never knew Sumner, but he did know the Massachusetts senator was a "great champion of liberty . . . a sympathizer with human sorrow." In his name, Northerners and Southerners should "lay aside the concealments which serve only to perpetuate misunderstandings and distrust." If Sumner could speak from the dead to both sides, Lamar declared, he would say: "My countrymen! *Know one another and you will love one another.*"

When Lamar finished, the House sat for a moment in shocked silence, and then a loud and spontaneous burst of sustained applause rolled across the floor. Speaker James G. Blaine did not raise his gavel, and in fact did nothing to check the hearty cheering, mainly because tears were streaming down his face.

✳ ✳ ✳

Lamar's eulogy marked an important Reconstruction turning point in the relations between North and South, and it elevated the Mississippi congressman to statesman status. The *Boston Advertiser* declared it "the most significant and hopeful utterance that has been heard from the South since the war." Not to be overshadowed, the relatively new *Boston Globe* claimed: "We do not know of *any parallel in history* to a recognition like this."

Even many Southern newspapers praised Lamar, though some vigorously criticized him. But he was willing to bear the negative reports. To his wife, he wrote: "Our people have suffered so much, have been betrayed so often . . . that it is but natural that they should be suspicious of any word or act of overture to the North by a Southern man." Some Northerners and modern historians attributed a purely cynical motive to Lamar—his hope that praise for Sumner would result in better treatment of the South by the U.S. government. But in his heart, Lamar was confident that his sentiments had served his region and his constituents well.

Still, he vowed, if enough people disagreed with his actions, Lamar would abide by the will of voters and "will calmly and silently retire to private life." But his fellow Mississippians eventually came to understand and accept Lamar's message, or at least they respected him for speaking honestly about his feelings. In 1876, Mississippi's Democratic state legislature elected him to the U.S. Senate; Lamar had strong support from blacks and whites, Republicans and Democrats.

In early 1877, he became the first former Confederate leader to be seated by the U.S. Senate.

* * *

Charles Sumner's cherished civil rights bill, whose fate worried him even on his deathbed, was finally passed and signed into law by President Grant in 1875, albeit with the desegregated school section deleted. Like its sponsor, the bill was far ahead of its time, and it served as a fitting tribute to Sumner's perseverance and leadership.

But it did not last long. In 1883, the U.S. Supreme Court ruled large portions of the Civil Rights Act unconstitutional, especially sections that forbade discrimination in hotels, trains, restaurants, and other private establishments. Essentially, the court held that the Fourteenth Amendment guaranteeing equal protection under the law applied only to *public* institutions and the regulation of states and not to private businesses or individuals. The *Plessy v. Ferguson* case in 1896 all but eroded Sumner's signature bill when the Supreme Court—relying largely on the argument of Massachusetts justice Lemuel Shaw in the 1850 Sarah Roberts decision—upheld the legality of "separate but equal" laws imposed by states in most public settings, including in schools.

Despite his enormous role in ending slavery and promoting equal rights, Sumner never lived to see his lifelong desire "to close forever the great question . . . so that there shall be no such words as 'black' or 'white' but that we shall speak only of citizens and of men."

✳ ✳ ✳

It was not only Supreme Court decisions that postponed the fulfillment of Charles Sumner's legacy on the question of equal rights.

The infamous Compromise of 1877—convoluted, cynical, largely unwritten, and hammered out partially in secret in a Washington, D.C., hotel—served the dual purposes of deciding the winner of the 1876 presidential election and ending Reconstruction.

And it did far more harm to Sumner's dream.

The fight for the presidency between Republican Rutherford B. Hayes, governor of Ohio, and Democrat Samuel J. Tilden, governor of New York, devolved into chaos soon after Election Day in 1876. Tilden seemed to win 203 electoral votes, when only 185 were needed for victory. But Republicans disputed the electoral votes of Louisiana, Florida, and South Carolina, states they controlled; without these states, Tilden had only 184 electoral votes, one short of the number needed to win. If Hayes received the electoral votes from these states, he would become President. By disqualifying enough Democrat ballots, election boards in the three disputed states certified Hayes as the winner and sent their results to Congress.

Democrats cried fraud, a charge that was likely true, but one more than counterbalanced by white Democrat intimidation, violence, and terror that kept thousands of black voters from the polls who would have undoubtedly voted for Hayes (many counties with large black majorities recorded no Republican votes at all, a virtual impossibility unless freedmen voted unanimously against their own interests, or far more likely were prevented from voting at all). Democrats sent their own sets of returns to Congress declaring a Tilden victory.

To resolve the crisis of two sets of returns, Congress created an electoral commission composed of five senators, five representatives, and

five Supreme Court justices. The commission was supposed to be politically balanced, with seven Democrats, seven Republicans, and one Independent, the latter being Justice David Davis. But Davis removed himself
after he was elected to the Senate, and he was replaced by Justice Joseph
P. Bradley, a Republican.

With an 8–7 majority on the commission, the Republicans resolved
every disputed ballot in favor of the fifty-four-year-old Hayes, giving him
the 185 electoral votes he needed to become the nineteenth president of the
United States.

Furious Democrats refused to go quietly. During secret negotiations at the Wormley Hotel in Washington, which Hayes did not attend,
Democrats pledged not to contest the election further only if Hayes
agreed (among other things) to end military occupation of the South—
specifically, to remove federal troops that still supported the state governments of Louisiana and South Carolina, the last Republican regimes
in the region. Republicans agreed.

With the compromise in place, Hayes was declared elected on March
2, 1877, and the new President—who was, ironically, a supporter of African American rights—made good on the promise to remove federal
troops from the South. It marked the end of Reconstruction, and along
with it, the end of protection of freedmen from violence and racist policies. The emergence of Democratic-supported Jim Crow laws, the Ku
Klux Klan, restrictive voting practices, and physical violence against
African Americans all flowed from the premature removal of a federal
presence in the South.

Reconstruction had ended, and with it—only three years after his
death and for decades to come—so had Charles Sumner's lifelong and
elusive dream of equality under the law.

✳ ✳ ✳

What, then, of Charles Sumner's lasting contribution to the nation—his
legacy, as it were?

The Compromise of 1877 surely delayed for decades Sumner's dream
of full equality under the law, but it neither diminished nor destroyed it.
It took one hundred years, but the arguments about freedom and racial
equality that Charles Sumner made during his twenty-five years in public
life, from 1849 to 1874, were the identical arguments made in *Brown v.*

Board of Education in 1954 and by leaders such as Martin Luther King, Jr., throughout the civil rights movement of the 1950s and 1960s. Sumner's language of the 1850s and 1860s found its way into the Civil Rights Acts of 1964 and 1965 and the Voting Rights Act of 1965.

It is difficult today to imagine the Herculean odds Sumner faced in the 1850s when he went to Washington to battle the slaveocracy. Then, the slave system was entrenched not just across the plantations of the American South but in the economic DNA of the North and within the political corridors of Washington, D.C. In Congress and throughout the executive branch, slavery had been "managed" for decades by a series of compromises by all political parties, but it was not opposed in any meaningful or substantive way. In the North and the South, slavery was considered a normal part of "doing business." Sumner upended the economic and social applecarts—and he did so without remorse and without permission.

Describing Sumner's task as an uphill battle is woefully inadequate; it required an exertion of sweat and labor and personal and political capital akin to digging a deep well with nothing more than a spoon. Yet he never stopped digging, and for that alone, America owes him a deep and permanent debt of gratitude.

In the face of repeated insults, ridicule, personal setbacks, and a devastating physical attack, Charles Sumner's voice and ideas moved a nation, slowly, even grudgingly at first, but eventually with a surety that accompanies righteousness.

A year before he died, Charles Sumner explained his lifelong quest to a friend: "My hope has been to help mankind, and advance the reign of justice on earth."

✳ ✳ ✳

For Charles Sumner, freedom and equality were America's *national* birthrights, and slavery and racist laws were a perversion of those ideals. He saw the government's tolerance and support for the growth of slavery as an ignorant misreading of the country's founding documents, not an inevitable condition flowing from them.

Dour and disconsolate as he often appeared, he was an optimist at heart. As one congressional eulogist declared, Sumner "believed in his country, in her unity, her grandeur, her ideas, and her destiny."

He believed in it as he held up a mirror to its flaws and challenged the country to live up to the vision of its founding. He believed in it as he ferociously battled slavery and inequality. He believed in it as he endured and recovered from a vicious beating for speaking his mind.

Charles Sumner told all who would listen that his lonely fight to create a more perfect union was a burden well worth shouldering—that the fulfilled promise of America would literally change the world.

ACKNOWLEDGMENTS

Since I published my first book two decades ago, I have been amazed by the number of people who have donated their time and talent to make my work easier and better. For this, my eighth book, the story is the same. Many professionals, family members, and friends have helped me get *The Great Abolitionist* into your hands—this book would not have been possible without their contributions.

First and foremost, I'd like to offer my deepest thanks to you, dear reader, because it's you who make all books possible. I'm honored by your support of my work through the years. I'm humbled by your encouragement and inspired by your kind words. A simple "thank you" seems inadequate, but I hope you recognize the heartfelt manner in which I convey it. You have given me that rare and often elusive gift that all authors hope to receive—loyal readership. I hope you found *The Great Abolitionist* worthy of it. Communicating with you is one of the joys of being an author—please continue to reach out to me at spuleo@aol.com, through my website at www.stephenpuleo.com, on Facebook at facebook.com/stephenpuleoauthor, or on Instagram at Instagram.com/puleosteve.

Now to others who have supported me as I worked on *The Great Abolitionist* (my first full biography!) and have accompanied me through some or all of my author journey.

My editor **Tim Bartlett** at St. Martin's Press has my deepest thanks for his support of this book. This is our third book together—Tim also edited my *Voyage of Mercy* and *American Treasures*—and I'm grateful to be in such good hands. Tim is the consummate pro; he knows when to bring a light touch and when to exert a heavier editorial hand. He cares about history, he cares about books, and everything he does is done with an eye toward making the book better. What more can an author ask for? *The Great Abolitionist* is a much better book because of him. I'm also grateful to St. Martin's associate editor **Kevin Reilly** for his assistance and thoroughness every step of the way. Tim, Kevin, and the entire team at St. Martin's are a pleasure to work with, including **Rob Grom**, who provided the book's stunning jacket, and **Meryl Sussman Levavi**, who created the compelling overall design.

My agent, **Joy Tutela**, has been with me for my entire career as an author, which is a true blessing for me. Joy's belief in me from day one and her passion for my first book, *Dark Tide,* launched my author's journey, and the ride has been spectacular. Through the years, I have benefitted beyond words from Joy's enthusiasm, encouragement, loyalty, and professionalism—and I have valued her friendship most of all.

I am the beneficiary of unwavering support from so many talented friends and family members whose interest and encouragement inspire me and make me a better author. It is impossible to list them all, but I would like to mention a few for all they've done—I am truly honored that they are members of the "Puleo team."

Paula Hoyt, who regularly edits my work, once again shared her wonderful talents to make this book better. As she has with several of my books, Paula read the manuscript in its entirety, ensuring that it was smoother and cleaner before I submitted it for publication. Her interest in my work is a source of inspiration, as is her dear and deep friendship with my wife, Kate, and me.

Sue Hannan lends her considerable marketing and communicating skills to my work by expertly managing content and navigation for my aforementioned website—I'm biased, but I think it's one of the best!—as well as my author Facebook page, and other parts of the social media and marketing outreach portion of an author's job. Her creative and thoughtful ideas and insights, sound judgment, and excellent communication skills help me connect with readers in the best possible way. All important, for sure, but most important of all is the cherished friendship Sue and her family share with Kate and me.

For more than four decades, **Ellen Keefe** has selflessly offered Kate and me a deep reservoir of friendship, support, encouragement, wisdom, and love that we've drawn from often. She helps us celebrate joyful moments and offers solace and support when times are tough. It's such a bonus that she also edits my manuscripts (this one included), constantly spreads the word about my books to family and friends, and shares my love for history and reading. She is and always has been there for us—we are eternally thankful for a friendship so rare.

I hope all authors have an unsung hero in their lives—someone who stands beside them every step of the way, always offers encouragement, and can be counted on to inject needed enthusiasm into accomplishments and progress, large or small. For me, that person is my friend and sister-in-law **Pat Doyle**, who has accompanied me on the author journey from the first day. I am so grateful for her bedrock support, whether it's in the form of a simple inquiry on how my writing is going, her attendance at a large number of my nearly 670 author appearances, or the many wonderful photographs she has contributed to my website, Facebook page, and e-newsletters to readers. Kate and I are most grateful and thankful for the love we share with Pat.

I had the great pleasure of working for the first time with my friend **Charlotte Hannan**, who assisted me with the research on this book and did an outstanding job. Charlotte is a student at Harvard and a student of history, a thorough and intuitive researcher with an eye for what's important. I've known Charlotte for a long time, and when she is trusted with a project her work is excellent, and she takes the greatest care to get it right. Her work here was no exception—creative, thorough, well organized, and shrewdly analyzed. I'm immeasurably proud of Charlotte for her contributions to *The Great Abolitionist* and—to echo a theme—blessed by the friendship she shares with Kate and me.

My mom, **Rose Puleo**, passed away while I was working on this book, which makes this my first book published without either of my parents being here to celebrate (I lost my dad, Anthony, in 2009). They were there for me always and provided constant support, interest, pride, and love throughout my whole life. I miss them dearly, but I'm aware of their love and comforting presence always—when I'm writing or doing anything else, I feel them on my shoulder and in my heart. I will never be able to thank my parents for all they have done. We also lost Kate's parents while I worked on the research and writing of this book; we offer profound thanks for the lives they lived, the example they set, and the love they shared.

Saving the best for last . . .

The love and friendship **Kate** and I have shared for more than four decades is my greatest joy and most profound blessing. We are true partners in so many things, including book writing—she is the first to hear my ideas, the first to offer insights, the first to read my manuscripts, the first to know when things are going smoothly or if I've hit a rough patch. She is, simply, "present on every page" I've written. Her gifts are many, and she shares them constantly with me, family members, and friends. Throughout her professional life as a teacher and principal, she inspired thousands of students to reach their full potential; in her personal life, her strength of character and compassion inspire scores of others. She inspires me each and every day. I am proud of all she is and all she's done, proud to share our dreams, and I thank her for everything—always. *The Great Abolitionist* is dedicated to her from the bottom of my most grateful heart.

BIBLIOGRAPHIC ESSAY

The Great Abolitionist is a biographical history that rests on a sturdy foundation of scholarship and research, layered with an array of primary and secondary sources. This essay lists the sources and explains how I used them in the narrative. I have grouped them into topical categories and, where possible, listed them in chronological order.

I have received many favorable comments from readers that this approach is more appealing—and revealing—than traditional bibliography and notes sections in which sources are simply listed.

It's important to clarify up front that every word in this story is true. Everything that appears between quotation marks is contained in a diary, letter, speech, government document, congressional record, newspaper, magazine article, journal, pamphlet, or book. My narrative and conclusions are based on an examination and interpretation of the sources and my knowledge of the real-life characters and events; these also provide the underpinnings for any conjecture that I engage in. In those instances when I do speculate about people or events—as all historians and nonfiction authors must do from time to time—I make it clear to the reader.

In cases where there are several sources about a topic, I have done my best to give greater weight to the source chronologically closest to the event for greatest accuracy and veracity. When I rely on sources that were created well after an event they reference, I signal the reader with a phrase such as, "Years later, Sumner wrote . . ."

I have tried to tell Charles Sumner's story, which for all intents and purposes is the story of America during its most dire and defining period, with as much accuracy and narrative drama as the historical record allows.

* * *

For nearly twenty-five years, Charles Sumner was at the center of almost everything of importance that happened in the United States—as well as the dissolution of the Union between 1861 and 1865—and for that, I am grateful that he was a prolific writer and speaker.

Sumner wrote often—frequently several letters a day—on broad topics to a vast array of people. He seemed incapable of *not* writing; it is difficult to find a day Sumner did not put quill to paper. Just as rich are the thousands of letters people wrote *to* him during his career; those offer a wonderful look into the tenor and tone of the times from around the country. I've examined a few thousand of Sumner's letters, hundreds of letters he received, and virtually all of his speeches and related commentary in his *Works*.

Diaries, letters, memoirs, and papers of several other historical figures, including Abraham Lincoln, also proved integral to building the narrative, and these are cited in this essay.

The *Congressional Globe*, the precursor to the *Congressional Record*, contains Senate (and House) debates on all major events cited in this book. I referred to it often through the Library of Congress website (https://memory.loc.gov /ammem/amlaw/lwcg.html), focusing on the years Sumner served as senator. This is a great source to understand the depth of feeling of Northern and Southern lawmakers during this period in American history.

Throughout the book, I drew on hundreds of articles from several nineteenth-century newspapers as secondary sources. In the narrative, I mention newspapers I relied on most often, and I also examined other publications for background. Among the most important when it comes to Sumner is the Boston press, which includes the *Evening Transcript, Morning Post, Daily Advertiser, Daily Whig, Courier*, the *Commonwealth*, and Garrison's *The Liberator*. New York papers of importance include Horace Greeley's *Daily Tribune*, as well as the *Times, Evening Post*, and *Evening Sentinel*. The *Times* of London presents a decidedly anti-Sumner British perspective, and scores of pro-slavery Southern journals present virulent anti-Sumner articles; most important are the *Charleston (SC) Mercury* and the *Standard*, the *Edgefield (SC) Advertiser*, the *Macon (GA) Messenger*, the *Montgomery (AL) Journal*, the *New Orleans Times-Picayune*, and the *Richmond Whig*.

One other note: When an author writes about a subject that touches this profound era—the run-up to the Civil War, the war itself, Reconstruction, and the aftermath—he can't help but rub elbows with some of America's greatest historians. The articles and books I list here under "secondary sources" are a fraction of the thousands written about the Civil War era, but in my view they are among the best and most important, and they provided me with invaluable material for this work.

Charles Sumner

PRIMARY SOURCES

To understand and analyze this brilliant, mercurial, courageous, and complex man, I drew extensively on the enormous collection of letters to and from Sumner contained in *The Papers of Charles Sumner, 1811–1874*. These comprise letters contained in the Charles Sumner Papers at Harvard's Houghton Library, plus letters located in nearly two hundred other repositories in the United States, Great Britain, France, and Canada.

More than nine hundred of Sumner's most significant letters are published in the masterful *The Selected Letters of Charles Sumner*, volumes 1 (1830–1859) and 2 (1859–1874), produced by editor Beverly Wilson Palmer (Boston: North-eastern University Press, 1990). These volumes were my constant companion throughout the writing of this book. Palmer, a Sumner scholar, did an excellent job choosing letters that revealed Sumner's character and his beliefs, and she annotated the letters thoroughly, making it possible to align historical events of the day with Sumner's letters.

Sumner's speeches and many other writings are also contained in his fifteen-volume collection, *The Works of Charles Sumner* (Boston: Lee and Shepard, 1875), or *Works*. Sumner worked on these exhaustively during his later years, and they are an invaluable source. I used them with care, since, as I mentioned in the narrative, Sumner sometimes altered his past writings for clarity or to portray himself in a better light.

I made the decision to include in the "primary source" section, and found indispensable, the contemporaneous four-volume work by Edward Lillie Pierce, *Memoir and Letters of Charles Sumner* (Boston: Roberts Brothers, 1878–93). Although technically an authorized biography of Sumner, Pierce's valuable work contains many primary sources—speeches, letters to and from Sumner, letters contributed by Sumner's friends and colleagues—and Pierce's eyewitness and up-close analyses. Pierce's narrative is overly charitable in places, but he does delve into Sumner's shortcomings, and the memoirs are comprehensive and well written.

Numerous collections of Sumner's contemporaries were essential in reconstructing his life: the *Papers of Salmon P. Chase*, available digitally at the Library of Congress at https://www.loc.gov/collections/salmon-p-chase-papers/about--this-collection/; the *Frederick Douglass Papers*, available at https://www.loc.gov/collections/frederick-douglass-papers/about-this-collection/; the expansive *Edwin McMasters Stanton Papers, 1818–1921* at https://www.loc.gov/collections/edwin-mcmasters-stanton-papers/about-this-collection/; the extensive *William Henry Seward Papers* ("Seward Family Digital Archive") at the University of

Rochester (accessed at https://sewardproject.org/TheProject); *The Letters of Henry Wadsworth Longfellow*, 5 vols. (Cambridge, Mass.: Harvard University Press, 1966–82), edited by Andrew Hilen; *The Letters of William Lloyd Garrison, 1805–1879*, 5 vols. (Cambridge, Mass.: Harvard University Press, 1970–79), edited by Walter M. Merrill and Louis Ruchames; *The Collected Works of Abraham Lincoln* (1953), edited by Roy P. Basler, made available digitally by The Abraham Lincoln Association at https://quod.lib.umich.edu/l/lincoln/; and *The Papers of Ulysses S. Grant*, edited by John F. Marszalek and John Y. Simon (1967), made available digitally at the Ulysses S. Grant Presidential Library at https://www.usgrantlibrary .org/collections/digital#:~:text=University%20Press%2C%201967.-,The%20Pa- pers%20of%20Ulysses%20S.,a%20small%20number%20of%20photographs.

SECONDARY SOURCES

Articles, Essays, and Periodicals

I made use of the following secondary research to develop the overall personal and political character of Charles Sumner.

Carl M. Fraser's "Charles Sumner and the Rights of the Negro," *The Journal of Negro History*, Vol. 13, No. 2 (April 1928), pp. 126–149.

Arnold Burgess Johnson's "Recollections of Charles Sumner, Part 1," *Scribner's Monthly* (May 1874–October 1874), pp. 475–490; and "Recollections of Charles Sumner, Part II," ibid. (November 1874–April 1875), pp. 101–114. A. B. Johnson, who served as Sumner's secretary, offers invaluable information on Sumner's personal and work habits, his home, and his relationship with friends.

Andrew F. Rolle's "A Friendship Across the Atlantic: Charles Sumner and William Story," *American Quarterly*, Vol. 2, No. 1 (Spring 1959), pp. 50–57.

Louis Ruchames's "The Pulitzer Prize Treatment of Charles Sumner," *The Massachusetts Review*, Vol. 2, No. 4 (Summer 1961), pp. 749–769; and Louis Ruchames's "Charles Sumner and American Historiography," *The Journal of Negro History*, Vol. 38, No. 2 (April 1953), pp. 139–160. In these articles, Ruchames accuses Sumner biographer David Donald and prior historians of giving too much weight to Sumner's arrogance, insensitivity, and egotism while failing to recognize and highlight his moral courage, integrity, and dedication. I concur with Ruchames's conclusion.

Books

The most comprehensive "modern" biography on Sumner is the two-volume work by David Herbert Donald. This work includes: *Charles Sumner and the Coming of the Civil War* (Chicago: University of Chicago Press, 1960), which covers his early life, coming of age, first election, and caning; and *Charles Sumner and the Rights of Man* (New York: Alfred A. Knopf, 1970), which covers Sumner during the Civil War, Reconstruction, and afterward. My book is the first full treatment of Sumner since Donald's second volume.

The only biographical work in between is a short book by Frederick J. Blue entitled *Charles Sumner and the Conscience of the North*, written as part of the American Biographical History Series (Arlington Heights, Ill.: Harlan Davidson, Inc., 1994). Prior to Donald and Blue, the last full biography on Sumner was written in 1910—fifty years before Donald's book—by Walter G. Shotwell and titled *Life of Charles Sumner* (New York: Thomas Y. Crowell & Company).

My 2012 book, *The Caning: The Assault That Drove America to Civil War* (Yardley, Penn.: Westholme), provides a limited biographical look at Sumner for the years up to the 1856 attack by Preston Brooks.

Before Shotwell, several early biographies of Sumner were published. From the most recent, these were: George H. Haynes's 1909 book *Charles Sumner*, part of American Crisis Biographies (Philadelphia: George W. Jacobs & Company); Sumner's secretary Moorfield Storey's 1900 volume, *Charles Sumner: American Statesman* (Boston and New York: Houghton Mifflin Company); and two books published upon his death in 1874: Jeremiah Chaplin's and J. D. Chaplin's *Life of Charles Sumner* (Boston: D. Lothrop & Co.); and Elias Nason's *The Life and Times of Charles Sumner: His Boyhood, Education, and Public Career* (Boston: B.B. Russell Publishers).

The *Pearl* Attempted Slave Escape and the Sarah Roberts Case

In addition to the sources that follow, much of the narrative for these events was drawn from Sumner's letters.

PRIMARY SOURCES

The best account of the dramatic *Pearl* episode is recounted colorfully and in detail in the *Personal Memoirs of Daniel Drayton, for Four Years and Four Months a Prisoner (For Charity's Sake) in Washington Jail Including a Narrative of the Voyage and Capture of the Schooner Pearl* (Boston: Bela Marsh; New York: American and Foreign Anti-Slavery Society, 1854). The captain's memoir explains Sumner's contribution to Drayton's release and is available as a PDF at the Library of Congress: https://tile.loc.gov/storage-services/service/ll/llst/008/008.pdf.

Harriett Beecher Stowe describes the *Pearl* incident that partly inspired her internationally acclaimed *Uncle Tom's Cabin* in her *A Key to Uncle Tom's Cabin: Presenting the Original Facts and Documents Upon Which the Story Is Founded, Together with Corroborative Statements Verifying the Truth of the Work* (Boston:

John P. Jewett & Co., 1853). Part 2, Chapter 6 describes, in Stowe's own words, the *Pearl* incident and the Edmondson family.

Frederick Douglass and M. R. Delaney comment on the *Pearl* incident in several issues of *The North Star*, an African American newspaper that was published between December 1847 and April 1851. Relevant excerpts run approximately from late April 1848 (just after the *Pearl* episode occurred) to June 1849.

For the decision that set up the *Roberts* appeal, see Boston City Document, No. 23, *Report to the Primary School Committee on the Petition of Sundry Colored Persons for the Abolition of the Schools for Colored Children, with the City Solicitor's Opinion,* dated June 15, 1846 (Boston: J. H. Eastburn, City Printer).

For the decision against Sarah by the Lemuel Shaw Supreme Judicial Court, see *Sarah C. Roberts v. The City of Boston, November term, 1849; 59 Mass. 198, Cush. 198,* accessible here: https://cite.case.law/mass/59/198/. Chief Justice Lemuel Shaw's opinion, delivered in the March 1850 term, can be found at the same location.

The Robert Morris Papers are housed at the Boston Athenaeum and offer a look at the lawyer's life and legal cases; they can be accessed at https://cdm .bostonathenaeum.org/digital/collection/p16057coll56.

It is worth noting that Sumner's brilliant speech *"Equality Before the Law; Unconstitutionality of Separate Colored Schools in Massachusetts"—argument of Charles Sumner, Esq., Before the Supreme Court of Massachusetts in the Case of Sarah C. Roberts vs. The City of Boston, December 4, 1849* can be found not only in his *Works* but also in numerous repositories around the country, including the Library of Congress. It is easily accessed here: https://archive.org/details /equalitybeforela00sumn/page/n1/mode/2up.

SECONDARY SOURCES
Unpublished Works
Mary Sarah Bilder and Laurel Davis's "The Library of Robert Morris, Antebellum Civil Rights Lawyer and Activist" (Boston College Law School Research Paper 536, June 24, 2020), provides a look at the *Roberts* case and many of Morris's other cases, as well as his philosophy on family, faith, and citizenship.

Articles, Essays, and Periodicals
Several newspapers covered the story of the near escape by Washington, D.C., slaves aboard the *Pearl* (the *Boston Daily Bee* and the *Examiner* of Louisville, Kentucky, were just two examples). In addition, the following articles were useful in my efforts to reconstruct the event:

John H. Paynter's "The Fugitives of the *Pearl*," in *The Journal of Negro His-*

tory, Vol. 1, No 3 (July 1916), offers a fine summary of the event sixty-eight years after it occurred.

An outstanding recap of the event appears in Stanley C. Harrold, Jr.'s "The *Pearl* Affair: The Washington Riot of 1848," in *Records of the Columbia Historical Society*, Washington, D.C., Vol. 50, 1980, pp. 140–160.

Mary Kay Ricks wrote an excellent article in the *Washington Post* on August 12, 1998, 150 years after the *Pearl* incident, entitled "Escape on the *Pearl*," which she expanded to a book a decade later (see below).

Erin Blakemore recounted the *Pearl* incident in an August 23, 2017, History .com article entitled "The Largest Attempted Slave Escape in American History," which included the tagline, "The failed escape attempt inspired *Uncle Tom's Cabin*."

Thomas J. Fleming authored an article, "The Flight of the *Pearl*," in *American Legacy* (Summer 2000 issue).

One of the best analyses of Sumner's argument and speech in the *Roberts* case was provided by Arthur Burr Darling in his piece "Prior to Little Rock in American Education: The 'Roberts' Case of 1849–1850," in *Proceedings of the Massachusetts Historical Society*, Third Series, Vol. 72 (October 1957–December 1960), pp. 126–142.

James Oliver Horton and Michele Gates Moresi did an effective job of comparing eras and related cases in "'Roberts,' 'Plessy,' and 'Brown': The Long, Hard Struggle Against Segregation," in the *Organization of American Historians' Magazine of History*, Vol. 15, No. 2, "Desegregation" (Winter, 2011), pp. 14–16. Leonard V. Levy and Harlan B. Philips offered a more thorough treatment in "The *Roberts* Case: Source of the 'Separate but Equal' Doctrine," in *The American Historical Review*, Vol. 56, No. 3 (April 1951), pp. 510–518 (note that this article was published before *Brown v. Board of Education*).

A nice summary of *Roberts* was entitled "A Century Before Brown v. Board of Education: In 1849, a Young Black Girl Challenged the Separate but Equal Doctrine" (author not stated), in *The Journal of Blacks in Higher Education*, No. 18 (Winter 1997–1998), p. 138.

Books

Historian Don E. Fehrenbacher offers a shrewd analysis of the *Pearl* affair in *The Slaveholding Republic: An Account of the United States Government's Relation to Slavery* (New York: Oxford University Press, 2001). He does so in Chapter 3, entitled "Slavery in the National Capital."

As mentioned above, a decade after her article in the *Washington Post*, Mary

Kay Ricks wrote her book *Escape on the Pearl: The Heroic Bid for Freedom on the Underground Railroad* (New York: HarperCollins, 2008).

An outstanding full treatment of the Roberts case was Stephen Kendrick's and Paul Kendrick's *Sarah's Long Walk: The Free Blacks of Boston and How Their Struggle for Equality Changed America* (Boston: Beacon Press, 2004).

Other works consulted include Richard Kluger's 1975 work *Simple Justice: The History of* Brown v. Board of Education *and Black America's Struggle for Equality* (New York: Random House), and Stanley Schultz's 1973 book, *The Culture Factory: Boston Public Schools, 1798–1860* (New York: Oxford University Press).

The Caning of Charles Sumner

In the interest of space, I have truncated this section of the Bibliographic Essay to include just a few key primary sources. For a full list of sources on the caning of Charles Sumner by South Carolina congressman Preston Brooks, please see my own previously mentioned 2012 book: *The Caning: The Assault That Drove America to Civil War.* Alternatively, readers can email me and request the full bibliography for this section at spuleo@aol.com.

KEY PRIMARY SOURCES

The entire episode, including testimony of the House of Representatives investigation; follow-up speeches from lawmakers; testimony from Sumner, Preston Brooks, and other witnesses; and the Brooks expulsion hearing, is contained in the *Congressional Globe.* A wealth of information is included in the *Alleged Assault upon Senator Sumner* (House Report, No. 182, 34th Congress, 1st Session, 1856), and extensive additional information appears in the appendix and other places within the *Congressional Globe.*

In addition, the *Journal of the House of Representatives* (July 15, 1856) contains the resolution calling for Brooks's ouster and outlines the arguments regarding his actions.

I also examined the U.S. Senate report from the "Select Committee appointed to inquire into the circumstances attending the assault committed upon the person of Hon. Charles Sumner, a member of the Senate" in *The Reports of the Committees of the Senate of the United States* (First Session of the 34th Congress, 1855–1856).

Much of the material on Brooks (including his funeral) can be found in his papers at the University of South Carolina in Columbia—specific citations are mentioned in *The Caning.*

Kansas and John Brown

Scores of Charles Sumner's letters and multiple pages in the *Congressional Globe* deal with the debate about Kansas and with John Brown—both Brown's murderous rampage in Kansas and his raid on Harpers Ferry.

PRIMARY SOURCES

There was rich and valuable information on the dire situation in territorial Kansas at www.territorialKansasonline.org, which contained diaries, letters, legislative proceedings, and other primary sources. That site was "retired" in January 2022, but an archives is available here: https://web.archive.org/web /20210511225228/https://territorialkansasonline.ku.edu/index.php.

In addition, the Assumption College E Pluribus Unum Project, a collection of documents and analyses of three American decades (1770s, 1850s, 1920s), contained some excellent primary sources that helped analyze the situation in Kansas. Though the project is now retired, I accessed this collection frequently at http://www1.assumption.edu/ahc/ (which is the project's "cover page").

Similarly, there is a fine collection of sources, including affidavits and testimony from the families of John Brown's murder victims in Pottawatomie, at West Virginia's online Archives and History site: www.wvculture.org /history.

Senator Stephen Douglas's committee's lengthy report (March 1856) relative to the "Affairs of Kansas" is available in the *Congressional Globe* (34th Congress, 1st Session).

SECONDARY SOURCES

Unpublished Works

For an interesting and well-researched look at the relocation of New Englanders to Kansas Territory, I found helpful Tracee M. Murphy's history master's thesis, "The New England Emigrant Aid Company: Its Impact on Territorial Kansas, 1854–1857" (Youngstown State University, 1999).

Articles, Essays, Periodicals

Of the plethora of articles on John Brown and Kansas, I found the following particularly helpful.

Stanley Harold's "Border Wars," in *North & South*, Vol. 12 (January 2011), pp. 22–31.

Tony Horwitz's "Why John Brown Still Scares Us," in *American History* (December 2011), pp. 38–45.

Douglas O. Linder's "The Trial of John Brown: A Commentary," in Univer-

sity of Missouri at Kansas City online faculty projects at https://irlaw.umkc.edu
/popular_media/78/.

Gunja SenGupta's "Bleeding Kansas," in *Kansas History* (Kansas Historical
Society), Vol. 24, No. 4 (Winter 2001–2002), pp. 318–341.

Marvin Stottlemire's "John Brown: Madman or Martyr?" in *Brown Quarterly*, Vol. 3, No. 3 (Winter 2000), http://brownvboard.org.

Books

Virtually every book about the run-up to the Civil War deals with the Kansas
issue and with John Brown—I have listed many of these in other sections of this
essay.

Two that deal specifically with Brown that I found invaluable were: Tony
Horwitz's *Midnight Rising: John Brown and the Raid That Sparked the Civil War*
(New York: Henry Holt, 2011), which focuses on Harpers Ferry; and David S.
Reynolds's excellent biography, *John Brown: Abolitionist* (New York: Alfred A
Knopf, 2005).

The *Dred Scott* Decision and the Emergence and Growth
of the Republican Party

PRIMARY SOURCES

A wonderful digital collection of primary sources in the *Dred Scott* case is available from Washington University in St. Louis, entitled *The Revised Dred Scott
Case Collection*. The collection contains more than 110 documents and is fully text
searchable. I accessed it at https://libguides.wustl.edu/c.php?g=47391&p=303604.

For a document that straddles the line between a primary and secondary
source, see Samuel Tyler's *Memoir of Roger Brooke Taney, LL.D.* (Baltimore: John
Murphy & Co.), an 1872 account that contains numerous primary sources, including letters to and from Taney, bridged by Tyler's narrative.

For a fine collection on the growth of the Republican Party, see *Proceedings of
the First Three Republican National Conventions of 1856, 1860, and 1864, including
proceedings of the antecedent national convention held at Pittsburg [sic], in February, 1856, as reported by Horace Greeley* (Minneapolis: Charles Johnson, 1893).

For a wide range of primary sources, opinion pieces, and letters, see the contemporaneous *The Republican Scrap Book: containing the platforms, and a choice
selection of extracts, setting forth the real questions in issue, the opinions of the
candidates, the nature and designs of the slave oligarchy, as shown by their own*

writers, and the opinions of Clay, Webster, Josiah Quincy, and other patriots, on slavery and its extension (Boston: John P. Jewett & Co., 1856).

I also made use of the University of Pennsylvania's Schoenberg Center for Electronic Text and Image collection entitled: *The Crisis of the Union: Causes, Conduct and Consequences of the U.S. Civil War,* available at https://web.archive .org/web/20220426022516/http://sceti.library.upenn.edu/sceti/civilwar/index .cfm.

SECONDARY SOURCES
Articles, Essays, Periodicals
For the Dred Scott portions of the book, see James McPherson's "Politics and Judicial Responsibility: *Dred Scott v. Sandford,*" in Robert P. George, ed., *Great Cases in Constitutional Law* (Princeton, N.J.: Princeton University Press, 2000), pp. 90–93; Cass R. Sunstein's "*Dred Scott v. Sandford* and Its Legacy," in Robert P. George, ed., *Great Cases in Constitutional Law* (Princeton, N.J.: Princeton University Press, 2000), pp. 63–89; and Sally Denton's "Frémont Steals California," *American Heritage,* Vol. 60, No. 4 (Winter 2011), pp. 30–39.

For the emergence and growth of the Republican Party, see Don E. Fehrenbacher's "The Republican Decision at Chicago," in Norman A. Graebner, ed., *Politics and the Crisis of 1860* (Urbana: University of Illinois Press, 1961); and Fehrenbacher's "Comment on Why the Republican Party Came to Power," in George H. Knoles, ed., *The Crisis of the Union, 1860–1861* (Baton Rouge: Louisiana State University Press, 1965).

Also, William Gienapp's "Formation of the Republican Party," in L. Sandy Maisel and William G. Shade, eds., *Parties and Politics in American History* (New York: Garland Publishing, 1994), pp. 59–81; and Gienapp's "The Crime Against Sumner: The Caning of Charles Sumner and the Rise of the Republican Party," in *Civil War History* (September 1979), pp. 218–245.

Books
For *Dred Scott,* Don E. Fehrenbacher's *The Dred Scott Case: Its Significance in American Law and Politics* (New York: Oxford University Press, 1978), is an excellent analysis of the major constitutional questions this landmark case sparked.

Also, see Mark A. Graber's *Dred Scott and the Problem of Constitutional Evil* (Cambridge, England: Cambridge University Press, 2006); Walker Lewis's *Without Fear or Favor: A Biography of Chief Justice Roger Brooke Taney* (Boston: Houghton Mifflin, 1965), a largely sympathetic work of the man whose career and historical legacy was defined by *Dred Scott*; Corinne J. Naden's and Rose

Blue's *Dred Scott: Person or Property?* (New York: Benchmark Books, 2005); and Charles W. Smith, Jr.'s *Roger B. Taney: Jacksonian Jurist* (Chapel Hill: University of North Carolina Press, 1936).

For the Republican Party's growth, see William E. Baringer's *Lincoln's Rise to Power* (Boston: Little Brown, 1937); Andrew Wallace Crandall's *The Early History of the Republican Party, 1854–1856* (Boston: Gorham Press, 1930); and Eric Foner's *Free Soil, Free Labor, Free Men: The Ideology of the Republican Party Before the Civil War* (New York: Oxford University Press, 1970).

Abolitionists, Secession, Slavery, and the Run-up to the Civil War

These topics are covered in detail in several of the sources I've already cited. This section includes additional documents that I examined in connection with this topical heading.

PRIMARY SOURCES

For Daniel Webster's famous March 7, 1850, speech on the Fugitive Slave Law, and several responses, see the appendix to the *Congressional Globe*, beginning on page 269. I also referred to two handbills that helped crystallize the debate and provide context for Sumner's viscerally negative reaction to Webster. The first, published in May of 1850 by Gideon and Co. in Washington, D.C., was titled *Letter from Citizens of Newburyport, Mass., to Mr. Webster in Relation to His Speech Delivered in the Senate of the United States on the 7th of March, 1850, and Mr. Webster's Reply.* The second, published in August 1850, also by Gideon and Co., was entitled *Correspondence Between Mr. Webster and His New Hampshire Neighbors.*

For a comprehensive look at the depth of the opposition to the Fugitive Slave Law in Sumner's hometown of Boston, see the nineteen-page Massachusetts Senate Report No. 51 (March 24, 1851), titled *Joint Special Committee on So Much of the Governor's Address as Relates to Slavery and on Petitions Praying to the Legislators to Instruct Their Senators and to Request Representatives in Congress to Endeavor to Procure a Repeal of the Fugitive Slave Law.*

For a powerful overview of the Fugitive Slave Law and the Thomas Sims case, see the collection of writings from Thomas Wentworth Higginson, edited by Howard N. Meyer, titled *The Magnificent Activist: The Writings of Thomas Wentworth Higginson, 1823–1911* (New York: Da Capo Press, 2000). In addition, see *Massachusetts Senate Document No. 89*, April 9, 1851, for an in-the-moment account of Sims's capture and confinement just days after his arrest.

For more about the abolitionist movement and slavery, I made use of the *Frederick Douglass Papers*, many of which are online from the Library of Con-

gress at https://www.loc.gov/collections/frederick-douglass-papers/about-this
-collection/. In addition, numerous writings, speeches, and illustrations of notable abolitionists and other antislavery champions are available at the Massachusetts Historical Society's *Images of the Anti-slavery Movement in Massachusetts*
at https://www.masshist.org/features/abolition. I accessed both sites to immerse
myself in Charles Sumner's world.

For the secession crisis, I relied on a number of primary sources, including
*The War of the Rebellion: A Compilation of the Official Records of the Union and
Confederate Armies* (Washington, D.C., 1880–1902), available through the Cornell University Making of America series at http://ebooks.library.cornell.edu/m
/moawar/waro.html. Also, see Yale Law School's Lillian Goldman Law Library's
The Avalon Project: Documents in Law, History and Diplomacy, which includes:
*Confederate States of America: Declaration of Immediate Causes Which Induce
and Justify the Secession of South Carolina from the Federal Union* at http://avalon
.law.yale.edu/19th_century/csa_scarsec.asp.

Also, two illuminating secession documents were included as an appendix to
Charles B. Dew's *Apostles of Disunion: Southern Secession Commissioners and the
Cause of the Civil War* (Charlottesville: University of Virginia Press, 2001). These
included: a speech in pamphlet form titled "Address of Hon. W. L. Harris, Commissioner from the State of Mississippi, Delivered Before the General Assem-
bly of the State of Georgia, on Monday, Dec. 17th, 1860" (Milledgeville, Georgia,
1860); and "Letter of Stephen F. Hale, commissioner from Alabama, to Governor
Beriah Magoffin of Kentucky, Dec. 27, 1860."

SECONDARY SOURCES
Articles, Essays, Periodicals
Countless articles and essays have been written about this broad topic. However,
I relied on the following for direct references and background reading:

Elaine Brooks's "Massachusetts Anti-Slavery Society," in *Journal of Negro
History*, Vol. 30, No. 3 (July 1945), pp. 311–330.

Michael Fellman's "Theodore Parker and the Abolitionist Role in the 1850s,"
in *Journal of American History*, Vol. 61, No. 3 (December 1974), pp. 666–684.

Linck C. Johnson's "Liberty Is Never Cheap: Emerson, the Fugitive Slave Law,
and the Antislavery Lecture Series at the Broadway Tabernacle," in *New England
Quarterly*, Vol. 76 (December 2003), pp. 550–592.

Leonard W. Levy's "Sims' Case: The Fugitive Slave Law in Boston in 1851," in
Journal of Negro History, Vol. 34, No. 1 (January 1950), pp. 39–74.

James W. Loewen's "The First to Secede," in *American Heritage*, Vol. 6, No. 4
(Winter 2011), pp. 13–16.

Jane H. Pease's and William H. Pease's "Confrontation and Abolitionism in the 1850s," in *Journal of American History*, Vol. 58, No. 4 (March 1971), pp. 923–937.

David Von Drehle's "The Civil War 1861–2011: The Way We Weren't," in *Time* (April 18, 2011), pp. 40–51.

Caroline E. Vose's "Jefferson Davis in New England," in *Virginia Quarterly Review* (Autumn 1926), pp. 557–568, accessed February 6, 2012, at http://www .vqronline.org/articles/1926/autumn/vose-jefferson-davis/.

Books

In addition to the books already listed that cover the abolitionist movement, I found helpful Tilden G. Edelstein's *Strange Enthusiasm: A Life of Thomas Wentworth Higginson* (New York: Atheneum, 1970), a work about one of Boston's most militant abolitionists; Louis Filler's *The Crusade Against Slavery, 1830–1860* (New York: Harper & Row, 1960); Henry Mayer's comprehensive and electrifying biography *All on Fire: William Lloyd Garrison and the Abolition of Slavery* (New York: St. Martin's Griffin, 1998); Wendy Hamand Venet's *Neither Ballots nor Bullets: Women Abolitionists and the Civil War* (Charlottesville: University of Virginia Press, 1991); and Albert J. Von Frank's *The Trial of Anthony Burns* (Cambridge, Mass.: Harvard University Press, 1998).

For books focusing on secession, I relied on some outstanding works, including: Shearer Davis Bowman's *At the Precipice: Americans North and South During the Secession Crisis* (Chapel Hill: University of North Carolina Press, 2010); David Detzer's fast-moving *Allegiance: Fort Sumter, Charleston, and the Beginning of the Civil War* (New York: Harcourt, 2001); William W. Freehling's excellent overview, *The Road to Disunion, Vol. 2: Secessionists Triumphant* (New York: Oxford University Press, 2007); and Maury Klein's *Days of Defiance: Sumter, Secession, and the Coming of the Civil War* (New York: Alfred A. Knopf, 1997).

I was also assisted immeasurably by comprehensive works that focused specifically on slavery. These included: John W. Blassingame's *Slave Community: Plantation Life in the Antebellum South* (New York: Oxford University Press, 1972), which discusses the rich cultural and family life that many slaves deliberately kept hidden from their masters; David Brion Davis's excellent *Inhuman Bondage: The Rise and Fall of Slavery in the New World* (New York: Oxford University Press, 2006); Anne Farrow, Joel Lang, and Jennifer Frank's *Complicity: How the North Promoted, Prolonged, and Profited from Slavery* (New York: Ballantine Books, 2005); and Eugene D. Genovese's classic and exhaustive analysis of slavery, *Roll, Jordan, Roll: The World the Slaves Made* (New York: Random House, 1972).

Works by some of America's best historians provided me with insights on the run-up to the Civil War. These works included Bruce Catton's *The Coming Fury* (New York: Doubleday & Company, 1961); Catton's *This Hallowed Ground: The Story of the Union Side of the Civil War* (New York: Doubleday & Company, 1955), William Catton's and Bruce Catton's *Two Roads to Sumter* (New York: McGraw Hill, 1963); and Avery Craven's *The Coming of the Civil War* (Chicago: University of Chicago Press, 1942). Also, David Donald followed his classic (and critical) Sumner biography with a more balanced biography years later of the sixteenth President, simply titled *Lincoln* (New York: Simon & Schuster, 1995).

Ernest B. Furgurson details the chaos in the nation's capital during the war in *Freedom Rising: Washington in the Civil War* (New York: Alfred A. Knopf, 2004). I also found invaluable Constance McLaughlin Green's *Washington: Village and Capital, 1800–1878* (Princeton, N.J.: Princeton University Press, 1962), to get a feel for life and conditions in D.C. during Sumner's time.

It is hard to imagine learning about the causes of the Civil War (or the war itself) without consulting James M. McPherson's one-volume masterpiece, *Battle Cry of Freedom: The Civil War Era* (New York: Oxford University Press, 1988). Nor is it possible to overlook Allan Nevins's *The Emergence of Lincoln* (New York: Charles Scribner's Sons, 1950), and his two-volume *Ordeal of the Union* epic: *Fruits of Manifest Destiny, 1847–1852* and *A House Dividing, 1852–1857* (both New York: Charles Scribner's Sons, 1947).

For other fine and important books on the national run-up to war, see David M. Potter, *The Impending Crisis, 1848–1861* (New York: Harper & Row, 1976); Kenneth M. Stampp, *America in 1857: A Nation on the Brink* (New York: Oxford University Press, 1990); Stampp, *The Imperiled Union: Essays on the Background of the Civil War* (New York: Oxford University Press, 1980); and Erich H. Walther, *The Shattering of the Union: America in the 1850s* (Wilmington, Del.: Scholarly Resources, 2004).

Lincoln, the War Years, and the Lincoln Assassination

Again, these topics are covered in great detail in several of the primary sources I've already cited (Sumner papers, Lincoln papers, papers of Lincoln' cabinet members, etc.).

PRIMARY SOURCES

The *John G. Nicolay Papers* at the Library of Congress consist of fifty-five hundred items (more than fourteen thousand images) of the papers of Lincoln's secretary and biographer. It can be accessed here: https://www.loc.gov/collections/john-g -nicolay-papers/about-this-collection/.

Tyler Dennett edited a volume published in 1939 entitled *Lincoln and the Civil War in the Diaries and Letters of John Hay*, which provides interesting observations from Lincoln's other secretary, primarily on events through the Civil War years and Reconstruction (New York: Dodd, Mead & Company). I include it in the "primary sources" section because of the amount of firsthand material from Hay.

Hay and Nicolay produced an iconic ten-volume biography on their boss, entitled *Abraham Lincoln: A History* (New York: The Century Co., 1914), which includes firsthand quotes from Lincoln, letters, etc. The work is an up-close account of Lincoln and the nation in the Civil War.

In similar fashion, I include in this section Frederick Seward's book on his father, William Seward, *Seward at Washington, as Senator and Secretary of State: A Memoir of His Life, with Selections from His Letters, 1846–1861* (New York: Derby and Miller, 1891), because of the volume of primary source material included. Frederick Seward also offers a powerful firsthand account on the assassination attempt at his house on the night of April 14, 1865.

In 1949, Norma B. Cuthbert edited a volume based almost entirely on primary sources focusing on the plot to kill President Lincoln as he made his way to Washington in 1861 for his first inauguration—*Lincoln and the Baltimore Plot, 1861: From Pinkerton Records and Related Papers* (San Marino, Calif.: The Huntington Library). The volume collects and collates the key sources relating to the conspiracy, mostly Pinkerton records and other letters.

Sumner's other personal secretary, Moorfield Storey, described the night of Lincoln's assassination during a February 1868 dinner hosted by Sumner, which included Edwin M. Stanton and Charles Dickens. His account was reprinted in "Dickens, Stanton, Sumner, and Storey," published in *The Atlantic Monthly* (1857–1932; April 1930), pp. 463–465.

Virtually every topic in this biography is covered in the *Congressional Globe* and Sumner's papers, but it is worth calling out that the "Prayer of One Hundred Thousand" petition brought to the Senate floor in 1864 is described in a rich and colorful way.

A fascinating step-by-step account of the 1865 assassination conspiracy against Lincoln, Seward, and others was delivered during the trial of the conspirators and published in *Argument of John A. Bingham, Special Judge Advocate, in Reply to the Arguments of the Several Counsel for Mary E. Surratt, David E. Herold, Lewis Payne, George A. Atzerodt, Michael O'Laughlin, Samuel A. Mudd, Edward Spangler, and Samuel Arnold, Charged with Conspiracy and the Murder of Abraham Lincoln, Late President of the United States* (Washington, D.C.: Government Printing Office, 1865). The document can be accessed and downloaded from the Cornell University Library's digital collection at https://digital.library .cornell.edu/catalog/sat2606.

SECONDARY SOURCES

Articles, Essays, Periodicals

In addition to sources already cited, these articles and essays assisted me in the preparation of this section:

No author listed, "The Baltimore Plot to Assassinate Abraham Lincoln," in *Harper's New Monthly Magazine*, Vol. 37, No. 244 (June 1868), pp. 123–128.

No author listed, "Four Lincoln Conspiracies: Including New Particulars of the Flight and Capture of the Assassins," *The Century Illustrated Monthly Magazine*, Vol. 51 (November 1895–April 1896), pp. 889–894.

Henry Adams provides a strong analysis of the British position and includes key letters from British officials in "Why Did Not England Recognize the Confederacy?" included in *Proceedings of the Massachusetts Historical Society*, Third Series, Vol. 66 (October 1936–May 1941), pp. 204–222.

Historian Edward Ayers adapted a keynote address delivered in 2011 at the 150th anniversary of the Battle of Bull Run (First Manassas) at the Manassas Battlefield Park in Virginia in "The Meaning of Bull Run," published in the *New York Times* on July 24, 2011.

Nicholas Basbanes looks at death, including Fanny Appleton's and the death of the Longfellows' daughter, in "A Beautiful Ending: On Dying and Heaven in the Time of Longfellow," in *Humanities*, Vol. 41, No. 3 (Summer 2020), which can be accessed here: https://www.neh.gov/article/beautiful-ending.

Lincoln historian Michael Burlingame wrote an analysis of Lincoln's elections of 1860 and 1864 for the Miller Center at the University of Virginia titled "Abraham Lincoln: Campaigns and Elections" (undated), which can be accessed here: https://millercenter.org/president/lincoln/campaigns-and-elections.

Bradley Gottfried writes a powerful analysis on how Bull Run (First Manassas) impacted both North and South in "An End to Innocence: The First Battle of Manassas," published by the *American Battlefield Trust* in Spring 2011 and accessible here: https://www.battlefields.org/learn/articles/end-innocence.

For a well-researched and well-written piece on Abraham Lincoln's evolutionary thinking on the subject of emancipation, see "The Shifting Attitudes Toward Abraham Lincoln and Emancipation," in the *Journal of the Abraham Lincoln Association*, Vol. 34, No. 1 (Winter 2013), pp. 18–39.

Books

Most of the books I've already listed in this essay cover some of the topics in this section. In addition, I found these works helpful (in alphabetical order by author):

Edward Achorn's *Every Drop of Blood: The Momentous Second Inauguration of Abraham Lincoln* (New York: Atlantic Monthly Press, 2020); contemporaneous journalist Noah Brooks's *Washington in Lincoln's Time* (New York: The Century Co., 1895), which offers a rich description of the nation's capital during the Lincoln administration; Adam Goodheart's *1861: The Civil War Awakening* (New York: Vintage Books, 2011); and S. G. Gwynne's outstanding *Hymns of the Republic: The Story of the Final Year of the American Civil War* (New York: Scribner, 2019).

Also, Thomas Wentworth Higginson's *Henry Wadsworth Longfellow* (Boston and New York: Houghton, Mifflin, and Company, 1902); Margaret Leach's classic *Reveille in Washington, 1860–1865* (New York: Harper & Row, 1969); John Matteson's riveting *A Worse Place Than Hell: How the Civil War Battle of Fredericksburg Changed a Nation* (New York: W. W. Norton, 2021); Brad Meltzer's and Josh Mensch's *The Lincoln Conspiracy: The Secret Plot to Kill America's 16th President— and Why It Failed* (New York: Flatiron Books, 2020); and Stephen B. Oates's *With Malice Toward None: The Life of Abraham Lincoln* (New York: Harper & Row, 1977).

Also, David Ryan's excellent *Four Days in 1865: The Fall of Richmond* (Richmond: Cadmus Communications Corporation, 1993); James L. Swanson's vivid recount and juxtaposition of Lincoln's funeral and Jefferson Davis's efforts to flee Union troops in *Bloody Crimes: The Funeral of Abraham Lincoln and the Chase for Jefferson Davis* (New York: HarperCollins, 2010); Noah Andre Trudeau's *Lincoln's Greatest Journey: Sixteen Days That Changed a Presidency, March 24–April 8, 1865* (El Dorado Hills, Calif.: Savas Beatie LLC, 2016); Ted Widmer's compelling account of Lincoln's trip from Springfield to Washington to begin his presidency in *Lincoln on the Verge: Thirteen Days to Washington* (New York: Simon & Schuster, 2020); and Jay Winik's splendid *April 1865: The Month That Saved America* (New York: HarperCollins, 2001).

Reconstruction and the Impeachment of Andrew Johnson

Vast amounts of material on these topics are included in the papers already cited (Sumner's papers, Grant's memoirs, the *Congressional Globe*, among others). Here are additional sources I found helpful:

PRIMARY SOURCES

Carl Schurz's exhaustive examination on end-of-war conditions in the South for freedmen can be found in his *Report on the Condition of the South*, 39th

Congress, Senate, Ex. Doc. 1st Session, No. 2 (1865). The document is full of firsthand accounts from virtually every Southern state and is indispensable in understanding the hardships faced by freedmen after fighting ended.

A marvelous collection of documents is available at *The Freedmen's Bureau Online: Records of the Bureau of Refugees, Freedmen, and Abandoned Lands*, available at https://www.freedmensbureau.com/. I made use of many reports at this site, including: *Records of the Assistant Commissioner for the State of Tennessee,* "Reports of Outrages, Riots, and Murders, January 15, 1866–August 12, 1868," and similar reports for Texas, Georgia, and Louisiana; eyewitness statements and affidavits on violence in the South; and onerous laws and statutes from many states imposed upon freedmen that restricted their movements, ability to work, and places where they were allowed to settle.

The Library of Congress has compiled numerous documents related to the Civil War and Reconstruction, including the three Reconstruction amendments, which can be accessed here: https://www.loc.gov/rr/program/bib/ourdocs/civilwarrecon .html.

A good way to understand the tone and tenor of the Senate on the Andrew Johnson impeachment debate is to review the *Supplement to the Congressional Globe Containing the Proceedings of the Senate Sitting for the Trial of Andrew Johnson, President of the United States, Fortieth Congress Second Session* (Washington City: F&J Rives & George A. Bailey, Reporters and Printers of the Debates of Congress, 1868). It can be found through the Library of Congress here: https://memory.loc.gov/ammem/amlaw/lwcg-imp.html. The page also includes important background aspects of the impeachment trial and the process in general, as well as links to numerous academic institutions and archives that provide more information on this topic.

For more on Andrew Johnson, see *The Papers of Andrew Johnson*, 1808–75, edited by Leroy P. Graf, Ralph W. Haskins, and Paul H. Bergeron (1967–2000).

The exhaustive weekly coverage by *Harper's Weekly* of the impeachment proceedings, which includes columns, news stories, speeches, letters, and editorial/opinion pieces, can be found here: https://www.impeach-andrewjohnson .com/.

Elizabeth Cady Stanton, Susan B. Anthony, and Matilda Joslyn Gage edited a three-volume work entitled *History of Woman Suffrage* (Rochester, N.Y.: Charles Mann, 1887). Each book is full of letters, documents, and other primary sources, which is why I include it in this section. I made particular use of Volume 2, which covers the years 1861–76, to research the debate over the Fifteenth Amendment.

SECONDARY SOURCES

Articles, Essays, Periodicals

Historian and previous Sumner biographer David Herbert Donald offers an interesting analysis in "Why They Impeached Andrew Johnson," in *American Heritage,* Vol. 8, No. 1 (December 1956), which can be accessed here: https://www.americanheritage.com/why-they-impeached-andrew-johnson.

The Fourteenth Amendment debate and the South's overall attitudes and reactions were analyzed shrewdly by Joseph B. James in "Southern Reaction to the Proposal of the Fourteenth Amendment," in *The Journal of Southern History,* Vol. 22, No. 4 (November 1956), pp. 477–497.

Joseph H. Mahaffey examines Carl Schurz's letters during his Southern tour in "Carl Schurz's Letters from the South," in *The Georgia Historical Quarterly,* Vol. 35, No. 3 (September 1951), pp. 222–257.

The Freedmen's Bureau and its ability to provide protection for former slaves is discussed by Donald G. Nieman in "Andrew Johnson, the Freedmen's Bureau, and the Problem of Equal Rights, 1865–1866," in *The Journal of Southern History,* Vol. 44, No. 3 (August 1978), pp. 399–420.

Richard A. Primus writes an illuminating piece for the *Harvard Law Review* entitled "The Riddle of Hiram Revels," Vol. 119, No. 6 (2006), pp. 1–52.

For a look at how the discussion of the Fifteenth Amendment divided the women's suffrage movement, see Robert E. Riegel's "The Split of the Feminist Movement in 1869," in *The Mississippi Valley Historical Review,* Vol. 49, No. 3 (December 1962), pp. 485–496.

For an excellent account of the violence faced by freedmen in the reconstructed South, see Jeff Strickland's "The Whole State is on Fire: Criminal Justice and the End of Reconstruction in Upcountry South Carolina," in *Crime, History, and Societies,* Vol. 13, No. 2 (2009), pp. 89–117.

Ryan A. Swanson examines presidential Reconstruction policy in "Andrew Johnson and His Governors: An Examination of Failed Reconstruction Leadership," in the *Tennessee Historical Quarterly,* Vol. 71, No. 1 (Spring 2012), pp. 16–45.

Elizabeth R. Varon analyzes President Andrew Johnson's domestic policies in a piece she wrote for the Miller Center at the University of Virginia entitled "Andrew Johnson: Domestic Affairs" (undated). It can be found here: https://millercenter.org/president/johnson/domestic-affairs.

The Senate Historical Office (no author listed) provides a good summary of Hiram Revels's journey to the Senate in "Hiram Revels: First African American Senator," written in February 2020, and accessible here: https://www.senate.gov/artandhistory/senate-stories/First-African-American-Senator.htm.

Books

In addition to the numerous books already cited, I referred to these books for the topics in this section:

Eric Foner's thorough *Reconstruction: America's Unfinished Revolution, 1863–1877* (New York: Harper & Row, 1988). It is possible to disagree with some of Foner's conclusions while still admiring the depth of his scholarship and research.

A. J. Languth writes a compelling narrative of "what might have been" in his *After Lincoln: How the North Won the Civil War and Lost the Peace* (New York: Simon & Schuster), 2014. The book covers the period immediately after Lincoln's assassination through the Compromise of 1877 and the Jim Crow era beyond.

Historian and Constitution expert David O. Stewart writes about the landmark trial of Andrew Johnson in *Impeached: The Trial of President Andrew Johnson and the Fight for Lincoln's Legacy* (New York: Simon & Schuster, 2010).

The Trent Affair, the *Alabama* Claims, and the Treaty of Washington

These occurred at different periods chronologically, but I decided to group them since they both focus on U.S.-British relations during and after the Civil War. This section contains sources not previously listed.

PRIMARY SOURCES

Charles Sumner delivered two major speeches on these events: "The *Trent* Case and Maritime Rights: Speech in the Senate on the Surrender of Mason and Slidell, Rebel Agents, taken from the British Mail Steamer Trent, January 6, 1862"; and his speech delivered in executive session and published afterward entitled "The *Alabama* Claims: Speech of the Honorable Charles Sumner Delivered in Executive Session of the United States Senate on Tuesday, April 13, 1869 against the Ratification of the Johnson-Clarendon Treaty for the Settlement of the *Alabama* and Other Claims." Both are available in his *Works*, and the 1869 speech was also published in pamphlet form in London and elsewhere.

The *Trent* case, including details on the capture of Mason and Slidell, is recounted in *Official Records of the Union and Confederate Navies in the War of the Rebellion*, Series 2, Vol. 3 (Washington, D.C.), 1922.

The September 1872 decision and report of the international tribunal that decided on the *Alabama* claims award, as dictated by the Treaty of Washington of May 8, 1871, can be found here: https://legal.un.org/riaa/cases/vol_XXIX

/125-134.pdf. The tribunal's decision can also be found in *Papers Relating to the Foreign Relations of the United States, Transmitted to Congress with the Annual Message of the President*, Part 2, Vol. 1 (December 2, 1872).

SECONDARY SOURCES

Articles, Essays, Periodicals

Charles Francis Adams, Jr., provides an invaluable and illuminating look at the first event that nearly drove the United States and England to war in "The Trent Affair: An Historical Retrospect," a paper he prepared for the Massachusetts Historical Society in 1911 and printed in the Society's *Proceedings* in 1912 (Vol. 45, pp. 35–76).

James Phinney Baxter III tackled the subject of the Treaty of Washington for the Massachusetts Historical Society in "The British High Commissioners at Washington in 1871," published in *Proceedings* in June of 1934 (Vol. 65, pp. 334–357).

Tom Bingham examines the legal ramification of the *Alabama* claims in "The *Alabama* Claims Arbitration," in *The International and Comparative Law Quarterly*, Vol. 54, No. 1 (January 2005), pp. 1–25.

Kenneth Bourne digs into the British perspective during the *Trent* Affair in "British Preparations for War with the North, 1861–1862," in *The English Historical Review*, Vol. 76, No. 301 (October 1961), pp. 600–632.

Victor Cohen looks at the *Trent* Affair from the Confederate perspective in "Charles Sumner and the *Trent* Affair," in *The Journal of Southern History*, Vol. 22, No. 2 (May 1956), pp. 205–219.

W. L. Morton examines the difficulty England had controlling Canada and other parts of the Americas in "British North America and a Continent in Dissolution, 1861–1871," in *History*, Vol. 47, No. 160 (1962), pp. 139–156.

Books

Several books already mentioned deal with the *Trent* Affair and the Treaty of Washington. In addition, I highly recommend James Tertius deKay's *The Rebel Raiders: The Astonishing History of the Confederacy's Secret Navy* (New York: Ballantine Books, 2002).

Grant Administration, Sumner's Death, and Beyond

Charles Sumner fully documents in his letters his distaste for and rocky relationship with President Grant, and Grant's frustration with the Massachusetts senator is evident in Grant's papers. The *Congressional Globe* debates on the civil rights bills and the Fifteenth Amendment also convey this tension. Other sources are included here.

PRIMARY SOURCES

Eleven members of the House of Representatives and nine senators spoke eloquently upon Sumner's death, and their remarks were compiled in *Memorial Addresses on the Life and Character of Charles Sumner (a Senator of Massachusetts) Delivered in the Senate and House of Representatives, Forty-Third Congress, First Session, April 27, 1874, with Other Congressional Tributes of Respect* (Washington, D.C.: Government Printing Office, 1874).

Lucius Quintus Cincinnatus Lamar's tribute speech to Sumner after Sumner's death is reprinted in several places. I made use of the version at www.bartleby .com/268/10/6.html, and also of extensive excerpts about Lamar in President John F. Kennedy's *Profiles in Courage* (reprint, New York: Pocket Books, 1961).

Details of Sumner's state funeral in Washington, D.C., are available in *Order of Proceedings for the Funeral of the Hon. Charles Sumner, Late a Senator of the United States from the State of Massachusetts, March 12, 1874*, are accessible from the Library of Congress here: https://www.loc.gov/item/rbpe.0740190a/.

Charles May's eulogy on Sumner, delivered at Kalamazoo College, was printed in *Charles Sumner—A Eulogy, Delivered Before the Faculty and Societies of Kalamazoo College, June 16, 1874* (Kalamazoo, Mich.: *Daily Telegraph* Printing House, 1874).

Sumner's colleague Carl Schurz's eulogy, delivered at the Boston Music Hall on April 29, 1874, is printed in *Eulogy on Charles Sumner by Carl Schurz* (Boston: Lee and Shepard Publishers), 1874.

SECONDARY SOURCES

Unpublished Works

Archibald H. Grimke delivers a positive address on Charles Sumner on the occasion of the centenary of his birth for *The American Negro Academy*, Occasional Papers No. 14 (Washington, D.C.: Published by the Academy, 1911).

Articles, Essays, Periodicals

For an excellent analysis of the election of 1876 and the Compromise of 1877, see Michael Les Benedict's "Southern Democrats in the Crisis of 1876–1877: A Reconsideration of Reunion and Reaction" in *The Journal of Southern History*, Vol. 46, No. 4 (November 1980), pp. 489–524.

Marianne L. Engelman Lado examines the Supreme Court's 1883 decision declaring that the 1875 Civil Rights Act was unconstitutional in "A Question of Justice: African-American Legal Perspectives on the 1883 Civil Rights Cases— Freedom: Constitutional Law," in the *Chicago-Kent Law Review*, Vol. 70, No. 3 (April 1995), pp. 1123–1194.

Ronald B. Jager examines Charles Sumner's final legislative effort in "Charles Sumner, the Constitution, and the Civil Rights Act of 1875," in *The New England Quarterly*, Vol. 42, No. 3 (September 1969), pp. 350–372.

John A. Mayne posits less-than-charitable motives to L. Q. C. Lamar for his historic speech in "L. Q. C. Lamar's 'Eulogy' of Charles Sumner: A Reinterpretation," in *The Historian*, Vol. 22, No. 3 (May 1960), pp. 296–311.

Earl Maltz writes about the subject of separate-and-unequal in "*Brown v. Board of Education* and Originalism," in Robert P. George, ed., *Great Cases in Constitutional Law* (Princeton, N.J.: Princeton University Press), 2000.

Books

For an interesting period look at Lucius Q. C. Lamar, see Edward Mayes's *Lucius Q. C. Lamar: His Life, Time, and Speeches, 1825–1893* (Nashville, Tenn.: Publishing House of the Methodist Episcopal Church, South, 1896).

Much has been written about Ulysses S. Grant, soldier and President. Two works that I relied on for this book were Brooks D. Simpson's *Ulysses S. Grant: Triumph Over Adversity, 1822–1865* (Boston: Houghton Mifflin Company, 2000); and Ronald C. White's excellent biography, *American Ulysses: A Life of Ulysses S. Grant* (New York: Random House, 2016).

For a well-done analysis of the landmark Supreme Court decision that borrowed from Charles Sumner's arguments in *Sarah Roberts*, see James T. Patterson's *Brown v. Board of Education: A Civil Rights Milestone and Its Troubled Legacy* (New York: Oxford University Press, 2001).

Miscellaneous

For a look at the antislavery work that influenced Charles Sumner at a young age, see abolitionist Lydia Maria Child's *An Appeal in Favor of That Class of Americans Called Africans* (Boston: Allen and Ticknor, 1833).

For a good primary source on the John W. Webster–George Parkman murder case that occupied Lemuel Shaw and the Massachusetts Supreme Judicial Court, see *Report of the Case of John W. Webster, Indicted for the Murder of George Parkman Before the Supreme Judicial Court of Massachusetts* (Boston: Little and Brown, 1850). This work contains the entire court transcript, including witness testimonies.

Two books on the Webster-Parkman case are important to examine, both published in the same year. These are Robert Sullivan's *The Disappearance of Dr. Parkman* (Boston: Little, Brown and Company, 1971); and Helen Thomson's *Murder at Harvard* (Boston: Houghton Mifflin Company, 1971).

INDEX

abolition, 2–6, 15
  Bleeding Kansas, 138–51
  Compromise of 1850, 83–87
  Dred Scott v. John F. A. Sandford,
    189–92, 293, 383–84
  Mexican War, 37–42
  Sims case, 98–104
abolitionism of Sumner, 2–6, 11,
    17–19, 32–42, 57–58, 92–95,
    108, 275–76, 286–88
  antislavery education, 14–17
  Burns case, 131–34
  Constitution and, 3, 5, 17, 18–19,
    108, 119–21, 134, 215, 289
  Fugitive Slave Law, 87–88, 91,
    92–93, 105, 108, 111, 115–25
  influence and legacy, 4–8, 401–4
  Kansas-Nebraska Act, 126–31
  Mexican War, 37–42
  Pearl incident, 49–50, 111–14, 115
  Roberts case, 51, 52, 55, 58–77,
    88, 94
  as Senator. *See* Senator of
    Massachusetts
  Sims case, 100, 103–4
  speeches. *See* speeches of Sumner
  Texas annexation, 33–37
  Wilmot Proviso, 41–42, 50
Acorn, 102, 103
Adams, Charles Francis, Jr., 106

Adams, Charles Francis, Sr., 106, 222,
    363
Adams, Henry, 106
Adams, John Quincy, 25, 213
Affairs of Kansas (report), 142–43
Agassiz, Louis, 391
Alabama, 13, 49, 219, 336, 372
Alabama claims, 254–58
Albany, 16
Alcott, Amos Bronson, 124
Alcott, Louisa May, 124
American Anti-Slavery Society, 287,
    290, 381
American Literary, Scientific, and
    Military Academy, 23
American Revolution, 24, 57, 92, 103,
    229, 258
Anderson, Robert, 224–26
Andrew, John, 218, 227, 271, 276, 338
angina pectoris, 195, 349, 388
Anglo-African, 269
annexation of Santo Domingo, 387,
    388
annexation of Texas, 33–37
Anthony, Henry, 397
Anthony, Susan B., 4, 286–87, 380
anti-Catholicism, 57
*Appeal in Favor of That Class of
    Americans Called Africans, An*
    (Child), 15

Appleton, Fanny. *See* Longfellow, Frances Appleton "Fanny"

Appleton, Isabella Mason, 354

Appleton, Nathan, 39, 40, 41

Appomattox Court House, 2, 324–25, 326, 357

Aquia Creek, 185

Argyll, Elizabeth Campbell, Duchess of, 296, 353

Arkansas, 227, 336, 372, 379

Armory Square Hospital, 284

Army of the Potomac, 262, 319, 329

Asperger's syndrome, 26n

Atchison, David, 129, 139

Bacon, John, 98–99

Badger, Edmund, 122

Balfour, Isabella "Bell," 351–52, 353, 358, 362–63

Bancroft, George, 353

Banks, Nathaniel P., 309–10

"Barbarism of Slavery" speech, 205–12, 213–14

Barber, Thomas, 140

Barnes, William, 341

Barnum's City Hotel, 228–29

Bartlett, Sidney, 104

Batchelder, James, 132

Bates, Edward, 253

Battle of Antietam, 273–74

Battle of Atlanta, 299, 302–3

Battle of Ball's Bluff, 248

Battle of Cedar Creek, 304

Battle of Cold Harbor, 304

Battle of First Manassas, 238–42

Battle of Fort Sumter, 224–26, 231, 233, 269

Battle of Fredericksburg, 277

Battle of Gettysburg, 256, 285

Battle of Spotsylvania, 304

Battle of the Wilderness, 304, 318

Battle of Vicksburg, 256, 382

Beacon Hill, 23–24, 53, 54, 70

Beauregard, P. G. T., 225

Beecher, Henry Ward, 199, 390

Bell, Daniel, 45

"better angels of our nature," 223

Bill of Rights, 66, 140, 289

Bismarck, Otto von, 363

"Black Codes," 343–44

"black laws," 140–41

Blaine, James, 388, 399

Blair, Francis P., 167–68

Bleeding Kansas, 138–51, 163, 165–66, 200
  Sumner's "Crime Against Kansas" speech, 145–51, 152, 155, 200

Bleeding Kansas that, 5

"Blind Memo," 300

Booth, John Wilkes, 1–3, 326–27, 328, 330

"border ruffians," 140, 148, 166

Bossuet, Jacques-Bénigne, 27

Boston
  Burns case, 131–34
  Emancipation Proclamation celebrations, 276–77, 279–81
  Roberts case, 51, 52, 55, 58–77
  segregation in, 52–77
  Sims case, 98–104

Boston Advertiser, 96, 281, 395, 400

Boston Atlas, 183

Boston Bar Association, 62

Boston Common, 229

Boston Globe, 400

Boston Herald, 102–3

Boston Music Hall, 277, 332

Boston Primary School Committee, 53–55, 58–60, 66–70, 72–75

Boston School Board, 55, 64

Boston Tea Party, 102

Boyle, Cornelius, 159, 165

Bradley, Joseph P., 402

Brahmins, 56

Brazil, 255, 275–76

Briggs, George N., 89

Bright, John, 252, 253, 254, 330, 335, 353
Britain. *See* Great Britain
Brooks, James, 363
Brooks, Noah, 317
Brooks, Preston
  Bleeding Kansas and, 143–44, 171
  caning of Sumner, 79, 153–59, 164, 192, 194, 388, 394
    aftermath, 171–72, 174, 175, 176, 205, 398
  death of, 184–86
  expulsion resolution, 166, 169–70
  legal proceedings against, 168–69
  Sumner's "Crime Against Kansas" speech, 145, 149, 151, 152
Brown, Albert, 382
Brown, E. P., 140
Brown, George Washington, 141
Brown, John, 141, 163, 199–200
Browning, Orville, 278
Brown-Séquard, Charles-Édouard, 194–95, 196
Brown v. Board of Education, 76, 402–3
Buchanan, James, 181, 185, 187, 192, 202, 218
Burlingame, Anson, 178, 209, 210
Burns, Anthony, 131–34
Burnside, Ambrose, 277
Burnside Bridge, 273–74
Butler, Andrew P., 110, 116, 143–44, 205, 218
  caning of Sumner, 154, 156, 172
  death of, 200
  Sumner's "Crime Against Kansas" speech, 148–52, 155, 200

Calhoun, James, 303
Calhoun, John C., 13, 129, 213, 218, 398
  Compromise of 1850, 83–84

California, 379
  statehood, 82–83, 84
California Gold Rush, 81–82
caning of Sumner, 3–4, 79, 153–59, 398
  aftermath of, 164–80
  background to, 145–52
  convalescence, 164–65, 167–68, 178–80, 186–87, 188–89, 193–98
    Brown-Séquard's treatment, 194–95, 196
  legal proceedings and expulsion resolution of Brooks, 166, 168–70
  politics of, 172–77
  return home to Boston, 178–80
Cape May, New Jersey, 168, 171
Carpenter, Matthew, 390, 394
Cass, Lewis, 50, 150
Chandler, Peleg W., 55–56, 59, 338
Channing, William Ellery, 25
Chaplin, William, 45
Charles River Bridge, 392
Charleston Courier, 196
Charleston Harbor, 224, 226, 246
Charleston Mercury, 217
Chase, Salmon P., 51, 109–10, 127
  Civil War, 274, 322–23, 326
  death of, 391
  Fugitive Slave Law and, 123
  Johnson's impeachment, 368, 370
  Kansas-Nebraska Act, 130
  Lincoln and, 274, 317, 326
  Sumner and, 51, 70, 77, 109–10, 123, 322–23, 326, 339, 348, 353
Chesapeake Bay, 43
Chesnut, James, 208–9, 225–26
Chester, T. Morris, 321–22
Child, Lydia Maria, 15, 390
Christmas Carol, A (Dickens), 366
Churchill, Winston, 7
City Point, Virginia, 319–20, 323

Civil Rights Act of 1883, 389–90, 393,
    394, 400–401
Civil Rights Acts of 1964 and 1965,
    403
Civil War, 224–58, 298–99. *See also*
    specific figures
  Battle of Antietam, 273–74
  Battle of Atlanta, 299, 302–3
  Battle of Cedar Creek, 304
  Battle of First Manassas, 238–42
  Battle of Fort Sumter, 224–26, 231,
    233, 269
  Battle of Fredericksburg, 277
  British treachery, 246–58
    Alabama claims, 254–58
    Trent Affair, 5, 246–54
  Lee's surrender, 2, 324–25, 326
  Lincoln's City Point visit, 320–23
  Lincoln's Independence Day
    address of 1861, 234–37
  secession crisis and prelude to,
    219–20, 221–22
  wounded soldiers, 284–85
Clay, Henry, 13, 83, 84, 110, 218
  Compromise of 1850, 83–84, 110
Clemens, Jeremiah, 122
Cobden, Richard, 250, 252, 253
Cockburn, Alexander, 257
Cole, Cornelius, 378
Colfax, Schuyler, 307, 352, 383,
    384
Colored Troops, U.S., 281, 288, 295,
    315
Comet of 1861, 235
Commonwealth, 106
compensated emancipation x, 84,
    262–70
Compromise of 1850, 83–87, 89, 100,
    130
  Fugitive Slave Law and, 84–88, 89,
    91, 98, 105, 118
Compromise of 1877, 401–3
"Compromise Whigs," 91

Confederate States of America (CSA),
    219, 227, 246–47, 299, 321–22,
    398
Confiscation Acts, 242, 272–75
Congressional Globe, 368
Congressional Joint Committee on
    Reconstruction, 343–44, 357
Conness, John, 326–27
Conscience Whigs, 36, 38, 40–42, 91,
    93
Constitution of Massachusetts, 64–66
Constitution of the United States,
    285. *See also specific amendments*
  abolitionism of Sumner, 3, 5, 17,
    18–19, 108, 119–21, 134, 215, 289
  slavery and, 3, 5, 17, 18–19, 94–95,
    108, 213
Cooper Union Institute, 213–14, 283
Cornfield Harbor, 46
Cotton Whigs, 36, 37, 41, 42, 44, 50,
    89, 91, 96, 102, 107
Craft, William and Ellen, 100
Crawford, Thomas H., 168
Cresson, Pennsylvania, 168, 171
"Crime Against Kansas" speech,
    145–51, 152, 155, 200, 205
Crittenden, John J., 158–59, 218
Cuba, 247, 275–76

Dana, Mary Rosamond, 176
Dana, Richard Henry, 176, 244–45,
    249, 390
Davis, David, 402
Davis, Jefferson, 3, 110, 330, 344, 382,
    398
  Civil War, 224–26, 246–48, 299,
    320–23
Declaration of Independence, 3, 5, 13,
    17, 35, 64–65, 94–95, 119, 215,
    285, 289
Delaware, 231–32, 303, 379
Delaware Canal, 43
Delaware River, 43

Democratic National Convention (1856), 145

Democratic National Convention (1864), 300–301

depression of Sumner, 20, 21, 29, 188

Devens, Charles, 229–30

Dickens, Charles, 366

Diggs, Judson, 45–47

District of Columbia Compensated Emancipation Act of 1862, 266–70

divine law, 92, 121, 274

Dix, Dorothea, 113, 114, 219

Dodge, Augustus C., 122

Dodge, Mary Abigail, 366

Don Quixote (Cervantes), 148–49

Doolittle, James, 264–65

Douglas, Stephen, 122
   Bleeding Kansas, 142–43
   caning of Sumner, 158, 174–75
   Civil War, 226
   election of 1858, 201–2
   election of 1860, 202–3
   Kansas-Nebraska Act, 126–27, 128–31, 143, 148
   Lincoln debates, 201
   Sumner's "Crime Against Kansas" speech, 148–49, 150–51

Douglass, Frederick, 4, 221, 239, 267, 277, 279–80, 389, 393

Downing, George T., 393

Drayton, Daniel, 43–50, 111–14, 115

Dred Scott v. John F. A. Sandford, 189–92, 293, 383–84

Eastburn, Manton, 354

Edgefield, South Carolina, 185, 186

Edmonson, Amelia, 45–47

Edmonson, Paul, 45

Edmonson, Samuel, 45–46

Edmundson, Henry, 153–56, 166, 170

égalité devant la loi, 59–60

election of 1848, 38, 41, 50–51

election of 1851, 9, 89, 90–97, 104–7

election of 1852, 112, 113–14, 127

election of 1854, 128

election of 1856, 163–64, 173–74, 177, 180–81, 211

election of 1857, 182–85

election of 1858, 201–2

election of 1860, 201, 202–4, 213–17
   Sumner's campaign speeches, 213–16

election of 1862, 276

election of 1864, 298–305

election of 1866, 343–44, 347

election of 1868, 372

election of 1869, 373, 374–75

election of 1872, 389

election of 1876, 401–2

Elizabeth, 88

emancipation, 125, 231, 233, 236–40, 242–43, 262–70

Emancipation Proclamation, 5, 272, 274–82, 398

Emerson, John, 189–90

Emerson, Ralph Waldo, 87, 124, 277, 392, 393

Empire State, 290

English, Chester, 43–44

"equality before the law," 6, 59–60, 64, 65–66, 69, 74–77, 94, 290–91

Equality Before the Law (Sumner), 51, 52, 59–60

"equal protection," 6, 74–76, 400

"Equal Rights of All, The" speech, 346–48

Everett, Edward, 217

Faneuil Hall, 33, 130, 275
   death of Sumner, 394–95
   Sumner's speech of 1845, 34–35
   Sumner's speech of 1851, 92–93, 97
   Sumner's speech of 1860, 215–16
   Sumner's speech of 1870, 386
   Whig convention of 1846, 40–41

Fessenden, William, 343–44, 348, 352, 370

Fifth Amendment, 191

Fifteenth Amendment, 375, 376–81

Fillmore, Millard, 42, 89, 92, 97, 100, 103, 112–13, 114, 175

First Amendment, 121

First Battle of Bull Run, 238–42

First Inaugural Address of Lincoln, 222–23

Fish, Hamilton, 353, 379, 387

Fletcher, Richard, 61–62

Florida, 219, 336, 372, 401

Foote, Henry, 110

Ford's Theatre, 1–3, 327

Fort Pillow, 295

Fort Wagner, 295

Fort Washington, 48

Foster, Daniel, 102

Founding Fathers, 3, 18, 119, 213

Fourteenth Amendment, 6, 74–75, 344, 345–49, 357, 372, 376, 383–84

France
  during Civil War, 246–47
  Revolution of 1848, 44
  Sumner's trips to, 16–17, 187, 188, 193–95, 198

"franking," 155

Franklin, Benjamin, 4, 119

Freedmen's Bureau, 296–97, 341, 356–57

"Freedom National; Slavery Sectional," 116–25, 127

Free Soil Party, 42, 50–51, 89, 90, 108, 109–11, 127, 183, 202
  Bleeding Kansas and, 140–41, 142
  election of 1848, 50–51
  election of 1851, 90, 91–97, 105–6

Free-Stater, 140–42

Frémont, John C.
  election of 1856, 164, 173, 175, 178, 180–81, 211
  election of 1864, 298–99

Fugitive Slave Law, 5, 75, 84–88, 89, 92, 98, 133
  repeal efforts, 115–25, 133, 134, 237–38, 294–97
  Sims case, 98, 99, 100, 102–4
  Sumner's anti-Fugitive Slave Law speech, 115–27
  Sumner's motion to repeal, 115–23, 134
  Webster's "Seventh of March" speech (1850), 84–87, 105

Fulton, 187

Gage, Matilda Joslyn, 380

Gardiner, Henry J., 179, 180

Garfield, James A., 381

Garrison, William Lloyd, 15, 17–18, 33, 381
  Brown's execution, 199
  Civil War, 227
  Sumner and, 70, 113, 287, 374–75

Georgia, 219, 336, 372

Gerry, Elbridge, 119

Gettysburg Address, 215, 285–86, 317, 332

Gladstone, William, 188

Gott, Daniel, 50, 150

"gradualism," 281

Grant, Ulysses S., 367
  Civil War, 299, 304, 314
    Lee's surrender, 2, 324–25, 326
    Lincoln visit, 320
  election of 1868, 372
  Lincoln's assassination, 331
  presidency of, 387–88, 389–90, 400
  Sumner and, 387–88, 389–90, 393, 400

Great Britain, 233, 245, 246–58, 266
  Alabama claims, 254–58
  Trent Affair, 5, 246–54

Great Comet of 1861, 235

Great Famine of Ireland, 57

Greeley, Horace, 273, 389

Greenleaf, Simon, 11, 14–15
Grimes, James W., 211
Grimes, Leonard, 331
Gurley, Phineas D., 2
gutta percha, 153–54

Haiti, 266, 272, 387
Hale, John Parker, 110, 123, 127, 318
Hale, Lucy Lambert, 318
Hall, Lydia, 140, 141
Halleck, Henry, 328
Hamilton, Alexander, 4
Harpers Ferry raid, 199–200
Harvard College, 23–24, 56, 62, 63, 392
Harvard Law School, 11, 16, 19, 24–25, 63–64
Harvard Medical College, 71
Hastings, Julia, 27, 29, 30, 109, 271, 283, 350
Hawthorne, Nathaniel, 124
Hay, John, 233–34, 236, 262, 264, 277–78, 312
Hayes, Rutherford B., 401–2
Henderson, John B., 290
Herald of Freedom, 141
Higginson, Thomas Wentworth, 105, 132
Hillard, George, 20, 36, 391
Hoar, George F., 398
Holden, William W., 336
Holmes, Oliver Wendell, 26, 390, 392
Holstein, Friedrich von, 360–63, 365
Hood, John B., 302–3
Hooker, Isabella Beecher, 380
Hooper, Samuel, 351–52, 359–60, 364
House Committee on Territories, 128
Howe, Julia Ward, 26–27, 350, 380
Howe, Samuel Gridley, 26–27, 271
    Sumner and, 26–27, 109
        caning aftermath, 175, 193–94, 195

    letters, 110, 111, 175, 203, 283, 353, 364, 374
Hunter, Robert, 117, 123

Illinois, 181, 189, 191, 232
impotence of Sumner, 363–64, 365
Indiana, 181, 202, 232
interracial marriage, 56–57
Iowa, 111, 287
Irish immigrants, 57

Jackson, Andrew, 13, 33
Jackson, Robert M., 171
James, Henry, 365
James River, 321
Jay, John, 75, 77, 223
Jewett, John P., 124–25
Jim Crow laws, 75, 402
Johnson, A. B., 210, 330
Johnson, Andrew, 345, 347, 349
    Fourteenth Amendment, 345, 347, 349
    Harpers Ferry raid, 200
    impeachment trial of, 5, 367–71
    Lincoln's assassination, 328, 330, 331
    provisional governments, 338, 356–57
    Reconstruction, 344, 345, 354, 355, 356–57, 371
        betrayal, 335–43
    swearing in as vice president, 316
    Tenure of Office Act, 355–56, 365, 367, 368

Kalamazoo College, 397
Kansas. See Bleeding Kansas
Kansas-Nebraska Act, 5, 126–32, 134, 136, 138, 147–48
Keitt, Laurence, 145, 153, 157, 159, 166, 170
Kentucky, 231–32, 303, 379
Key, Francis Scott, 13

King, Martin Luther, 4, 7, 403
Ku Klux Klan, 402

Lafayette Square house, 360, 365–66
Lamar, Lucius Quintus Cincinnatus, 398–400
Lawrence, Amos, 133
Lawrence, Kansas, 140, 141–42, 147, 165
Lecompton, 141, 200
Lecompton Constitution, 200
Lee, Robert E., 199, 227
    surrender of, 2, 324–25, 326
Libby Prison, 322
Liberator, The, 15, 18, 70, 113
Liberia, 266, 272
Lieber, Francis, 15–16, 19, 20, 25, 338, 353, 358
Lincoln, Abraham
    assassination of, 1–3, 326–32
    assassination plot, 221
    "Blind Memo," 300
    caning of Sumner, 163
    Civil War, 2–3, 231–40, 242, 272–74, 277, 298, 301–2, 319–20, 324
        Battle of Fort Sumter, 224–26, 231, 233
        City Point visit, 320–23
        Independence Day address of 1861, 234–37
    compensated emancipation, 263–64, 265–66, 268–69
    Confiscation Acts, 242, 272–75
    Douglas debates, 201
    Dred Scott decision, 191
    election of 1860, 5, 201, 204, 215–17, 218
    election of 1862, 276
    election of 1864, 298–305
    Emancipation Proclamation, 272, 274–82, 398
    first inauguration of, 221–23
    Freedmen's Bureau, 296–97

Fugitive Slave Law, 295–96
Gettysburg Address, 215, 285–86, 317, 332
"Last Public Address" of, 326
"lost speech" of, 163
Reconstruction, 308–12, 323, 325–26
    Louisiana debate, 309–13, 325–26
secession crisis, 219–20, 221–22
second inauguration of, 307, 313, 315–18, 332
Sumner and. See Lincoln, Abraham, and Sumner below
Thirteenth Amendment, 305–6, 313–14, 332
Trent Affair, 251–53, 262
Willie's death, 261–62
Lincoln, Abraham, and Sumner, 3–4, 231–35, 307–9, 312–14
    assassination, 1–3, 326–32
    "Barbarism of Slavery" speech, 211
    City Point visit, 319–20, 323
    Civil War, 231–35, 242, 262, 319–20, 322–23
    Confiscation Acts, 272–73
    election of 1860, 215–16, 218
    election of 1864, 298–99, 302–5
    Emancipation Proclamation, 263–64, 275–76, 278–89
    first inauguration, 222–23
    Fugitive Slave Law, 237
    Independence Day address, 237, 234–35
    Reconstruction, 308–9, 312–14, 325–26
    Richmond visit, 322–23
    secession crisis, 221–23
    second inauguration, 307–8, 313–14, 318
    Trent Affair, 252–53, 262
    Willie's death, 262

Lincoln, Mary Todd, 1–3, 261, 307–8, 320, 322–23, 325, 330, 331, 353
Lincoln, Theodore "Tad," 261
Lincoln, William "Willie," 261–62
Lincoln General Hospital, 284
literacy tests, 378
Livermore, George, 132
Longfellow, Charles "Charley," 28
Longfellow, Edith, 244
Longfellow, Frances Appleton "Fanny," 27, 39–40, 178
    fire and death of, 243–45
Longfellow, Henry Wadsworth, 20, 29–30, 124, 323, 389, 390
    fire and death of Fanny, 243–45
    Sims case, 100
    Sumner and, 27, 39–40, 106, 178, 181, 193, 243, 283, 350, 358, 365, 389, 390
        death, 392, 396
        letters, 7, 29–30, 167, 176, 217, 223, 295, 350, 353, 363, 365, 373, 374, 390, 391
Louisiana, 372, 379, 401
    Reconstruction, 309–13, 325–26, 336
    secession, 219
    segregation, 74, 75
    slavery, 13, 42, 128, 190
Louisiana Purchase, 190
Louis Philippe I of France, 44
Louisville Journal, 103
Lovejoy, Owen, 237–38
Lowell, Charles R., 304
lynchings, 341, 356–57
Lyons, Richard, 1st Earl, 252, 254
Lyons-Seward Treaty of 1862, 266, 272

McClellan, George, 248, 262
    election of 1864, 300–302, 303
Madison, James, 18, 119, 293
Maine, 128, 287

Malvern, 321, 322
Marshall, John, 63
Marshall, Thurgood, 76
Maryland, 13, 14, 84, 231–32, 379
Mason, James, 110, 116, 148, 246–47, 249–54
Massachusetts
    literacy tests, 378
    Sumner as Senator of. See Senator of Massachusetts
    Texas annexation and, 33–34
Massachusetts First Infantry Regiment, 394
Massachusetts Third Rifle Battalion, 229–30
Massachusetts Fifth Infantry Regiment, 229
Massachusetts Sixth Infantry Regiment, 227, 229, 230
Massachusetts General Hospital, 283
Massachusetts Supreme Judicial Court, 51, 52, 53, 58–75
Massachusetts Whig Party, 33, 37, 40–42, 130
Mayer, Henry, 125
Mayflower, 213
Medical College of Virginia, 194
Melville, Herman, 62, 124
Mexican War, 37–42, 155
Michigan, 202, 287
Minkins, Shadrach, 100
Minnesota, 200
Mississippi, 42, 219, 336, 372, 382
Mississippi State Constitutional Convention, 398
Missouri, 128–29, 143–44, 189–90, 231–32
Missouri Compromise of 1820, 87, 126, 128, 129, 130, 132, 133, 189, 190, 191
Missouri Supreme Court, 189–90
M&JC Gilmore, 98
Montgomery (AL) Journal, 139

Morgan, Edwin, 158, 159

Morris, Robert, 52–53, 55–61, 63–64, 69

Mount Auburn Cemetery, 245, 283, 350, 392, 396–97

Mount Vernon, 13

Murray, Ambrose, 158

National Mall, 13, 14, 284

Nebraska, 355. *See also* Kansas-Nebraska Act

"Negro question," 381

Nell, William Cooper, 70

Nevada, 74, 326, 379

New England Emigrant Aid Company, 139, 142–43

New Jersey, 202, 214, 303

New Mexico, 83, 84, 219

New York, 202, 241, 287, 299

New York Express, 363

New York Herald, 235, 312

New York Times, 157, 171, 172, 183

New York Tribune, 273, 396

Nicolay, John, 235, 261, 262, 264, 277–78, 312

"Nigger Hill," 53, 54

Nineteenth Amendment, 381

"No Property in Man" speech, 293–94, 295

North Carolina, 227, 372, 379

Nullification Acts, 214

Nye, James, 384

Ohio, 202, 232, 287, 379

Ohio River, 232

Ordinance of Secession, 218, 398

Oregon, 74, 200, 379

"Origin, Necessity, and Permanence of the Republican Party, The," 213–14

original sin, 34

Orr, James L., 153, 169–70

Otis School, 55

Overland Campaign, 304

Palmerston, John, 251, 254

Pardoning Power of the President, The, 113

Paris, 16–17, 187, 188, 193–95, 198

Parker, Theodore
    Fugitive Slave Law, 100, 133
    Sumner and, 114, 115, 126, 142, 144, 187, 188, 193, 198

Parkman, George, 71–72

Partridge, Alden, 23

Pearl incident of 1848, 43–50, 111–14, 115, 269

Pendleton, George, 301, 302

Pennington, Alexander, 169–70

Pennsylvania, 181, 202, 241, 299, 378

Pennsylvania Avenue, 13, 133, 145, 159, 315

Perry, Marshall S., 164–65, 167

Pettus, John J., 217

Phi Beta Kappa, 132

Philadelphia Evening Telegram, 379

Philadelphia Press, 322

Phillips, Wendell, 55, 112, 114, 173, 380, 390

Phillips School, 53–55

Pickens, Andrew, 226

Pierce, Edward L., 95, 107, 117, 210, 351, 373, 390, 391, 396

Pierce, Franklin, 126–27, 128, 130, 141, 142, 143, 147–48, 185

Pierpont, Francis Harrison, 336

Pinkerton, Allan, 221

Plessy, Homer, 75

Plessy v. Ferguson, 74–76, 400–401

Point Lookout, 46, 47

Polk, James K., 33, 34, 36, 38, 246

post-traumatic stress disorder (PTSD), 197

Potomac River, 14, 43, 46

Potter, James, 98–99, 101, 104

Potter, John Fox, 274
Powell, Lewis, 328–29
"Prayer of One Hundred Thousand,"
    286–87, 290, 291
Prescott, William, 37–40, 41
psychoanalysis, 21
Puerto Rico, 275–76

Quincy, Edmund, 107

Radical Republicans, 5, 151, 310, 311,
    345, 355, 356, 377
Rainey, Joseph, 397–98
"Ransom of Slaves at the National
    Capital" speech, 267–68
Raymond, Henry, 299–300
Reconstruction, 3–4, 5, 264, 308–12,
    323, 354, 356–58, 372–73
    Johnson's betrayal, 335–43
    Louisiana debate, 309–13, 325–26
Reconstruction Acts, 357–58, 372
Report on the Condition of the South,
    341–42, 356–57, 366
Republican Party, 3, 5, 135–36, 192,
    203
    election of 1856, 173–74, 180–81
    election of 1858, 201–2
Revels, Hiram, 381–85
Revolutionary War, 24, 57, 92, 103,
    229, 258
Rhode Island, 241, 378
Richmond Enquirer, 163
River Queen, 321, 323, 324
Roberts, Benjamin, 53–55, 58–60, 70,
    72, 75
Roberts, Sarah, 53–55, 56, 58–60,
    65–68, 69, 72, 291
Roberts v. The City of Boston, 51, 52,
    55, 58–77, 88
Ropes, Hannah, 138, 142

Salem, 47–48
Sanford, John F. A., 189–90

San Jacinto, USS, 247–48
Santo Domingo, 387, 388
Sargent, John Singer, 365
Saulsbury, Willard, 295
Sayres, Edward, 43–44, 46, 48–49,
    111–14, 115
school segregation, 52–77, 400
    Brown v. Board of Education, 76,
        402–3
    Roberts v. The City of Boston, 51,
        52, 55, 58–77
Schurz, Carl, 341–42, 356–57,
    366
Scott, Winfield, 114
secession crisis, 219–20, 221–22
Second Confiscation Act, 272–75
Second Inaugural Address of Lincoln,
    237, 317–18, 332
sectionalism, 108, 118
Senate Foreign Relations Committee,
    223, 231, 360, 362
    Sumner's removal as chairman,
        387–88
Senate Judiciary Committee, 237,
    290–93
Senate Select Committee on Slavery
    and Freedom, 287, 291
Senator of Massachusetts
    abolitionism. See abolitionism of
        Sumner
    Bleeding Kansas, 138, 141–52, 155,
        200
    British treachery, 249–58
        Alabama claims, 256–58
        Trent Affair, 5, 249–53
    caning of Sumner. See caning of
        Sumner
    Civil War, 2–3, 227–33, 241–43,
        272–73, 284–85, 304, 319–20
        Richmond visit, 322–23
    Compensated Emancipation Act of
        1862, 266–70
    Confiscation Acts, 242, 272–75

Senator of Massachusetts (*continued*)
  death threats and safety concerns,
    126, 133, 209–10, 228–29
  Dred Scott case, 192
  election of 1851, 9, 89, 90–97,
    104–7
  election of 1857, 182–85
  election of 1863, 276
  election of 1864, 302, 303–4
  election of 1869, 373, 374–75
  emancipation, 231, 233, 236–40,
    242–43, 262–70, 274–89
  Fourteenth Amendment, 344,
    345–49
  Fifteenth Amendment, 375, 376–81
  Fugitive Slave Law, 92, 111, 112,
    115–25, 294–97
    motion to repeal, 115–23, 134
  Grant and, 387–88, 389–90, 393,
    400
  Johnson and, 328, 330, 344,
    355–57, 365
    impeachment, 5, 367–71
    Reconstruction betrayal,
      335–42
  Kansas-Nebraska Act, 126–27,
    128–31, 134, 136
  Lincoln and. *See* Lincoln,
    Abraham, and Sumner
  "Prayer of One Hundred
    Thousand," 286–87, 290, 291
  Reconstruction and civil rights,
    3–4, 5, 264, 308–12, 323,
    325–26, 356–58
    Johnson's betrayal, 335–42
    Louisiana debate, 309–13,
      325–26
  as senator-elect, 106–8
  "state suicide" theor4y, 264–65
  Tenure of Office Act, 355–56, 365,
    367, 368
  Thirteenth Amendment, 289–94,
    305–6, 313–14

Thirty-Second Congress, 109–14
Thirty-Third Congress, 127–31,
  134–35
Thirty-Fourth Congress, 142–59,
  169–70
Thirty-Fifth Congress, 192–93,
  197, 198
Thirty-Sixth Congress, 200–202,
  204, 205–9, 223
Thirty-Seventh Congress, 235, 237,
  242, 263–70, 272–75
Thirty-Eighth Congress, 264–65,
  286–88, 290–97, 305, 311, 312
Thirty-Ninth Congress, 342–49,
  352, 354–58
Fortieth Congress, 367–72
Forty-First Congress, 374–85,
  387–88
"separate but equal," 6, 56, 74–76,
  310, 401
Separate Car Act of 1890, 75
"Seventh of March" speech (Webster),
  84–87
Seward, Augustus, 329
Seward, Frances, 135, 146, 328, 329
Seward, Frederick, 328–29
Seward, William H., 250, 306, 314
  assassination attempt, 327–29
  British
    Trent Affair, 252–54
  carriage accident, 323, 324
  Civil War, 223, 250, 252–54, 279,
    323, 324
  election of 1860, 204
  Sumner and, 135, 146, 168, 314
Shaw, Lemuel, 62–77, 99–100, 401
Sherman, John, 210, 295
Sherman, Roger, 119
Sherman, William Tecumseh, 299,
  302–3, 318, 329, 393
Sibley, John Langdon, 99, 102
siege of Petersburg, 299, 304
Silver Spring, 167–68

Simonton, James W., 157
Sims, Thomas, 98–104
Sismondi, Jean Charles Léonard de, 16–17
Slack, Charles W., 280
Slidell, John, 246–54
Smith Street School, 59
Sorbonne, 17
South Carolina, 74, 143, 185, 311, 336, 372, 379, 401
  secession, 218–18, 219
speeches of Sumner, 13, 17, 22, 373–74
  "*Alabama* claims," 257
  "Barbarism of Slavery," 205–12, 213–14
  "Crime Against Kansas," 145–51, 152, 155, 200
  Faneuil Hall of 1845, 34–35
  Faneuil Hall of 1851, 92–93, 97
  "Freedom National; Slavery Sectional," 116–25, 127
  "No Property in Man," 293–94, 295
  "Ransom of Slaves at the National Capital," 267–68
  Texas speech of 1845, 36
  "The Equal Rights of All," 346–48
  "The Origin, Necessity, and Permanence of the Republican Party," 213–14
  Worcester speech of 1854, 135–37
Springfield Republican, 396–97
Stamp Act, 92
Stanton, Edwin M., 2, 279, 324, 326, 329–30, 356, 366, 367–68
Stanton, Elizabeth Cady, 286–87, 380
"Star-Spangled Banner, The" (song), 13, 325
"state suicide" theory, 264–65
Stevens, Thaddeus, 336, 348, 373
Stewart, William M., 326–27
Stone, James, 176
Storey, Moorfield, 363–64

Story, Joseph, 11, 13, 16, 24–25
Stowe, Harriet Beecher, 125, 277, 380
Sumner, Albert, 30
Sumner, Alice Mason Hooper, 351–54, 358, 359–65
  divorce of, 364–65
  Holstein affair, 360–63, 365
  marital discord of, 359–64
  marriage of, 353–54
Sumner, Charles
  abolitionism of. *See* abolitionism of Sumner
  antislavery education of, 14–17
  background of, 23–24
  Boston to Washington journey, 11–12
  burial of, 396–97
  Burns case, 131–34
  caning of. *See* caning of Sumner
  death of, 392–400
  early legal career of, 16, 19–20
  early life of, 21
  education of, 11, 16, 19, 23–24
  election of 1848, 50–51
  election of 1851, 9, 89, 90–97, 104–7
  European travels of, 16–17, 25, 187, 188, 193–98
  family of, 21–25, 27–32, 88–89, 271, 349–50
    brother Charles's death, 283–84
    father's death, 25
    mother's death, 349–50
    sister Mary's death, 28–31
  friendships of, 25–28. *See also specific friendships*
  health of, 28–30, 388, 389–91
  legacy and influence of, 4–8, 401–4
  Lincoln and. *See* Lincoln, Abraham, and Sumner
  Mexican War, 37–42

Sumner, Charles (*continued*)
  personality of, 20, 21–23, 25–28,
    26*n*, 31, 37, 352
  popularity of, 134–35, 136, 176
  Senate career of. *See* Senator of
    Massachusetts
  speeches of. *See* speeches of
    Sumner
  Texas annexation, 33–37
  Webster and, 13, 85–86, 89, 91–93,
    105–6
  Winthrop affair, 37–40, 41
  women and marriage, 26–27.
    See also Sumner, Alice Mason
    Hooper
Sumner, Charles Pinckney, 15, 23–24,
  25
Sumner, George, 22, 29, 30–31, 34,
  40, 72, 106, 108
  ill health and death of, 271, 283–84
Sumner, Horace, 88–89
Sumner, Jane, 22
Sumner, Mary, 22, 28–31, 32
Sumner, Matilda, 21, 22
Sumner, Relief Jacob, 21–22
  death of, 349–50
  ill health of, 271, 283–84, 349
Sutherland, Harriet Sutherland-
    Leveson-Gower, Duchess of, 16
Sutter's Mill, 81–82
Swisshelm, Jane, 171, 172

Taney, Roger, 190–91
tariffs, 34, 40, 186–87
Taylor, Zachary, 35–36, 38, 41–42,
  50, 89
Tennessee, 227, 336, 357
Tenure of Office Act, 355–56, 365,
  367, 368
Texas, 219, 336, 372
  annexation of, 33–37
Thackeray, William, 188
Theodora, 246–48

Thirteenth Amendment, 269, 289–94,
  305–6, 310, 313–14, 332
Thomas, Lorenzo, 368
Thoreau, Henry David, 57, 124, 132
Three-Fifths Compromise, 18
Ticknor, George, 39
Tilden, Samuel J., 401–2
Tocqueville, Alexis de, 188
transcontinental railroad, 128
Traveller, 136
Treaty of Washington, 257, 258
Tremont Temple, 276–77, 279
Trent Affair, 5, 246–54
Trumbull, Lyman, 290–93
tuberculosis, 21, 28, 29, 30, 261
Tukey, Francis, 99–100, 101
Tyler, John, 33
typhoid, 22, 89, 155, 261, 316

Uncle Tom's Cabin (Stowe), 125
Underground Railroad, 331
Union blockade, 227, 246, 250, 253,
  255
universal suffrage, 309–13, 318,
  322–23, 345–48, 354
Utah, 83, 84

Van Buren, Martin, 33, 50
Vickers, George, 383
Virginia, 13, 14, 227, 372
Voting Rights Act of 1965, 403

Wade, Benjamin, 123, 150
War of 1812, 250, 258
Washington, D.C.
  Pearl incident, 43–50
  slavery and slavery trade, 13–15,
    32, 43–44
  Sumner's first visit, 12–15
Washington, George, 120
Washington Star, 132
Webster, Daniel
  Compromise of, 81, 85–86

Compromise of 1850, 81, 83–87,
103, 105
death of, 127
election of 1848, 41
Fugitive Slave Law, 84–87, 91,
92–93, 105
"Seventh of March" speech (1850),
84–87
Sumner and, 13, 85–86, 89, 91–93,
105–6
Texas annexation, 33
Webster, John, 71–72
Weed, Thurlow, 299
Weller, John, 122
Welles, Gideon, 249
West Virginia, 336, 379
Whig Party, 33, 36, 40–42, 50, 110,
130, 150
White House of the Confederacy,
321–22

Whitman, Walt, 87, 315–16
Whittier, John Greenleaf, 90–91,
181–82, 389, 392, 396
Wilkes, Charles, 247–48, 249, 253–54
Willard's Hotel, 221–22
Willey, Waitman T., 264
Wilmot Proviso, 41–42, 50
Wilson, Henry, 113, 115–16, 150, 159,
209–10, 382, 390, 392, 396
Winthrop, Robert, 37–40, 41, 60, 63,
89, 96, 97
Wisconsin, 189, 202, 287
Women's National Loyal League
(WNLL), 286–87
women's suffrage, 380–81
Worcester speech of 1854, 135–37
Wright, Henry C., 290
Wright, Paulina, 380

Young Men's Republican Union, 214